To D~ Orlovsky

with best wishes

Oxford

6.7.1999

Bernard Wasserstein

VANISHING DIASPORA

BERNARD WASSERSTEIN

Vanishing Diaspora

The Jews in Europe since 1945

HAMISH HAMILTON · LONDON

HAMISH HAMILTON LTD

Published by the Penguin Group
Penguin Books Ltd, 27 Wrights Lane, London w8 5tz, England
Penguin Books USA Inc., 375 Hudson Street, New York, New York 10014, USA
Penguin Books Australia Ltd, Ringwood, Victoria, Australia
Penguin Books Canada Ltd, 10 Alcorn Avenue, Toronto, Ontario, Canada m4v 3b2
Penguin Books (NZ) Ltd, 182–190 Wairau Road, Auckland 10, New Zealand

Penguin Books Ltd, Registered Offices: Harmondsworth, Middlesex, England

First published in Great Britain by Hamish Hamilton Ltd 1996
3 5 7 9 10 8 6 4 2

Filmset in 12/14pt Monophoto Bembo
by Datix International Limited, Bungay, Suffolk

Printed in Great Britain by Clays Ltd, St Ives plc

A CIP catalogue record for this book is available from the British Library

ISBN 0–241–13619–9

Contents

LIST OF TABLES   vi
PREFACE   vii
ACKNOWLEDGEMENTS   xvi
ABBREVIATIONS   xvii
GLOSSARY   xix

1. Displaced Persons   I
2. Stalin's Last Victims, 1945–53   36
3. Revival in Western Europe, 1945–73   58
4. The Impact of Israel   85
5. Facing the Past   103
6. Jews and the Christian Problem   131
7. Three Germanies and the Jews   159
8. The Soviet Jewish Revolt   180
9. East European Shadows, 1953–89   206
10. West European Dilemmas, 1973–89   227
11. Jews in the New European Disorder   253

AFTERTHOUGHTS   280
NOTES   291
BIBLIOGRAPHY   312
INDEX   324

List of Tables

1. Jewish Populations in Europe   viii
2. Immigration to Israel from Europe, 1948–94   92
3. Jewish Emigration from the USSR and CIS, 1948–94   200

Preface

The Jews are vanishing from Europe – and not only because of Hitler. In 1939 there were nearly 10 million Jews in Europe; during the war more than half were murdered. By 1994, emigration and a surplus of deaths over births had reduced Europe's Jewish population again by more than half, to under 2 million. Demographic projections for the next two or three decades vary greatly, depending on such factors as the rate of emigration from the former Soviet Union; but the range of possibilities extends only downward – at best the Jews in Europe face slow diminution, at worst virtual extinction. Here and there pockets of ultra-orthodox Jews, clinging to the tenets of the faith, will no doubt survive – a picturesque remnant like the Amish of Pennsylvania. Perhaps too some Europeans of the twenty-first century may point with pride to strands of Jewish ancestry as some white Americans today boast of partial Amerindian descent. Since the dawn of the modern era European Jews, as individuals shaped by a common spiritual and cultural tradition and as communities moulded by a shared historical destiny, played vitally important political, economic and intellectual roles in all the major European societies; a realistic forecast now is that within a few generations they will disappear as a significant element in the life of the continent.

Yet although the Jews are disappearing, the Jewish question has not gone away. On the contrary, it has re-emerged in different forms in the politics of most European countries since the war. Even in countries such as Poland and Austria, where there are hardly any Jews left, it has been a significant theme in public

Table 1: Jewish Populations in Europe

	1937	1946	1967	1994
Austria	191,000	31,000*	12,500	7,000
Belgium	65,000	45,000	40,500	31,800
Britain	330,000	370,000	400,000	295,000
Bulgaria	49,000	44,200	5,000	1,900
Czechoslovakia	357,000	55,000	15,000	7,600†
Denmark	8,500	5,500	6,000	6,400
Estonia	4,600	§	§	3,500
Finland	2,000	2,000	1,750	1,300
France	300,000	225,000	535,000	530,000
Germany	500,000	153,000*	30,000	55,000
Greece	77,000	10,000	6,500	4,800
Hungary	400,000	145,000	80,000	56,000
Ireland (Republic)	5,000	3,900	2,900	1,200
Italy	48,000	53,000*	35,000	31,000
Latvia	95,000	§	§	18,000
Lithuania	155,000	§	§	6,500
Luxemburg	3,500	500	500	600
Netherlands	140,000	28,000	30,000	25,000
Norway	2,000	750	1,000	1,000
Poland	3,250,000	215,000	21,000	6,000
Portugal	–	4,000	1,000	300
Romania	850,000	420,000	100,000	10,000
Spain	–	6,000	6,000	12,000
Sweden	7,500	15,500	13,000	16,500
Switzerland	18,000	35,000	20,000	19,000
Turkey¶	50,000	48,000	35,000	18,000
USSR/CIS¶	2,669,000	1,971,000	1,715,000	812,000
Yugoslavia	71,000	12,000	7,000	3,500‡
TOTAL	**9,648,100**	**3,898,350**	**3,119,650**	**1,980,900**

Note: These figures, collated from many sources, are of varying reliability and in some cases are subject to a wide margin of error and interpretation. This warning applies particularly to the figures for 1946, a year in which there was considerable Jewish population movement. It must also be borne in mind that the boundaries of many European countries changed between 1937 and 1946.

* Includes 'Displaced Persons' † Total for Czech Republic and Slovakia ‡ Total for former Yugoslavia § Baltic States included in USSR between 1941 and 1991 ¶ Excludes Asiatic regions

discourse at critical political junctures since 1945. In the Soviet Union, home of the largest Jewish community to survive Hitler, the Bolshevik claim to have eliminated the Jewish question was proved to be bogus; indeed, the Soviet failure to solve the problem was one of the factors that galvanized opposition to the regime in its last two decades. In the Eastern European lands dominated by Soviet imperialism between 1945 and 1989, the large pre-war Jewish communities have all but disappeared, yet antisemitism remained and remains a live force. In Western Europe the emancipation of the Jews, first achieved in France under the Revolution, seemed to provide a secure position for Jews within liberal democracies. But during the Second World War the collusion of the administrations of occupied countries in the deportation of Jews to the death camps, the indifference of most Germans and many (though not all) occupied populations to the fate of their Jewish neighbours, as well as the inaction of the British and other Allied governments in the face of Nazi mass murder, revealed holes in the effectiveness of the liberal umbrella as a protection for Jews. With the establishment of Israel in 1948 a new ideological pole of attraction was created, as well as a new, apparently successful formula for resolving the Jewish problem. To a considerable degree it did provide such a solution – both for its own Jewish citizens and for Diaspora Jews threatened by persecution. But the establishment of the Jewish state, while stimulating a sense of collective pride and self-confidence, also gave rise in the 1950s and 1960s to new accusations of double loyalties or of disloyalty and in the 1970s and 1980s exposed Jews in the Diaspora to bloody terrorist attacks.

Why will the Jewish question not go away? Why is it that neither Hitler's 'Final Solution' nor the communist, liberal or Zionist prescriptions for grappling with the problem succeeded in eliminating it from the political and social agenda? Why is it still today a disturbing element in the politics of many European countries? The main purpose of this book is to address this cluster of questions and to suggest some new answers.

The passage of half a century since the end of the war, the collapse of communist rule in Eastern Europe and the movement towards a comprehensive Arab–Israeli peace settlement furnish a convenient vantage point for thinking about these questions afresh and assessing how history has answered them in the post-war period.

First, some problems of definition.

Who is a *Jew*? According to Jewish religious law, a Jew is a person born to a Jewish mother. This definition, however, is too restrictive to satisfy contemporary social realities. Another definition was offered by Jean-Paul Sartre in his *Réflexions sur la question juive*, published in 1946: the Jew was quite simply a man whom other men took for a Jew. By 'other men', Sartre meant particularly antisemites. 'If the Jew didn't exist,' he wrote, 'the antisemite would invent him.'[1] While the definition has the merit of being almost all-inclusive, it obviously fails to satisfy the desire of most Jews to define their own collective identity – not to mention the desire of a few to hide it from others or from themselves or to secede from the collectivity. In most West European countries the question may be resolved for most people on a purely voluntary basis: within certain limits they may choose whether or not to be Jews. A person of Jewish ancestry may decide to merge totally into the larger society – in the nineteenth century the process commonly involved conversion; in the secular societies of post-war Europe no such rite of passage is required. Many assimilate implicitly, some explicitly; thus, for example, in Britain some years ago, the Liberal MP for Ely, Clement Freud, bearer of one of the most illustrious Jewish names of the century, let it be known that he did not wish to be included in counts of Jewish MPs drawn up after each election by the *Jewish Chronicle*. In general, in liberal societies, no particular advantage is gained, nor any significant odium incurred by such actions which are viewed as matters of private preference. As for choosing to become Jewish, this is a matter of little public import. The would-be convert must meet the necessary conditions (stringent for entry to the orthodox community, much more lax in the case of Liberal and Reform congregations) but the state takes no interest in the matter. Elsewhere, particularly as one moves east, however, matters are rather different. In the countries of the former USSR, for example, Jews have always been regarded as members of a national as well as a religious group and are registered as such on their identity documents. Once so registered, ethnic status is not easily changed. In the case of Soviet Jews, through much of the post-war period such public registration and ready official identification provided a basis for thinly disguised policies of discrimination – for example, in access to higher education. On the other hand, in the 1970s, official recognition as a Jew provided a basis in the USSR for possible emigration – a goal of many besides Jews – so that what was a disadvantage in one way might become an asset in another. The problem of definition is thus of more than linguistic import. This book is concerned in the broadest sense with all those who considered themselves or were considered by others as Jews.

What is the *Jewish community* – that vague and fleetingly discerned entity whose very existence is denied by some writers? The word community implies some shared collective life which may or may not approximate to social reality. In some countries the Jewish community has a legal definition. In the Federal Republic of Germany, for example, members of the community are formally registered as such by public authorities and a proportional share of their taxes is paid towards communal expenses. In other countries, for example Great Britain, the community is a purely voluntary body although recognized under the law for certain purposes, such as the registration of marriages. Yet other countries occupy a middle position – France, for example, although a secular state, in some senses militantly so, nevertheless recognizes the Consistoire, the main synagogal authority in France, as having a legal status. In all the secular societies (which is to say all the societies) of contemporary Europe, however, there are large numbers of people on the fringe. A study of Dutch Jewry around 1960 estimated that about a third of the Jews in the country 'do not desire to be considered members of a Jewish religious community'.[2] Although such persons may not be formal members of any Jewish institution, they may still consider themselves in some sense Jewish – perhaps in an ethnic or cultural sense, sometimes for some residual religious purposes such as burial. Some sociologists and demographers distinguish between a 'core' Jewish community whose members actively identify as Jews and a 'larger aggregate of all current Jews, former Jews, other persons of recent Jewish descent, and any other related non-Jewish persons who share household ties with Jews'.[3] Here too this book adopts, for most purposes, a broadly inclusive rather than a narrow definition – but the reader should bear in mind throughout that 'community' is, in most cases, a convenient shorthand rather than an accurate description of social reality. Most Jewish populations in Europe in the recent past were divided – by political ideology, by geography, by social class or economic standing, or by religious commitment – into discrete and some-times mutually hostile elements. Community should not, for the purposes of this book, be held to imply unity. As a French Jewish writer noted in the summer of 1945: 'Jewry of the Diaspora is a body perpetually torn apart. It cannot find a single direction.'[4]

What is *antisemitism* and who is an *antisemite*? The very spelling of these words has aroused controversy. Yehuda Bauer, the noted historian of the Holocaust, has suggested that they should not be hyphenated; to do so, he argues, involves a conceptual error since, after all, there is no such doctrine as 'semitism'. The centre for the study of antisemitism at the Hebrew University of Jerusalem, founded by Bauer, accordingly deletes the hyphen. This form no doubt has the merit of logical consistency and might also help counter such absurd pseudo-semantic notions as that presented by some anti-Zionist controversialists who have occasionally main-tained that Arab 'anti-semitism' is impossible since, after all, Arabs, like Jews, are 'semites'. For the purposes of this book antisemitism is understood as both an ideological doctrine and a set of prejudicial attitudes. The doctrine combines disparate fea-tures from many sources: traditional Christian teaching and Nazi neo-paganism, integral nationalism and populist demagogy ('the socialism of fools'), hostility to Jews as capitalists and to Jews as communists. As a set of attitudes it fulfils a variety of psychological needs both collective and individual, generally of a psychopathic nature. The antisemite, consequently, may be a sophisticated intel-lectual or a boor, a militant atheist or a Christian crusader, a communist or a reactionary. All these types appear in what follows. This is not, however, a study of antisemites – though sadly they repeatedly force their way on to the stage – but of Jews. And in spite of everything it is not, taken as a whole, the story of Jews as victims of the hatred of their neighbours but rather as victims of their kindness – of the processes of integration and assimilation that have succeeded, at least in Western Europe, to such a degree as to threaten the collective survival of Jews on the Continent.

What, in the context of a discussion of the Jewish question in modern Europe, is *assimilation*? The late Maurice Freedman, one of the pioneers of contemporary Jewish sociology, pointed out that the term can have many meanings. For example, he wrote,

> To be an Englishman and a Jew, which is probably the aim of a very large proportion of Jews born in England, depresses Judaism to the level of one faith among many in a predominantly secular society. Here assimilation implies the state in which Jew, Protestant and Catholic stand in similar relationship to the social entity which comprises them all. It is debatable whether Jews have in fact reached this kind of position . . .[5]

That was written in 1955. Since then Jews, at least in England, have moved much closer to such a position – for better or for worse. Many Jews, particularly the orthodox religious and Zionists, would say for worse. Such Jews, indeed, often use the word 'assimilation' almost as a term of abuse, as in 'he's totally assimilated' (meaning 'he has lost his Jewish identity'). For that reason I emphasize that my use of the word carries no opprobrious connotation.

One might proceed further to attempt a definition of such terms as 'Diaspora', 'Zionism', 'Holocaust' and so on. But in these cases, as with the terms already mentioned, even to raise the question of definition immediately involves broaching critical problems of substance. It seems more sensible, therefore, to address these issues at appropriate points in the narrative. As an aid, however, to the understanding of a few other such terms and non-English expressions I have provided a short glossary.

The primary themes of this book are social and political: the evolving shape of the Jewish problem in different national or ideological contexts, the impact on attitudes towards Jews of collective memories of the Second World War, the revolutionized collective imagery of the Jew arising from the creation and growth of Israel, the rapidly changing social character of the major Jewish communities, the impact of new Christian approaches to Jews and Judaism, and the reactions to all these developments of European Jews themselves. Let me also say what this book is not: it is not concerned with Jewish 'contributions', whether to European cultures or economies; I deal only to a limited degree with the internal communal histories of European Jewries and hardly at all with their inner spiritual and intellectual currents — save in so far as such discussion is necessary for my central argument.

To the best of my knowledge this is the first attempt to write a history of European Jewry in the post-war period. In writing about the very recent past I have had to rely to a considerable degree on published sources, first and foremost the Jewish press. The great period of Yiddish journalism in Europe ended in 1939 but there are still dozens of lively Jewish newspapers appearing all over the continent, among which the London *Jewish Chronicle*, the oldest Jewish paper in the world (it was founded in 1841), approaches the status of a newspaper of record. I have also made use of some archival materials for the early part of the period and have had access to valuable unpublished analytical reports and memoranda prepared by various research bodies and organizations (all listed in the Notes and the Bibliography). Perhaps my most important source, however, has been personal observation over the past three decades.

A great deal of what has been published hitherto on various aspects of the subject has inevitably had a certain polemical thrust arising from the emotions of the post-war period, the ferocity of the Arab–Israel conflict and the pervasive context of the Cold War. As the Second World War generation dies out, as the Middle East conflict winds down and as the Cold War recedes into the black hole of memory, it becomes possible, perhaps for the first time, to write on this subject *sine ira ac studio* (a momentary lapse from this impossible ideal may be observed in the footnote on p. 64). Much of the book is about conflict — between antisemites and Jews, Zionists and anti-Zionists, assimilationists and those who placed some value on collective Jewish survival, and so on. I do not pretend to a neutrality in any of these disputes. Nevertheless, I have tried, no doubt with only limited success, to jettison the implicit assumptions and special pleading characteristic of much of what has previously been written on the subject. This book is conceived in neither the spirit of Job nor that of Cassandra. It draws its inspiration rather from the example of the first generation of Jewish sociologists, demographers and contemporary historians such as Arthur Ruppin, Jacob Lestchinsky and Emmanuel Ringelblum. The world they delineated was dead by 1945. Its heirs form the subject of this book.

Jerusalem
November 1994

Acknowledgements

I wish to acknowledge the help I have received from all the archives and libraries in which I have worked while preparing this book. In particular I should like to thank the Centre de Documentation Juive Contemporaine in Paris, the Institute of Jewish Affairs in London, the Jüdische Gemeinde in Berlin and the Institute of Contemporary Jewry of the Hebrew University of Jerusalem. I am also grateful to Jonathan Frankel, Gregory Freeze, Avraham Greenbaum, Antony Polonsky and Geoffrey Wigoder for reading and commenting on portions of the book. Ari Paltiel of the Israel Central Bureau of Statistics kindly compiled the data for Table 2. I owe a special debt of gratitude to my indefatigable agent, Bruce Hunter, and to my energetic publisher, Andrew Franklin. My greatest debt is to my late father, my mother and my brother for their close readings of the book.

Abbreviations

AJDC	American Jewish Joint Distribution Committee (the 'Joint')
AJYB	*American Jewish Year Book*
CBF	Central British Fund for World Jewish Relief records
CRIF	Conseil Représentatif des Israélites de France (later known as the Conseil Représentatif des Institutions Juives de France): the main French Jewish representative body
DP	'Displaced person', refugee
FSJU	Fonds Social Juif Unifié: the main French Jewish welfare organization
HIAS	Hebrew Immigrant Aid Society: American Jewish welfare organization
IJARR	Institute of Jewish Affairs Research Report
IRO	International Refugee Organization
JC	*Jewish Chronicle*
JJS	*Jewish Journal of Sociology*
JTADNB	Jewish Telegraphic Agency Daily News Bulletin
NYT	*New York Times*
PRO	Public Record Office, Kew
SJA	*Soviet Jewish Affairs*
UNRRA	United Nations Relief and Rehabilitation Administration
USNA	United States National Archives, Washington, DC

Glossary

Agudas Yisroel (*Agudat Yisrael*) Anti-Zionist political party of orthodox Jews, founded in Kattowitz in 1897. Hence Agudah, Agudist, etc.

Ashkenazim Jews of German origin: more generally, all Jews of Central or East European origin except those of the Balkans.

Bund Jewish socialist-autonomist party, founded in Vilna in 1897. Strong in inter-war Poland but virtually destroyed during the Second World War.

Diaspora The dispersion of the Jews outside Israel.

Hasidim Followers of the revivalist hasidic movement, founded in the eighteenth century, generally adhering to a specific rabbinical dynasty (Belzer, Lubavitcher, Satmarer, etc.). Hasidim are strict observers of Jewish religious laws. Most hasidim today live in the USA or Israel, although some are found in London (Stamford Hill and Golders Green), Paris, Antwerp and a few other European cities. Male hasidim generally do not shave, cover their heads at all times and wear distinctive dress – most commonly wide-brimmed black hats and long black coats.

'Joint' American Jewish Joint Distribution Committee: the major charity involved in distribution of relief to European Jews.

Knesset The Israeli parliament.

Ladino Also known as Judaeo-Spanish: language of the Sephardim (q.v.) in Turkey and the Balkans. Basically fifteenth-century Castilian written in Hebrew characters (in modern Turkey in Latin characters).

Mizrachi Religious Zionist political party founded in Vilna in 1902.

Revisionists Right-wing Zionist party founded by Vladimir Jabotinsky.

Sephardim Jews of Spanish or Portuguese origin: descendants of Jews expelled from Spain and Portugal in 1492 and 1497 respectively. The main Sephardi settlements were in Turkey and the Balkans (particularly Salonica). Old Sephardi families also lived in Amsterdam, London and Hamburg. By extension the term is often applied also to all Jews of non-European origin, especially Middle Eastern and North African Jews.

Yeshiva College of talmudic learning.

Yiddish Language of the Ashkenazim (q.v.). Basically Middle High German written in Hebrew characters with an admixture of vocabulary from Hebrew, Slavonic and some other sources. Widely spoken in Russia, Poland, Lithuania and much of East–Central Europe until the Second World War; its use is now largely confined to ultra-orthodox communities.

Yom Kippur The Day of Atonement, a fast, the holiest day of the Jewish year; also date of the outbreak of the 1973 Arab–Israel war.

CHAPTER ONE

Displaced Persons

On 27 January 1945 Russian forces operating in Upper Silesia captured the Nazi prison camp and mass-murder centre at Auschwitz. The place already had a sinister reputation. More than 1.1 million people had been killed there, at least 960,000 of them Jews. The Red Army found only about 3,000 alive. A Polish officer reported that they did not 'look like human beings; they are mere shadows'.[1] A few days earlier, most of the remaining prisoners who were able to walk had been moved by their captors to the German hinterland where the Nazis made their last stand. In April and early May 1945, as American and British forces advanced from the west, other concentration camps were liberated one by one. These had been prisons rather than death camps like Auschwitz, Majdanek, Treblinka, Sobibor and similar establishments in the East. They were nevertheless places of the utmost horror. Hundreds of thousands of prisoners had been killed in Dachau, Bergen-Belsen, Buchenwald and the other camps in the West. Many were shot in the final days before the arrival of Allied troops. Although the Russians had published extensive details of what they had found at Majdanek upon its liberation in July 1944, the Western Allies were totally unprepared for what they found in the camps in the West.

The shocking first encounter with the human evidence of the Nazi genocidal machine produced a mixture of compassion and repulsion. 'I had tried to visualize the interior of a concentration camp, but had not imagined it like this,' wrote the first British officer to enter Belsen. 'Nor had I imagined the strange simian throng who crowded the barbed-wire fence surrounding the compounds, with their shaven heads and their obscene prison suits, which were so dehumanizing.'[2] An American army report on 25 April 1945 described the so-called 'little camp', a barbed-wire enclosure in the centre of Buchenwald where the worst horrors were encountered:

> Even now, a trip through the little camp is like a nightmare. On the sight of an American uniform a horde of gnomes and trolls seems to appear like magic, pouring out of doorways as if shot from a cannon. Some hop on crutches. Some hobble on stumps of feet. Some glide like Oriental genies. Almost all wear striped convict suits, covered with patches, or grey-black remnants of Eastern clothing. The universal covering is a little black skull cap. They doff these ceremoniously to the visitors. Some are crying, others shouting with joy.[3]

These reactions were typical in their mingling of conventional, and no doubt genuine, sympathy with a disturbed sense of aversion to something so ugly as to be outside the normal range of human experience.

The reaction was natural, for not only the physical but the mental worlds of survivors and liberators were utterly different. Richard Crossman, a former Oxford don, at that time a British army officer, visited Dachau in early May 1945 and described the scene in his diary:

> As we entered the camp we turned left to see the crematorium. We passed a long line of bullock carts – with sullen peasants standing by. The carts were laden with corpses taken from the crematorium . . .
>
> As I had previously suspected, corpses in themselves are not particularly horrible, even half-starved corpses. After the first shock one fails to react to what is so obviously not alive and so apparently not human. Just by the crematorium there were half a dozen camp inmates sitting in the shade of a pine tree, nonchalantly watching the corpses being arranged with pitchforks on the carts. Obviously they were completely immune to any sense of horror at the sight, and even their sense of smell apparently had been deadened . . .

The abyss which separates the outside world from the concentration camp influences both sides equally. Even the most sensitive and intelligent people whom we met in Dachau seemed to accept it as the only reality and to think of the outside world as a mirage. Similarly, the incoming troops, after the first uprush of indignation, seemed to slump back into accepting Dachau, not as 32,000 fellow human beings like themselves, but as a strange monstrosity to be treated on its own standards. How else can one explain that ten days after the liberation no one thinks it strange that there are no trucks to carry the dying to hospital and no proper diet in the hospital? If a town of 32,000 people had been struck by a cyclone, an immense rescue apparatus would be organized. But these 32,000 outcasts are so remote from civilization as we know it that we are content to leave them as they are, improving slightly their living conditions.[4]

The situation at Dachau was mirrored elsewhere.

In default of any easily available alternative, many of the former concentration camps continued to house their former inmates, sometimes in former SS barracks. They were fed and clothed and allowed to move about freely, but thousands were in such poor condition that they died within days or weeks of liberation. At Bergen-Belsen, captured by British forces on 12 April, 40,000 starving inmates were on the verge of death. Five days passed before the first medical units were brought in. Malnutrition was so advanced that it was decided 'to select individuals as to chances for recovery'. The result was, as an army report put it, that even after liberation 'those individuals so obviously near death will receive no care'.[5] A similar lack of preparedness led to thousands of post-liberation deaths at Mauthausen, liberated by the Americans, and Theresienstadt, liberated by the Russians.[6]

Most of the Nazis' victims (though only a minority of the survivors) were Jews, most of the liberators gentiles; but the ambivalent reaction was not restricted to gentiles. Among Jews there was a widespread if seldom explicitly voiced suspicion that those who had survived against overwhelming odds must have done so by ignoble or corrupt means. This line of thinking was particularly prominent among Zionists, whose ideology impelled them almost instinctively towards contempt for Diaspora Jews. David Ben Gurion, leader of the Palestinian Labour Zionists, expressed a widely held view: 'Among the survivors of the German camps were people who would not have been alive were they not what they were – hard, mean and selfish – and what they have been through erased every remaining good quality from them.'[7]

The survivors were a small remnant of the large pre-war Jewish communities of Eastern and Central Europe. In Poland, home of some 3.2 million Jews in 1939, nearly 90 per cent had been murdered by the Nazis and their local collaborators during the German occupation. In the former Baltic states, White Russia and the Ukraine, a similar proportion of the pre-war Jewish populations had been killed between 1941 and 1944. In Hungary, Romania and Bulgaria, which had preserved a shadowy semi-independence under Nazi domination, a higher percentage had survived, but hundreds of thousands had nevertheless been deported to their deaths, as had three-quarters of the Jews of Czechoslovakia and the great majority of those in Austria and Yugoslavia. In Western Europe only the 370,000 Jews in Britain, the small Jewish communities of neutral Ireland, Switzerland and Sweden, and the 8,500 Danish Jews (most of whom had been transported overnight by the Danish Resistance to sanctuary in Sweden) survived virtually intact. The 300,000 Jews of France had been subjected to discriminatory laws by their own government in 1940; two years later French police rounded up thousands and handed them over to the Germans for deportation to Auschwitz, where about 75,000 died. Three-quarters of Dutch and two-thirds of Belgian Jews were killed. Fascist Italy had protected its own Jews, as well as some of other nationalities; but after the fall of Mussolini in July 1943 and the occupation of most of the country by the Germans, thousands of Italian Jews were deported to their deaths. As for the 500,000 Jews who had lived in Germany itself in 1933, about half managed to leave before the outbreak of the war. But immigration restrictions everywhere limited possibilities for departure. Only a handful of those who were still in Germany in September 1939 survived the war in camps or in hiding. Altogether fewer than a million

Jews in former Nazi-occupied Europe outside the USSR were still alive in 1945.

Beyond the millions of individual lives extinguished, what had also been destroyed was a collectivity that had preserved a distinctive, if richly variegated, identity. In Western Europe, where Jews had been emancipated for several generations, Jewish social and cultural separateness was often attenuated, sometimes virtually non-existent. In Central Europe too, where Jews had played a major part in shaping the modernist culture of cities such as Prague, Vienna and Budapest, they had seemed to be assimilating fast in a fruitful symbiosis. But the great mass of European Jews in 1939 still lived in what had been for centuries the Jewish heartland: Eastern Europe, particularly Poland and the western provinces of Russia. In this region Jews had been formally emancipated after the First World War but the alien concepts of liberal individualism had not taken root and the Jews were still generally regarded as a national no less than as a religious group.

To a considerable degree this was merely a recognition of reality. The Jews in inter-war Europe lived, for the most part, in dense urban concentrations in predominantly peasant societies. Some retained a rigorous attachment to religious orthodoxy and not only prayed but dressed and ate in ways that immediately marked them out from their gentile neighbours. Among these the traditional religious leadership, based in the yeshivas (talmudic colleges), still commanded an influence that radiated throughout the Jewish world. But more modernized Jews too generally differed from most of their neighbours in their level of education, their economic functions and often their political outlook. In some countries, such as Poland, Jews, like other minorities, had their own political parties. Some among them had abandoned a specifically Jewish identity, seeking to merge in a socialist internationalism founded on class rather than nationality; so many Jews, indeed, were attracted to the revolutionary left that, rather than losing their identity, they found to their chagrin that they imprinted it on the movement as a whole, which was often accused by its enemies of being Jewish-controlled. The majority of Jews, however, were neither communist nor socialist but people of

bourgeois values and aspirations. Atheist or ultra-orthodox, socialist or Zionist, Polish, Russian or Romanian, most of the Jews of
Eastern Europe spoke the same language: Yiddish, still the lingua
franca of the overwhelming majority of Jews in the region in the
1930s. In this richly expressive demotic tongue, which even its
speakers sometimes despised as a 'jargon', they created, in the two
or three generations before their extinction, a unique culture that
found expression in sentimental drama on stage and film, in
haunting folk-songs and in a dynamic newspaper press out of
which grew one of the world's great literatures. All this too ended
at Auschwitz.

On orders from the Commander-in-Chief of the Allied armies
in the West, General Eisenhower, the proofs of Nazi brutality
were given wide publicity. Delegations of bigwigs descended on
the camps for tours of inspection. A British parliamentary delegation visited Buchenwald shortly after its liberation and reported:
'Such camps as this mark the lowest point of degradation to which
humanity has yet descended. The memory of what we saw and
heard at Buchenwald will haunt us ineffaceably for many years.'[8]
The British press provided considerable coverage of these and
similar findings, although shortages of newsprint and the welter of
other news precluded much detail. Some papers in any case
considered the specifics too shocking to inflict on their readers.
The London *Daily Express*, reporting the liberation by General
Patton's 4th Army Division of Ohrdruf, a subcamp of Buchenwald, where the bodies of 3,000 recently killed inmates were
discovered, published a photograph that was said to be 'the only
picture fit to print' of the many that had been taken there.[9]
Newsreel companies in Britain were given extra allowances of
film stock in order to include full coverage of the camps in their
reports. The images shown of piled-up bodies, of emaciated prisoners and of German civilians being frog-marched past the evidence
of the crimes committed in their name, lodged in the public
consciousness, although retention of the image was not always
accompanied by an apprehension of its meaning – in Britain for a
generation 'Belsen' became an epithet thrown cheerfully by school-
boys at unusually thin or undernourished-looking contemporaries.

With their liberation, those among the camp inmates who were physically able to move were, once military considerations permitted, free to go. Chaotic transport conditions made travel difficult, particularly in the East, but some former prisoners, mainly those from Western Europe, did make the journey home almost immediately. They met with a surprisingly cool reception. The eighteen-year-old Simone Jacob (later, as Simone Veil, a French government minister and president of the European Parliament) arrived in Paris in late May 1945 after a year in Auschwitz, where she had lost most of her family. She found people did not want to hear about her experiences. They preferred to talk to her sister, who had fought in the Resistance: 'People wanted to hear tales of glory and heroism of the Resistance. Auschwitz didn't interest them.'[10] Another young Jew who returned from Auschwitz at the same time, Jean-Marie Lustiger (later Archbishop of Paris), recalled: 'What was quite extraordinary was that it was such a taboo subject that nobody spoke about it and nobody wanted to speak about it.'[11]

Dutch survivors too encountered incomprehension and incredulity, and responded with silence. One woman recalled trying to explain to an acquaintance what had happened to her family: 'I told her my story. She looked at me as if I were lying and said she did not believe me. Then I said goodbye to her and walked on. For years I did not tell anyone anything about my experiences during the war. My lips were sealed. People don't understand, or they don't believe you.'[12] About 5,000 Jews returned to the Netherlands between April and July 1945, the largest groups arriving from Auschwitz, Bergen-Belsen and Theresienstadt. The Dutch government was slow in organizing their return and, on principle, gave no special help to Jews. Bureaucratic formality rather than compassion was the order of the day. Some Jews faced demands for payment of rent or insurance premiums for the period of their deportation. The former resistance magazine *De Patriot* adjured returning Jews to 'demonstrate their gratitude by assuming responsibility for making amends to those who became victims themselves for helping Jews'.[13]

In many cases former deportees found upon arrival that their homes had been occupied by other people who were unwilling to move out. Some had gone back to their pre-war places of residence only to encounter black holes where Allied bombs or German flamethrowers had destroyed towns and villages. East European Jews were often afraid to return, terrified of the reception they might encounter from local populations. In Poland, the Ukraine, Slovakia and elsewhere, returning Jews were often met with hostility or violence. At Krasnik, near Lublin, the 300 Jewish survivors (out of a pre-war community of 5,000) who returned after the liberation were ordered out of town within twenty-four hours by the mayor. At Polaniec, near Kielce, Bolkow, near Lodz, and in many other small Polish towns, returning Jews were murdered.[14]

The conduct of the Red Army in the areas of Eastern Europe that it occupied was often rapacious and brutal. This too led Jewish survivors from the East to join the general westward stampede of millions of people fleeing to the safety of the Western powers' occupation zones of the former Third Reich. Upon arrival there the Jews found themselves back in camps, this time as refugees rather than prisoners and with British and American forces as protectors rather than German gaolers. These were the 'displaced persons' whose disposition became a major headache for the occupation forces in post-war Germany and Austria.

'Displaced persons' were formally defined by the International Refugee Organization (IRO), formed in 1947, as 'victims . . . of the Nazi or fascist . . . or . . . quisling regimes . . . [or] persons who were considered refugees before the outbreak of the second world war, for reasons of race, religion, nationality, or political opinion . . . who [have] been deported from, or obliged to leave [their] country of nationality or of former habitual residence'.[15] As so often in history, the invention of an ugly neologism was a revealing indicator of political frustration. The British and American governments, who found themselves primarily responsible for dealing with the problem, hesitated to use the word 'refugee' since that might imply acceptance that the person in question could not return to his home country. They were reluctant also to use the word 'Jew' if it could possibly be avoided, since that might suggest an invidious singling-out of one racial group among many. Hence the term 'displaced persons', which was not only ethnically neutral but seemed to suggest that the people described had got involved in some demographic traffic jam which might easily be sorted out if only they would all just follow the policemen's signals and go home. As the numbers of 'displaced persons' grew, with the arrival of new refugees from the East, the British Cabinet Office created a new category, 'infiltrees', although in real life these perforce merged into the general refugee problem.

Initially objects of pity, then instruments of propaganda, the 'displaced persons' were soon transformed into a millstone round the neck of the Allied authorities. Most had nowhere to go and those responsible for their welfare had no idea where to send them. The Jewish 'displaced persons', or 'DPs' as a world in a hurry came to refer to them, were not a majority of European Jewry in 1945. They numbered, in the beginning, no more than 100,000 or so out of around 4 million Jews in Europe. But they were a living symbol of the torment that all Jews in occupied Europe had endured and a reminder, initially disturbing, then frustrating, ultimately profoundly irritating, of the crime against humanity that continued to trouble the European conscience for long after the war.

The Jews had incontestably suffered more than any other group among the heterogeneous crowds of fugitives clamouring for attention in the summer of 1945. But they were neither the most numerous nor the most popular. From the outset the occupying powers worried about the political consequences of allowing Jews to receive any specially favourable treatment. When a Jewish organization, in early May 1945, sought permission from officials in London to arrange for the dispatch of food supplies from Sweden to Jews in liberated Europe, the Ministry of Economic Warfare expressed concern that 'those responsible for the feeding of civilians and refugees in western Germany may be glad to have extra supplies or may, on the other hand, consider that extra supplies for a particular class of refugee only is a source of embarrassment'.[16] A few weeks later Professor Selig Brodetsky, President of the Board of Deputies of British Jews (the main

Anglo-Jewish representative body), offered to form a consultative committee of Jewish organizations to assist the British occupation authorities in Germany in solving Jewish problems. The Foreign Office poured cold water on the idea. One official minuted:

> I do not think we should take lightly the difficulties which recognition of a Jewish body as advisers on Jewish interests in Germany [. . .] would cause.
>
>   The extermination of Jews in Germany is believed to have reduced their number from 660,000 to about 50,000. The Jewish problem being thus no longer *local*, the Jewish representatives would not be of assistance in dealing with practical problems but would no doubt use their position to interfere in general policy. Taking advantage of their curious privilege of being British subjects when it suits them and members of an extra-territorial community when this suits them better, they would form a pressure group and, having representatives actually in Germany, they could justly claim knowledge equal to that of the official Military Government. It is reasonable to suspect that the influence of the pressure group would be lent to most critics of our zonal policy who could use it for their own ends.[17]

The response to the offer was perhaps ungenerously expressed but it was not untypical. Within eight weeks of VE Day the Jews had thus been transformed in the minds of their liberators from victims of enemy atrocities into a troublesome 'pressure group'.

The official perception was in an important sense correct and the concern justified. For unlike the millions of Germans who fled from ancient areas of German settlement in the East, the Jews had influential friends. The Jews of the United States, more than 5 million in number and a powerful force within President Truman's Democratic Party, now found themselves the largest and most important Jewish community in the world. Most were immigrants or children of immigrants from Eastern or Central Europe. Many had lost relatives to the Nazi onslaught. During the war they had been told by the Allied governments and by most of their leaders that there was little or nothing that could be done to help the Jews in Europe except to win the war as soon as possible. Now the war was over, and it seemed there was still little or nothing that could be done. They were well organized (perhaps over-organized) in such groups as the American Jewish Committee and the World Jewish Congress. They also had experienced and effective welfare bodies, particularly the American Jewish Joint Distribution Committee (AJDC), popularly known as the 'Joint', to which very large sums of money were contributed. After years in which they had been condemned to observe impotently the mass murder of the Jews of Europe, these bodies were chafing at the bit, anxious at last to justify their existence and to give succour to the surviving remnant. Yet they found endless obstacles in their path.

The 'Joint' was the largest and richest American Jewish charitable organization, with a sophisticated staff of welfare administrators. It eschewed political involvement or publicity. Overall, between 1945 and 1948 it spent a total of $229 million, most of it on refugee relief and most of it in Europe. But its initial attempts to conduct welfare activities in the liberated areas under American and British control were hampered by the military occupation authorities, who objected to independent activity by what was regarded as a sectarian group. Thus the 'Joint' was able to begin operations in Buchenwald only on 13 June 1945, two months after its liberation.

In startling contrast to the obstructive attitude of the British (and to a lesser extent American) military occupation authorities to such requests from Jewish relief organizations, the Soviet Union manifested a readiness to cooperate, at least in the transportation of relief to Jews in liberated Poland and Czechoslovakia. The 'Joint' began shipments to Poland, via Teheran, as early as the end of 1944. In Czechoslovakia 'Joint' representatives began operations at Bratislava in April 1945 and in Prague a few days after its liberation in early May. The USSR had an underlying political motive: glimpsing an opportunity to increase the legitimacy of the Soviet-sponsored, communist-dominated Lublin Committee (which the Western powers refused to recognize as the government of Poland), it insisted that all aid be channelled through that body.[18]

The plight of the Jewish survivors and the sluggish response of the Western Allies quickly aroused protest. In July 1945, when

Churchill, Truman and Stalin met at Potsdam, the World Jewish Congress issued a public appeal, alleging that nearly three months after liberation many Nazi victims were still detained as virtual prisoners 'in conditions of the most abject misery' and were 'being treated with a callous and shameful neglect and indifference' by the Allied military control authorities.[19] The Post Office in London refused to accept the message for telegraphic transmission to Potsdam and it was eventually sent by diplomatic bag, although the Foreign Office considered it 'tendentious'.[20]

The British government's response to such interventions on behalf of Jewish survivors was not specially sympathetic. 'Jews,' wrote the Prime Minister, Clement Attlee, in September 1945, were to be treated in the same way as everybody else rather than as 'a special category at the head of the queue'.[21] British policy on the issue was dominated by the worsening situation in Palestine, ruled by Britain under a League of Nations mandate since the end of the First World War. By the late 1930s the mandate had degenerated into a political morass. Since 1939 Britain had limited Jewish immigration in the hope of damping down Arab hostility throughout the Middle East. Even before the end of the war the Zionists were secretly organizing illegal Jewish immigration from south-eastern Europe and Jewish terrorist groups were mounting attacks on British targets. Britain had become increasingly dependent during the war on Middle East oil and less able to maintain large forces in the Middle East to hold down local populations, whether Arab or Jewish. The Labour Party, which formed a government in July 1945, had supported Zionism outspokenly in earlier times but was now persuaded that British interests dictated a different policy. Immigration restrictions into Palestine were therefore maintained at an upper limit of 1,500 per month. In fact, as a result of illegal immigration, the average of monthly Jewish arrivals from all quarters was 1,870 between January 1946 and May 1948. More than 50,000 Jews, including illegal immigrants, arrived in Palestine from Europe between the end of the war and 14 May 1948. This number, however, was inadequate to meet the growing pressure of refugees seeking an exit from Eastern and Central Europe. As a result, some alternative destination for the displaced persons was required. No such outlet seemed to be available.

The difficult post-war economic and social position in Britain seemed to preclude the admission of large numbers of Jews there. The country already held more than 50,000 Jewish refugees from Germany and Austria who had arrived between 1933 and 1939. Pressure for repatriation of these refugees had arisen immediately after VE Day. On 15 May 1945 Austin Hopkinson, MP, asked the Prime Minister in the House of Commons 'whether in view of the destruction of National Socialism, arrangements can be made for the immediate repatriation of all Jewish refugees who had been the victims of persecution in their country of origin'. Responding on the basis of a Foreign Office brief, Churchill replied, 'No, sir', and referred to the 'very considerable practical difficulties'. When Hopkinson pressed the issue, reminding the Prime Minister that successive home secretaries had given assurances 'that these men were to be repatriated at the earliest possible moment', Churchill added that repatriation 'still remains the desire, but Europe is in a state of frightful confusion at the moment'.[22] Given the hostility to Jewish refugees who were already in the country, the British government felt unable to open its doors to a new influx. A flurry of inquiries into various far-fetched proposals for Jewish settlement in remote corners of the empire or the globe revealed a host of obstacles – as had similar investigations before the war. In default of any alternative, the British hit on the notion that the latest wave of Jewish refugees should return to their countries of origin and reconstruct their lives there, in common with the rest of the population of Europe. It was a policy that appealed to basic liberal principle and apparently to common sense. But it did not work.

The United States government had no solution either. The country's highly restrictive and racially inspired immigration laws prevented the entry of large numbers of East European Jews. Congressional opinion, after the war as before, remained hostile to new immigration legislation. President Truman, however, was pressed strongly by Jewish organizations to do something. He

ordered an on-the-spot investigation. Earl G. Harrison, a former
US Commissioner of Immigration who was Dean of the University of Pennsylvania Law School, was appointed on 22 June 1945
to undertake the task. He visited the DP camps and submitted his
findings to Truman with extraordinary dispatch on 1 August.
Harrison's report was a damning indictment of the conditions
faced by the DPs and of the policies of the Allied authorities
responsible for their welfare:

> Three months after V E Day . . . many Jewish displaced persons . . .
> are living under guard behind barbed-wire fences . . . amidst
> crowded, frequently insanitary and generally grim conditions, in
> complete idleness, with no opportunity, except surreptitiously, to
> communicate with the outside world, waiting, hoping for some
> word of encouragement and action in their behalf . . .
>
> Many of the Jewish displaced persons, late in July, had no
> clothing other than their concentration camp garb − a rather
> hideous striped pajama effect − while others, to their chagrin, were
> obliged to wear German SS uniforms . . .
>
> Beyond knowing that they are no longer in danger of the gas
> chambers, torture and other forms of violent death, they see − and
> there is − little change . . .
>
> The first and plainest need of these people is a recognition of
> their actual status and by this I mean their status as Jews . . . The
> general practice thus far has been to follow only nationality lines
> . . . There is a distinctly unrealistic approach to the problem.
> Refusal to recognize the Jews as such has the effect, in this
> situation, of closing one's eyes to their former and more barbaric
> persecution, which has already made them a separate group with
> greater needs.
>
> As matters now stand, we appear to be treating the Jews as the
> Nazis treated them except that we do not exterminate them. They
> are in concentration camps in large numbers under our own
> military guards instead of the SS troops. One is led to wonder
> whether the German people, seeing this, are not supposing that we
> are following or at least condoning Nazi policy.

Harrison proposed a number of administrative reforms, designed
to bring about an immediate improvement in living conditions in
the camps. For the longer term he urged that Truman press the

British government to admit 100,000 people from the camps to Palestine.[23]

A British observer noted rather condescendingly that Harrison's report was 'filled with misleading innuendo and truths out of context. The shocked civilian, fresh from the undisturbed comforts of modern living, is apt to find himself somewhat bewildered on a war-torn continent, and it might be charitable to suppose that this, rather than deliberate misreporting, gave rise to the confusion.'[24] The dark picture painted by Harrison was perhaps overstated but it contained several grains of truth. On one point, the attitude of some of the occupation chiefs, Harrison may even be said to have pulled his punches. General Patton, for example, whose area of command in southern Germany contained the largest number of DPs in the American occupation zone, commented in his diary on 15 September: 'Harrison and his ilk believe that the DP is a human being, which he is not, and this applies particularly to the Jews, who are lower than animals.'[25] A pamphlet issued by the US War Department in late 1946 attempted to inculcate a sympathetic attitude towards DPs among lower ranks, but in so doing disclosed some of the prevalent hostility. The pamphlet admitted that, on their first encounter with DPs, the average GI

> found it difficult to understand and like people who pushed, screamed, clawed for food, smelled bad, who couldn't and didn't want to obey orders, who sat with dull faces and vacant staring eyes in a cellar, or concentration camp barrack, or within a primitive cave, and refused to come out at their command ... When people are reduced to the animal level their reaction to suggestion and situations is on that level.

After outlining the harsh conditions in which most of the DPs had lived, the pamphlet argued that there was 'little wonder that the resultant product of this systematic starvation and enforced slavery should present a picture of apathy, chronic weakness, lack of coordination, and warped mentality'.[26]

Truman and Eisenhower took immediate action to implement the main recommendations in Harrison's report. The US zonal authorities established twelve all-Jewish camps, dismantled the barbed wire and watch-towers, recognized Jews as a separate, favoured category and increased their standard food ration to 2,300, later 2,500, calories a day. Although the ultimate responsibility for the camps remained that of the occupying armies, direct administration was taken over in October 1945 by the United Nations Relief and Rehabilitation Administration (UNRRA). Jewish advisers were appointed to the US military government and the 'Joint' was enabled to carry on its welfare work in the camps with relative freedom. The British disliked the idea of segregating Jewish DPs but they were compelled to follow the American example. Similar measures were taken in the French zone and in all three Western occupation zones in Austria.

One reason for the irritation of the Allied governments with the volume of Jewish protest was that it seemed disproportionate to the larger refugee problem in Europe. Jews formed only a small part of the millions of refugees who were attempting to move from Eastern to Western Europe. A British estimate in September 1945 counted a total of 1,888,000 displaced persons, excluding ethnic Germans. Only 53,000 of these were said to be Jews in camps in Germany, Austria and Italy. The Jews jostled for attention with Germans fleeing the Russian occupation of East Prussia and the Polish annexation of Silesia; Volksdeutsche, members of long-established German communities in Czechoslovakia, Romania, Hungary and Yugoslavia, who were expelled by those states; Baltic, Ukrainian and other former collaborators, who feared vengeance at the hand of the Soviets; Cossacks and Russian turncoats, who had engaged as volunteers in Nazi military units; anti-communists of all nationalities, who found themselves branded as class enemies by the newly installed Soviet puppet governments. The focus, particularly in the American press, on the Jewish aspect of the displaced persons problem greatly annoyed the British occupation authorities, who came to suspect the hidden hand of American Jewish influence on the media.

In the later part of 1945, however, the number of Jewish DPs began to increase even as many of the non-Jews began to be absorbed in Germany and Austria. Jewish departures from Eastern Europe, particularly Poland, were stimulated by repeated outbreaks of anti-Jewish violence. A total of 353 Jews are estimated to have been killed by Poles between May and December 1945. Violent antisemitic propaganda, produced by extreme right-wing groups, appeared in many Polish cities. Pogroms broke out in Rzeszów in July and Cracow in August.

A clandestine organization of Palestinian Zionists, the Mossad le-Aliyah Bet, with its headquarters in Paris, was instrumental in channelling the movement of Jews out of Eastern Europe and towards Palestine. Already in June 1945 members of the Jewish Brigade of the British Army stationed in Italy, mainly Palestinians, had begun moving boatloads of illegal Jewish immigrants to Palestine. Jan Masaryk, the notably pro-Jewish Foreign Minister of Czechoslovakia, arranged for nine trains to be furnished to carry Jews from the Polish border across his country to the US zone of Germany. During the summer and autumn of 1945 tens of thousands of Jewish survivors from Eastern Europe began to trek towards the Western occupation zones of Germany and Austria, adding to the magnitude of the problem. Some were organized by the Zionists; others moved on their own. The DP camps in Italy were soon full to overflowing and pressure on those in Germany and Austria steadily increased. At the all-Jewish camp of Feldafing in Bavaria, army barracks suitable for 2,500 persons were housing 6,000. At Landsberg, also in Bavaria, conditions were so crowded that some residents had to sleep two to a bed. In August the British occupation authorities, fully realizing that the ultimate intended destination of the refugees was Palestine, closed the Italo-Austrian border to refugees. In December they prohibited any movement of Jews into or through their zone of Germany via Berlin. The flow of refugees continued regardless.

The British reacted with bafflement verging on fury. General Sir Frederick Morgan, chief of UNRRA Operations in Germany, complained at a press conference in Frankfurt on 2 January 1946 of a 'well-organized plan to get [the Jews] out of Europe'. He expressed scepticism regarding the 'monotonous story about pogroms', asserting that the Jews who arrived from Poland were 'well dressed and fed, rosy-cheeked; and have plenty of money. They certainly do not look like persecuted people.'[27] The remarks (later half-repudiated) provoked outrage among Jews, particularly in America. If Morgan's statements displayed a certain lack of sensitivity, on one point at any rate he had been right: the exodus was planned and organized. Where he was wrong, however, was in imagining it could be stopped. The British Embassy in Warsaw, closer to the realities, meanwhile reported that it was 'nonsense' to imagine that there was any prospect for a revival of Jewish life in Poland; the remaining Jews there would leave *en masse* 'whatever His Majesty's Government or anyone else may say'.[28]

The Warsaw embassy, however, was not heeded. The bulk of British officials and politicians concerned with the issue resorted to a conspiracy theory in order to explain the exodus – an easy but in large measure self-deceiving interpretation. They suspected their fellow occupiers, Russians, French and Americans alike, of complicity in the Jewish refugee movement. The suspicions were fully justified. All three powers, it seemed, had reason to wish to embarrass the British in the Middle East. The Russians saw Palestine as the weak point in Britain's imperial armour in the region and hoped to exploit it to expel the British from the area altogether. They therefore allowed Polish Jewish refugees in Russia to leave the USSR. In July 1945 an agreement was concluded between the Russian and Polish governments permitting Poles and Jews from the former eastern Polish borderlands acquired by the Soviet Union to renounce Soviet citizenship acquired during the war and return to Poland. The repatriates began to arrive in Poland in February 1946 and by the following July an estimated 157,000 had arrived. Most had little interest in remaining in Poland and immediately sought (and, with the help of Zionist agents, found) means of moving west. The USSR also seems to have encouraged, or at least allowed, Eastern European governments to permit continued movement of Jewish refugees west towards the British and American zones of Germany and Austria and south towards Palestine.

The American administration was sensitive not only to Jewish electoral pressure but also to the charge that American democracy was now being used as a buttress for British imperialism. They therefore pressed the British to admit Jewish refugees to Palestine but would not send US troops there to uphold continued British rule. Meanwhile, some American Jewish military personnel, as well as Jewish relief administrators, collaborated with the Zionists in organizing the flow of refugees aiming to go to Palestine.

In fact, Russian and American motives were rather more complex than some British conspiracy-theorists granted. While the Soviet government undoubtedly wished to add to British embarrassment in the Middle East by helping to stimulate the refugee tide, it had no wish to legitimize Jewish nationalist activity within its own domain. Moreover, the many Jews among its communist protégés in Eastern Europe were vehement opponents of the Zionists and cooperated with them very much à contrecoeur. The Americans had no wish to add to the burdens of occupation and therefore were sometimes ready to cooperate with the British in seeking to limit the exodus from the East.

As for the French, they bitterly resented British pressure on them to fulfil wartime commitments to grant independence to Syria and Lebanon and consequently took an undisguised Schadenfreude in Britain's predicament in Palestine. Public sentiment in France, sensitive to the plight of the Jewish DPs, was reflected in the blind eye that French border and port officials often turned to the passage of refugees. All over Europe, therefore, Russian, American and French military officers, bureaucrats and agents, sometimes for reasons of personal sympathy, often as a matter of policy, facilitated the Jewish refugee movement that, as a result, became ever larger and more of an annoyance to the British.

As there appeared to be no means of dissolving the DP camps, they developed into semi-permanent settlements. Gradually some semblance of normality returned as the camp residents, no longer clad in striped prison clothes, were restored, thanks to UNRRA medical care and adequate food rations, to at least the outward appearance of physical health. Daily life inside the camps acquired some sense of purpose as the inmates engaged in education, sports such as football and boxing, music, theatre and other recreational activities. Political organization also resumed, generally along the lines of the pre-war Jewish parties of Eastern Europe − orthodox, Bundist and Zionist. The urge for expression found outlets in a number of newspapers, mostly in Yiddish; owing to the non-availability of Hebrew type, however, these were initially printed in Latin characters. Their contents reveal a gradual return to normalcy in, for example, an increasing number of marriage announcements. But they also contained grim reminders of recent horrors in long columns of 'Missing Relatives' notices. As 1945 wore into 1946, these papers also bore eloquent and sometimes angry testimony to the frustration of the camp-dwellers. Generally they were Zionist in orientation and, as the Palestine conflict grew fiercer, they became increasingly hostile to Britain – particularly those papers published in the American zone.[29]

The British suspected that the Zionists were using undue influence or even strong-arm tactics to persuade DPs to declare that Palestine was their only desired destination. There was some localized evidence to support this. But overall the sentiment in the camps was heavily Zionist and became more so as months in the camps turned into years, as the prospect of returning to live in Eastern Europe became ever less attractive and as the USA, Canada and Britain were disinclined to admit Jewish refugees. Zionist emissaries in the camps were themselves impressed by the fervour they encountered. When David Ben Gurion visited the camps in late 1945 he found that 'despite everything, people are healthy, both in the physical sense and in the spiritual sense. The majority are precious Jews, precious Zionists with deep Zionist instincts, ready to undergo again all troubles if this is what Zionism requires – with fervour for the unity and survival of the Jewish people.'[30] No doubt there was an element of wishful thinking in this. When it suited his purpose of the moment, Ben Gurion reverted to a negative evaluation of the Zionist potential of the survivors. The displaced persons were, in truth, a palimpsest on which all those involved could imprint their values, hopes and obsessions.

But the camp-dwellers also spoke with their own voices. Committees emerged in each camp and an umbrella organization known as She'erit ha-Pletah (The Surviving Remnant) was formed. These bodies were rent by constant feuds, political differences and a tendency towards hysteria born of memories of past agonies and increasing desperation about a clouded future. They lodged complaints and demands with the occupation authorities, UNRRA, the 'Joint', IRO, the press, the Jewish Agency – anybody who would listen, and many who would not. An American Jewish aid worker noted:

> the average leader of these various Jewish barracks, or camps, is a young, defiant, militant Jew . . . I happened to place my hands on the shoulder of a meek-appearing Jew of about 35 or 38. He turned to me and said, 'nemt arunter di hent fun mir' [take your hands off me!]. It was not how he said it, it was the look in his eye of defiance.[31]

The main political beneficiary of this mood was Zionism. The impact of Ben Gurion's visit to Landsberg in October 1945 was recorded by the camp commander in his diary:

> To the people he is God. It seems he represents all of their hopes of getting to Palestine . . . The first I knew of his coming was when we noticed the people streaming out to line the street leading from Munich. They were carrying flowers and hastily improvised banners and signs . . . I don't think that a visit by President Truman could cause as much excitement.[32]

A survey found that 90 per cent of Jewish DPs questioned said they wanted to emigrate to Palestine. A poll taken in a Bavarian DP camp in early 1946 showed that of 22,000 people, thirteen wished to stay in Europe, 596 hoped to go to the USA, the British Commonwealth or Latin America, while almost all the others said they wanted to go to Palestine.[33] In May 1946 UNRRA carried out a poll of DPs in assembly centres in Germany and concluded that the Jews 'expressed a unanimous desire' to emigrate, 'the majority of them either to Palestine or to the U.S.'. The UNRRA report added:

> By far the largest number of Polish and Ukrainian Jews express a desire to go to Palestine . . . Although many would perhaps prefer to go to some western country, the emigration quotas to these lands will be so low as to allow only a trickle of immigrants to enter. Palestine appears to be the only solution to the problem.

Hundreds of ballots showed just one word as an explanation for not returning home: 'Palestine'.

The report cited some typical comments on ballots by Jewish DPs:

Palestine is my fatherland.

Poland is covered with Jewish blood; even now the Poles are persecuting Jews. We can visit the cemeteries, but we cannot live there. Therefore I want to immigrate to the U.S. to join my relatives in the best democracy in the world.

I have nobody left at home.

My husband was murdered by the Germans. I spent three years in the KZ [concentration camp]. My relatives are in foreign countries. They will take care of me.

All my relatives were killed in Auschwitz. I can't live among the murderers of my parents.[34]

As time went on, the Zionist tendency in the camps had become pronounced and was reflected in elections to representative committees. These revealed strong support for Zionists of all hues, including the militant Revisionist Zionists. The mood of the period was indicated by the alliance of convenience in many camps, where joint electoral lists were offered by the Revisionists and the ultra-orthodox Agudas Yisroel party, who were theoretically anti-Zionist although most of their adherents in the camps evidently wanted to go to Palestine.

In the hope of drawing the Americans into some form of constructive commitment to help in a solution, the British persuaded Washington in October 1945 to agree to the establishment of an Anglo-American Committee of Inquiry into the issue. The scope of the inquiry was to cover not only Palestine but also the Jewish refugees in Europe. The American members of the committee included Joseph C. Hutcheson, a Texas judge, Bartley C. Crum, a California lawyer, and James G. McDonald, former League of Nations High Commissioner for Refugees. Among the British was Richard Crossman, an ambitious and intellectually agile young Labour MP who was strongly sympathetic to the Jewish cause; he wrote a vivid account of the committee's investigations in both Europe and Palestine.[35] The committee was not granted permission by the Russian occupation authorities to visit Hungary or Romania, but some of its members visited Poland and others inspected DP camps in Austria and Germany. In Poland the committee's investigations were conducted in what one member described as 'an atmosphere of conspiracy, lawlessness, violence, robbery, forces of foreign power, espionage and Government disliked by most and loathed by many'.[36] The Austrian Minister of the Interior told the committee that the allocation of special accommodation and rations to DPs was producing resentment and antisemitism: 'You have taken all the best hotels in our most beautiful resort, Bad Gastein, for these poor migrants from Poland. That may be tolerable for a year. But longer . . .'[37]

The Anglo-American Committee's report in April 1946 pleased almost nobody. It angered the British and the Arabs by calling for the immediate admission of 100,000 Jewish refugees from Europe to Palestine. At the same time it infuriated the Zionists by rejecting their demand for a Jewish state and by recommending the disbandment of the Jewish underground armed forces in Palestine. The Truman administration greatly annoyed the British by seizing on the recommendation for 100,000 refugee admissions to Palestine, an echo of Harrison's proposal the previous summer, and urging its immediate implementation. The British response was to announce that no such measure could be entertained without the disarmament of the Jewish underground forces. This decision was ill-received in the United States but the British Foreign Secretary, Ernest Bevin, with undiplomatic bluntness, suggested that the 'agitation in the United States, and particularly in New York . . . was because they did not want too many of them [the Jewish DPs] in New York'.[38] The remark did not enhance Bevin's popularity among Jews, nor did it assist British diplomatic efforts in Washington.

The result was stalemate and an additional long period of uncertainty for the residents of the camps. In April–May 1946 the Economic and Social Council of the United Nations held a conference in London on the problem of refugees and DPs, but no practical solution emerged. Meanwhile, the Jewish position in Eastern Europe deteriorated.

At Kielce, north of Warsaw, on 4 July 1946, the 200 Jewish survivors of a pre-war Jewish community that had numbered 18,000 were attacked by an angry crowd. The Jews were accused of having abducted a Christian boy with a view to killing him for ritual purposes. Soldiers and policemen joined in the attack on a house in which Jewish *halutzim* (Zionist pioneers) were living. The chairman of the Jewish community was shot dead in the back of the head by a soldier while trying to telephone to the city authorities to appeal for help. Forty-one Jews were killed and fifty injured – some shot, others killed by axe-blows or stoned to death. Further deaths and injuries occurred in separate incidents in and around the city. One of the survivors later recalled:

> When I came to I was lying naked among corpses. Shortly before-hand, I had been vaguely aware of being stripped of my wrist-watch and shoes by a soldier. This was the guard who was watching over the Jewish corpses. I was saved from being buried alive by Dr Balanowski, who noticed that I was moving my arm. I was taken, seriously wounded, to a hospital in Lodz where I was laid up for two months.[39]

One hundred people were arrested for participation in the massacre and nine were sentenced to death. The cemetery in which the victims were buried was later turned into a football field. By mid-1947 the Jewish death toll in such incidents in Poland since the end of the war had risen to over 1,500.

The responses of the Polish government and the Roman Catholic Church in Poland to these events were deeply coloured by the virtual civil war which was still continuing between communists and their enemies in the country. Cardinal Hlond, the Catholic Primate, condemned the killings at Kielce, but he added that 'they cannot be attributed to racialism. They arose on an entirely different, painful and tragic foundation.' His further elaboration made it plain that he placed much of the responsibility on the shoulders of the Jews themselves:

During the time of the exterminating German occupation, the Poles, in spite of the fact that they themselves were being exterminated, aided, hid, and saved Jews, endangering thereby their own lives. Many a Jew in Poland owes his life to Poles and to the Polish clergy. The responsibility that this good relationship is deteriorating lies in great measure on the Jews who remain in Poland on preferential bases in governmental affairs and who tend to impose forms of organization which the enormous majority of the people do not want. That is a harmful game, because from this dangerous tensions arise. In fatal armed encounters on the political battle front in Poland some Jews perish, I regret to say, but far more Poles perish.[40]

This statement clearly aligned the Polish Church with the enemies of the 'Zydo-Komuna' (Jewish communist ramp), as the Jewish communists came to be called. It also demonstrated, incidentally, that 'Jews' and 'Poles' remained distinct categories in the mind of Hlond as of most Poles. Jews, in other words, whether communists or not, assimilated or not, Yiddish- or Polish-speaking, could never, so far as Hlond was concerned, be Poles in the full sense. In this Hlond faithfully reflected the outlook of the great majority of his flock.

A different (though to many Jews no less disturbing) outlook was evinced by Professor Olgierd Górka, an official of the Polish Foreign Office specially assigned to handle Jewish matters. In a conversation with an American diplomat a few days after the events in Kielce, Górka outlined the government's view. He admitted that soldiers and militia had been involved in the riot and that the authorities in Kielce had not taken effective action. He attributed the disturbances to antisemitism, but there was a point of convergence with Hlond's view in Górka's reference to 'resentment which existed on the part of some of the people because of the Jews in the government'. He particularly mentioned the failure of the Roman Catholic clergy to join in resistance to racism.[41] The full-blown official version, developed later under communist rule, explained the pogrom as a 'large-scale anti-Jewish provocation' by 'an organized reactionary group'.[42]

The Kielce pogrom and smaller-scale similar outbreaks elsewhere led further large numbers of Jews to move out of Eastern Europe, particularly Poland. The Polish government reached an informal understanding with Palestinian Zionist agents that it would not impede the outflow. An UNRRA report in late July 1946 indicated that the illegal departure of Jews from Poland across the so-called 'green frontier' with Czechoslovakia had increased from about seventy a week to 700 a day. An American diplomatic dispatch explained:

> Movement of Jews over the whole route is facilitated, although illegally, by all local authorities involved. Polish border guards allow Jews to cross the Polish frontier. The Czech authorities transport them across Czechoslovakia. The Soviets assist their transit of the Soviet zone in Austria as far as Vienna. From this point they make their way into the American zone, whence U.S. military authorities, being unable to care for them themselves, permit them to cross the border into the American zone [of] Germany.[43]

Between June and September 1946 an estimated 100,000 Jews left Poland; most travelled through Czechoslovakia to the DP camps in Germany.

This was a spontaneous emigration; it was also highly organized. Altogether it has been estimated that of the quarter of a million or so Jewish refugees who fled Eastern Europe between 1945 and 1948, about four-fifths were brought out under Zionist auspices. Many of these were subsequently moved to Palestine aboard boats sailing from a number of Mediterranean ports, from Bulgaria to France. In all, sixty-five ships set sail, but most were intercepted and boarded by the British, who interned the passengers, at first in a camp in Palestine and, from August 1946, in Cyprus. Eventually more than 50,000 Jewish refugees were detained in Cyprus, among them at least 6,000 children. Camps, administered by the 'Joint', were established at Caraolos near Famagusta and at Xylotymbou near Dhekelia. The pace of arrivals was so hectic that many were housed in tents or obliged to sleep on the ground. Photographs of these prisoners, including many children, once again behind barbed wire, aroused worldwide indignation – not only among Jews. But

British officials dismissed protests based on what they saw as grossly inflated Zionist propaganda.

The British deceived themselves, however, in thinking that the Jews fled as a result of misleading 'propaganda' activity by the Zionists. There was, of course, such propaganda, but in truth the Jewish populations in Poland and elsewhere in Eastern Europe needed little persuasion to leave. By late 1946 they were in a state bordering on mass hysteria. Observing the mounting hostility of the surrounding non-Jewish populations towards them, they recalled that they had made the mistake in the recent past of staying put until it was too late. Most were resolved not to repeat the error. The British government, fearful that the migrants would seek to enter Palestine, pressed the Czechoslovak government to refuse to allow them to cross Czechoslovak territory. The government in Prague formally acceded to the British request. But, as an American diplomat in Prague noted in October 1946, the movement of Jewish refugees continued, although 'on a reduced scale'. The reason for the failure to close the border completely was said to be 'the benevolent attitude of the Czechoslovak Minister of the Interior and of General [Joseph] McNarney [Eisenhower's successor as American army chief in Europe]'.[44]

The quickened pace of Jewish emigration from Eastern Europe changed the dimensions of the Jewish DP problem and heightened the urgency of finding a solution. The number of Jewish DPs receiving UNRRA aid in Germany, which was 18,361 in December 1946, increased to 97,333 by June 1946 and 167,531 a year later. By then nearly a quarter of a million Jewish refugees in Germany, Austria and Italy were dependent on UNRRA for their survival.

In September 1946 a confidential report by the US zone headquarters of UNRRA in Germany warned of the danger of creating a '"barrack race" – a demoralized, hopeless mass of stranded humanity'. The same report noted that the DPs were 'held in the greatest contempt by the Germans' and were also despised by many American occupation soldiers. 'The DPs are generally considered by military personnel as "lousy Poles" and

"Goddam DP" who should be sent back where they came from whether they like it or not.' The report continued:

> In so far as it has affected and continues to affect the DP situation, we can state authoritatively that the US military establishment has broken down completely. The directives of General Eisenhower have not been and are not being properly implemented in the field. The majority of officials are woefully ignorant of the problem and the few officers remaining who have knowledge of and sympathy for it are unable to make their influence felt at the troop level.
>
> That the contempt for the DP and forgetfulness of his proper status has also permeated the higher echelons is evidenced by recent policies [. . . such as] the granting of authority for the use of German police in carrying out raids and searches in DP installations. [. . .]
>
> This policy has provoked several serious situations and has culminated in the incident at Stuttgart, where over 200 armed German police, under the supervision of a few MP [military police] with *no* commissioned officer, using a number of dogs on leashes, surrounded and attempted to search a camp of approximately 1,500 Polish-Jewish Displaced Persons. This resulted in the shooting to death by the German police of one Polish-Jew (survivor of a concentration camp and only recently reunited with his wife and two children) and the wounding by gunshot of three other DPs.[45]

A relatively fair-minded British observer gives eloquent testimony to the deteriorating relations between the British authorities and Jews in the camps in the British zone:

> Most of the Jews ... were, understandably, in an unbalanced emotional condition. But even though rational behaviour could hardly have been expected, their mental state was frequently so abnormal and offensive that it required a real effort for even the most friendly non-Jews to keep from being goaded into discriminatory action. Jews complained about being segregated, as this suggested the ghetto and Nazi methods. Yet when not segregated they complained about being separated from their own kind. They complained about crowding in the centres, and yet it was the unexpected and illegal infiltration of thousands of Jews which had

caused the crowding. They complained about the shortage of food
and other supplies, and yet their rations were larger than other
United Nations displaced persons, and their supplies were plentiful
enough to enable many to engage in large-scale black market
operations ... They conducted sit-down and hunger strikes to
pressure the authorities to rectify complaints, many of them imagi-
nary. And they shouted jeers and taunts at those in authority. It is
to the credit of the Western military, and their Jewish advisers, that
they handled so tactfully the many incidents that arose, minimized
the friction, and found day-to-day solutions in this emotionally
surcharged atmosphere.'[46]

Each of these strictures was based on a kernel of truth – but the
deep frustration on both sides that gave rise to such relations arose
from a reality that was less 'to the credit' of the two powers
centrally involved: their utter failure to find any solution to a
problem that grew steadily in size and in its international
ramifications.

The longer the displaced person problem dragged on, the more
insistent were the British that the Jews must not be accorded any
special or separate treatment. 'Any discriminatory treatment on
behalf of Jews runs counter to the fundamental principle of the
Foreign Office policy.'[47] Palestine was only one reason. Behind the
British attitude lay also a broader feeling that the efforts after the
First World War to protect Jews and other minorities in Eastern
Europe by so-called 'minority treaties' had proved a failure. At the
Paris peace conference in 1919 a number of Jewish organizations
had been represented and had played an important part in securing
the passage of such treaties. Towards the end of the Second World
War the World Jewish Congress and other Jewish organizations
formed a joint committee to press the powers to incorporate
Jewish concerns in the peace treaties to be imposed on the defeated
powers. They called for the outlawing of fascist movements, the
punishment of war criminals, the recognition of the right of Jews
to maintain 'their collective ethnic, religious, linguistic, and cultural
identity and institutions', as well as the return of confiscated
Jewish property and freedom of Jewish emigration. But the representatives of Jewish organizations who presented these demands at

the 1946 Paris peace conference encountered less receptive ears than their predecessors in 1919. Then 'world Jewry' had been courted as a power and the Zionist leader, Chaim Weizmann, had been received as a statesman who represented an important political force. Now Jewry was reduced to a remnant of petitioners and the Jewish organizations' representatives were paid little attention. One of them, Israel Cohen, commented on the 'depressing contrast' with 1919. He and his colleagues were received with 'effusive sympathy' but their proposals were, for the most part, ignored: 'The representatives of Romania, Hungary and Bulgaria issued separate statements for the purpose of proving to the conference that the Jewish amendments [to the draft peace treaties] were unjustified and might, if adopted, tend to "create" antisemitism in their countries.'[48] In Bulgaria Jews themselves were induced by the government to organize protests against the proposed protective clauses. The British oscillated on the issue. While they resisted the concept of specific Jewish interests, they wished to encourage the resettlement of Jewish DPs in their countries of origin – which necessitated the creation of conditions that would induce Jews to return. They therefore moved in September 1946 to insert an amendment in the Romanian peace treaty that would prohibit any form of discriminatory legislation. It was approved over the objections of the Romanian government, which complained that it was humiliating and anyway superfluous, as were similar amendments to the Hungarian and Bulgarian treaties. The treaties with Hungary and Romania, when they finally emerged, did, as a result, include provisions for the restitution of property of victims of racial or religious persecution.

With Palestine in mind, however, the British Foreign Office still resisted any proposal that might seem to recognize the existence of a Jewish nation. Thus in 1947, when the Foreign Office was considering a draft peace treaty with Austria, officials immediately rejected proposals from Jewish organizations that the treaty include specific provisions against 'anti-Jewish activities', as well as protective clauses for Jewish displaced persons. 'Protection and immunities designed to cover the Jews alone are likely to aggravate any hostility to them which exists,' minuted one Foreign Office official. And another: 'Refugee Dept. do not welcome any proposals which would tend to give Jewish displaced persons and refugees privileges which are not enjoyed by other persons in the same unhappy plight.'[49] So disturbed were the British occupation authorities in Germany over the mass influx of Jews from the East that at one point they proposed to their American counterparts that rations for Jewish DPs in both zones should be reduced to the standard for Germans, that they should be compelled to work in the German economy and placed under German legal jurisdiction. The opposition of UNRRA and the US authorities prevented these proposals being put into practice.[50]

The British refusal to treat the Jews as a distinct category led to a mass movement of Jewish DPs from the British to the American occupation zone in Germany. Soon the overwhelming majority of Jewish DPs were concentrated there. Between August 1945 and April 1947 the American authorities announced repeatedly that no new Jewish refugees would be admitted to DP camps in their zone, but pressure of numbers from refugees fleeing Poland and Romania compelled them again and again to extend the deadline.

The melodramatic saga of the ship *Exodus 1947*, which sailed for Palestine in the summer of 1947 with 4,515 refugees on board, marked the climax of the British–Zionist struggle over immigration to Palestine. The ship was boarded when it arrived at the shore of Palestine and three people were killed in fighting with British troops. The refugees were refused admission to Palestine and were sent back to France. The French government would not permit them to land. Bevin, in a disastrous fit of pique, decided to make an example of them, and ordered their return to Germany, where they were forcibly disembarked and once again placed in camps under military guard. The resulting tumult was attributed by British officials to 'Zionist propaganda'. But no great promotional skill was required by Zionist advocates to turn this episode into a signal moral victory for their cause. Desultory discussions continued in London and Washington, but it was only with the decision of the United Nations in November 1947 to partition Palestine into Jewish and Arab states that a resolution of the interrelated problems of Palestine and the DPs at last appeared on the horizon.

The British withdrawal from Palestine on 14 May 1948 and the proclamation that day of the independent state of Israel opened the Zionist-controlled areas of the country to free Jewish immigration. On the first day of the state's existence 1,700 Jews arrived. By December more than 100,000 had entered and by the end of 1951 the total number of immigrants since independence had reached 687,000. Of these more than 300,000 came from Europe, the largest numbers being Poles (118,940) and Romanians (103,732). The refugees on Cyprus were gradually released by the British, although men of military age and their families were not permitted to go to Israel until January 1949.

Meanwhile, the United States too opened its doors – but only gradually and with many reservations. Truman demonstrated considerable personal concern for the DPs but he was unable to do much by executive action to alter the country's highly restrictive immigration policy. In May 1946 two ships carried the first group of 1,215 Jewish DPs to America. Forty thousand people were admitted between 1946 and 1948 as emergency immigrants under the 'Truman Directive'. Of these 12,849 were Jews. Legislative proposals became bogged down in acrimonious debate and it was not until July 1948 that the Displaced Persons Act opened American doors to the refugees. The act permitted the admission of nearly 250,000 DPs per annum, a ceiling that was raised in 1950 to 415,000. But the act set a cut-off date of 22 December 1945: Jews who had arrived in Germany or Austria after that date were ineligible for admission. The relevant clause was amended only in June 1950. The act was, in fact, primarily designed to facilitate the admission not of Jews but of anti-communist Balts and Germans; pressure from Jewish organizations nevertheless enabled an estimated 63,000 Jews to enter under the act. Altogether, between 1945 and 1952 an estimated 137,450 Jews immigrated to the United States, of whom about half were classified as DPs.★ Among

---

★ No exact count of Jewish immigrants to the USA was made in official immigration statistics after 1943; these figures are therefore estimates.

these were many European Jewish refugees who had found shelter during the war in remote corners of the earth, from Havana to Shanghai.

The remainder of the DPs scattered to other countries. At least 20,000 Jews from Europe settled in Canada between 1946 and 1953. Latin American states took in about 15,000 and Australia 11,000. Some European states too admitted Jewish refugees: France, Belgium, Sweden and the Netherlands took more than 5,000 each.

The British contribution was less impressive. Although over 200,000 East European refugees, including Balts, Ukrainians and Yugoslavs, some of whom had fought in SS and other German units during the war, were admitted to Britain in the period 1945–50, the number of Jewish DPs admitted is estimated at under 3,000. Jews were accorded a low priority for settlement in Britain, apparently for fear that they might move on to Palestine. There were also other reasons. Major-General Winterton, second-in-command of the British military administration in Austria, wrote to Lord Pakenham in April 1949:

> It seems to us, however, much more simple and more effective to recruit from the whole body of DPs without regard to nationality, except that we should exclude Jews and Polish men because of the opposition from public opinion at home, and persons whom we acknowledge to be Soviet citizens, because of the certainty of trouble with the Soviets if we recruit such people.[51]

The last stage of the Jewish DP problem in Europe was a sorry, at times sordid, affair. In December 1950 there were still 39,000 Jewish DPs in camps in Germany, Austria and Italy, but thereafter the numbers were rapidly reduced. When IRO closed its operations in January 1952, only 12,000 Jewish DPs remained in Germany. In the autumn of 1955, 322 were still living in camps in Austria and 999 at Föhrenwald, the last Jewish DP camp in Germany. These were regarded as the 'hard core' of DPs, many of whom had become so accustomed to camp life that they refused to leave. Some were tuberculosis cases who would not go to Israel and could not go to any other country. Others were mentally ill. Others again saw the camp as a 'golden bridge' for securing better compensation terms from the German government. The camp population also included some 'illegal' residents who had returned to the camps from Israel. The Israeli government had sought to prevent such re-emigration by stamping the documents of departing citizens 'not to be used to enter Germany' but they left anyway and threw away their passports, thus turning themselves once again into stateless persons.[52] At that period Zionist ideology attributed *yerida* (emigration from Israel) to weakness of character and even moral obliquity. The equation was too simple. The motives of the emigrants were generally mixed: some found economic conditions in the Jewish state too difficult. Others missed what they regarded as the security of camp life. Some were indeed 'flotsam and jetsam, ne'er-do-wells, irresponsibles, and not infrequently gangster types' (the description is from a confidential 'Joint' report in August 1953[53]). Altogether about 3,500 former DPs had returned to Germany by 1953. The problem of what to do with them was rendered more acute by the refusal of the USA, Canada and most other countries of settlement to regard them as refugees since they had voluntarily left Israel.

Welfare officers of the 'Joint' became exasperated with the obduracy of the elected leaders of the remaining Jewish DPs. Charles Jordan, head of the organization's Paris office, called the Föhrenwald committee 'a curse for the camp population'.[54] Another 'Joint' official pronounced the camp's leader 'a criminal surrounded by gangsters'.[55] Fierce squabbles broke out constantly among the camp-dwellers and with the German authorities. In May 1952 armed German police with dogs raided the camp to curb alleged illegal activities. 'Joint' officials ultimately felt obliged to resort to what amounted to psychological warfare techniques, 'shock therapy',[56] in order to persuade the residents to leave voluntarily. As a 'Joint' representative put it in October 1956: 'Camp life is a state of suspended animation where time stands still and where one can postpone indefinitely coming to grips with conflicting feelings and hard decisions which have to be made about one's future.' He noted the disturbing effect of the impending closure of the camp on mentally ill residents: 'As familiar faces and landmarks disappear, these tragic and solitary figures seem to lose their precarious hold upon their shreds and patches of reality – anxieties become unbearable, paranoid trends more pronounced, retreat into the shadows less accessible.'[57] In February 1957 Föhrenwald camp was at last closed – over the objections of the remaining residents.

With this squalid epilogue, the Jewish refugee problem in Europe seemed to have been solved. In fact, hardly had the remnants of Jewish war victims been cleared away than new refugee movements suddenly began that were to recast the shape of European Jewry.

CHAPTER TWO

Stalin's Last Victims, 1945–53

Throughout Eastern Europe the surviving Jewish populations at the end of the war were living in conditions of wretched poverty, disease, fear and misery. An observer in Lodz, shortly after its liberation, wrote that 'Jews besieged the Jewish Committee, crying, shouting, complaining, begging for a suit of clothes, a crust of bread, a place to sleep.'[1] In the former Budapest ghetto thirty-five children died of hunger in a single apartment building during the first two months after the liberation. Across the whole region the Jewish population balance was abnormally skewed. In Hungary, for example, there were reckoned to be 1,500 female to every 1,000 male survivors. There were only 7,712 Jewish children under fourteen, while there were 27,256 people over the age of sixty. In Poland too, very few Jewish children were alive at the end of the war, although there very few old people had survived either.

The most urgent and desperate needs, for food and medicine, were met by the 'Joint', which mounted a large-scale relief operation to support Jewish survivors. In the early post-war months more than 85 per cent of the Jews in Budapest were dependent on food from public kitchens furnished by the organization. It employed more than 3,000 people in the city and spent over $10 million in Hungary during the first year after the war. Its budget for worldwide operations in 1946 was more than $53 million, of which 86 per cent was spent in Europe, particularly in the DP camps. More than 180,000 people in Germany received assistance, over 200,000 in Romania, 120,000 in Hungary, 65,000 in Poland

and 42,000 in Austria. Between 1945 and 1950 the 'Joint' funnelled money and supplies worth $20 million to Poland alone. In Romania, it provided aid to nearly half the Jewish population in 1946.

Although the Soviet authorities permitted Western Jewish relief organizations such as the 'Joint' to operate in Eastern Europe, they were much more suspicious of bodies that had any kind of political tinge. At the end of the war the Board of Deputies of British Jews sought to establish contact with the Jewish community in Bulgaria. The Bulgarian king and parliament had resisted Nazi attempts to deport the country's Jews (except for those in Bulgarian-occupied Thrace). Although most Bulgarian Jews came out of the war with their lives, many had lost their livelihoods and their homes. A British consul who visited the Jewish quarter in Sofia in May 1945 reported that the appearance of Jews there was

> little short of lamentable: many of the women are dressed in old pieces of Bulgarian soldiers' uniforms, and some are dressed in every kind of patched and tattered material ... one man was building a bed out of bricks and packing cases ... One soon got used to seeing holes and patches in their clothes. I particularly remember one man who had an enormous hole in the seat of his trousers, through which a bit of black underclothes was sticking out like a turkey's tail ... All the buildings smell of humanity in tatters (not of drains); many of the inmates had been in concentration camps. No doubt I was shown the worst; but bad it is.[2]

So depressed was the condition of the community that some of its members maintained privately that they preferred the wartime fascist regimes to the ruling communist-dominated government.

The British government, however, did not wish to allow the Jewish question to complicate its already delicate relations with the Russians in south-east Europe. Its political representative in Sofia was 'emphatic that, in view of Soviet antagonism, it would be very inopportune for the Board [. . .] to attempt to assist Jews in Bulgaria at least so long as Bulgaria is under the Armistice regime administered by the Soviet Govt.'.[3] He pointed out that 'whatever the Board [. . .] might be able to achieve for the Jews in Bulgaria, such assistance could never be enough to warrant the injury that might be caused to general and local Anglo-Soviet relations if it were pressed in the face of Soviet reluctance to allow it'.[4]

On another occasion an orthodox Jewish organization complained to the British Foreign Office about restrictions placed in the way of Jews attempting to reconstruct communal life in Hungary. A reply was sent reporting that the British political representative in Budapest had looked into the matter and had discussed it with a reliable local informant who stated 'that this allegation is completely groundless'. As evidence, he offered (and the Foreign Office accepted) the facts that the Communist Party leader, Mátyás Rákosi, and the Minister of Transport, Ernö Gerö, as well as other prominent communists, were Jews.[5]

With foreign governments generally unwilling and Jewish organizations often unable to intercede on behalf of Jews in Eastern Europe, the shattered remnants could wield little independent power of their own. They thus found themselves with minimal means of protection at a period when they were still sometimes under attack. This was true even of Czechoslovakia, where the communists did not take full control until 1948 and where anti-semitism was much weaker than in most of the rest of the region.

Before the war Jews in Czechoslovakia had generally identified with the language and culture of the old ruling nationalities – German in the Czech lands, Hungarian in Slovakia. Some of those who returned from the camps found that the liberation brought no relief from their troubles. Accused of having registered in pre-war censuses as of German or Hungarian nationality, they were lumped together with the millions of gentile members of these minorities. The Czechoslovak government, by way of revenge for the collaborationism of many of their non-Slav citizens, persecuted these mercilessly and in the case of the Germans deported almost all. At first, no differentiation was made between Jews and non-Jews. 'German' Jews had to exchange their yellow stars for white armbands with the letter 'N' (for 'Němec' = German); they received German food rations – equivalent to the miserable quantities that had been allowed during the occupation by the Nazis to Jews.

This policy had some tragic consequences. One such case is described by Peter Meyer in his study of Czechoslovak Jewry in this period:

> Dr M. Ungerová, a physician, escaped to England during the war. She served voluntarily in a hospital for Czechoslovak soldiers. Immediately after the war she volunteered to go to the Terezín [Theresienstadt] concentration camp to fight the typhus epidemic there. Later she applied for Czechoslovak citizenship. The Commission on Internal Security of the National Committee in Prague unanimously decided *not* to recommend her application for the following reasons: Ungerová and her parents were Germans, although of the Jewish faith. She had studied medicine at the German university in Prague. She considered German as her mother tongue ... She had no 'positive ties' with the Czech nation and had taken a Czechoslovak passport only in order to flee to England. Dr Ungerová committed suicide after this decision. The reasons quoted were given in an official statement published after her death. The Commission resolutely denied any antisemitic bias, but declared that 'one cannot pass over circumstances caused by the friendly attitude of many Jews towards Germanization'.[6]

One could speculate on what might have been the fate, under these conditions, of Czechoslovakia's greatest writer, a Jew of German cultural orientation, had he not died at a young age in 1924. Kafka would certainly have appreciated the cruel irony of such policies. After Jewish protests, some concessions were made in September 1946, but it was not until October 1947 that the 2,000 Jews affected recovered their Czechoslovak citizenship.

Meanwhile, another group of Jewish citizens of the country had encountered difficulties. These were residents of the former easternmost province of Czechoslovakia, Subcarpathian Ruthenia, which was annexed by the Soviet Union as the price of the country's liberation. Under an agreement between the USSR and Czechoslovakia in June 1945, persons in the ceded area who had declared themselves Czech or Slovak by ethnicity (as distinct from the majority Ukrainian population) before the war could opt for repatriation to Czechoslovakia. About 12,000 Jews, virtually the whole surviving Jewish population, took the opportunity to move west. Most of these, however, were strictly speaking ineligible for repatriation since they had declared themselves Jews by ethnicity before the war. They were not made welcome in Czechoslovakia. The Minister of Information, Václav Kopecký, called them 'bearded Solomons' and 'Jewish scum'.[7] One truckload of these unfortunates was driven back to the frontier for deportation, but Soviet border guards refused to admit them. Some were eventually allowed to settle in Czechoslovakia but at least 6,000 fled to the American occupation zone of Germany, where their fate was subsumed in the larger DP problem.

Two dominant political facts shaped Jewish life almost everywhere in Eastern Europe in the early post-war years. The first was Soviet occupation. The Soviet troops were ordered not to discriminate against ethnic groups. But as a Hungarian Jewish observer noted, 'this was interpreted by many officers to mean that no distinction was to be made between Jews and Nazis'.[8] In Budapest this meant that Jews, like the rest of the population, found themselves victims of large-scale looting and rape at the hands of the liberating army.

The Soviet attitude towards Jews had always been riven with contradictions. On the one hand, Jewish emancipation had been one of the earliest legislative acts of the Bolshevik regime after the October Revolution (the provisional government, installed by the February Revolution, had already abolished all discriminatory legislation based on religion). On the other, the new regime's anti-religious edicts inevitably brought it into conflict with the great mass of staunchly orthodox Jews within its territories. Jews had always played an overwhelmingly disproportionate role in the Russian socialist movement, but they were attracted less to the Bolsheviks than to their Menshevik opponents, a large number of whose leaders were Jews, as well as to the Jewish socialist Bund and the socialist Zionists. With the elimination of the legal existence of opposition parties by 1921, many of these Jewish socialists joined the Communist Party. But their earlier histories rendered them a potentially suspect and vulnerable element and many perished in the purges of the 1930s – as did 'Old Bolsheviks' of Jewish origin such as Zinoviev and Kamenev.

The Soviet approach to Jewish nationalism, while generally hostile, was ideologically confused and politically variable. Zionism was denounced as a manifestation of bourgeois nationalism and after the late 1920s all Zionist activity and even Hebrew literary expression were suppressed. Yet the Jews were recognized as a distinct national minority within the Soviet Union; a Jewish section of the party, *Evsektsiya*, was established, and Yiddish, still the vernacular of the majority of Jews, was for a while officially promoted in opposition to Hebrew as a supposedly 'proletarian' tongue. Yiddish schools, newspapers and theatres flourished, although perforce operating within the narrow ideological limits permitted by the regime.

In 1928 the Jews were even accorded an 'autonomous area' (promoted after 1934 to 'autonomous region') in Birobidzhan, a remote area of Central Asia near the Chinese border. A few thousand pioneers were induced to emigrate there and establish collective farms. Pro-Soviet organizations in the United States also raised money to help settle Jews on farms in 'national districts' in Ukraine and the Crimea. A handful of disappointed Zionists even returned from Palestine to join such enterprises. But the Jewish population of Birobidzhan never exceeded 30 per cent of the total in the region, and was never more than 1 per cent of the total number of Jews in the USSR. Soviet propagandists in the 1930s displayed photographs of enthusiastic Jewish pig farmers in Birobidzhan and the Crimea in order to demonstrate that the Soviet Union rather than Palestine had achieved a solution to the Jewish problem. The Ukrainian and Crimean Jewish settlements were all annihilated during the German sweep through the region in 1942, but Birobidzhan survived as a strange relic into the 1990s.

The Soviet annexations of eastern Poland, the Baltic states and Bessarabia in 1939 and 1940 brought large new Jewish populations under Soviet rule. During this period the USSR, faithful to its pact with Hitler, suppressed news of the Nazis' anti-Jewish persecutions, although dark rumours filtered through.

Jews suffered more heavily during the Nazi occupation than any other population group in the USSR. Of the approximately 5 million Jews in the territories ruled by the Soviets in June 1941,

at least 2 million were murdered by the Nazis. In the later part of
the war the Soviet regime made an effort to harness Jewish
solidarity to the Soviet war effort. In December 1942 the Soviet
Ambassador in London, Ivan Maisky, a Jewish ex-Menshevik,
took the initiative in arranging a joint Allied declaration denouncing Nazi crimes against the Jews and promising retribution to the
perpetrators. Friendly overtures were even made to the Zionists.
In October 1943 Maisky visited Palestine and held cordial discussions with Zionist leaders. Meanwhile, leaders of the 'Jewish Anti-
Fascist Committee', composed of prominent Soviet Jewish figures,
were dispatched to the United States and other Allied countries to
propagandize for a 'Second Front' and other Soviet objectives.
For a while the committee served as a quasi-representative body
for Soviet Jewry both externally and internally.

Soviet power thus arrived in Eastern Europe without a clear
ideological position or a consistent policy record on the Jewish
issue. In the initial post-war phase the primary Soviet objective
was the consolidation of communist authority. The Jewish question, like all others, was subordinated to that aim. But the communists who took power in every country in the region between
1945 and 1948 soon found that the political culture of their new
empire impelled the Jewish issue to the fore of the agenda.

The second political fact shaping Jewish life all over Eastern
Europe was a political culture in which popular antisemitism was
deeply ingrained. Hostility to Jews long antedated the Nazi occupation. It was an outgrowth partly of traditional Christian hostility
to Christ-killers, particularly in the Roman Catholic and Russian
and Romanian Orthodox Churches, and partly of right-wing
nationalist ideologies that had burgeoned as a result of the social
and economic upheavals of the inter-war period. After 1945 a
further element exacerbated anti-Jewish feeling: the special relationship between Jews and communism.

Jews had always played a disproportionate role in the communist
parties of most East European countries. The most highly urbanized and best-educated element in these largely peasant societies,
Jews had the biggest stake in ideologies based on some principle
other than ethnicity or religion. In countries such as Poland,

Hungary and Romania, the party had never attracted mass follow-ing, even among the small proletarian class before the war, whether because of government repression or the intrinsic lack of appeal of its ideology. Educated Jews thus came to play an outstanding role in these small parties. In Poland at least a quarter of the party's members and more than half of its leaders in the 1930s were Jewish.

After 1945 the new communist rulers imposed by the Russians in Eastern Europe generally divided into two distinct groups: the 'internal' communists, who had remained in the country during most of the inter-war and wartime periods and had often partici-pated in anti-Nazi underground resistance; and the 'externals', who had spent recent years in exile – for the most part in the Soviet Union. Given the special danger for Jews of life under Nazi occupation, it was inevitable that they were represented much more heavily among the 'externals' than among those who had remained in their homelands. Since the exiles had often received intensive ideological training in the Soviet Union and had established contacts among the Soviet hierarchy, they were more trusted by Moscow and in the initial phase of communist rule were conse-quently often accorded prominent places in the new governments.

In Poland, for example, the communist leadership included Roman Zambrowski, Hilary Minc and Jakub Berman, who held the security portfolio in the politburo. The head of the notorious 'Tenth Department' of the Ministry of Public Security, established in 1949, was a Jew, Anatol Feigin. It was a sign of the unpopularity of the Jews – and of the displacement of anti-communist feeling on to the traditional enemy, the Jew, that some of the most hated communist figures, such as the Minister of Police, Radkiewicz, were falsely rumoured to be Jewish. Another such indication was the fact that gentiles in Poland who were honoured for having helped Jews during the war complained that such publicity exposed them to revenge at the hands of angry neighbours.

In the first three years after the war antisemitism bubbled over into violence in many parts of the region. In addition to the large-scale pogroms in Poland, there were serious anti-Jewish distur-bances in Slovakia between 1945 and 1948. At Kundamaras in

Hungary three people were killed in a riot in May 1946. In Slovakia there were riots at Presov and Topolcany in 1945 and at Bratislava in 1946 and again in 1948. In Hungary and Slovakia, as in Poland, rumours spread that Jews were abducting Christian children; in Hungary they were said to be using them to manufacture sausages.

As a result of the emigration wave after the Kielce pogrom, the number of Jews in Poland fell precipitously. In June 1946 there were 240,489 Jews registered in the country – the actual Jewish population may have been 10–15 per cent lower because of multiple registrations; on the other hand, some Jews feared to register as such. By 1948 the number of Jewish registrations was only 88,257. Some effort was made by the government and by Jews who believed there might yet be a Jewish future in Poland to absorb Jews repatriated from the Soviet Union in the early postwar years. Most were resettled not in their own former homes, now generally occupied by Poles, but in places vacated by expelled Germans, particularly in Silesia and Pomerania. Breslau, now renamed Wrocław, formerly an important German Jewish centre, which had become *Judenrein* as a result of Nazi massacres, now acquired a small new Polish Jewish community. These new settlements did not, however, strike root in what, it became clear, was deeply unreceptive soil.

A survey of the attitudes of Polish Jews carried out in the period 1947–50 indicates the basic insecurity that impelled most of them to leave. There was a deep and pervasive fear of antisemitism. A forty-seven-year-old Jewish physician in Lodz told an interviewer: 'In the long term I don't believe in Polish–Jewish co-existence even in a socialist regime.' An unemployed thirty-year-old Jewish woman in Dzierzoniów, a small town unique in post-war Poland in that about a third of the population was Jewish, said:

> I think Jews should have their own state at any price, for they are the most unfortunate people, constantly humiliated. Up until the war, I hadn't thought as much about Palestine as I do now. I am one of the Kielce victims who survived by a miracle and this has convinced me even more. I admit that in today's democratic Poland Jews are treated equally with Poles. The government's

attitude towards the Jews is favourable, but still, the Jewish people should have their own state, especially after all we went through; we are not Gypsies after all. The time has come to put an end to our wanderings. After all, we have our traditions and culture.[9]

The deep insecurity of Polish Jews showed itself in other ways. Many thought it prudent to conceal their Jewishness or to practise their religion secretly. Some were careful not to speak Yiddish in the street. A religious Jewish woman told an interviewer that she didn't light candles on Friday night 'in order not to be conspicuous'.[10] Some changed their names to more Polish-sounding ones in the hope of merging into the general population.

Most of the remaining Polish Jews were non-practising, but in the atmosphere of anxiety, bordering on terror, small events could trigger waves of collective emotion; according to several accounts, the broadcast of the Kol Nidrei prayer (the most solemn moment in the Jewish religious calendar) by Warsaw radio on Yom Kippur 1947 had a deep effect even on many non-religious Jews.

The political culture that had evolved in the inter-war period was the main source of one kind of antisemitism in Eastern Europe. But the further phenomenon of antisemitism promoted by communists themselves requires some other explanation. At one level this, like everything political in Eastern Europe at the time, can be understood as an emanation from Moscow. Beyond that, however, it can be seen as an integrative mechanism deployed by deeply unpopular politicians who were regarded as alien by most of their countrymen. Just as anti-Dreyfus feeling in France at the turn of the century had 'brought the Duke closer to his coachman', as Sartre put it,[11] so now antisemitism brought the new communist ruling class closer to its hostile and suspicious subjects.

Conspiracy theorists have suggested that Stalin deliberately fostered a Jewish preponderance in the Polish party leadership, but there is little evidence to support this and it is hard to see what motive he could have had for such a policy. There is no doubt, however, that in the minds of most Poles in the immediate post-war period Jews and communists were virtually synonymous.

Although Jews were indisputably prominent among the Polish communist leadership, most Jews in Poland were not communists. They tended to support social-democratic, liberal, Zionist or ortho-dox Jewish parties. In a region where the mass political movements tended to be either agrarian or nationalist, however, such sympa-thies placed the Jews in a relatively narrow section of the political spectrum and often left them without effective allies on issues that particularly affected them.

A case in point was the highly contentious problem of restitution of Jewish property, both communal and individual, confiscated under anti-Jewish laws during the war. Jewish-owned real estate had often been turned over to other users and in the case of residential property was often occupied by non-Jews who were reluctant to make way for former owners. In Lodz an observer reported: 'I met Jews who had lived all their lives in Lodz and whose homes and workshops had not been destroyed but were occupied by Poles. I also met some who have recovered their homes and workshops by legal action but who have left them again upon receipt of threatening letters.'[12] Jews soon discovered that an unholy alliance of right and left combined to oppose them on this issue. The right opposed restitution on familiar antisemitic grounds; the communists, on the other hand, often did so too out of a wish not to enrich people they regarded as belonging to the former 'possessing classes'. In Hungary the communist paper Szabad Nép urged Jews to demonstrate understanding by sharing their apartments with their current occupants.[13] In Czechoslovakia, parliament passed a law in 1947 under which all heirless assets, including large amounts of property formerly owned by Jews, accrued to the state. Jan Masaryk was outraged, but his democratic influence was by now too small to affect the issue. The central council of the trade union movement rejected Jewish claims for restitution out of hand:

The declaration of the Jewish communities is based on a wrong principle. It does not defend the interests of the citizens of Jewish faith, it defends the private interests of a capitalist. Should the Jewish communities continue this way, they would commit the gravest error possible. We ask the citizens of Jewish religion to decide whether they agree when their representatives lead them into the ranks of the enemies of united labour.[14]

Hungarian Jews too found themselves caught between the fascist hammer and the Soviet anvil. Many, including women, had been forcibly drafted into labour battalions as virtual slaves during the war. After the arrival of the Soviet army, they were regarded as enemy prisoners-of-war and were deported to camps, first in Romania, later in the Soviet Union. The total number of such Jewish deportees may have been as high as 35,000. In June 1947 Stalin released about 50,000 Hungarian POWs, among whom were about 1,000 Jews. By 1949 another 1,000 or so Jews had been released. But large numbers of the deportees were sent to Soviet prison camps and never heard from again.

Communist economic policies affected Jews more directly and more damagingly than almost any other group. Jews in the East European states had been overwhelmingly concentrated in petty commerce and in the professions. In many parts of Eastern Europe they had dominated these spheres in the inter-war period, often encountering bitter nationalist hostility as a result. In the initial phase of communist rule nationalization was mainly confined to the extractive and heavy-industrial sectors, in which Jews were less involved. But from about 1949 most light industry in Hungary and elsewhere was nationalized and retail trade too was brought under state control. Of 1,721 retail stores nationalized in Hungary in 1949, 1,504 were Jewish-owned. The communist-controlled Jewish newspaper *Uj Élet* explained the new dispensation to its readers in an article on 8 September 1949:

> The middle classes as such have now terminated their historic role. Whether they like it or not, they are retiring from the scene of history, yielding place to upsurging social classes: the workers and peasants . . . Let us speak frankly: within the Jewish middle classes, too, there are elements that still fail to see the situation clearly, people who do not understand the call of the times even today. These elements do not want to give up the remains of their middle-class style of life . . . The paramount truth is that whoever

would consider the old economic order and absolute middle-class style of life worthy of preservation is insisting upon a condition which may lead only to a new Auschwitz and to new mass murders.[15]

The old Jewish commercial middle class was effectively eliminated. Many Jews were virtually ruined.

In the formerly free professions such as medicine and law too, communist rule made the earning of a livelihood increasingly hard. Many Jewish lawyers were disbarred. Jews once again encountered restrictions on their entry to universities – in effect a revival of the old *numerus clausus*, this time allegedly based not on racial or religious origin but on class background.

In 1951 large numbers of Jews were deported from Budapest and other large towns on the ground that they were capitalists. One of the deportees, Dezső Sator, aged sixty-four, Budapest agent for a London company, later related that the deportees were given twenty-four hours to prepare for the move to country villages, where they were billeted with peasant families. The deportees' flats and belongings were expropriated. They remained in enforced rusticity until 1953. Sator, whose wife had emigrated in 1947, finally secured permission to join her in the United States in January 1955.[16] His case was sadly typical of many. Jews were also heavily represented among businessmen and non-communist politicians deported to labour camps. 'No tears will be shed [wrote *Uj Élet*] for the Jewish capitalists who, interested only in their profits, have been allies of the slaveholding lords and the flayers of the common people.'[17]

As the communists gradually extended their control over all aspects of life in Eastern Europe, the Jews found that their communal institutions too were infiltrated and eventually taken over by communist sympathizers. The process was a microcosm of the larger developments affecting society as a whole.

In the Jewish community, as in government and trade unions, the favoured communist mechanism for achieving dominance was the so-called 'united front'. In Romania, for example, a Jewish Democratic Committee was formed in June 1945, composed of communists, social democrats, left Zionists and some provincial Jewish elements. By early 1948, however, some members of the committee were accused of 'themselves sliding down the road to Bundism'.[18] The communists eventually forced out the established Jewish leadership, headed by Wilhelm Filderman, and gained control of Jewish organizations and communal assets. Filderman fled the country, as did the anti-communist Chief Rabbi, Alexander Safran. The Bulgarian Chief Rabbi, Dr Hananel, was more accommodationist than his Romanian counterpart. He fell into disfavour in 1948, when an incautious reference to the Temple in Jerusalem was judged to have political overtones. He ate humble pie, declaring himself 'a faithful servant of the Fatherland Front [the communist front organization]' and was forgiven, although subsequent offences led to his imprisonment in 1962.[19]

The Central Committee of Polish Jews, formed at Lublin in late 1944, originally had a clear Zionist majority. In 1946 its composition, a product of intra-party agreement, not elections, was still similar: thirteen Zionists, four Bundists, seven communists and one non-party member. (The orthodox Agudist and Mizrachi parties, which also had significant support among Polish Jews, refused to join the committee unless it agreed to observance of the Sabbath and of *kashrut* in all Jewish institutions.) Four non-communist representatives of Jewish parties served in the Sejm (parliament). But communist pressure soon led to the emigration of the head of the committee, Dr Emil Sommerstein, a Zionist, as well as of other non-communist Jewish leaders. By October 1948 the committee had been brought under full communist control.

By 1950 not only representative bodies but all subsidiary Jewish institutions such as newspapers, synagogues, schools and theatres had been either closed or deprived of their last shreds of autonomous existence. The independent Jewish press in Poland had been a vital force in politics and society in pre-war days and had enjoyed a brief resuscitation in the immediate post-war period. More than twenty Jewish newspapers were published in Poland between 1945 and 1948, mainly in Yiddish. *Dos Nyeh Lebn*, organ of the Central Committee of Polish Jews, was the first to appear, from 10 April 1945. It had a communist editor but an editorial board that included Zionists and Bundists. By 1947, however, deep rifts had appeared between the Zionists and the communists, with the former insisting on the priority of emigration while the latter maintained that Jewish departures should not be on such a scale as to endanger the survival of Jewish life in Poland itself.[20] With the communist take-over of the committee in 1948, *Dos Nyeh Lebn* too fell under party control and in 1950 merged with the communist *Folksshtime*.

In Hungary the Neolog (Reform) and orthodox Jewish communities were forcibly combined (for a while the orthodox were allowed to maintain a separate section under the global umbrella). The teaching of Hebrew was suspended in 1949. At the same time nearly all Jewish schools were taken over by the government. Most forms of Jewish cultural activity were snuffed out or rigorously supervised. In Poland the two existing Jewish theatre troupes were nationalized and united into the State Jewish Theatre in 1949. On 1 January 1950 all Jewish children's homes and schools in the country were nationalized. In Romania the 122 Jewish schools were taken over in 1948. In Bulgaria all Jewish schools and libraries and all but three synagogues were closed. Of course, the departure of much of the Jewish population from many parts of Eastern Europe provided a justification for some of these closures, but often this was a pretext rather than a reason. The Bulgarian government went further and banned celebration of most Jewish festivals, including Passover and Rosh Hashana (the New Year); these were said to be 'reactionary', as distinct from holidays such as Purim and Hanukah.★

These events took place against the background of a sudden darkening of the Jewish situation within the USSR itself. The

---

★ The reasoning is unclear and may have been based on ignorance: Passover, with its central theme of the liberation of the Hebrew slaves in Egypt, could be argued to have a 'progressive' message, whereas Hanukah, a celebration of the Hasmonean revolt in Palestine, might be regarded as having dangerously nationalist connotations. Perhaps the explanation lay in the high religious importance attached to Passover and Rosh Hashana and the relatively secular nature of the other two holidays.

first signs of a change for the worse in the internal position of Soviet Jews came in the autumn of 1946, when a series of press articles appeared attacking Jewish nationalist deviations by Soviet Yiddish writers.

The attacks continued even as the USSR, in its external policy, gave crucial assistance to the nascent Jewish state. On 14 May 1947, in a speech to the UN General Assembly, Andrei Gromyko indicated that the USSR might be prepared to support the partition of Palestine into separate Jewish and Arab states. By the time of the critical vote in the General Assembly on 29 November 1947, the Soviet position had moved towards outright support for partition. Soviet backing for the new state was registered by the immediate recognition it accorded to Israel in May 1948 and by the green light that was given to the communist-controlled Czechoslovak government to sell arms to Israel at a critical point in Israel's war of independence against the surrounding Arab states. Evidently the requirements of internal and external policy were very different; no doubt, also, the government wished to issue an unsubtle warning to Soviet Jews that Russian diplomatic support for Zionism did not imply any freedom for Zionist activity within the country.

In 1948 a sustained 'anti-cosmopolitan' campaign began, orchestrated by the Soviet cultural supremo, Zhdanov. There were widespread denunciations of 'rootless cosmopolitans' in the intelligentsia, among whom, it emerged, were a large number of Jewish writers and artists. Those denounced as cosmopolitans lost their jobs, were unable to publish, were expelled from the Communist Party and removed from positions of influence. A parallel campaign against 'bourgeois nationalism' resulted in the elimination of most remaining vestiges of Jewish cultural expression. All Yiddish schools, newspapers (except the small-circulation Yiddish paper in Birobidzhan), theatres and most other Jewish institutions, including many synagogues, were closed. The Jewish Anti-Fascist Committee was disbanded in late 1948 and its newspaper, *Eynikeyt*, stopped publication. A few months earlier, on 13 January 1948, the committee's chairman, the actor Shlomo Mikhoels, had been murdered under suspicious circumstances while on an official visit to Minsk.

More than 100 leading Jewish cultural activists were arrested and deported to prison camps.

These anti-Jewish actions were followed by a switch in the Soviet diplomatic posture regarding Zionism. On 21 September 1948 *Pravda* published a front-page article, signed by the prominent Soviet Jewish writer Ilya Ehrenburg – apparently he wrote it under party pressure. The article attacked Israel and Jews who saw Israel as their homeland and suggested that the DPs return to their countries of origin and help build socialist societies there rather than emigrate to Israel. The new policy found ideological expression in the 1952 edition of the *Great Soviet Encyclopaedia*, which defined 'Jews' as 'the name given to different peoples having a common origin in the ancient Hebrews'. It insisted that 'the Jews do not comprise a nation' and that 'from an ethnographical point of view the Jews approximate to those peoples in whose midst they live (although not to the same degree everywhere)'.[21]

Why the sudden change in the Soviet attitude? Once the Zionists had achieved their objective of ejecting the British from Palestine, it soon became clear to the Soviets that the best hope for further progress in eliminating Western influence in the Middle East was Arab nationalism; Soviet policy accordingly adjusted. Another factor may have been alarm at the enthusiastic reception accorded by Moscow Jews to the first Israeli Minister in Moscow, Golda Meir.

The switch in party line was quickly detected and as quickly replicated in the Soviet satellites. In December 1948 the Romanian party politburo published a resolution condemning 'the attempt of the Jewish bourgeois nationalists to spread the idea of "Jewish unity" and deny the existence of class differentiation among the Jewish population'. Ominously, the resolution warned that such efforts were a 'diversion by which they attempt to harness the Jewish working masses to the wagon of reactionary Jewish big business in the service of the Anglo-American imperialists'.[22]

As Soviet policy turned against Israel, Zionist parties in Poland and other satellites were dissolved. Zionist leaders in Hungary and Romania were arrested. The Bund, which still claimed thirty branches and 2,000 members in Poland in February 1947, supported the communists in their hostility to Zionism, but this did not save them. In November 1948 a conference of Jewish communists in Poland resolved:

> Although our party evaluated correctly the character and role of Jewish nationalism – Zionism and Bundism – we did not oppose with sufficient energy the Zionist-nationalist ideology, which is foreign to us . . . Submission to the pressure of Zionist nationalism led some comrades into a deviation of a specifically Jewish character [as part] of the general right-nationalist deviation apparent in the leadership of the party.[23]

With the dissolution of the Bund in January 1949 all non-communist Jewish political activity ceased.

Antisemitism and anti-Zionism coalesced between 1949 and 1953 in a spectacular purge of the East European communist leadership in which many prominent Jews were victims. A series of show trials in Hungary began, in September 1949, with the indictment of the (non-Jewish) communist leader László Rajk, accused of treasonous contacts with Zionists and American espionage services.

In Czechoslovakia the hunt for a 'Czechoslovak Rajk' was headed by the General-Secretary of the Communist Party, Rudolf Slánský, a Jew. After several batches of socialists and Catholics had been arrested, the purge switched to the Communist Party. In mid-1951 Slánský himself came under suspicion. He was demoted to Deputy Prime Minister and submitted to self-criticism. With thirteen others, he was tried on charges of high treason, espionage and sabotage. Of the fourteen, eleven were Jews. As usual in show trials, the script was finalized in advance of judicial proceedings – the prosecutor many years later admitted as much.

After failing in an attempted suicide, Slánský yielded to his interrogators and made a grotesquely grovelling confession of guilt. Although none of those arrested had any Jewish communal connections, let alone the slightest tincture of sympathy for Zionism, they were induced to admit involvement in an absurd *mélange* of conspiracies involving Israel, the 'Joint', Trotskyism and Western intelligence agencies. Perhaps to lend colour to the accusations, a visiting Israeli politician, Mordechai Oren, leader of the pro-communist faction of the leftist Mapam party, was also arrested. Massive publicity surrounded the Slánský trial, much of it stressing, by unsubtle hints and references, the Jewish origin of most of the accused. *Pravda*, the organ of the Slovak Communist Party, for example, explained:

> It is in the service of the class enemy that the Zionists have wormed their way into the Communist parties in order to disrupt and undermine them from within. Certain members of our party, too, have come under the influence of Zionism. They have succumbed to the ideology of cosmopolitanism and Jewish bourgeois national-ism, and do not judge events from the viewpoint of the working class, of the struggle for socialism.[24]

In his final summation the prosecutor declared:

> The criminals in the dock have shamelessly abused the Czechoslo-vak people's traditional abhorrence of anti-semitism . . . This abhor-rence was abused by various Jewish hucksters, manufacturers, and bourgeois elements in order to infiltrate the Communist Party, to suppress any kind of criticism, and to hide their faces, the faces of obstinate class enemies, behind the suffering of Jews under Nazi rule.[25]

The verdicts were decided in advance by the communist leadership in consultation with Moscow. Three of the accused were sentenced to life imprisonment. Slánský and ten others were sentenced to death and executed in December 1952. According to one account, the ashes were handed over for disposal to a driver and two interrogators. They put them in a potato sack and drove out into the country to scatter them in the fields. But as the roads were icy, they spread them instead on the roadway. The driver later joked 'that he had never before carried 14 people in his little Tatra, three living and 11 in the sack'.[26]

The small remaining Jewish community in Czechoslovakia ob-served the Slánský affair with mounting consternation and terror. Shortly after the start of the trial, the secretary of the Prague Jewish community, E. Kohn, committed suicide, together with his wife. Among Jews sentenced in subsidiary trials was the writer Eduard Goldstuecker, later to play a prominent part in the Prague Spring of 1968. In Hungary a wave of arrests in early 1953 swept up, among others, a number of political figures of Jewish origin such as Péter Gábor, head of the secret police, and Stephen Szirmai, head of the state radio. Also arrested were non-political figures such as Louis Stoeckler, president of the Budapest Jewish community, who had collaborated closely with the communist authorities, and Ladislas Benedek, chief physician of the Budapest Jewish hospital. In Romania the Foreign Minister, Ana Pauker, said to be the daughter of a rabbi, was purged in 1949. She was fortunate, however, in not facing trial, perhaps because of her sex. She died in her bed in 1960.

Meanwhile, the deepening East–West rift led one communist government after another to order Western Jewish relief organizations to cease contact with Jews in Eastern Europe. In late 1949 the 'Joint' was forced to halt its support for Jewish welfare institutions in Poland. By 1950 it had also been compelled to suspend operations in Bulgaria, Czechoslovakia and Romania. In 1953 it was forced out of Hungary too. Among communist states, only Yugoslavia under Tito's maverick leadership permitted it to continue to dispense relief to the small surviving Jewish community there. Contact with the World Jewish Congress, in which the Central Committee of Polish Jews and some other Jewish bodies in Eastern Europe had been allowed to participate between 1944 and 1948, was likewise halted.

The campaign against the Jews reached a bloody climax during the final year of Stalin's life. In July 1952 a group of 110 prominent Soviet Jewish intellectuals, among them the writers Itzig Feffer, David Bergelson and Peretz Markish, were subjected to a secret trial on charges of espionage, 'bourgeois nationalist activity' and 'armed insurrection with the aim of severing the Crimea from the Soviet Union and establishing there a Jewish bourgeois and Zionist republic to serve as a base for American imperialism'.[27] The charge regarding the Crimea arose from representations that had been made by the Anti-Fascist Committee about the possible settlement of Jewish refugees in that area, where the pre-war Jewish colonies had been eradicated by Hitler, rather than in the Ukraine, where there was local resentment at the return of Jews. Mikhoels was posthumously denounced and accused of being an American agent. On 12 August, thirteen of the accused were executed.[28] What little remained of Yiddish culture in the USSR was snuffed out. The last Yiddish school in the country, in Vilna, former 'Jerusalem of Lithuania', closed in 1950. Not a single Yiddish book was published in the USSR between 1949 and 1958. Yiddish radio broadcasts ceased. Until the late 1960s the Soviet Jews became, in Elie Wiesel's phrase, 'the Jews of silence'.[29]

The final stage of the anti-Jewish drive came with the so-called 'Doctors' Plot'. On 13 January 1953 a TASS communiqué announced that nine Moscow doctors had been arrested on charges of murdering Zhdanov and another leading communist and of plotting to murder other senior figures. Six of the nine were said to have been 'connected with the international Jewish bourgeois nationalist organization, "Joint"', which, according to the news agency, was engaged, under the direction of American intelligence, in espionage, subversion and terrorism in the Soviet Union.[30] Preparations were made for a show trial of the accused physicians and alarmist rumours were rife that Stalin planned a forced removal of the entire Jewish population to Siberia. According to Khrushchev's later account, Stalin told the official responsible for the investigation: 'If you do not obtain confessions from the doctors we will shorten you by a head.'[31] As one expert later put it, 'For the first time since the October Revolution the smell of pogroms was in the air.'[32] Only Stalin's death on 5 March 1953 halted what appeared to be a Jewish slide into another abyss.

With the simultaneous elimination of the greater part of the Soviet Yiddish cultural intelligentsia, most of them loyal communists, and of nearly all the leading Jewish communists in Eastern Europe, a significant type disappeared from the European political stage: the revolutionary Jew, for the previous two generations a source of right-wing paranoia and a stereotype of antisemitic propaganda, but also a fact. Most Jews had not been revolutionaries and most revolutionaries had not been Jews. Yet the contribution of Jews to the revolutionary movement in Europe, both democratic socialist and communist, had been profound. They had been among its foremost ideologues – from Marx and Hess to Bernstein, Luxemburg and Lukács. They had been among its most prominent leaders – from Lassalle to Martov and Trotsky. In some countries, notably France, some Jews stuck to a Communist Party that clearly wished to disembarrass itself of them. But they were a declining breed. Apart from a brief resurgence in the New Left of 1968, the Jewish revolutionary now survived only in confessional memoirs or (in the English version) as a pub bore reminiscing about street battles against fascism. Thus ended a proud, sometimes heroic, more often self-deluding and self-destructive, political tradition.

CHAPTER THREE

Revival in Western Europe, 1945–73

The fundamental dividing line among West European Jews after
1945 was between those who had endured Nazi occupation and
those who had not. The latter included the Jews of Britain, as well
as neutral countries such as Sweden and Switzerland, which had
only small communities but had given shelter to several thousand
Jewish refugees from Nazism. Most of the rest of Europe had
suffered Nazi occupation and the mass murder of Jewish populations. The gulf between those who had experienced Nazism
firsthand and those who had merely read about it or witnessed its
end was almost unbridgeable. The human and material destruction
of the war years had left the once formidable Jewish communal
structures of most of Western and Central Europe shattered almost
beyond repair. Decades were to elapse before they recovered even
a shadow of their former authority and influence. In many places
they could never do so.

In France, Italy and Belgium large numbers of Jews, particularly
orphans and old people, depended critically on the 'Joint' for
survival in the bleak post-war years. Along with Jewish populations, the institutions of Jewish life had been destroyed and in most
countries the survivors had to attempt to rebuild from scratch. In a
few cases, however, some Jewish institutions had survived underground. In the Netherlands, for example, a Jewish Coordination
Commission for the Liberated Territories, founded in January
1945, had sent precious aid to surviving Jews in the northern part
of the country, which remained under German occupation until
May. They did so with the help of money provided by the 'Joint'.

When an American social worker employed by the 'Joint' visited the leaders of the Dutch Jewish underground at Eindhoven in the spring of 1945 she found:

> They looked thin, undernourished, worn, wan – they looked pale, but they came out of it with some kind of pride. They had been receiving monies in the usual way in which the JDC sent them to the Jewish communities under the occupation, and while we never expected any real accounting ... it was shocking and amazing to see on the very first visit we had with this group in Eindhoven, van Amerongen ... had his accounts up to date ... The Dutch Jews told me practically from the beginning: 'Here is what you sent us. Here is how we spent it. Here are the receipts. We may need help for a very short time but we do not expect the JDC to support the remnants of Dutch Jewry *ad infinitum.*'[1]

Dutch Jewry succeeded in rebuilding its institutions relatively quickly; other communities never did so.

In Salonica (Thessaloniki), a city that within living memory had had a majority Jewish population and where the primary language at the turn of the century had been Ladino, only a few hundred Jews remained after the war. Thanks to the resources it inherited from the past, the community had no need of outside financial aid; but a report to the 'Joint' in 1956 noted sadly that the survivors had 'not succeeded in reaching an accord among themselves and establishing an authority capable of putting an end to the squandering of [their] immense communal wealth'.[2]

For all the Jewish communities in formerly occupied Europe, the aftermath of the war required not only a huge effort at reconstruction but a traumatic coming to terms with the past. Among the most painful issues was that of Jews who were accused of having collaborated with the Nazis. They were only a handful of people but many of them owed their own survival to dubious wartime behaviour and the question arose what should be done with them. Part of the difficulty lay in defining collaboration. Were all Jews who had served on Nazi-appointed 'Jewish Councils' automatically to be regarded as collaborators? For the most part, such people had had no choice in the matter. They had been ordered to serve on the councils and many had genuinely, if naïvely, believed that they might be able to better the lot of their fellow Jews marginally by agreeing. In the event, for the most part they turned out to be cogs in the machine of mass murder – in some instances selecting Jews for deportation to death camps.

One such case was that of Abraham Asscher. A diamond merchant, he had been a prominent member of the pre-war Jewish community in Amsterdam and president of the union of Ashkenazi congregations in the city. He had also been active in Dutch politics as a member of the Liberal Party and was a leading supporter of Zionism. When Chaim Weizmann visited the city in 1921 Asscher was his host: 'a fine man with a really good Jewish background', the Zionist leader called him.[3] In the 1930s he had headed a committee that gave help to Jewish refugees from Nazi Germany who settled in the Netherlands. In 1941 Asscher was appointed by the Nazi occupation authorities as co-chairman of the Joodsche Raad (Jewish Council) in Amsterdam. Whatever may have been his original motives in consenting to serve, he eventually found himself obliged to participate in the submission to the Nazis of lists of names and addresses of Jews to be deported to death camps. Some other Jews placed in similarly impossible positions baulked at carrying out such tasks and were either murdered or, as in the case of Adam Czerniakow, chairman of the Jewish Council in Warsaw, committed suicide. Asscher, however, carried on. In 1943 he himself was sent to a concentration camp, but emerged alive from Bergen-Belsen at the end of the war. After the liberation Asscher was not prosecuted but faced judgement by a Jewish 'court of honour' and was condemned – though he refused to accept the verdict. No *cherem* (excommunication order) was issued against him of the sort that had been promulgated against Baruch Spinoza in the same city in 1656; nevertheless, regarded as a pariah, he excluded himself from the Jewish community. On his death in 1955 he was buried in a non-Jewish cemetery.

Another disturbing case in the Netherlands was that of Dr Friedrich Weinreb, a Polish-born Jew who had persuaded fellow Jews during the war to pay him large sums of money, in return for which he undertook to arrange for them to be placed on lists of persons supposedly eligible for exchange via neutral countries. A few such exchanges were actually effected between Britain and Germany, but none involving the so-called 'Weinreb lists'. Altogether Weinreb received £87,200 from Jews hoping to escape. In fact, the persons listed were deported to Auschwitz and killed. An exhaustive post-war investigation by the Netherlands Institute for War Documentation concluded that at least 118 people had been betrayed by Weinreb, of whom seventy were murdered. Weinreb was sentenced to six years' imprisonment in 1948, though he served less than four. After his release he moved to Zurich, where he wrote memoirs protesting his innocence.[4]

In the aftermath of the war some of the survivors in Europe found Jewishness an unsupportable burden. A few seceded from Jewish communities, as in the case of a number of Danish Jews who, upon their return from wartime refuge in Sweden, felt 'tired of being Jews'.[5] Others were baptized. The most extraordinary case of this kind was that of Israel Zolli, Chief Rabbi of Rome. In 1943, when the German army occupied the Italian capital, Zolli had sought refuge in the Vatican. His congregants regarded him as having abandoned them at their moment of greatest need. After Rome was liberated in September 1944, Zolli attempted to resume his functions but was repudiated by his community. For a second time he took flight to the Vatican and in February 1945 announced his decision to convert to Christianity. He spent his remaining years in Rome as a professor of Hebrew.

The largest surviving Jewish community in formerly occupied Western Europe in 1945, about 225,000-strong, was that of France. The wartime experience, in which 75,000 Jews had been murdered in the death camps, had deeply scarred French Jewry. In particular, it heightened the antagonism between Jews of Russo-Polish origin and the old French Jewish establishment, a few of whom were tainted by collaborationism on account of their participation in the Union Générale des Israélites Français (UGIF), the French version of the Jewish Councils. The readiness of the Vichy regime, headed by Pétain and Laval, to collaborate with the Germans in the deportation of foreign, mainly East European Jews (according to Laval, a necessary sacrifice in order to save Jews who were citizens of France) inevitably led to the suspicion, partially justified, that some leaders of the French Jews themselves had collaborated in this 'sacrifice'. Many East European Jews in France, including, for the nonce, the communists, tended to be pro-Zionist, whereas members of the longer-established groups often feared lest support for Zionism compromise their identification with the French Republic, to which (forgetting its betrayal of them between 1940 and 1944) they still felt they owed a special debt on account of its emancipation of their ancestors in 1790 and 1791. During the occupation, in 1943, a new representative body, the Conseil Représentatif des Israélites de France (CRIF) had been founded, with members drawn from the Consistoire Central, the rabbinate, Zionists, the socialist Bund, Jewish communists and resistance groups. The first open meeting of CRIF took place at Lyons a few days after its liberation in September 1944.

Post-war French Jewry remained stratified along lines of geographical origin, often following but sometimes cutting across divisions of social class. An old Sephardi element was mainly descended from the wealthy Jewish merchant community of Bordeaux, who had been the first to be emancipated by the French Revolution. Many of them had assimilated in the course of the nineteenth century and converted to Christianity. Some, however, remained Jews, among them a future Prime Minister of the Fourth Republic, Pierre Mendès France, descendant of Sephardim of Bayonne and Bordeaux. There were also several thousand Sephardi Jews of more recent immigrant origin, mainly from North Africa and Turkey. It was not until the 1960s, however, with their augmentation by huge numbers of immigrants from Tunisia, Morocco and Algeria, that these began to play a role in communal affairs.

A second stratum consisted of long-established Ashkenazi elements, notably the French branch of the Rothschilds. This group included members of the important Jewish communities of Alsace and Lorraine, now again restored to French sovereignty. Some of these, like Simone Jacob, had survived the war in concentration camps; others, such as the young Annie Besse (later Kriegel), had fought in the Resistance; and others again, like the political writer

Raymond Aron, had worked with de Gaulle in London. What they all shared was a deeply patriotic outlook. Some of these too had left the Jewish community – for example, Robert Debré, son of a Chief Rabbi of Strasbourg and father of a Prime Minister of the Fifth Republic, Michel Debré. But most of the Alsatian Jews remained orthodox and rather disdainful of the lax practices permitted by the only nominally orthodox Consistoire in Paris. Until after the fall of the Fourth Republic in 1958 the 'great families', composed almost exclusively of members of these two upper strata, still ruled French Jewry's central institutions: the Consistoire, CRIF and the welfare organization, the Fonds Social Juif Unifié (FSJU), formed in 1949.

A third stratum, the largest, consisted of the masses of East European Jews, immigrants or children of immigrants from Russia and Poland. In the case of France, unlike Britain, such immigration, particularly from Poland, had continued throughout the inter-war period, with the result that Yiddish was still spoken in France on a significant, albeit diminishing, scale in the early post-war period. After 1945 this group began to undergo a process of rapid *embourgeoisement*. Nevertheless, a self-consciously proletarian element endured that gave political support to the Communist Party or to the remnant of the Jewish socialist Bund. The East Europeans provided a continuing audience for the Yiddish press, which flourished into the 1950s, partly thanks to the government-subsidized cheap newsprint enjoyed by all newspapers in post-war France. Paris in consequence became the only city in Europe with three Yiddish daily newspapers, one communist, one Bundist, one Zionist, engaged in fierce competition and ideological conflict with one another.

The Slánský trial and the 'Doctors' Plot' had their reflections in the communist movement in France, of which large numbers of Jews, particularly former resistance fighters and young intellectuals, were members. The antisemitic reverberations of these episodes caused the first rumblings of disquiet that later led many to desert the party. Some, however, were unperturbed and signed statements denouncing Slánský and the Kremlin doctors. Annie Besse, at the time a leading Paris *militante* charged with propaganda among intellectuals, contemptuously rejected allegations of Soviet anti-semitism as a 'typical social democrat calumny'. Arguing, in an article published in 1953, that the Jewish question must be inter-preted in terms of class conflict, she placed the 'Jewish bourgeoisie' in the dock. She charged that Hitler had been careful to spare the Jewish *'haute bourgeoisie'* and by way of example cited the former socialist Prime Minister who had survived the war in a concentration camp: *'Qui oubliera jamais que Léon Blum, des fenêtres de sa villa, aux côtés de sa femme, contemplait la fumée des fours crématoires?'*[6]★ Even some veteran Jewish communists who had stomached the show trials of the 1930s and the Nazi–Soviet pact of 1939 found this style of political discourse hard to digest; but the 'thaw' in the USSR after the death of Stalin brought for most a renewal of faith in the movement and reassur-ance that the antisemitic campaign had been but a passing aberration.

French Jews in general remained much more at home politically on the left than on the right in the Fourth as in the Third Republic. A number rose to high ministerial positions. Pierre Mendès France, the most dynamic premier of the Fourth Republic, assumed office in mid-1954. His Jewishness proved to be a lightning conductor for hostility from the right, a hatred that was personal, not merely political – as had been the experience of Blum a generation earlier. The populist demagogue Pierre Poujade led a protest movement of small shopkeepers that won ephemeral electoral support with an appeal that included a strong dose of antisemitism. Mendès France's efforts to combat France's high rate of alcoholism gave Poujade a convenient opening. Alluding to a photograph of the Prime Minister at an international conference sipping a glass of milk, Poujade roared:

★ Mme Kriegel herself appears to have 'forgotten' this outburst.[7] In any event, a little later, finding that she was the victim of an anti-Jewish current in the French Communist Party, she abandoned it and turned her talent for invective against her former comrades and to the service, as she now saw it, of the Zionist cause.

Admit that you don't care a damn about the health or the blood of our people . . . If you had a drop of Gallic blood in your veins, you who represent our France, world producer of wines and champagnes, you would never have dared to have a glass of milk served to you in an international situation! On that day, Monsieur Mendès, you dealt every Frenchman a smack in the face![8]★

Specifically racial hostility was not restricted to the right. In June 1954, when Mendès France disdained to include the communists in his parliamentary majority, Jacques Duclos, the communist second-in-command, exploded: 'He is a coward, a scared little Jew who chatters away and is afraid to act! He is a shit but without the silk stockings.' The incident led the Yiddish daily *Unzer Vort* to taunt its fellow-travelling contemporary *Naie Presse* mercilessly and relentlessly, finally provoking the latter to retort: '*Unzer Vort*'s calumnies against the Parti Communiste Français, worthy of the Judenrat [the collaborationist wartime Jewish Council], are arousing a mighty anger amongst the Jewish masses.'[9]

Like Blum, Mendès France made no apology for his Jewishness. Though a non-believer he declared, 'I am deeply aware that I am Jewish . . . I remain intrigued and impressed by the fact of Jewishness.'[10] Once, when he was dining in a restaurant, he heard a man at a neighbouring table say in German, 'That is the Jew Mendès.' The former Prime Minister rushed over and punched him. Whether, as some have argued,[11] antisemitism was one of the reasons for his fall from power is more doubtful. Mendès France himself is reported to have explained his refusal to stand for the presidency of the Fifth Republic in 1965 on the ground that his Jewishness would arouse opposition; but he had other reasons for not allowing his name to be placed on the ballot.

The three years of acute political crisis following Mendès France's fall from power in 1955 were dominated by the Algerian

★ In Britain, world producer of beer and spirits, such matters are ordered differently. When Churchill was photographed in his cups, he took care to conceal the evidence under the table beneath a napkin. Of course, no opponent would have dared to accuse the half-American Churchill of being less than 100 per cent English.

war of independence, which divided French Jews as it divided the
French nation as a whole. Jewish communists and fellow-travellers
supported Algerian independence. Some, like the classical historian
Pierre Vidal-Naquet, campaigned vigorously against the use of
torture by the French army. Perhaps some Jewish socialists were
influenced by their sympathy for Israel in their inclination to
support the Mollet government's strong line against Egypt in the
Suez crisis of 1956 and in the struggle against the Algerian rebels.
Raymond Aron was unusual on the right in recognizing at an
early stage that the war could not be won. But neither Aron nor
Vidal-Naquet took up his position *qua* Jew.

Although French Jews generally repudiated the notion of a
specifically Jewish reaction to the crisis, there undeniably existed a
Jewish dimension in the form of the 140,000 Jewish inhabitants of
Algeria. Most were French citizens, thanks to the Loi Crémieux of
1870.* The Algerian Jews found themselves caught between two
warring communities: on the one hand, the Muslim majority,
who, in spite of protestations to the contrary by the leaders of the
revolutionary FLN, were not prepared to accept the Jews as
fellow citizens; and on the other, the European minority, who
were deeply impregnated with antisemitism and whose embrace
of the Jews was a transparently tactical manoeuvre rather than an
affair of the heart. The great majority of Algerian Jews nevertheless
supported the French and a few even joined the terrorist OAS. A
handful, mainly communists, threw in their lot with the nationalist
movement; but their expectation of finding a place within a
secular nationalist society after 1962 was disappointed and all left
shortly after independence.

The Algerian endgame produced political effects that were
worrying to Jews. Upon independence in 1962 nearly a million
Europeans moved to France. These *pieds noirs* provided the
base of support for an upsurge of right-wing political activity.

---

* Not all, as is often stated: the decree applied only to Jews born in those
parts of Algeria that were annexed by France by 1870 and to their descendants.
Foreign-born Jews were excluded, as were Jews of the Oasis region and of the
Algerian–Moroccan border areas annexed between 1872 and 1906.

French Algeria had been a hotbed of antisemitism ever since the 1890s. The extreme right in France, it was feared, would now be emboldened to revive antisemitic themes that had been taboo since the end of the war. Such concern turned out to be misplaced. The *pieds noirs*, perhaps in recognition of the pro-French attitude of Algerian Jews, seemed to moderate their traditional antisemitism. Tixier-Vignancour, standard-bearer of the far right against de Gaulle, did not betray any anti-Jewish tendencies. Some evidence, indeed, suggested that the chief locus of antisemitic feeling was moving to the far left rather than the right. A poll in 1967 showed that communists evinced anti-Jewish attitudes in greater proportion than supporters of any other party.[12]

Meanwhile, Algerian independence in 1962 produced a sudden wave of Jewish emigration: virtually the entire community left within a few months. North African Jewish migration to France had begun in 1952-4, when disturbances in Tunisia led an initial wave of Jews to move to France. During the 1950s an estimated 75,000 Jews arrived from North Africa (mainly Tunisia and Morocco). Unlike the Moroccan and Tunisian Jews, many of whom, particularly the poor, had gone to Israel, few Algerian Jews felt attracted to the Jewish state; not more than 10,000 settled there permanently. As French citizens, they felt much more at home in French society and French culture. At least 80 per cent chose to move to France. Altogether during the 1960s, 145,000 Jewish immigrants from North Africa settled in France. Together with the earlier arrivals from Tunisia and Morocco, they roughly doubled the size of the French Jewish community.

The arrival of the North African Jews totally changed the character of French Jewry. In formerly Yiddish-speaking Ashkenazi areas of Paris such as the quartier St Paul (the fourth *arrondissement*) and Belleville (the twentieth) the new lingua franca was Judaeo-Arabic. The odours of couscous and *rahat-loukoum* replaced those of herring, pickles and *cholent*. Although often seen from the outside as a single group, the North Africans divided in certain respects according to their country of origin. Like many immigrant groups, the Tunisians and Moroccans congregated in neighbour-hoods within the Paris city limits where relatives or friends from the same country had settled previously. The Algerians tended to move to the Paris suburbs and the provinces. Many provincial Jewish communities were reinvigorated by the influx. The Jewish population of Marseilles rose from 12,000 in 1955 to over 65,000 by 1968; that of Lyons from 6,000 to 20,000. Smaller communities that had been moribund were suddenly revivified. For example, the old community of Bordeaux, with its rich Sephardi heritage, more than doubled in size.

The influx changed the demographic outlook for French Jewry, but only in the short term. As might be expected, the fertility of North African Jewish women was much higher than that of French natives and the average family size of the immigrants was much larger than that of the indigenous community. But in North African Jewish families, as in French, the number of children steadily declined. Jewish fertility in the 1960s, in fact, declined rapidly. By 1967–71 the average Jewish woman in France had 1.4 children – well below population replacement level.

The contact between the newcomers and the settled communities was initially often marked by incomprehension. Most of the North African Jews were poor; even many of the middle-class Algerian Jews arrived penniless, having had to abandon their property before leaving. Whereas more than a third of French-born Jews had been to university, only a small proportion of the immigrants had a higher education. Many of the Tunisian Jews were very poorly educated; some, unusually among Jews, were illiterate. The social habits of the newcomers were also different: unlike the East European Jews, the North Africans were not averse to the bottle – in this more closely resembling the general French population.

Nevertheless, the newcomers integrated fairly easily and quickly. Most of the Algerians had received French education, often in the schools of the Alliance Israélite Universelle, and felt fully at home in French culture. Within a few years the new immigrants displayed a marked upward social mobility. Following the pattern of the Ashkenazi Jews, they tended to move between generations from the ranks of artisans and small businessmen into the professions. A survey of Jews in Paris and its suburbs in the early 1970s indicated that 20 per cent were employed in liberal professions and '*cadres supérieurs*'; only 6 per cent in Paris (9 per cent in the suburbs) were artisans; 19 per cent in Paris (13 per cent in the suburbs) were '*commerçants*'. Only 11 per cent overall were '*ouvriers et personnel de service*'. The extent of social movement between generations was indicated by the fact that of those born in France, 28 per cent were in the liberal professions and '*cadres supérieurs*', as compared with only 14–15 per cent of those born in North Africa.[13]

The newcomers were generally more religious in outlook than the native French Jews. The number of kosher butchers in the Paris region rose from four in 1965 to more than sixty by 1983, the number of synagogues from thirty to 100. The North Africans were also less embarrassed about asserting a distinctive Jewish ethnicity. Their traditionalism should not, however, be exaggerated. Like earlier waves of Jewish immigrants, many shed some of their religiosity after settling in France. As early as 1963 half of those questioned in a survey said that they were less religiously observant in France than they had been in North Africa. The second generation attended synagogue less frequently, was less scrupulous in observance of the Sabbath and less resistant to eating non-kosher food.

Such changes reflected the larger secularizing tendencies in French society and among French Jewry as a whole. Only a little over half of Jewish students in Paris, questioned in a survey in 1964, fasted on Yom Kippur (an elemental form of religious observance). Just under half ate *matzah* (unleavened bread) during Passover. Only 29 per cent made any distinction between the Sabbath and other days. As for synagogue attendance, only 11 per cent attended services regularly, although another 43 per cent did so occasionally. A larger proportion, 46 per cent, did not believe in God than believed in Him (41 per cent).[14]

The North Africans' greater religious commitment and their numerical weight, particularly in many provincial centres, diminished the power of the old ruling establishment and the dominance of Paris in the country's Jewish institutions. Before their arrival, only Strasbourg Jews, with their staunch tradition of Ashkenazi orthodoxy, had maintained an attitude of hauteur towards their more liberal brethren in the capital; otherwise the Paris Jewish notables had ruled French Jewry in a highly centralized and autocratic manner. Now a slow process of democratization began. In this as in other ways French Jewry followed a pattern of development similar to the other major Jewish community of Western Europe.

Anglo-Jewry, in the immediate post-war years, still bore the aspect of an oligarchy. As late as 1960 a writer in the recently established *Jewish Journal of Sociology* could plausibly maintain: 'It is another symbol of the Conservative continuity that the principal communal charities concerned with the Jews of the country are largely directed by members of the old-established aristocracy. The hereditary principle is strong in Anglo-Jewry as in English public life and evokes a sense of responsibility in the hundred families.'[15]

British Jews were divided not only by class but also by a quadripartite stratification based on the successive waves of Jewish immigration to Britain. The smallest, most select group consisted of Sephardim, expelled from Spain and Portugal in 1492 and 1497 respectively, who had come to England, mainly from Amsterdam, in the wake of the tacit 'readmission' of the Jews to England by Cromwell in 1656. Many of these families still bore names harking back to their Iberian origins: Henriques, Carvalho and Bueno de Mesquita. In the eighteenth century they had been joined by other Mediterranean Jews, such as the Montefiores and the D'Israelis. Further non-Ashkenazi Jews, particularly Syrian merchants from Aleppo, had joined the Sephardim in London and Manchester in the nineteenth century. The Sephardim founded the oldest and most beautiful synagogue in London, Bevis Marks. Some made fortunes in the City of London and a few, such as the Sassoons (of Baghdadi origin), had entered high society.

The second stratum were Ashkenazim, descendants of immigrants from Germany in the eighteenth and early nineteenth centuries, many of whom had also prospered in the City. The most notable of these families were the English branch of the Rothschilds. Others, Cohens, Samuels, Montagus and Franklins, belonged to the closely knit group known as the 'Cousinhood',[16] among whose members were such figures as Edwin Montagu and

Herbert Samuel, prominent in Liberal politics in the early part of the century. Samuel, made a viscount in 1937, was regarded until his death in 1963 as the lay head of the community. These two groups, comprising no more than a few hundred families, represented the 'aristocracy' of the community.

At the base of the social pyramid were Jews of Russo-Polish origin who had immigrated between 1881 and 1914 and whose descendants formed the overwhelming majority of Anglo-Jewry. The second generation no longer spoke Yiddish and was gradually moving up the social scale. Little was left of the old Jewish proletariat with its revolutionary socialist inclinations. Its offspring, like the children of many revolutionaries, was decidedly conformist; most were *petit bourgeois* in terms of occupation and (critics sometimes complained) outlook. The Yiddish press in Britain, unlike in France, had all but disappeared. Next to nothing remained of Yiddish publishing but the ghostly presence around the edges of Anglo-Jewish cultural events of the elderly Whitechapel poet A. Stencl, bravely peddling copies of his little magazine, *Loshn un Lebn*.

A fourth stratum, occupying an intermediate position between the old patriciate and the East Europeans, consisted of Jews, mainly from Germany, Austria, Hungary and Czechoslovakia, who had arrived in Britain as refugees from Nazism. About 50,000, including 10,000 unaccompanied children, reached the country between 1933 and 1939; several thousand more arrived during and after the war. In their home countries these had been mainly upper-middle-class business and professional people. They included some notable scholars brought to Britain by the Academic Assistance Council, which helped them to find positions in British universities. Although Ashkenazim, they had little in common, culturally or socially, with the East Europeans, whom they had tended to look down on in Berlin and Vienna as uncultivated 'Ostjuden'. The descendants of Russian Jews in Britain by and large reciprocated the dislike for the Central Europeans, who were regarded as stuck-up and priggish.

Relations among these four groups were uneasy. In general, leadership positions in the community were still the exclusive preserve of the old Sephardi and Ashkenazi patriciates, although a *coup d'état* during the war had brought the Zionist Selig Brodetsky, born in the East End of London of Russo-Jewish parentage, to the presidency of the Board of Deputies of British Jews. As in France, the older-established sections of the community tended to be lukewarm or hostile in their attitude to Zionism and lax in their practice of religion. It was from within these groups that the Liberal Judaism movement had been formed in 1902. The East European Jews, on the other hand, included many orthodox and ultra-orthodox elements. The recently immigrated Central European Jews included an important ultra-orthodox minority, though their orthodoxy took a different form from the East Europeans – modern in dress, more sophisticated in outlook, though no less strict in observance; the majority, however, were liberal or secular in their attitude to religion. In their home countries they had generally had little to do with Zionism but the refugee experience had in many cases led to a more favourable view of the Jewish enterprise in Palestine. In the late 1940s they were, in general, too recently arrived and too few in number to play a major part in community politics. The East Europeans, by contrast, were beginning to compete with the old establishment, aroused particularly by the issue of Zionism. But the social deference that they imbibed as part of the process of anglicization delayed their take-over of the reins of the community until the 1960s.

British Jewry was the one community of significant size in Western Europe that had survived the war intact. A weight of responsibility consequently descended on its shoulders for the fate of its continental brethren. Moreover, the British government's role as the ruling power in Palestine and in the British occupation zones of Germany and Austria gave London a pivotal role in determining the Jewish destiny over the next few years. Although the American Jewish community was ten times as numerous as Anglo-Jewry and very much richer, leaders of the British community, like British society in general, had not yet adjusted to their reduced circumstances and still sometimes behaved as if they had imperial pretensions. The religious head of the United Synagogue, the large grouping of orthodox synagogues, was still styled until

1953 'Chief Rabbi of the British Empire' – although the communities in Canada, Australia and South Africa paid decreasing heed to his authority.

In spite of its strong centralized institutions – the Board of Deputies, the United Synagogue and the Chief Rabbinate – Anglo-Jewry displayed a cautious defensiveness towards general society that was reflected in the choice of a new Chief Rabbi in 1948, following the death of the previous incumbent, J. H. Hertz. The most impressive candidate was undoubtedly Alexander Altmann, a distinguished scholar and Communal Rabbi of Manchester. But Altmann had been born in Hungary and educated in Germany and some of the lay leaders, whose votes decided the election, considered that the choice of a foreign-born Chief Rabbi might render the community's patriotism open to question. They therefore decided to elect Israel Brodie, less of a scholar but an Oxford man (educated at Balliol College) with an impressively Anglican style of public speaking.

Anglo-Jewry attained its demographic peak in the early 1950s, when there are estimated to have been 410,000 Jews in the country.* A trickle of Jewish immigration continued – about 2,000 from Hungary after the 1956 revolution, a similar number from Egypt following the Suez crisis and others from Aden after 1967. Immigration did not, however, compensate for natural population decline. As early as 1950 the average number of children in the Anglo-Jewish family was estimated at 1.4 or even lower. Many possible explanations were offered, none by itself wholly satisfactory. That Jews were more urbanized and more middle-class than the general population did not alone explain the trend, since Jews had a particularly low reproduction rate even when compared with other urban or middle-class groups. There was some evidence that Jewish women in the UK used birth control earlier and on a larger scale than other groups. But this begs the question why. The fact that Jewish women married on average later than others might help to explain lower Jewish

* Contemporary estimates, which were about 10 per cent higher, are now regarded as exaggerated.

fertility. A significant factor in Britain, as elsewhere in Europe, was increasing out-marriage, although its level was difficult to quantify.

The social geography of the community was changing rapidly as the children and grandchildren of the immigrant generation abandoned the characteristic 'Jewish trades' such as tailoring and cabinet-making and moved into larger-scale businesses and the professions. The Anglo-Jewish community by the late 1950s was quite affluent. In a survey of readers of the *Jewish Chronicle* in 1959, 86 per cent of households possessed televisions and more than half had cars. Nearly half went abroad on holiday – a rate six times higher than that for the general population. 'It does seem,' wrote an Anglo-Jewish sociologist, 'that Jews have taken up the twentieth-century mode of life even more than their Gentile neighbours.'[17] Large fortunes were made by the founders of department-store empires such as Marks and Spencer (the Marks and Sieff families) and Great Universal Stores (Sir Isaac Wolfson) and by property tycoons such as Charles Clore and Jack Cotton. A list in 1967 of 110 millionaire property developers in Britain who had made their fortunes since the war included about seventy Jews.

Other evidence confirmed the rapid upward social mobility of the Anglo-Jewish population. An analysis of the Jewish population of England and Wales in 1961 suggested that 44 per cent of Jews fell into the Registrar-General's social class I (professional: doctor, accountant, clergy, university teacher, etc.) or II ('intermediate': most self-employed, shop manager, company director, engineer, hairdresser, nurse, etc.), as compared with 19 per cent of the general population in these two classes. At the other end of the scale, 0 per cent of Jews fell into social class V (unskilled workers).[18]

In spite of the upward social movement, the political alignment of Anglo-Jewry remained distinctly left of centre until the late 1960s. This was reflected, perhaps exaggerated, in Jewish parliamentary representation: at the 1945 general election one Communist, twenty-six Labour MPs but only one independent Conservative were elected. A number of Jews served in senior positions in the

Labour governments of 1945–51: George Strauss as Minister of Supply, Emanuel Shinwell as Minister of Defence. Phil Piratin, the Communist MP for Stepney, disappeared from parliament at the 1950 election. By that time the old Jewish communist concentration in the East End of London had disintegrated. But Jews remained a disproportionate, although declining, element in the tiny Communist Party of Great Britain (as in the much larger French Communist Party): as late as 1965 they were estimated to constitute 10 per cent of the party's membership. Labour retained a virtual monopoly of Jewish MPs over the next several elections. Jewish Labour representation in the House of Commons reached a peak in the 1966 general election, when thirty-eight of the forty Jewish MPs were Labour Party members. As they moved into the upper middle class, however, Jews began to vote in increasing numbers for the Conservatives. By the late 1960s the lopsided Jewish Labour representation in the House of Commons was a historic residue rather than a reflection of contemporary Jewish voting patterns. The change finally began to register in the House of Commons in the 1970 election, when the number of Jewish Conservatives increased from two to nine, while Jewish Labour representation shrank to thirty-one.

As in France, religious observance among Anglo-Jewry slowly declined. The food rationing system in Britain in the early post-war years provides us with unusually exact statistics for observance of the laws of *kashrut*: in London in 1950, 161,000 individuals were registered with kosher butchers, of whom there were 300 in the city, plus seventy-five kosher poulterers. Well over half the Jewish population of the capital, estimated at about a quarter of a million, thus ate kosher meat. Although the end of meat rationing prevents any precise comparison, there is no doubt that these figures shrank steadily over the following decades. The decline in the number of kosher butchers was one sign of this. Moreover, an increasing tendency developed for people to buy kosher meat for home consumption but to eat non-kosher food outside the home. In Leeds in 1958 under half of Jewish schoolchildren ate kosher lunches. Whereas religious law draws very clear lines between what is and what is not kosher, social practice represented a spectrum running from the ultra-strict or *glatt* kosher to the totally non-observant, with much of the Jewish population strung along at various intervening points. One social observer in 1955 quoted an inform-ant who said: 'Yes, I do eat bacon but I draw the line at rabbit.'[19]★

The percentage of Jews joining synagogues nevertheless rose steadily. In 1933 only 35 per cent of London Jews were estimated to belong to a synagogue; in 1955 membership was estimated at 'between a third and a half of all Jewish adult men';[20] by 1965 the proportion had risen to 61 per cent. The increase was attributed not so much to heightened Jewish observance as to greater afflu-ence and consequent ability to pay high membership fees. In fact, over half the respondents in a survey of Jews in the London suburb of Wembley confessed that they were less observant than their parents had been.[21]

These trends were confirmed by one of the most searching social studies of a Jewish community in Western Europe in the post-war period, conducted by Ernest Krausz in the north-west London suburb of Edgware in 1963. This was an area to which a large number of Jews, particularly young couples, had moved since the war. Although Jewish settlement was fairly recent, Jewish households were found to constitute 38 per cent of the total number in the area – one of the densest Jewish concentrations in Britain. The district was regarded as 'trend-setting', so the findings of the survey were taken as indicative of broader changes in Anglo-Jewry. In some respects Krausz found that the Jews brought with them to the suburb patterns characteristic of life in the older Jewish areas. Thus, for example, he found that two-thirds of economically active Jews in Edgware worked on their own account, as against a mere 7.4 per cent for the UK population as a whole. Jewish women were still primarily housewives: only 22.3 per cent worked outside the home, as against 39.6 per cent for the general population in Edgware.

But in other respects there were clear signs of inter-generational social mobility. In the primary areas of Jewish settlement, such as

★ An otherwise strongly traditionalist Jew told this writer that he enjoyed eating ham and bacon but drew *his* line at roast pork!

the East End of London in the pre-war period, Jews had mainly rented their homes. In Edgware 95 per cent of Jewish householders owned their homes (as compared with only 65 per cent of the general population of the area). Of Jews in Edgware with children under the age of fifteen, no fewer than 85 per cent said that they intended their children to go to a college or university – this at a time when only a tiny fraction of the population was receiving higher education.[22]

Jewish religious observance in Edgware remained fairly high: 100 per cent of respondents observed Jewish law regarding male circumcision, 90 per cent the practice of *shiva* (mourning ritual) and recital of *kaddish* (mourning prayer); similar percentages celebrated the Passover and the barmitzvah rite of passage; 86 per cent of households lit candles on Friday night; 80 per cent of Jewish adults fasted on Yom Kippur; and 79 per cent observed *kashrut* at home, though only 31 per cent did so at all times. The pressures of maintaining small businesses were probably what led 70 per cent to work on the Sabbath. Only 11.2 per cent did not travel on the Sabbath. Although these figures showed some weakening compared with the parent generation, they indicated a higher level of observance than was common in Anglo-Jewry as a whole – probably connected with the high Jewish density of population in the area.

Religion, however, was not the only form of Jewish identification in Edgware. In their patterns of social interaction, Jews there exhibited a strong tendency to mix mainly with other Jews. Israel was also an important identifying factor: although only 16 per cent of Jews in the district had visited the Jewish state, half of all households regularly contributed to Israeli causes and another 41 per cent did so occasionally.

The increasing importance of affluent suburban communities such as Edgware began by the 1960s to be reflected in a democratization of the central institutions of Anglo-Jewry, especially the United Synagogue. Its lay head in the early post-war period was still a member of the patrician 'Cousinhood', Sir Robert Waley-Cohen. But in 1962 the last such president, Ewen Montagu, was replaced by the department-store magnate Sir Isaac Wolfson, born in Glasgow to Russian Jewish parents. The change involved more than a passing of the baton from an earlier immigrant group to a later; it reflected a changed religious climate in the community. The easygoing, tolerant ways of the old leadership, who prided themselves on keeping the United Synagogue firmly positioned in the 'middle ground', gave way to an attempt to enforce more rigorous orthodoxy. Montagu had been a fierce critic of the ultra-orthodox; his successor, who was personally more orthodox, determined to shape Anglo-Jewry in his own image.

These religious and social tensions within Anglo-Jewry came to a head in the early 1960s in what became known as the 'Jacobs affair'. The central protagonist in this imbroglio, Rabbi Louis Jacobs, was an independent-minded figure whose thought was close to that of the Conservative Judaism movement in America – the centrist group between orthodox and Reform. Jacobs's book *We Have Reason to Believe* (London, 1957), which was the main ground of orthodox hostility to him, had questioned the literal truth of the biblical account of the Sinaitic revelation but was not otherwise heretical. One critic complained that Jacobs 'rather gratuitously emphasized his modernism and combined this with a certain indifference to minor matters of ritual such as keeping his head covered'.[23] Inevitably the press compared him with the heterodox (and, according to some, heretical) Bishop of Woolwich, a modernist Anglican thinker of the time.

The 'Jacobs affair' was performed in two acts, with an interval between. In the first, in 1962, Chief Rabbi Brodie refused to approve the appointment of Jacobs as principal of Jews' College, the main seminary for training of Jewish ministers in England. In the second act, two years later, the Chief Rabbi issued another veto, this time forbidding the New West End Synagogue to appoint Jacobs as its rabbi. The New West End was the most fashionable synagogue in London and its membership included a large number of the old Ashkenazi patriciate. Encouraged by the *Jewish Chronicle*, which championed Jacobs vociferously, 300 members of the synagogue decided to secede and form a new congregation, of which Jacobs was appointed rabbi. The New London Synagogue soon attracted a large membership and by a remarkable expedient was able to effect the secret purchase of the old and beautiful building of the Chief Rabbi's own former 'seat', the St John's Wood Synagogue, which had recently built a new and rather ugly house of worship nearby.

For a moment it seemed as if Britain was about to witness the creation of a traditionalist third force in Judaism on the pattern of the American Conservative movement. The critical issue was the authority of the Chief Rabbi and of the United Synagogue. Many of the newer member congregations of the United Synagogue could not contemplate splitting away because they owed large sums to the central body for their buildings. But some of the older, established synagogues, particularly in the provinces, had no such standing obligations and seriously considered joining Jacobs's movement. The two that came closest were Singer's Hill in Birmingham and Garnethill in Glasgow. On the face of things, both were ideal candidates for secession. Singer's Hill committed the sin in the eyes of the orthodox of allowing mixed seating. Garnethill had a mixed choir* and its enlightened rabbi was held by the strict constructionists to have been over-lenient in his attitude to questions of Jewish marriage. Both of these central-city congregations resembled the New West End in being 'cathedral synagogues' of the old-established Jews. Jacobs succeeded in attracting many of the patriciate, grown moderate and accommodating in their attitudes to religious questions, but he did so precisely at the moment when their influence in Anglo-Jewry was coming to an end. Ultimately not a single other congregation seceded from the United Synagogue to follow Jacobs.

The combative behaviour of the orthodox establishment in the 'Jacobs affair' arose from a defensiveness based on a not unjustified fear that orthodoxy in Britain was steadily losing ground. Similar anxieties dictated the virtual excommunication of Jews who joined the Liberal or Reform synagogues. In Cardiff, for example, the local kosher butcher was forbidden, for a while, to sell meat to Reform customers. There and elsewhere some members of Reform

* In which, in his childhood, the present writer, then a soprano, sang to the Lord.

synagogues were refused burial in Jewish cemeteries. Rabbi Ber Rogosnitzky, the militantly orthodox rabbi of Cardiff, denounced the Reformers as 'new assimilationists, one of whose objects is to legalize intermarriage'.[24]

As a matter of sociological observation the remark was hard to fault, since the receptiveness of the Reform and Liberal movements to intermarried couples was one of their main drawing cards. The orthodox insisted on applicants for conversion meeting stringent requirements (in the case of males including circumcision), proving their 'sincerity' (by showing that conversion was not desired simply on account of marriage to a Jew), undergoing thorough educational preparation and waiting for extensive periods (the process rarely took less than five years). By contrast, Reform and Liberal rabbis would generally help to arrange for conversion of a non-Jewish spouse with relative ease and speed. Unlike many of their counterparts in the USA, however, they would not officiate at mixed marriages.

Strangely, whether through genuine conviction or, as seems more likely, a mixture of inertia and vague affection, akin to that of many Anglicans for the Church of England, most British Jews remained content to belong to the orthodox United Synagogue and its dependencies, even while, in their practices, they moved steadily away from the central tenets of the faith that it preached.★ For a long time, therefore, Jacobs remained a lone voice in Anglo-Jewry and his congregation took on the aspect of an anomaly rather than a portent.

Patterns of demographic change, social mobility and religious practice among Jews in France and Britain in the post-war period were thus remarkably similar. Many social developments, indeed, were replicated across much of non-communist Europe with extraordinary similitude.

The old distinctively Jewish districts in the centres of many

---

★ In 1955 the United Synagogue had about 31,000 members in London; two smaller orthodox groups had together about 20,000; a further 2,000 families belonged to Sephardi synagogues (also orthodox). The Liberal and Progressive movement had a total of 8,350 members in the country as a whole.

European cities were vacated – whether as a result of wartime bombing, redevelopment or social mobility. The East End of London, the Leylands in Leeds, the Gorbals district of Glasgow, the 'Pletzl' in the centre of Paris and the ancient Jewish ghetto in Rome all lost much of their former Jewish characters as their occupants moved to Golders Green, Moortown, Giffnock, the *'petite couronne'* and the *borgate*. The new centres of settlement lacked the intensive Jewish street life of old immigrant areas – the market stalls, Yiddish signs, immigrant *landsmanshaftn*, the radical political groups, Hasidic *shtiblech* (conventicles) and so forth. But the Jewish population in the new suburbs was often no less concentrated. A perceptive observer of the Anglo-Jewish scene noted in 1962: 'As they grew more prosperous they moved further north [in London] not [. . .] because they were running away from their fellow Jews, but because they were seeking a Jewish environment of a higher social standing.'[25]

The smaller Jewish communities suffered negative demographic trends comparable to those in Britain and France. In Switzerland, for example, there were 8,993 Jewish deaths between 1942 and 1973 but only 6,894 births.[26] The intermarriage rate was high in these communities. In Switzerland it was estimated at 40.9 per cent in the period 1961–73.[27] In Rome the rate was only 13.3 per cent in 1965, but in Milan it was 29.5 per cent and in smaller Italian communities over 40 per cent.[28] In the Netherlands a survey in 1966 estimated that Jewish fertility in the country was only about half the average for the population as a whole.[29] At the same time the high average age of Dutch Jews produced a death rate well above the national average. There as elsewhere, the demographic scissors were steadily clipping away at the Jewish population.

Almost everywhere Jewish religious observance was on the decline. In Amsterdam, for example, a survey in 1962 showed that only 21 per cent of Jews lit the festive candles on Hanukah, as against 45 per cent of their parents who did so. Meanwhile, 22 per cent of the respondents had Christmas trees in their homes, as against only 10 per cent of the previous generation; among those with small children, the proportion rose to 45 per cent. The traditional Friday night meal in honour of the Sabbath was eaten by just over half of all Jews, as compared with 84 per cent of the parents' generation. Only 46 per cent of those questioned affirmed a belief in God.[30]

The growing affluence of all these communities in the 1950s was attested by the growth of charitable endeavour as a central feature of communal activity. A sign of French Jewry's revival, for example, was its gradual emancipation from reliance on American Jewish money for its internal welfare programmes. By 1956 the FSJU was collecting nearly 200 million francs per annum from about 8,000 contributors. This provided about half of its total budget, the balance coming from the 'Joint' and from German reparations sources.

In general Jews in Western Europe felt increasingly secure. A sociologist of French Jewry writing in 1966 discerned

> a deep change in the way in which the Jew in France sees (or feels) himself as a Jew; and in the way he relates to other Jews and to non-Jews. [...] French society today is such that the Jew can fully accept his Jewish identity as a normal fact of existence. It is now possible to be a Frenchman, like other Frenchmen, and yet be different at the same time.[31]

Antisemitism was no longer a significant feature of the social or political landscape in most of Western Europe. In Edgware 78 per cent said they had experienced no antisemitism at all. In the 1950s some resort hotels and clubs (notoriously golf clubs) would not admit Jews, but such social antisemitism was regarded as a pinprick rather than an outrage. Jews happily formed their own golf clubs and stayed in hotels in Bournemouth, Brighton and Knokke that had predominantly Jewish clienteles. The reason was not only observance of *kashrut*: some of these hotels were only dubiously kosher. In a 1967 poll in France only 10 per cent of those questioned declared themselves antisemites, though 20 per cent showed evidence of antisemitic attitudes. Fifty per cent said they would prefer not to have a Jew as president of the republic and 33 per cent would not wish to be represented by a Jewish deputy. The depth of such opinions was perhaps questionable; interestingly, more respondents were disposed to accept a Jewish in-law than a Jewish president.[32]

Every now and again, however, some unexpected incident punctured Jewish complacency. A disturbing example was a peculiar episode in Orléans in 1968. A rumour, started nobody knew by whom, spread through the town that Jewish shopkeepers were kidnapping Christian girls and dispatching them off to white slavery. The sociologist Edgar Morin, who studied the affair, confirmed the persistence among some of the town's population of dark, traditional fears and prejudices about Jews.[33]

Jews were heavily represented among the rising bourgeoisie of the consumer societies of the 1960s. They were also disproportionately to be found in élite institutions of higher education in many countries of Europe. Not surprisingly, therefore, they were prominent among the leaders of the student rebels of 1968, particularly in France, where Alain Geismar, Alain Krivine and especially Daniel Cohn-Bendit, born in France of German, partly Jewish parentage, became for a brief period the best-known figures in the movement. When right-wingers attacked Cohn-Bendit as a 'German Jew' and chanted 'Cohn-Bendit à Dachau!' his supporters paraded with placards declaring, 'Nous sommes tous des juifs allemands!' Notwithstanding this episode, the Jews involved in the movement were rarely identified strongly as Jews, whether by themselves or others. Their Jewishness was a matter of ancestry but beyond that had little cultural or political significance for most of them. Unlike the Jewish revolutionaries of the previous generation, they did not speak Yiddish and there was no contemporary equivalent of the Bund. Some student rebels, as if to prove their internationalist credentials, became harshly anti-Zionist, such as the small group led by Tony Lévy in Paris. A few, like the Maoist Benny Lévy (brother of Tony) in France and the Angry Brigade in England (among whom were some Jews), hovered on the edges of terrorism, although they ultimately pulled back from the brink of acts such as those undertaken by the Red Brigades in Italy or the Baader–Meinhof gang in Germany. Benny Lévy, who worked for a time as Sartre's secretary, later announced that he was abandoning politics altogether and became a convert to religious ultra-orthodoxy.

In general, Jewish students were mildly reformist rather than revolutionary. Surveys of Jewish students in Paris in 1964 and Oxford in 1969 showed some interesting parallels.[34] In both cases the political balance was clearly to the left, particularly among those who were strongly committed: of the 12 per cent who belonged to a party in Paris, the largest number were communists and the next most popular party was the left-socialist PSU. In Oxford 49 per cent supported the Labour Party, compared with only 26 per cent support for the Conservatives. In both cases religious practice was steadily declining compared with the parental generation. Perhaps the most striking similarity was in attitudes towards Israel. Ninety per cent of those questioned in Paris thought Israel had brought something new to Jews in the Diaspora and an astonishing 72 per cent said they had at some time considered settling in Israel. The Oxford study concluded: 'There is nothing which unites, which concerns, and, we may say, which *identifies* Jewish students in England today as a group more than their relationship with the State of Israel.' A certain political altruism and a secular form of Jewish identification appeared to be driving Jewish students towards empathy with Israel. These surveys, one taken before, the other after the 1967 Six Day War, pointed to the most dramatic change that had taken place, not only among students but in Diaspora Jewry as a whole in the two decades since 1948: the rise of Israel to a position of centrality in Jewish life.

CHAPTER FOUR

The Impact of Israel

'The basic premise for the understanding of Jewish history is the continued unity of the Jewish nation even in the dispersion.'[1] Thus a Zionist historian. 'Jewish solidarity ... a subjective illusion.' Thus a sometime Jewish communist.[2] The world outlooks of most European Jews in the post-war period fell somewhere between the two poles represented by these competing interpretations of contemporary Jewish history. In the half-century after 1945 the general movement of opinion among Jews was towards the Zionist view. They were attracted to Zionism in spite of their successful integration, at least in Western Europe, into non-Jewish societies. How can this apparent paradox be explained and what were its implications for Jewish survival in Europe?

Zionism, a European nationalist movement, aspired to solve the Jewish problem in Europe. At one level it failed utterly: by 1948, when the Jewish state was declared, the greater part of the Jewish population of Europe, from among whom Zionism had grown up and whose predicament it sought to address, had been murdered. Yet Zionism could claim important successes in Europe in the post-war period. Its first and most notable achievement was in providing a refuge for the bulk of the Jewish 'displaced persons' and for other Jews who fled the darkening scene in Eastern Europe.

Before the Second World War Zionism had been a minority movement in world Jewry. In Britain and France the communal establishments tended to view it as an impractical enthusiasm that ran the risk of endangering rather than strengthening the position of Jews in the Diaspora, laying them open to accusations of double loyalty. In Germany and Central Europe, Zionism was seen by many as a movement of crackpots rather than a serious political force. In Russia it was banned altogether soon after the Bolshevik Revolution. Even among the 3.2 million Jews of inter-war Poland, where Zionism was strongest, it was merely one of several ideologies vying for support.

The rise of Hitler changed all this. Nazism turned some German Jews, almost in spite of themselves, into Zionists, when about 50,000 of them were compelled to emigrate to Palestine after 1933. The plight of Jews in the expanding Reich in the late 1930s and the refusal of most countries to accept them as immigrants lent force to the Zionist analysis of the Jewish problem and won new recruits to the cause. But it was only in the later part of the war that Zionism emerged as a majority movement among Jews in the United States and in non-occupied Europe. Some of its rivals, such as the Bund, were virtually destroyed by the Nazis, though small groups of nostalgic Bundists continued to gather from time to time in New York, Paris and Buenos Aires.

Although Zionism attracted widespread Jewish support in the period 1945–8, many Jews were still opposed and some indifferent towards it. The ultra-orthodox, greatly diminished in numbers and strength as a result of the destruction of Polish Jewry, remained hostile in principle, although the settlement in Palestine of some important rabbinic figures, including hasidic leaders such as the Belzer Rebbe, led them gradually to modify their attitudes in practice. The creation of Israel had paradoxical effects on ultra-orthodox Jewry. On the one hand, it intensified their anti-Zionism since the State of Israel, cast in a secular mould, represented in their eyes a heresy or even 'the incarnation of evil'.[3] Most hasidic rabbis, with the notable exception of the Belzer Rebbe, were deeply hostile to Zionism.* At the same time, however, Israel was

---

* This remained true, for example, of the Lubavitcher Rebbe, M. M. Schneerson, based in New York, who refused to set foot in Israel and declared that Jews living in the Holy Land were just as much in exile as those who lived in the Diaspora. His opposition to territorial concessions by Israel after 1967 was founded on religious considerations that had nothing to do with Zionism.[4]

one of only two remaining strongholds of extreme orthodoxy (the other being the United States) and the orthodox anti-Zionists there were perforce obliged to find some *modus vivendi* with the new state. In Europe only tiny redoubts of ultra-orthodoxy remained: in London, Gateshead, Paris and Antwerp. Self-isolated from surrounding society and even from surrounding Jewries, they exercised no influence on general European Jewish attitudes towards Israel in the post-war period. As for the greater part of orthodox Jewry, the so-called 'modern orthodox', some of whom had been sympathetic to Zionism even before the war, most embraced it wholeheartedly after 1948.

The Reform and Liberal Jewish movements, virtually non-existent in Eastern Europe except for the 'Neologs' in Hungary and much weaker in Western Europe than in the United States, had mixed feelings about Zionism. Since its birth in Germany in the mid-nineteenth century, Reform Judaism had been strongly antagonistic to Jewish nationalism, messianism and the idea of a return to the Holy Land. It condemned Zionism root and branch, in this single respect joining voices (though not hands) with the ultra-orthodox. In the United States some Reform Jews created a vehicle for anti-Zionist views, the American Council for Judaism, which propagandized outspokenly against the Jewish state. The use by anti-Zionist Jews of vocabulary, ideas and data often identical with and sometimes derived from Arab anti-Israeli sources increasingly discredited them in the Jewish world. Reform anti-Zionism, never as vociferous in Western Europe as in North America, dwindled after 1948. More than orthodox Judaism, Reform possessed within itself a capacity to evolve and to reinterpret doctrine. The ideological rejection of a Jewish return to Palestine was reformulated and narrowed into a hostility to the restoration of the Temple or of animal sacrifice, issues that were hardly on the agenda. By the 1960s Reform Jews in Western Europe were, by and large, as enthusiastic in their support for Israel as any others.

Liberal assimilationists did not share the Zionists' pessimism about the possibility of Jewish integration into Western societies. Some of them believed that Jews could survive as a religious group within these societies; others that group survival was unimportant, that individuals could make their own way. Such ideas remained strong in those countries, such as Britain and France, where, in spite of the rise of the welfare state, liberal individualism remained, in matters of political rights, the dominant ideology. But even many Jews in those countries now began to agree with Zionists that, in the light of what had happened in Nazi Europe and of events such as the Kielce pogrom, it was unrealistic to expect that the liberal solution could be exported to Eastern Europe and that surviving Jews could resettle in their countries of origin and face a bright future.

The internal Jewish debate over these questions reached its most intense point between 1945 and 1948 as British authority broke down in Palestine and the country descended into civil war. The 'double loyalties' charge inevitably affected Jews in Britain more than elsewhere because of the role of the British army in fighting the Jewish revolt in Palestine between 1945 and 1948. The violence briefly threatened to spread beyond Palestine. In the autumn of 1947 the Irgun Zvai Leumi, the underground Jewish terrorist organization led by Menahem Begin, set off bombs at several British military posts in Austria. The ensuing arms searches by British soldiers in the Admont DP camp did not endear them to the residents. There were even some attempts at parcel-bomb attacks in Britain. Although no injuries resulted from such incidents, the apparent broadening of the front of the terrorist campaign further envenomed relations between British military personnel and Jews, both in Palestine and in the British occupation zones of Germany and Austria.

The terrorist fringe of the Zionist cause generated next to no support in Anglo-Jewry. The *Jewish Chronicle* gave the extremists editorial backing for a short time; the result was the dismissal of the editor by the much more moderately Zionist editorial board. In France, on the other hand, some Jews, albeit a small minority, were attracted to the militantly anti-imperialist rhetoric of the Irgun Zvai Leumi and of the Stern Group (Lehi) – perhaps also by the violently anti-British tone of their propaganda.[5] A few even went to Palestine as volunteers to join in the war.

The anti-Zionists in Anglo-Jewry still counted among their number many of the community's patricians: Ewen Montagu, Robert Carvalho, Lord Swaythling, Leonard Montefiore and Sir Robert Waley-Cohen. These and some others joined to form the Jewish Fellowship, a body that insisted that the Jews were 'a religious community' as distinct from 'a politico-national group'.[6] The organization never exercised any real influence and, unlike the American Council for Judaism, soon dwindled away. After 1948 the anti-Zionists gradually transmogrified into non-Zionists and some were later reconciled to the reality of the Jewish state.

Although the Zionist struggle against the British and the Arabs in Palestine galvanized large-scale and effective worldwide support among Jews, Zionism as a personal ideology, requiring of its adherents a commitment to settle in the Land of Israel, engaged only a small minority in Western Europe. Most French Jews, except for some of those of recent East European origin, still regarded the French Republic as their promised land. 'Palestine? I hardly knew where it was!' recalls Simone Veil. 'It was perhaps a home for other Jews. Not for us.'[7] Raymond Aron wrote in *Le Figaro* that the birth of the Jewish state 'did not evoke any emotion in me' – though he later regretted having taken this position.[8] The French left in general supported Israel strongly at this time. Jacques Duclos, one of the most prominent leaders of the Communist Party (who was capable of antisemitic utterances★), declared at a mass meeting: 'We are entirely on the side of the Jewish people in its struggle. You will win!'[9] In this, of course, the party followed the (initial) signals from Moscow. But Jewish communists, who had devoted much of their lives to fierce argument against Zionism, were often wary and held aloof from seeming to over-identify with their brethren in Palestine. Jewish socialists too, with the notable exception of the aged Léon Blum, were often restrained in their enthusiasm. The French Jewish representative organ, CRIF, was at first reserved in its statements regarding Zionism. Nevertheless, it demanded free Jewish immigration to Palestine and after 1948, in spite of internal conflicts among

★ See above, p. 65.

its various constituents, became as outspokenly supportive of Israel as the Board of Deputies in Britain.

The ugly finale to Britain's mandate in Palestine and the numerous acts of Jewish terrorism against British troops and civilians in Palestine fanned antisemitism in Britain. A report by the Trades Advisory Council (TAC), an offshoot of the Board of Deputies that sought to harmonize relations between Jews and non-Jews in the business world, stated that 'even the most cynical and pessimistic could not have foreseen that during the past twelve months [1946–7] Britain would have been swept by such a wave of blatant and open antisemitism'.[10] The TAC was a sober and level-headed body not given to exaggeration. Its appraisal in this instance was probably correct. For the first time since the Mosleyite marches in east London in the 1930s, anti-Jewish riots erupted in Britain. In Liverpool some 5,000 people were estimated to have been involved. But there were no deaths or serious injuries and the disturbances soon petered out. The spasm of outrage soon passed and Jews in England did not feel seriously threatened. Interestingly, in Ireland, where neutrality and occasional pro-Germanism during the war had been accompanied by some manifestations of antisemitism, the Jewish struggle against the British in Palestine stimulated admiration and fellow-feeling among Irish nationalists.

While the 'double loyalties' charge was malevolently inspired and unrealistic (who but the single-minded fanatic has only one 'loyalty'?), the establishment of Israel did seem to confront Jews in the Diaspora with a dilemma. The Hungarian-born Jewish writer Arthur Koestler, who had taken refuge in Britain during the war, put it in its most succinct form when he argued that with the creation of the Jewish state Jews in the Diaspora had a simple choice: they could either go and live there or stop being Jews. Koestler's ideological odyssey had included a spell in a kibbutz in the 1930s. In 1947–8 he was a vocal supporter of the terrorist wing of the Zionist movement. His own decision was to remain in the Diaspora and he lived in London for the rest of his life. Whether he stopped being Jewish (he had never been a believer) is a matter of interpretation: he was not formally a member of the Jewish community, though he continued to write from time to time on Jewish issues. Like many secular Jews of the time, it seems, he could not altogether cut the umbilical cord. Real life is rarely susceptible to the short cuts of political chop-logic.

The very existence of Israel presented Diaspora Jews if not with a dilemma at least with a choice. In the early years of the state, when international tourism was still the preserve of the rich, few visited Israel. Later, as more and more Jews travelled there, curiosity often changed into a special intimacy. As Georges Friedmann, a French Jewish sociologist and a self-confessed 'marginal' Jew, wrote after his first trip there in 1963: 'Israel, to be sure, has an effect on every Jew, even the most peripheral or marginal. It may move him to enthusiasm or it may irritate him . . . Israel, besides, forces every Jewish observer, whatever his reservations, to ask himself what Jewishness is and what it means for him.'[11] Most Jews in Western Europe felt affected in some way by the existence of Israel but, rather than adopting one or other of the radical alternatives proposed by Koestler, resorted to a muddled middle position. The Zionist doctrine of *shelilat ha-golah* (negation of the Diaspora) was not really accepted; at the same time, Israel's security and welfare became a central concern, eventually almost a collective obsession, of Diaspora Jews.

Emigration to Israel from the relatively affluent Jewish communities of Western Europe was nevertheless very limited. Only about 3,000 Jews emigrated to Israel from France between 1950 and 1959. An estimated 31,000 British Jews did so between 1948 and 1992. Many of these, however, found the difference in standard of living too onerous and returned home after a few years. As for the majority who remained in Western Europe and became gradually less Jewish, their attachment to Israel nevertheless grew closer over the years. The successive crises of 1956, 1967 and 1973 heightened this feeling as Diaspora Jews became increasingly bound up in the Jewish state's travails as well as its successes. The relationship had in it some elements of the vicarious nationalism of Irish or Greek Americans. But it had more profound religious roots, a greater cultural resonance in the surrounding society, and it slowly acquired significant personal linkages.

The reaction of Jews in the USSR and Eastern Europe to the

Table 2: Immigration to Israel from Europe, 1948–94
By period of immigration and country of birth

	15 May 1948–51	1952–66	1967–79	1980–89	1990–94	TOTAL
Austria	2,632	1,011	1,215	356	168	5,382
Belgium	291	747	1,606	788	408	3,840
Britain	1,907	3,233	10,847	7,098	2,547	25,632
Bulgaria	37,260	2,336	256	180	2,489	42,521
Czechoslovakia	18,788	2,317	2,108	462	268	23,943
France	3,050	3,386	11,725	7,538	4,298	29,997
Germany	8,210	2,579	4,062	1,759	1,068	17,678
Greece	2,131	916	600	147	65	3,859
Hungary	14,324	11,447	2,073	1,005	1,180	30,029
Italy	1,305	714	1,353	510	279	4,161
Netherlands	1,077	1,139	2,147	1,239	510	6,112
Nordic countries*	85	349	1,571	1,178	638	3,821
Poland	106,414	46,531	14,011	2,807	1,708	171,471
Romania	117,950	108,478	28,586	14,607	3,904	273,525
Spain	80	427	475	321	109	1,412
Switzerland	131	536	1,237	706	443	3,053
Turkey	34,547	13,281	10,801	2,088	524	61,241
USSR/CIS†	8,163	22,283	157,970	29,754	530,767	748,937
Yugoslavia	7,661	481	287	140	1,447	10,016
Other countries	1,343	340	415	303	461	2,862
TOTAL	367,349	222,531	253,345	72,986	553,281	1,469,492
Percentage of total immigration to Israel	53.4	38.8	60.4	47.4	90.8	60.1

* Finland, Sweden, Norway and Denmark.

† In the 1970s *c*. 60 per cent of these immigrants from the USSR originated in European republics. In the 1990s *c*. 80 per cent originated in European republics.

Source: Israel Central Bureau of Statistics

creation of Israel was quite different. The very fact that the establishment of the Jewish state seemed to offer Jews a choice – and therefore a potential exit route from the misery of life under Stalinism – produced among many a feeling of excitement that was all the more explosive for being virtually pent up by the restrictions of communist rule. Free expression of Zionist sympathies was difficult though not, in the early years, impossible. So long as the Soviet Union supported Israel, such manifestations were permitted within limits, although the joy with which many Jews welcomed the creation of the state disturbed communist rulers. The Soviet Yiddish daily *Eynikeyt* celebrated the pro-Zionist speech delivered at the UN in May 1947 by Andrei Gromyko. A letter in archaic Hebrew written by 'an anonymous Soviet Jew' (Baruch Mordechai Weissman) 'to my brethren in the Land of Israel' expressed the view that the speech indicated that 'a new era had commenced for the Jews' and even that 'the Soviet Government would not look askance at those Jewish citizens who might wish to emigrate to their new homeland'.[12] As news of the foundation of Israel spread to Jews in Soviet prison camps, many of them too rejoiced. Even a former Bundist leader, Yerahmiel Weinstein, was reported to have declared 'Next year in Jerusalem' in a 'spiritual testament' that he left before his death in detention in 1949.[13]

The climax of this wave of Zionism in Russia came in the autumn of 1948 with an extraordinary display of enthusiasm by several thousand Jews in Moscow, shortly after the arrival of Golda Meir as the first Israeli Minister to the Soviet Union. '*A dank aich vos ir zeit geblibn yidn*' ('Thank you for having remained Jews') was her response to the crowd that surrounded her outside the main Moscow synagogue when she attended the service on the first day of the Jewish New Year on 4 October 1948. The Soviet switch in policy towards Israel soon afterwards may well have been partly prompted by official anxiety that such unprecedented public displays were getting out of hand. Soviet officials made it very clear to Israeli representatives that there could be no question of mass emigration of Soviet Jews; the only exceptions were Polish Jewish 'repatriates' and isolated cases of 'family reunion'.

The policies of East European governments towards Israel in the post-war period followed that of the Soviet Union in parrot-like fashion, as we have already seen. Only Yugoslavia and later Romania diverged from the path laid down by Moscow on this as on other matters. In the matter of Jewish emigration, however, Moscow allowed a certain latitude. Most Jews who wished to leave the Soviet satellites were able to go at some stage in the decade after 1948. Bulgaria, where the Jewish population had traditionally been strongly Zionist and where governments and population had generally been friendly towards the Jews, permitted free emigration from the outset. Most of the country's Jews, 32,781 out of 44,200, left for Israel in 1948 and 1949. By 1951 the communities in Czechoslovakia and Bulgaria had dwindled to a few thousand people.

In September 1949 the Polish government agreed to permit Jewish emigration to Israel and by December 1950 28,000 Jews had left the country, all but 2,000 going to Israel. The emigrants were permitted to take with them 'about $280 plus some pocket money, two rings, one watch, one overcoat, one nightshirt, two pillows, two blankets, a few pairs of shoes, one sheet, and five books'.[14] Poland permitted free emigration for Jews until 1951. For the following five years very few were permitted to leave. But after the 'Polish October' in 1956, when Władysław Gom-ułka's government regained a certain limited independence, emigration resumed. Over the next four years more than 42,000 Jews left for Israel, nearly 30,000 in 1957 alone. A further repatriation agreement between Poland and the USSR in 1957 led to the return to Poland of 18,000 Jews by 1959, of whom about a third left immediately for Israel.

In spite of its victory over all the neighbouring Arab states in the war of 1948–9, Israel still seemed in the early 1950s a small and vulnerable entity, highly dependent on the grace of great-power patrons. In the Suez crisis of 1956 Israel found itself out of favour simultaneously with both the United States and the USSR. Soviet hostility was expressed with a crude virulence reminiscent of the Stalin years. 'The government of Israel [the Soviet Prime Minister, Marshal Bulganin, warned on 5 November] is criminally and irresponsibly playing with the fate of its people. It is sowing a hatred for the State of Israel among the peoples of the east which cannot but leave its marks on the future of Israel, and calls into question the very existence of Israel as a state.'[15]

The crisis found West European Jews generally supportive of Israel. British opinion was deeply divided over the merits of British military involvement: much of the left condemned the 'collusion' of Britain and France with Israel in the attack on Egypt – although some distinguished between Israel's action, regarding it as a justifiable response to cross-border guerrilla attacks, and the Anglo-French 'police' operation, seen as an exercise in heavy-handed imperialism. While most British Jews still voted Labour, the anti-Suez and to some degree anti-Israeli position enunciated by Hugh Gaitskell, the Labour leader, did not find much Jewish backing – except in parliament. Jewish Labour MPs generally followed the party whip, though Barnett Janner, the President of the Board of Deputies of British Jews, and five others abstained on the key parliamentary votes. One of the abstainers, Emanuel Shinwell, said: 'Israel was right ... I have the utmost contempt for those Jews, including British MPs, who, though professed Zionists, claim to see in Israel's action an offence against international law. They ought to be ashamed.'[16]*

An acute observer of Jewish electoral behaviour has written: 'At Suez ... the special relationship between the Labour Party and Anglo-Jewry, so carefully built up on both sides in the 1930s and 1940s, was finally buried.'[17] This perhaps overstates the effect of the crisis on Jewish political attitudes. Jewish issues rarely determined Jewish votes in Britain. The strong opposition to the Suez enterprise of the liberal *Manchester Guardian*, historically a fervent supporter of Zionism and of Jewish causes, led to some cancellations of subscriptions, particularly among Jews in Manchester. But the paper attracted new readers in the south and overall increased

---

* The other four abstainers were: Austen Albu, Harold Lever, Moss Turner-Samuels, and David Weitzman. Shinwell's sudden access of Zionism was oddly at variance with his performance as a member of the Cabinet in the post-war Labour government.

its circulation during the crisis.[18] The episode was a foretaste of the gradual divorce after 1967 between Israel and its traditional liberal-left supporters.

The secret alliance of Israel with Britain and France, soon repudiated by the British, was perpetuated by the French in the form of a close relationship between the Israeli and French defence establishments. Over the next decade France supplied Israel with the Mystère and Mirage jet fighters with which she built the most formidable air force in the Middle East. The aircraft were produced by the Dassault aircraft company, whose owner, Marcel Dassault (formerly Bloch), was an ex-Jew.* The Franco-Israeli diplomatic alignment also affected the relationship between French Jews and Israel. In the warm atmosphere between the two countries, it now seemed highly patriotic to be pro-Israeli. Some members of the French Jewish establishment who had hitherto been standoffish in their attitude to Israel henceforth became more friendly.

This trend was accentuated by the arrival in France of the North African Jews in the late 1950s and early 1960s. Although they had, in a sense, voted against Zionism with their feet, the North Africans in France were, for the most part, fervently Zionist – at least in theory. When asked, in a survey in the winter of 1966–7, to say which foreign country they would most like to visit, 64 per cent said Israel – as against 24 per cent who named the USA and 7 per cent the USSR. When asked which country they would settle in if offered an interesting job, more than half chose Israel; only 13 per cent replied that they would prefer not to leave France; no other country received more than 10 per cent support.[19] These answers were the more remarkable given the weakness of support for Zionism among North African Jews prior to their emigration and also given the background, at the time of the survey, of serious economic difficulties in Israel.

In the crisis of May 1967 Israel once again appeared as a David threatened by surrounding Goliaths. Israel's substantial military

---

* Dassault converted to Catholicism in 1947. One of the most successful aircraft manufacturers of all time, he never flew – except on one occasion, his repatriation to France from Buchenwald in 1945.

superiority over the Arab states was not generally appreciated – except by Israeli military planners. The impressive performance of the Israeli army in the 1956 Sinai campaign had not altogether changed Israel's image, since the victory over the Egyptians was attributed in large measure to support from France and Great Britain, particularly French air cover for Israeli cities. The responses of Jews in the Diaspora, of public opinion in the West and to some extent of governments to the 1967 crisis were conditioned by this perception of Israeli weakness. During the weeks that followed President Nasser's expulsion of the UN Emergency Force from Sinai and his declaration of the closure to Israeli shipping of the Straits of Tiran (the only outlet from Israel's Red Sea port of Eilat), Israel seemed to be in danger of imminent attack and possible destruction. The decision of the UN Secretary-General, U Thant, to comply immediately with Nasser's demand for withdrawal of UNEF seemed like an abject capitulation to force, although it was pointed out that U Thant had no legal recourse except to comply. The failure in the succeeding weeks of the USA and Britain to organize a mooted multinational flotilla to test and challenge Nasser's blockade seemed to leave Israel alone and vulnerable. Parallels were drawn with the fates of Czechoslovakia at Munich and the Jews in Europe during the war.

During these weeks Diaspora Jewry underwent what amounted to a collective trauma. The prospect seemed real that, for the second time in a generation, they might witness a mass destruction of a large part of the Jewish people. Half-buried fears of 'a second Auschwitz' and suspicions of the intentions of non-Jews re-emerged. Some of the recent Jewish immigrants from North Africa in France supported Israel out of anti-Arab enthusiasm but the identification with Israel was not limited to this group. Even Jews who were far from Zionism and far from any form of Jewish identification, whether religious or secular, were moved to express some form of solidarity. Richard Marienstras, a secular, non-Zionist French Jewish intellectual, spoke of the challenge to Israel as something more than a political menace: it was, he said, 'an ontological threat that aimed at the very physical and cultural existence of Israel, that aimed at the destruction of its inhabitants, of the state, of the society. In short, what we feared was a cultural genocide and a genocide *tout court*.'[20] Another French Jewish intellectual, Alex Derczansky, a Zionist, compared the solidarity felt among Jews at that moment to the '*union sacrée*' in France in 1914.[21] Raymond Aron, paladin of the intellectual centre-right, avowed himself 'what people call an "assimilated Jew". As a child I wept for the misfortunes of France at Waterloo or Sedan, but not when I listened to the story of the destruction of the Temple.' Normally the epitome of the cool, unemotional analyst, never a Zionist, he wrote in the *Figaro Littéraire* on 12 June that within him too there mounted an irresistible feeling of solidarity: '*Peu importe d'où il vient. Si les grandes puissances, selon le calcul froid de leurs intérêts, laissent détruire le petit Etat qui n'est pas le mien, le crime, modeste à l'échelle du nombre, m'enlèverait la force de vivre, et je crois que des millions et des millions d'hommes auraient honte de l'humanité.*'

Most Marxist Jews maintained a critical attitude towards Israel. The distinguished French Jewish orientalist Maxime Rodinson wrote an impressive exposition of the Arab case against Israel in a special issue of the journal *Les Temps Modernes* that appeared on the eve of the war.[22] Aron commented with subtle irony that he respected his 'solitude': 'the Jews renounce him, the Arabs won't adopt him, and the French, pro- or anti-Israeli, regard him with suspicion: Christ or Judas?'[23] Other Jews took a less tolerant view of Rodinson's 'treason'. To which Rodinson replied: 'A small number of Jews of my kind feel that they have a special duty towards that people [the Arabs], despoiled by *some* Jews, and towards that fraction of it directly oppressed by *some* Jews. I prefer to attach myself to Judaism in this manner rather than in another.'[24] Other Jewish communists, however, found it difficult to emulate Rodinson's principled disinterestedness.

For many Jews the 1967 crisis made a deeper impression than those of 1948 and 1956. Unlike the previous two Middle East conflicts, the Six Day War was followed on television screens in most Jewish living-rooms in Europe. In 1967, unlike 1956, Israel stood alone. Protest meetings took place in major cities throughout Western Europe: the newly appointed British Chief Rabbi,

Immanuel Jakobovits, spoke at a mass demonstration at the Royal Albert Hall in London. Large sums of money were collected for Israel: Anglo-Jewry raised £2 million (a significant sum before the great inflation of the 1970s). Thousands of young Jews volunteered to go to Israel to fill jobs in fields and factories temporarily vacated by workers who had been mobilized into the armed forces.* Some of these later settled in Israel. Many were permanently marked by the experience.

Israel's swift and clear-cut victory over Egypt, Syria and Jordan in the second week of June led to a collective catharsis. Solidarity based on a certain sense of shame was now transformed into one based on pride. 'What the Six Day War showed [wrote the British political scientist Samuel Finer shortly afterwards] was that for the moment at least communities which had largely abandoned their religious observances felt a Jewish identity none the less keenly because they regarded the state of Israel as the *emblem* of their Jewishness, as their badge of pride.'[25] The Israeli triumph also produced a lasting change in its image in the West, from that of a small, vulnerable state dependent on great-power support and outside funding for its very survival to that of a dominant regional military power.

In the course of the crisis a sudden change had also taken place in Israel's diplomatic alignment which was to have a lasting effect not only on Middle East politics but on European Jewry. Since the Suez war Israel's chief diplomatic patron had been France. But on 2 June, before the outbreak of hostilities, President de Gaulle signalled that France's posture had changed when he placed an embargo on the export of arms to the Middle East and announced that France would oppose any country that attacked first. The effect of the embargo was severely disadvantageous to Israel, since France had hitherto been Israel's primary supplier of arms. Paradoxically, the decision almost certainly hastened Israel's decision to go to war, since her relative military position could be expected

---

* Altogether 8,232 such volunteers arrived in Israel in 1967. Of these nearly half were from Europe. The largest contingents came from Britain (1,749) and France (951).

only to deteriorate in the event of a prolonged ban on French arms exports.

De Gaulle felt personally slighted when the Israelis ignored his advice and attacked on 5 June, scoring a brilliant success within a few hours with their French-built planes. At a memorable press conference the following November, he sought to justify his policy, giving out, in the process, a comment on the Jews, whom he called 'an élite people, self-assured and dominating' (*'peuple d'élite, sûr de lui-même et dominateur'*).[26] De Gaulle was not an antisemite and he evidently came to regret the misjudgement that led him to utter the offending phrase. Later, in an effort to calm wounded spirits, he tried to explain to Chief Rabbi Jacob Kaplan that he had meant the observation as a compliment to the Jewish people. To some it had sounded very different.

Many French Jews who had invested much intellectual, emotional and charitable capital in Israel over the previous decade felt affronted and complained indignantly that their loyalty as French citizens had been impugned. Suddenly to be pro-Israeli seemed to be regarded as anti-patriotic. Raymond Aron, hitherto de Gaulle's most effective and dedicated champion in the press, wrote an eloquent riposte in which he dissected the president's 'poisonous, diabolical thesis'. The critique of de Gaulle was all the more telling since it was obviously written *à contrecoeur* by a political disciple. 'How many Jews, in France and abroad, wept after the press conference, not because they feared persecutions but because they had lost a hero!'[27] De Gaulle's *'petite phrase'* entered the political lexicon of French Jewry and was still being quoted (or misquoted) years later. This single remark and the furious reaction that it provoked heightened the self-consciousness of French Jews and their much greater collective assertiveness in French society in the following two decades.

The 1967 crisis also deeply affected the position of Jews in Eastern Europe. The USSR and its satellites not only backed Egypt and Syria in the war but broke off diplomatic relations with Israel. Large resupplies of tanks and aircraft were sent by the Soviet Union to Egypt and Syria to replace those destroyed or captured by Israel in the war. In the ensuing 'war of attrition' between Israel and Egypt in 1969–70 Russian pilots flew Egyptian planes that engaged in aerial combat with the Israelis. All this had serious effects on the position of Jews in communist Europe. Many came under pressure to make public statements denouncing Israel. The external propaganda offensive against Israel was reflected in internal public indoctrination. In Bulgaria, for example, talks on 'The Reactionary Essence of Zionism' were delivered at every Jewish club in the country during the month of November 1968. In Poland the war led to a dramatic *finis* to 900 years of Jewish history in the country. In Russia it gave birth to an extraordinary movement of Jewish revival and resistance.

After 1967 Israel basked in the sunshine of its military victory. Rather than taking the diplomatic initiative, however, the Labour-dominated governments of Levi Eshkol and Golda Meir took refuge in a policy of *attentisme*, waiting for a 'phone call' from Cairo or Amman in which the Egyptian president or the Jordanian king would consent to sign a peace treaty. No such call came. The Israeli government did not really believe in annexing the territories occupied in 1967 but thought to hold on to them temporarily as a gage to be used in eventual peace negotiations. The drawbacks of this policy became visible only later. For the time being, the Palestinian Arabs in the territories seemed docile and acquiescent. Meanwhile, the United States provided military and political aid; the economy boomed, expanding at a rate of 8 per cent per annum, reinforced by the availability of cheap Arab labour; and for the first time since the foundation of the state Jewish immigration from North America and Western Europe attained significant levels (see Table 2, page 92). In 1972, 3,000 Jews arrived from France and 1,381 from Britain. At last Israel seemed able to attract immigrants of choice rather than merely refugees.

Israel was no longer regarded as an 'experiment' and Israelis in the presence of Jewish visitors from abroad felt less like poor relations. The country's Jewish population continued to grow, while that of the Diaspora stagnated. From a small Levantine outpost of half a million in 1945, the Jews in the Land of Israel had been transformed by the 1970s into the second-largest Jewish community in the world. Israel, moreover, was increasingly recognized as the spiritual centre of world Jewry. One small sign of this was the adoption of the Israeli Sephardi pronunciation of Hebrew as the standard form for synagogue prayer even in Ashkenazi synagogues and schools in most of the Diaspora – though not in communist Europe. In some communities, particularly in Britain, there were fierce conflicts over this change, but the Israeli form eventually emerged in the ascendant.

Support for Israel among Diaspora Jewry after 1967 became virtually a civil religion. Indeed in an age of declining spiritual commitment, pro-Israeli activity, particularly fund-raising, provided a secular mode of Jewish identification and for some filled the void left by the abandonment of religious practice. The heads of fund-raising organizations became the most powerful figures in Jewish affairs in many West European countries. Since these were invariably the most affluent members of the community, democracy now gave way in many communal organizations to a new plutocracy. Critics of Israeli policy or of 'cheque-book Zionism' were shunted to the sidelines and often denounced as heretics or apostates.

An eloquent dissident view was expressed in the early 1970s by Richard Marienstras, exponent of a neo-Bundist ideology that affirmed the continued necessity and potential vitality of Jewish life in the Diaspora. The 'centrality' of Israel in Jewish life, he maintained, was 'an untenable ideological creation', a 'myth' that 'encourages Jews of the Diaspora to suspend the problem of their own identity and their institutions on the arms of a fictive coat-hanger: this political myth does not correspond to anything central in their traditions, to anything profound in their being'. The ideology of Israeli centrality, he argued, consigned the Diaspora to a secondary role. It required of the Diaspora that it deny its very being and, in the last resort, that it destroy itself.[28] At the time this was a voice in the desert. In the course of the next two decades, however, many leaders of Diaspora Jewry – and some Israelis too – would come to accept that the Israeli–Diaspora relationship was sick and required treatment.

CHAPTER FIVE

Facing the Past

The full meaning of the Nazi mass murder of the Jews took a long time to sink into the collective consciousness of both Jews and non-Jews in most of Europe. The confrontation with the past took place at many levels: physical, in the form of memorials and collections of documents and artefacts; imaginative, in the form of literature, film and drama; judicial, in the Nuremberg and other post-war trials of Nazi war criminals; economic, in the payment of restitution reparations by West Germany. All this could not suffice, however, to overcome the collective psychological trauma suffered by the Jews in Europe.

The enormity of the event, its disturbing implications, not only for surviving victims but for the whole of European society, as well as the lack of any moral, historical or theological frame of reference within which to place it, led the immediate post-war generation to avert its gaze. After the initial shock of the liberation of the concentration camps had abated, Europe got on with the business of reconstruction and devoted little attention to recent horrors. The news passed completely by even many well-informed people. Telford Taylor, chief American prosecutor in the later Nuremberg trials, confesses in a recent book: 'I myself did not become aware of the Holocaust★ until my exposure to the relevant documents and witnesses at Nuremberg.'[1]

★ The term 'Holocaust', although used occasionally during and after the war, did not enter into widespread use until the 1970s as a term for the destruction of European Jewry. At first the Hebrew/Yiddish word '*Hurban*' was used by many Jews. Later the established Hebrew form became '*Shoah*' (which was also used

The establishment of Israel and the consequent disappearance of the Jewish 'displaced persons' problem accentuated the amnesiac process. Until the 1960s there was little public remembrance of what had occurred. Few books dealt directly with the theme and general histories of the war often mentioned it only cursorily. The press, the cinema and broadcasting rarely referred to the subject. When they did so there was a perceptible tendency to broaden or universalize the depiction of the victims so as to hide the specifically Jewish character of the massacres, as if this were somehow an embarrassment. An exhibition of Nazi crimes organized in Paris in June 1945 gave the Jewish dimension only passing attention. Even in Israel there was a reluctance in the early years to lay too much emphasis on the Holocaust. The Israeli historian Dina Porat notes: 'In the absence of education, research, art forms, and human dialogue on the subject of the Holocaust, concern for the murdered European Jews seems to have been limited to formal state declarations' – though even there, she notes, there was a disturbing tendency to twist memory to fit the needs of Zionist ideology.[2] An annual memorial day, *Yom Hashoah*, was established in 1951 and observed with solemnity by the whole Jewish population. In due course it also came to be observed in much of the Diaspora. The orthodox establishment both in Israel and the Diaspora, however, refused to incorporate the day in the formal religious calendar.

Scholarly documentation centres on Nazism had been established in London before the war (the Wiener Library, originally founded in Amsterdam), in France before the liberation (the Centre de Documentation Juive Contemporaine) and in Jerusalem in 1953 (Yad Vashem). At the Jewish Historical Institute in Warsaw, founded shortly after the war, a small but devoted band of Jewish historians struggled in difficult conditions to assemble and preserve records of Jewish history in Poland and of Jewish life and death under Nazi rule. Their work was limited, however, by lack of funds and by the restrictive limitations of communist ideology.

by Pope John Paul II). 'Holocaust', with its root meaning of burnt offering or sacrifice, seemed inappropriate to many, including this writer, but it has now passed into general usage.

Public monuments to the Nazis' victims were slow to appear. In the former Warsaw ghetto a memorial, in the form of a group of figures by the Polish Jewish sculptor Nathan Rapaport, was unveiled on 19 April 1948, the fifth anniversary of the outbreak of the ghetto revolt. Conceived in the realist style acceptable to the communist authorities of the period, it became a focal point of remembrance, though with the passage of time it came to seem trite and inadequate to the tragic magnitude of the event it commemorated. At Auschwitz the Polish government created a museum and documentation centre. The emphasis was on the multinational nature of the tragedy: Jews, who had comprised the overwhelming majority of those killed there, figured as one among many groups of victims. Synagogues and Jewish institutions in various parts of Europe displayed memorial plaques, but there was at first a general sense that living institutions would serve as more fitting vehicles of remembrance than stone monuments. The project for a Mémorial du Martyr Juif Inconnu in Paris in the early 1950s aroused opposition from many sectors in the French Jewish community. Baron Guy de Rothschild expressed the view that such an edifice would be 'of sentimental value but without social contribution'. He was supported in this view by many of the East European Jewish organizations in the city, who favoured the construction of a community centre with a modest memorial.[3] A large monument was nevertheless built near the Seine in 1956. In London a Holocaust memorial garden was set up in Hyde Park in 1983; it was repeatedly daubed by vandals and for a time had to be placed under a permanent vigil.

At the sites of many of the massacres no memorial at all could be seen. A case in point was the refusal of the Soviet authorities to erect a memorial to the more than 50,000 Jews murdered by the Nazis at Babi Yar, a ravine near Kiev. The omission aroused protests from non-Jews as well as Jews. In 1959 the writer Viktor Nekrasov protested publicly against the absence of a memorial. In September 1961 the Russian poet and youth idol Yevgeni Yevtushenko published his poem 'Babi Yar', a bold protest not only against the lack of a memorial but also against the revival of antisemitism in the USSR. The poem caused a furore. Yevtushenko, hitherto something of a licensed rebel, fell under a cloud for a while and was denounced by the cultural establishment. In March 1963 Khrushchev himself engaged in a public argument with Yevtushenko when the poet read an extract from the offending poem in his presence. Yevtushenko was supported by the composer Dmitry Shostakovich, who incorporated the poem into his 13th Symphony in 1962. The work fell into official disfavour and for a time was not performed at all in the USSR.

In Western Europe the wartime horrors were discovered anew in successive decades by readers and audiences. The first work to make a major impression was *The Diary of Anne Frank*, written between 1942 and 1944 while the Frank family was in hiding in Amsterdam during the war. Anne had died aged fifteen with her sister at Bergen-Belsen in February or March 1945. Her father, Otto, was among the prisoners liberated at Auschwitz by the Russians in late January 1945. He returned to the Netherlands in June 1945 and, after the confirmation of his daughters' death, discovered the diary. This record of 'all kinds of things that lie buried deep in my heart' (entry for 20 June 1942) was first published in Dutch in 1947, then in many other languages (it was initially rejected by ten American publishers). It achieved an astonishing success: by 1989 it had appeared in thirty-seven countries and had sold more than 15 million copies. In 1955 it was turned into a Pulitzer-prize-winning play and in 1957 into a film. Neo-Nazis and antisemites, as well as the British military historian and self-publicist David Irving, attacked the diary, denouncing it as a forgery. A detailed analysis by the Netherlands Institute of War Documentation, however, conclusively established its authenticity.[4] The Anne Frank Foundation, established in 1956 at the Frank family's 'secret annexe' in Amsterdam, became a memorial visited by half a million people a year.

One of the earliest films about the concentration camps, *Nuit et Brouillard* (1956), was made by the French director Alain Resnais. In an attempt to underscore the general assault on human values, Resnais deliberately underplayed the Jewish aspect. By contrast, André Schwarz-Bart's novel *Le Dernier des Justes* (1959), which sold more than a million copies, sought to place the tragedy within the context of Jewish history in the Diaspora.

It was not until the 1960s, however, that writers and directors in several languages seemed to acquire the confidence to grapple with the theme. Giorgio Bassani's novel *Garden of the Finzi-Continis* (1962), which was made into a delicately affecting film, depicted the strange unworldliness and unwariness of upper-class Italian Jews under fascism. Jean-François Steiner's *Treblinka*, written by a half-Jewish Frenchman whose father had died in a death camp, aroused passionate debate on its appearance in 1966. The Czech film *Shop on Main Street*, in which Ida Kaminska, one of the last stars of the Yiddish stage, gave a touching performance in the central role, appeared in 1967. Perhaps the greatest impact on both the Jewish and the non-Jewish reading public was made by the autobiographical novel *Night* by Elie Wiesel. Born in Transylvania, Wiesel had been deported to Auschwitz as a child and witnessed there the death of his father. His early writings were published in French. Although he moved to the United States and became an American citizen, Wiesel continued to be widely read in Europe. His impact was, however, more as a personality and a human witness than as a writer. Less well-known but perhaps of greater literary weight were the poetry of Nelly Sachs, a German Jewish writer who had settled in Sweden, and the sober, sombre novels of Primo Levi, an Italian Jew who had survived Auschwitz.

In the 1970s and 1980s European cinema and television began to devote considerable attention to the theme of wartime collaboration and the persecution of Jews. Louis Malle's *Lacombe Lucien* (1974) and François Truffaut's *Le Dernier Métro* (1980) explored the psychology of collaboration. 'Genocide', a greatly extended version of an episode in Thames Television's *World at War* series (1975), was historically the most valuable documentary film ever made on the destruction of European Jewry. The facile and vulgarly exploitative American TV 'docudrama' *Holocaust* achieved record audiences in several countries, including West Germany. The most ambitious effort to encompass the subject on the cinema screen was the nine-hour-long *Shoah*, directed by Claude Lanzmann, a French Jewish intellectual and successor to

Sartre as editor of *Les Temps Modernes*. The film was initially banned in Poland, where it was condemned as anti-Polish. Elsewhere it was acclaimed by some as a masterpiece.

In the USSR the wartime persecution of the Jews was generally subsumed under the broader rubric of the sufferings of the Soviet people under Nazi rule. Immediately after the war Ilya Ehrenburg and Vasily Grossman edited *The Black Book*, a collection of documents designed to provide a comprehensive picture of the mass murder of Jews in the Soviet Union. The Russian edition, prepared under the auspices of the Jewish Anti-Fascist Committee, was announced as ready for publication in 1946, but various sections and eventually the whole work were banned by the Soviet authorities. It never appeared in print in the USSR, although abridged overseas editions were published in English and Romanian. Grossman's *Life and Fate*, a novel dealing with the Holocaust, was similarly banned. Among the few books on the Jewish fate in Nazi Europe to receive the commissars' imprimatur was a Russian edition of *The Diary of Anne Frank* – though even this appeared only in 1960. In 1966 Anatoly Kuznetsov's *Babi Yar* was published, but in a severely bowdlerized form. It was not until the move towards *glasnost* in the late 1980s that more open discussion of the Jewish tragedy became possible in Soviet literature.

Whereas the impulse towards literary and cinematic interpretation grew stronger with the passage of years, the judicial response to war crimes was initially vigorous and then seemed to fade. Following the joint Allied declaration on war crimes in December 1942, evidence with a view to future trials of suspected war criminals was assembled by the United Nations War Crimes Commission: by 1948 no fewer than 36,529 case files had been opened and became available to UN member governments in connection with specific war crimes investigations.* The first trials

---

* The files, which included all manner of unproven allegations, were not made available to the public. In May 1986 the Israeli representative at the UN demanded that they be opened to public access. He argued that their release was 'a supreme moral and historical imperative'.[5] The UN secretariat and the governments of the former member nations of the Commission were initially reluctant to change the established procedure but, after a lobbying campaign by

of Nazi war criminals in fact occurred during the war in the Soviet Union: at Krasnodar in July 1943 and at Kharkov the following December.

Though the principle of trial and punishment of war criminals had been agreed by the Allies and firmly established as policy during the war, the question of what legal steps should be taken against the perpetrators of the mass murder of Jews remained unclear in 1945. Many legal experts agreed with J. L. Brierly, Chichele Professor of Law and Diplomacy at Oxford, who argued in April 1945 that 'the acts of the Nazi leaders transcend mere legal justice and they can be fitly dealt with only by a high act of policy on the part of the Allied Governments'.[6] The issue was, however, resolved in August 1945 with an agreement among twenty-three former wartime allies on the trial and punishment of Axis war criminals.

The first big trial, of twenty-four 'major war criminals', among them Goering, Hess, Ribbentrop, Rosenberg, Frank and Speer, opened at Nuremberg before a panel of American, British, French and Russian judges, in November 1945. The defendants faced a lengthy indictment which included such items as the wilful launching of an aggressive war and, a new concept in international law, 'crimes against humanity'. The mass murder of Jews, of which voluminous evidence was assembled and presented to the court, was considered under the latter heading. A deficiency in the proceedings, at any rate from the historical point of view, arose from the restriction of the indictment to events during the war. Nazi persecution of the Jews between 1933 and 1939, in the form of economic boycotts and confiscations, the Nuremberg 'racial laws' of 1935, the *Kristallnacht* arsons and pogroms of November 1938, and the countless other instances of officially mandated expulsion, persecution and humiliation in the pre-war period were all excluded from the purview of the court.

The trial lasted for nearly a year and ended with the conviction of most of the defendants. Papen, Schacht and one other were

---

Israel and some Jewish organizations, their views changed and in November 1987 the archive was finally opened. No major disclosures resulted, nor did the release of the files produce any significant judicial results.

found not guilty. Twelve were sentenced to death, among them Goering, who cheated the executioner by swallowing a cyanide pill in his gaol cell. The rest were sentenced to varying terms of imprisonment. Speer, the only defendant who exhibited any remorse, served his full twenty years, and emerged from gaol in the mid-1960s to become a best-selling author. The former Deputy Führer, Rudolf Hess, who had been in British custody since his 'peace mission' flight to Scotland in 1941, was sentenced to life imprisonment. After the release of Speer he remained the sole inmate in Spandau Prison, under the joint control of the four Allied powers occupying Berlin. Hess was evidently deranged and there was some sentiment in Britain and the USA in favour of his release. But the Russians would not hear of it and he remained immured until his suicide four decades later.

A further twelve trials, known as the 'Nuremberg Subsequent Proceedings', took place before American judges between 1946 and 1949. These led to 177 convictions and twelve death sentences. Other trials were held in the British and French occupation zones of Germany. Altogether the Western occupation powers tried and convicted about 5,000 Germans; 806 received death sentences, of which 486 were carried out. A further 13,000 persons were tried in Austria and 1,000 in France (many of these *in absentia*). The latter figure does not include the thousands of alleged collaborators who were subjected to procedurally dubious instant justice during the post-liberation settling of accounts known as *l'épuration*.

In communist-controlled areas of Europe a more severe retribution was imposed. The USSR tried at least 24,000 Germans, as well as countless thousands of alleged collaborators. An estimated 40,000 persons were tried in Poland, of whom at least 1,200 received death sentences. Hungary tried a similar number, Czechoslovakia 19,000 and East Germany 12,000. In weighing these figures (which include trials for war crimes of all kinds, not only those against Jews), it should be borne in mind that the Allies had agreed during the war on the principle that war crimes should, in general, be tried in the country in which they had been committed; by far the greatest number of such crimes had been committed in the Nazi-occupied areas of Eastern Europe.

By 1948 public and official enthusiasm for further trials had diminished, particularly in Britain, where a certain distaste for what was increasingly seen as a victors' justice had begun to be felt. The writer Rebecca West assailed the trials as 'boredom on a huge historic scale'. Lord Birkett, who sat as a judge at Nuremberg, called them a 'shocking waste of time'.[7] On 31 July 1948 the Commonwealth Secretary, Philip Noel-Baker, informed the Canadian government that Britain would end prosecution of Nazi war criminals in the British occupation zone of Germany by 31 August: 'In our view, punishment of war criminals is more a matter of discouraging future generations than of meting out retribution to every guilty individual.'[8] Churchill, who had earlier been among the foremost advocates of punishment of war criminals, declared that the time had come to 'draw a sponge across the crimes and horrors of the past'.[9] After 1949 the British government took little further interest in the matter.

In West Germany, prosecutions for war crimes were hampered, at least until 1952, by legal restrictions imposed by the occupying powers. For a long time the authorities displayed little energy in investigating or prosecuting perpetrators of war crimes or atrocities against Jews. A Central Office for the Investigation of National-Socialist Crimes was set up at Ludwigsburg only in December 1958. Some important cases followed, in particular the trial of Auschwitz guards which opened at Frankfurt in 1963. Overall, however, the judicial results in the early years of the Federal Republic were meagre. By 1966 proceedings had been initiated in West Germany against a total of 61,761 persons. But guilty verdicts had been secured against fewer than 10 per cent of these. Fourteen received death sentences (before the abolition of the death penalty by the Basic Law of the Federal Republic in 1949), seventy-seven life sentences, 5,911 shorter gaol terms and 114 were fined.

In 1965 a long and ugly controversy began over the issue of whether the statute of limitations, which forbade the opening of new judicial cases after a certain period had elapsed since the crime, should be applied to Nazi war crimes. Under German law, prosecutions for murder could not be initiated after twenty years; for lesser crimes shorter periods were prescribed. A temporary solution was found in 1965 by a change in the law, setting the effective starting point for the statutory period at the foundation date of the Federal Republic in 1949 rather than the actual date of the crime. But this would still preclude any new cases being opened after 1969. A large body of opinion, particularly among Christian Democrats, opposed any further extension of the time limit. Public opinion polls indicated that two-thirds of the population favoured 'drawing a line' (*Schlussstrich ziehen*) at the twenty-year point. Under conflicting pressures, the German parliament approved a new law in July 1969 that abolished all time limits for prosecution on charges of genocide. At the same time the limitation period for murder was extended from twenty to thirty years. The extension did not, in fact, lead to a significant increase in the number of convictions. By 1986 a total of 90,921 cases had been opened but only 364 convictions had been secured since 1964. The rate of convictions declined from 9.9 per cent in the period 1945–64 to 1.5 per cent in the following decade. In many cases proceedings dragged on for years without ever being resolved.

Of the small number convicted in these later trials, many secured quite light sentences. The former Gestapo chief in Cologne, Emanuel Schaefer, who was convicted of deporting 13,000 Jews to death camps, received a three-month prison term. Kurt Asche, found guilty by a court at Kiel in 1981 of participating in the murder of 26,000 Belgian Jews at Auschwitz, was sentenced to seven years' imprisonment and walked free from the court pending confirmation of the sentence. The presiding judge, Dr Rudolf Dann, said no sentence could match Asche's crime and that the term imposed was merely a symbolic expression of the court's disapproval. The Asche case had continued for a total of eighteen years from the opening of proceedings to the verdict. In the interim one further defendant committed suicide and another was certified too sick to face trial.[10] Also in 1981, the trial of nine SS guards at Majdanek, seven men and two women, came to an end after proceedings that had lasted more than five years. The trial revealed yet more details of bestial behaviour but did not apparently create much of an impression on the German public, leading at least one Jewish commentator, Arthur Koestler, to wonder 'what is the point of continuing to stir up the sewers of the past?'[11]

Forty-five prosecutors and thirty policemen were nevertheless still at work in West Germany in 1987, building up files on war-crimes cases. In 1991 a former SS camp commandant, Joseph Schwammberger, faced trial at Stuttgart after being extradited from Argentina, where he had lived openly since 1948. In May the following year, aged eighty, he was sentenced to life imprisonment after what was expected to be the last such trial to take place in Germany.

In France, after the horrors of *l'épuration*, a tacit national understanding seemed to have been reached in the 1950s and 1960s to cast a veil over the uglier details of the wartime period. The 1971 documentary film *Le Chagrin et la Pitié*, made by the Jewish director Marcel Ophuls, was one of the first efforts to challenge that consensus by exposing the apathy and passive collaboration of much of the population during the war. Viewers were disturbed by the depiction of the banal, contemptible everyday compromises of life under occupation – the shopkeeper with the Jewish-sounding name who placed a notice in the local paper to announce that he was not Jewish, the two schoolteachers who tried to remember why they had said nothing when pupils suddenly vanished. The film was banned from French television for ten years on the ground, according to the director of the national broadcasting service, that 'myths are important in the life of a people and certain myths must not be destroyed'.[12]

Such deliberately contrived national amnesia began to dissipate only in the course of the 1970s. A turning point in the process was the trial of Klaus Barbie, who, as wartime Gestapo chief in Lyons, had been responsible for the killing and deportation to death camps of thousands of Jews, the torture of prisoners and the murder of the French Resistance chief Jean Moulin. Barbie was sentenced to death *in absentia* by a French military court at Lyons but remained in hiding under American protection – he served as an informant for the US Army Counter-Intelligence Corps in Germany from 1946 to 1951. French and West German efforts to arrest him were thwarted by American security officials in 1951, when they provided him with false identity documents and enabled him to escape to South America with the help of a Croat Catholic escape organization.[13] He spent most of the following three decades in Bolivia.

In February 1983, after long efforts to expose him by Beate Klarsfeld, a theatrical Franco-German 'Nazi hunter', he was flown back to France. During the long period of judicial preparation before his trial, Barbie's flamboyant lawyer, Jacques Vergès, a radical leftist, threatened to turn the tables on his client's accusers by exposing embarrassing secrets about wartime collaboration. The affair reawakened old demons in the French national conscience. 'Everyone wants to believe it was all a bad dream,' commented Bernard-Henri Lévy, a well-known Jewish intellectual.[14] The trial, which finally opened in Lyons in May 1987, furnished ample evidence of Barbie's guilt, but, contrary to the predictions of his lawyer, produced no sensational revelations. Barbie was found guilty and sentenced to life imprisonment; he died a prisoner four years later.

Three further long-drawn-out cases kept the issue of war crimes, and in particular of French collaboration in the persecution of Jews, in the public eye over the following decade. These were the cases of René Bousquet, Paul Touvier and Maurice Papon. Bousquet, a senior police chief in Vichy France, was accused of responsibility for the round-up of large numbers of Jews (in one instance of 194 children), who were deported to their deaths. At a trial in 1949 on charges of collaboration (all mention of antisemitic persecutions was struck from the indictment) he justified his conduct as a matter of defending French national interests and declared: 'I regret nothing and if I had to start over again under the same conditions I would behave in exactly the same way.'[15] He received a five-year sentence, suspended in recognition of services that he had rendered, in the later part of the war, to the Resistance. Thereafter he pursued a successful career as a banker and in 1957 was restored to the Legion of Honour.

In 1989 the lawyer Serge Klarsfeld (husband of Beate) filed a suit against Bousquet, alleging his involvement in crimes against humanity, but there were long delays in bringing the case to court. President Mitterrand was known to oppose such trials and a spokesman for the presidential office stated on his behalf: 'History has its rights, but so has civil peace.'[16] Later Mitterrand himself declared, 'One cannot continue to live on memories and resentments for ever.'[17] Mitterrand's comment was not published until three years later, in April 1994, when it evoked a strong protest by a group of leaders of Jewish organizations. The strange legal manoeuvres and delays evoked fierce criticism. Laurent Greilsamer commented in *Le Monde*: 'Nothing is more pitiful than this deliberately engineered paralysis of a judicial system going through the motions of busily performing its tasks, nothing more damaging for the honour of justice than this sham.'[18] Bousquet remained at liberty while the judicial investigations continued at a leisurely pace. He was still free in June 1993, when he was murdered in his Paris apartment. The French Chief Rabbi called for a posthumous trial 'at which everything that has been hushed up can finally be said'.[19] But the case was closed.

Paul Touvier had been chief of intelligence for a collaborationist militia in Lyons. He too was charged with responsibility for the deportation of Jews and with killing Resistance fighters. After the war he was sheltered for many years by right-wing Catholics. In 1949 he was sentenced to death *in absentia* but he remained in hiding until 1969, when the statute of limitations on such sentences expired. President Pompidou restored his legal rights and his property in 1971, later defending this action as a gesture towards national unity: 'Shall we for ever keep open the wounds of our national disagreements?'[20] The President's decision evoked outrage from former Resistance leaders and led in 1973 to the lodging of a new indictment alleging crimes against humanity that were not covered by the statute of limitations. Touvier returned to hiding for the next sixteen years but in 1989 he was captured in Nice, at a priory inhabited by followers of the schismatic traditionalist Catholic, Marcel Lefebvre.

In the course of the ensuing investigations it emerged that over the previous forty-four years Touvier had lived with his wife and two children in no fewer than fifty Catholic religious establishments – a fact that cast a lurid light on the relationship between the Roman Catholic Church and the Vichy regime. The revelations led the Archbishop of Lyons, Cardinal Albert Ducourtray, to appoint a commission of eight historians to examine the role of the Church in protecting Touvier. The commission, headed by René Rémond, delivered its report in January 1992. It was a damning indictment of some of the most senior figures in the post-war Church in France. *Le Monde* found it 'flabbergasting' and Cardinal Ducourtray declared himself 'deeply dismayed, saddened and puzzled'. 'How is it,' he asked, 'that so many in the Church, clergy for the most part, could have ignored the requirements of truth and justice to such a degree in the name of a certain conception of charity? What kind of charity is that?'[21]

Tortuous legal proceedings in the Touvier case culminated in April 1992 in a court decision to drop all charges against him on the ground that Vichy's anti-Jewish policies could not be considered 'crimes against humanity' since they did not involve 'ideological hegemony' – the peculiar criterion that had been laid down in French law as a necessary condition for defining such crimes. The decision evoked public uproar and 188 intellectuals signed a collective protest denouncing the judges as falsifiers of history. In November 1992 the highest French court threw out the lower court's ruling. Finally, in 1994, at the age of seventy-eight, Touvier was brought to trial again at Versailles, charged with responsibility for the execution of seven Jews during the war. The press dubbed him the 'French Barbie'. Insisting that he was a practising Catholic, Touvier denied that he was an antisemite. Portions of his diary that were presented to the court, however, in which he referred to two well-known French women as 'Jewish garbage', told a different story. He was found guilty and sentenced to life imprisonment.

The third such case was that of Maurice Papon, who had served as secretary-general of the Gironde region from 1942 to 1944. He was accused of having participated in the deportation to death camps of 1,690 Jews from Bordeaux (among them 233 children). From 1958 to 1967 he served as prefect of the Paris police and from 1978 to 1981 as a budget minister under President Giscard d'Estaing. Legal proceedings against Papon were initiated in 1982 but in this case too years passed without any trial. Meanwhile, Papon remained free. In 1995 he was still at liberty, aged eighty-five. It seemed unlikely that he would ever face trial, though he himself called for an opportunity to clear his name.

By this time attitudes in France had changed considerably. The angry debates arising from the Barbie, Bousquet, Touvier and Papon cases generated a greater public awareness of the extent to which the Vichy regime had been implicated in the deportation of Jews from France and a feeling that a full public accounting was necessary as a kind of national cleansing process. Some French Jews worried that the exhaustive media coverage of these cases might reinforce antisemitism. But many non-Jews and Jews alike suspected that the endless delays in bringing such men to justice indicated that something was being swept under the carpet. The issue became bound up with the broader question of the French attitude to half-buried aspects of the occupation period. It was not until 1992 that President Mitterrand reluctantly bowed to protests and discontinued his practice of sending an annual floral wreath to the tomb of Pétain on the Ile d'Yeu (he stressed that he was thus honouring the hero of Verdun, not the head of the Vichy state). Only in 1993 was an official day of national commemoration established to honour the victims of the 'grande rafle' of 16 July 1942 (when 13,152 Jews were arrested by the Paris police and transferred to the Germans for deportation to Auschwitz), as well as all victims of racist and antisemitic persecution.

Controversy over such issues reached a climax in 1994 with the publication of a book showing that President Mitterrand had been a supporter of the far right in his youth and had initially worked for and given full support to the Vichy regime.[22] Although the outlines of all this had been vaguely known for some time, public opinion on the left was shocked by some of the details that emerged, in particular Mitterrand's acknowledgement of his friendship, extending until the 1980s, with René Bousquet and his admission that he had intervened in the Papon case and slowed down the judicial investigation. In a television interview in September 1994 with the head of French state television, Jean-Pierre

Elkabbach (a Jew), Mitterrand explained that as late as 1942 he had 'not known at all' about Vichy's anti-Jewish measures – a remark that evoked acid comment among erstwhile supporters.[23] More than a distressing end to a distinguished political career, the episode again cast a piercing searchlight on the darkest hole of national memory.

In Britain the war-crimes issue remained strangely dormant until the 1980s, in spite of allegations that a handful of war criminals had found refuge in the country after the war under the guise of being refugees from communist oppression in Eastern Europe. Only in 1988, after public accusations against specific individuals were made insistently by the Simon Wiesenthal Center in Los Angeles, did the British government agree even to consider the matter. It was no accident that the initiative came from an American Jewish organization; the Anglo-Jewish establishment traditionally favoured quiet, backstairs activity and deplored the strident tone of the Wiesenthal Center's demands. But the issue was taken up by an all-party Parliamentary War Crimes Group and by the media. In Scotland the STV television channel broadcast a documentary laying out some of the most damning evidence against one alleged war criminal who was living in Edinburgh.

A Home Office committee of inquiry was established, headed by a former Director of Public Prosecutions, Sir Thomas Hetherington, which reported the following year, urging changes in the law that would facilitate prosecutions. The ensuing legislation gave rise to angry debates in both Houses of Parliament. Although the proposed law was personally favoured by the Prime Minister, Mrs Thatcher, many Conservatives opposed the measure. Some Jews doubted the value of new war-crimes trials. The columnist Bernard Levin wrote in *The Times*: 'The universe will not be a whit better or cleaner for purging itself of a dozen or two criminals with one foot in the grave.' And the *Jewish Chronicle*'s commentator, Chaim Bermant, agreed: 'There are, one feels, more wholesome outlets for Jewish emotions and more productive calls on Jewish energies.'[24]

The debate in the House of Lords was unusually passionate for that generally mild-mannered body. Some of the bill's opponents adduced arguments based on principled hostility to retrospective legislation. Others argued that the passage of time rendered successful prosecutions unlikely. Lord Hailsham, a former Lord Chancellor, thought that trials would be 'a gross perversion of justice' that would amount to little more than 'lynch law'.[25] Other opponents included Lord Shawcross, a former Nuremberg prosecutor, and Lords Soper, Longford, Callaghan, Grimond, Dacre (the historian Hugh Trevor-Roper), Carrington and Donaldson. The Bishop of St Albans, John Taylor, warned that trials might lead to increased antisemitism: 'I fear for the Jewish community in our midst.' Lord Mayhew, who as a junior Foreign Office minister in 1946 had been responsible for war-crimes policy, argued that the decision in 1948 to halt further prosecutions had been correct: 'The overriding reason was that we felt that retribution had gone far enough . . . The major difference between the policy we then established and the policy now recommended by the inquiry is that we thought that retaliation should end and the inquiry recommends that retaliation should be revived.' The Chief Rabbi, Lord Jakobovits, found himself in a minority with his argument that to allow war criminals to walk free would amount to 'handing the tyrant a posthumous victory'.[26]

The House of Commons eventually decided by 348 to 123 on a free vote to approve the inquiry's recommendations, but when the necessary legislation was presented to parliament the House of Lords put up further strong opposition. Lord Campbell of Alloway, a survivor of the Colditz prisoner-of-war camp, led the opponents to the bill, calling it 'no more than a cruel vendetta against frail old men'. Lord Beloff, a Jewish Conservative, aroused some indignation when he said: 'A degree of prejudice has crept into the matter that is very similar to that contained in the official documents of the wartime years.'[27] The bill was rejected twice by the Lords (technically by a wrecking amendment). It was eventually enacted only after use of the constitutional right of the House of Commons to overrule the upper chamber – a device used on only two previous occasions since 1911.

The 1991 War Crimes Act did not, however, produce any immediate prosecutions. In June 1994 the government announced that it was setting aside £8 million to finance the prosecution of up to ten suspected Nazi war criminals who were living in the United Kingdom. In addition, a further eighteen cases were still under investigation by the Scotland Yard war-crimes unit. Last-ditch opposition from backwoods hereditary peers persisted. The Earl of Lauderdale said that the act was a 'classic example of the folly of the House of Commons'.[28] In October 1994 the government announced that prosecution was being considered in seven cases, but by that time all the potential defendants were so old that it seemed unlikely any would ever face trial.

The controversy over the War Crimes Act helped bring to public attention the fact that large numbers of former war criminals had eluded capture and found refuge in the United States, Canada, Britain and elsewhere as a result of help they received from officials of Allied governments and, in some cases, from the Vatican. A US State Department report in 1947 called the Vatican 'the largest single organization involved in the illegal movement of emigrants'.[29] Although such allegations were denied by Church historians, evidence suggested that there was some basis for them. For example, Croats who had served in the fascist Ustaša militia during the war were aided in travelling to Argentina. Walter Rauff, an SS officer responsible for poison-gas killings of tens of thousands of Jews, was sheltered for eighteen months in monasteries in Rome before moving on to Syria, Ecuador and Chile.

Many Ukrainians and other East Europeans who had served as volunteers in Nazi armed units, including the SS, succeeded in persuading the Western Allies that they were anti-communists who deserved to be treated as refugees rather than as criminals to be returned to the USSR to face almost-certain death. The British and Americans did, in fact, abide by wartime agreements with Stalin to the extent of handing over large numbers of such Nazi collaborators (the so-called 'victims of Yalta'), who were imprisoned or killed in the USSR. But from early 1947 onwards, with the growth of Cold War animosities, a reluctance to continue with such transfers developed among British officials. The upshot was that suspected war criminals were indeed transformed into political refugees. Several thousand Latvians, Ukrainians and others in the British zone of occupation in Germany who had served in SS and other German units were granted DP status by the Foreign Office and recruited for work in Britain.

When former members of the Ukrainian volunteer SS Galizien division arrived in Britain in the summer of 1947, Richard Crossman, MP, forwarded to the Foreign Office a constituent's letter complaining of the arrival of '8,000 bloodthirsty cut-throats'.[30] The government responded with claims that 'cross-sections' of the immigrants had been screened, but such screening was in reality perfunctory and it subsequently emerged that many war criminals had slipped through the net. Soviet protests were dismissed. About 1,000 of the Ukrainians settled in Britain; the remainder moved elsewhere, particularly to Canada.

In 1979 the United States Justice Department established an Office of Special Investigations (OSI) with responsibility for identifying war criminals living in the United States and securing their deportation. The OSI achieved only limited results. By 1990 about thirty such persons had been deported, among them Karl Linnas, a sixty-seven-year-old former Estonian living on Long Island who was sent to face trial in the Soviet Union in April 1987. Linnas, who had secured admission to the USA from Germany in 1951 as a 'displaced person', had served as chief of a concentration camp at Tartu, where 12,000 people had died. He had been tried *in absentia* by a Soviet court and faced a death sentence but died while Soviet authorities were still considering his appeal.

The most troubling case of this kind was that of John Demjanjuk, a Ukrainian-born Cleveland auto worker accused of being 'Ivan the Terrible', a psychopathic guard at the Treblinka death camp. In 1988, after being extradited from the United States, he was convicted by an Israeli court and sentenced to death. The trial was followed with particular attention among the Ukrainian exile community in North America and in Ukraine itself, where the case fed extreme nationalist agitation. But after doubt was cast on some of the evidence, the verdict was reversed. Demjanjuk was released and returned to the USA.

The most important trial of a single individual for participation in the mass murder of Jews (and the only other one to take place before an Israeli court) was that of Adolf Eichmann in Jerusalem in 1961. Eichmann's capture in Argentina by Israeli agents and his surreptitious removal to Israel aroused criticism. But his trial was seen by the Israeli Prime Minister, Ben Gurion, as a means of providing an education in the realities of the Jewish fate in Nazi Europe for the generation of Israeli Jews who had come to maturity after 1945. The prosecution's massive assemblage of documentary evidence and the heart-rending testimony of large numbers of witnesses helped achieve that object.

The trial and execution of Eichmann (his is the only death sentence to have been carried out in the history of Israel) aroused bitter debate on a number of counts. The aged German Jewish philosopher Martin Buber, the best-known Israeli religious thinker of the time, opposed the carrying out of the sentence, but his view found little echo among the general public. The British publisher and writer Victor Gollancz argued that Israel should not have put Eichmann on trial. By far the most controversial response to the trial was Hannah Arendt's book (originally a series of articles written for the *New Yorker* magazine) *Eichmann in Jerusalem: A Report on the Banality of Evil*.[31] Arendt, a philosopher who had been compelled to flee Germany because of her Jewish origin, provoked a vehement reaction, particularly as a result of her denunciation of the role of the Judenräte (Jewish Councils). The book contained a large number of historical errors, exposed in merciless detail by the legal scholar Jacob Robinson.[32] Unfortunately, his rebuttal of Arendt lacked her seductive literary style. The immense publicity given to the trial throughout the world (British television, for example, broadcast special reports daily) revived interest in some of the profound moral and historical issues of the Nazi era. It also broadened understanding among gentiles of the unique horror of the Jewish fate in Nazi Europe and of the status of Israel as heir to the murdered Jewish communities.

That status had received recognition in international law and treaty a decade earlier in the Luxemburg agreement on reparations concluded between West Germany and Israel. Although there

were many precedents for the payment of reparations after wars
(for example, by the defeated powers after the First World War)
there could in the nature of things be no precedent for reparations
after the unique collective crime of the mass murder of European
Jewry. A legal distinction was drawn between *restitution*, for
example of real estate and other property, and *reparations* – compensation for the suffering, damage and crimes committed by the
Nazi regime and its accomplices. Restitution began in the late
1940s in occupied Germany when some Jewish properties were
restored to their owners – where these could be identified. The
authorities in the US military zone enacted a restitution law in
1947 and similar laws followed in the French and British zones.
The Soviets returned some Jewish properties, but in most cases the
owners were unable to take effective possession. The larger issue
of reparations, however, awaited the restoration of German sovereignty, which took place in stages between 1949 and 1955.

Prior to the establishment of Israel, the Jews had no effective
collective voice that could place the matter on the diplomatic
agenda; the efforts of Jewish voluntary organizations to do so in
the immediate post-war years had failed almost completely.★ Even
Israel's *locus standi* in the matter seemed doubtful in international
law since Israel had not been a belligerent against Germany. The
birth of the Federal Republic of Germany in May 1949, however,
opened new possibilities. The West German government made
clear from the outset its readiness to acknowledge responsibility
for the past. President Heuss declared in November 1949 that 'the
German people should feel collectively ashamed'.[33] But the initial
offer to Israel by the Federal German Chancellor, Konrad Adenauer, of 10 million marks as 'an immediate sign of Germany's
determination to redress the wrongs done to the Jews throughout
the world' struck an awkward note and evoked criticism among
Jews in the Diaspora. No response, either positive or negative,
came from the government of Israel.[34]

The reparations issue aroused deep feelings in both Israel and the
Diaspora. Many Jews were violently opposed to accepting what

★ See above, pp. 29–30.

was seen as 'blood money' from West Germany. Others argued that there was no ethical reason for allowing the Jews' murderers to become also their inheritors. The Israeli government at first tried to sidestep the emotional issues raised by such debates. In March 1951 it presented a formal demand, addressed not to Germany but to the four occupying powers. In this it demanded 'collective reparations on behalf of Israel and the Jewish people' based on 'the expenditure incurred and anticipated in connection with the resettlement of Jewish immigrants from the countries formerly under Nazi control'. The sum involved was estimated at $1.5 billion. The Western Allies replied that they were legally unable to enforce any such payment on the West German government and the USSR never replied at all. Israel was therefore compelled, though it went against the grain, to negotiate directly with West Germany. After preliminary talks between Israeli and German representatives, Chancellor Adenauer delivered a statement to the Bundestag on 27 September 1951 in which he announced formally that his government intended to negotiate an agreement on reparations with Israel.

Israel could, and did, claim to be the collective heir of the murdered Jews, but Israel alone in the early 1950s did not represent the Jewish people as a whole. The absence of diplomatic relations between the Jewish state and West Germany and the strong public hostility in Israel to any contacts with Bonn made direct, public talks between the two governments difficult. West Germany therefore required a negotiating partner that could plausibly claim to represent the survivors of the destroyed Jewish communities of Europe. Contacts had meanwhile been established between West German officials and leaders of the World Jewish Congress, which took the initiative in concerting a Jewish position on the issue. As a result a suitably representative body was formed, the Conference on Jewish Material Claims against Germany, of which the moving spirit was Nahum Goldmann.

The closest that Diaspora Jewry had to a leader in the post-war period, Goldmann was a man of many parts, many tongues and many passports. His combined leadership of the World Jewish Congress, the World Zionist Organization and the Claims Conference gave him a unique position in the Jewish world. Possessed of considerable charm, wit and an iconoclastic intellectual independence, Goldmann delighted in his friendships with the great and in breaking taboos. Some of his political efforts went astray, notably his attempt to break into Israeli politics by founding the centrist Liberal Party in the mid-1960s. Many of his political positions, unfashionable in their day, were later vindicated, such as his call for Israeli withdrawal from occupied territories after 1967. His greatest achievement was undoubtedly the negotiation of the reparations agreement with West Germany in which he represented both the State of Israel and that amorphous, disunited, semi-mythical body, world Jewry.

Following Adenauer's statement to the Bundestag, Goldmann brought together the major representative organizations of all the main European and ex-European Jewish communities in the non-communist world and in October 1951 they formed the Claims Conference. The task of securing a unified approach by all the Jewish participants was not easy. In France, for example, there were fierce debates within CRIF over whether to participate. Jewish communists, following the line dictated by Moscow, which was concerned about West German rearmament, did not wish to do anything that might help rehabilitate Germany. They denounced Goldmann as an American agent and argued that it was 'anormal et indigne de se mettre à table avec des assassins'. They were supported by the Bund, the left-Zionist Mapam party and by some ex-resisters. Only after 'longs débats houleux' did CRIF eventually agree to participate – on the condition that there would be no rehabilitation and no pardon offered by the Jewish people.[35]

On 6 December Goldmann held a private (and secret) meeting with Adenauer at Claridge's Hotel in London. Goldmann later wrote: 'Of all the important conversations I have had in the course of my work, this was the most difficult emotionally and perhaps the most momentous politically . . . If ever an encounter deserved to be called historic it was this one.' Adenauer said that he felt 'the wings of history beating in this room'.[36] Goldmann was not exactly a self-effacing character but the tragic solemnity of this encounter justified his picture of the occasion. The Chancellor immediately acquiesced to Goldmann's demand that the German government should confirm in writing its acceptance of moral responsibility and should take the Israeli government's indemnification proposal as a basis for negotiation. Adenauer wrote a letter to Goldmann to that effect the same day.[37]

After violent debates in the Israeli parliament and among Jews throughout the world, formal negotiations began at Wassenaar in the Netherlands in March 1952. The Israeli government and the Claims Conference negotiated jointly on behalf of the Jews with a German government delegation. At one point the talks came close to breaking down. The influential German banker Hermann Josef Abs, at that time heading the German delegation at an international conference in London on German debts, feared lest Germany's credit be adversely affected by large reparations obligations. He therefore pressed for a limitation of the amount to be paid and a stretching out of the payment period. When Bonn seemed to accept these proposals, the German negotiators at Wassenaar, Dr Otto Küster and Professor Franz Böhm, protested against the policy of their own government and threatened to resign. Talks were suspended for a time. In June, however, Adenauer intervened in support of the position taken by Küster and Böhm. Negotiations resumed in August and were successfully concluded shortly afterwards.

The agreement was signed in Luxemburg on 10 September 1952 by Adenauer, Moshe Sharett, the Israeli Foreign Minister, and Goldmann, representing the Claims Conference. The occasion was awkward for many reasons, one being the absence of formal relations between West Germany and Israel. Arab states protested vociferously against the economic support that Israel would receive under the agreement. For fear of terrorist attacks by right-wing Jews, the time and place of the ceremony remained secret until the last moment. To avoid embarrassment, no speeches were made. The Bundestag ratified the agreement the following March by a large majority (the communists opposed it and the liberal FDP abstained). The treaty provided for payment to Israel of 3 billion marks (then equivalent to $714 million) and to the Claims Conference of 450 million marks ($107 million). These payments were not 'reparations' *stricto sensu*; they were defined in the treaty as a partial recompense by the West German government 'within the limits of their capability' for the 'unspeakable criminal acts ... perpetrated ... during the National Socialist regime of terror'. Although these sums were smaller than those that had been originally demanded, the Jewish negotiators accepted them, since the West German government in addition undertook to enact legislation providing for large payments in compensation to individuals who had suffered or lost property as a result of Nazi persecution. The Claims Conference funds were used mainly for relief and welfare projects among Jewish communities in Europe: schools, synagogues, community centres, hospitals and cultural bodies all received grants.

The amounts eventually paid by the German government, to Israel, to the Claims Conference and to Jewish individuals, far exceeded those originally envisaged. In June 1956 an amended Indemnification Law was adopted in West Germany, extending eligibility for compensation to individuals. This was the first of several such amendments. By 1956 it was estimated that 1.2 million claims had been lodged, of which about 400,000 had been settled. A large legal apparatus helped victims of Nazi persecution press their claims. In 1956 the Claims Conference and its various offshoots, such as the United Restitution Organization, employed more than 1,000 persons around the world, including 217 full-time lawyers. At that time 131,000 claims were being actively prosecuted. By 1976 a total of 4,318,193 individual claims had been presented (in some cases multiple claims for different types of damage had been lodged by one claimant). By that time the aggregate of payments by the West German government was over 42 billion marks ($18 billion at the then rate of exchange). Much of this was in the form of annuities to Nazi victims – widows, orphans, people whose health had been damaged or careers disrupted by Nazi persecution. Others received payments for loss of civil service positions or compensation for forced labour. The beneficiaries were initially only German citizens, but in due course the categories were broadened to include some (but not all) other

Nazi victims. Separate legal processes were initiated for dealing with the problem of heirless Jewish property.

The question how to look back on the destruction of European Jewry was thus tackled on several levels – monumental, literary, cinematic, judicial and financial. On none of these levels was the outcome wholly satisfactory. How could it be? But the problem was at least addressed and serious efforts were made. In West Germany, in particular, the issue became a central concern both of public debate and among scholars. In the so-called *Historikerstreit* of the 1980s historians engaged in bitter academic controversy over the place of the mass murder of the Jews in Nazi ideology and German history. Some of the arguments adduced seemed to indicate a wish to 'relativize' the Jewish catastrophe – for example, the theses of Ernst Nolte, who compared Hitler's crimes with those of Stalin, as if to palliate the former. The rebuttals to Nolte, however, came not only from Israeli and British historians but most trenchantly from fellow Germans. In retrospect, the controversy indicated the maturity and sense of responsibility with which the greater part of the historical profession in the Federal Republic approached this sensitive issue.

Exactly the contrary was true of the ill-assorted collection of persons who engaged in the strange practice of what came to be known as 'Holocaust denial'. In Britain David Irving, who described himself as a mild fascist and said that he regarded Hitler's summer home at Berchtesgaden as a 'shrine', advanced at least half-way towards such a position. He maintained that Hitler could not be shown to have given any order for the 'Final Solution'. While conceding that Jews had been murdered, he suggested that this was the result of the 'clumsy and mindless brutality of Hitler's underlings'.[38] The notion that Auschwitz was, as it were, a 'sob story' invented by Jews to garner sympathy and strengthen support for Zionism gained currency in some circles in the late 1970s and early 1980s. In France Robert Faurisson, a lecturer in literature at the University of Lyons, went so far as to argue that the gas chambers had not existed.

How to deal with this grotesque phenomenon exercised many liberal minds: some argued in favour of applying legal sanctions against such propaganda; others contended that the self-styled 'revisionists' courted martyrdom and that to send them to prison would merely gratify their craving for publicity. Others again, such as the American Jewish scholar and radical activist Noam Chomsky, insisted that the right to free expression extended even to such cases; Chomsky allowed a statement of his to be printed as a preface to a book by Faurisson, evoking outrage in Jewish circles.

Eventually the persistence of the 'revisionist' propagandists and their links with the extreme right led several countries to pass legislation banning such publications. In West Germany the Supreme Court ruled in 1979 that denial of the Holocaust was an offence:

> It is part of the personal consciousness [*Selbstverständnis*] of the persecuted to be considered as belonging to a group that stands out because of the persecution suffered and to whom all other citizens bear a moral responsibility. This consciousness of being victims of persecution is a matter of their personal dignity. Respect for that consciousness is the guarantee against the repetition of similar discrimination in the future and an essential condition which makes their life in Germany possible. Whoever tries to deny the truth of past events denies to every Jew the respect to which he is entitled.[39]

Explicit legal sanctions against 'Holocaust denial' were applied, although in Mannheim in 1994 an extreme rightist was given a suspended sentence and congratulated by judges on his conduct in challenging the 'claims of the Jews'. The judges involved were temporarily removed 'on health grounds' and the German Chancellor, Helmut Kohl, declared the court's action shameful. But the incident left a sour taste. With a view to clarifying the law, the Bundestag passed a new bill in September 1994 that increased the maximum penalty to five years' imprisonment. In France the Loi Gayssot, passed in 1990, was used to prosecute Faurisson, who was convicted under its provisions and fined 30,000 francs. Others found guilty of publishing or distributing such works were sent to prison.

By the 1970s the Holocaust, as it had become generally known in English, had developed into a central feature of Jewish identity in the Diaspora. Some leaders, such as Chief Rabbi Jakobovits of Britain, deplored this development, warning against 'the sanctification of the Holocaust as a cardinal doctrine in contemporary Jewish thought and teaching'.[40] Jakobovits argued: 'The danger is acute that preoccupation with the Holocaust could easily distort the Jewish purpose, substituting the fear of national extinction for the hope of Jewish spiritual fulfilment as the supreme dynamic of Jewish life and ultimate goal of Jewish existence.'[41] In religious, social and intellectual terms, the argument was unexceptionable; but it was difficult to advance without arousing bitter feelings.

More than any other religion or people, Judaism and Jews are centrally concerned with collective historical memory. The desire to stare history unflinchingly in the face is in tune with Jewish tradition and arises, in its current form as applied to the Jewish catastrophe in Nazi Europe, from the most well-meaning of motives. Within limits the exercise is socially necessary and healthy. The problem is to define those limits. The central position that the Holocaust has come to occupy in contemporary Jewish self-understanding threatens to become an almost necrophiliac obsession. As in their relationship with Israel, here too European Jews have succumbed to a potentially destructive sickness.

CHAPTER SIX

Jews and the Christian Problem

The most important antisemitic institution in Europe in 1945, one in which anti-Jewish doctrine was deeply embedded in profound historical foundations, was the Roman Catholic Church. It is a sign of the revolution in consciousness within the Church and in the relationship between Judaism and Christianity that has taken place in the space of a generation that, from the vantage point of the 1990s, such a statement may seem far-fetched. In 1945 it was axiomatic to any unprejudiced observer.

To move back across the great historic watershed of Vatican II is to cross into a dark spiritual netherworld in which the Catholic Church was the most powerful engine of anti-Jewish ideologies and the foremost inculcator of scorn for the Christ-killers. Catholic priests and teachers routinely explained that the Jews were a cursed people who had turned their back on Christ. Every Good Friday the liturgy included a prayer calling for the veil to be lifted from the hearts of 'the perfidious Jews ... so that they too may acknowledge our Lord, Jesus Christ'. The authoritative Catholic periodical *Civiltà Cattolica*, well known as faithfully representing the views of the Pope, refrained during the war from any mention of Nazi persecutions of the Jews, denounced the Jews' 'injustice, impiety, infidelity, sacrilege' in March 1942, dwelt with sympathy between 1945 and 1952 on the travails of German refugees from the East while never once mentioning the liberated concentration camps, spoke of the 'pious' deaths of war criminals executed at Nuremberg in 1946, explained in 1951 that Satan had filled the hearts of the Jews with 'national egoism, racial pride, greed, desire for vengeance, hypocrisy, hardness towards their neighbour' and expressed regret in 1952 that Germany should be held responsible for war crimes and should have to pay restitution for confiscated Jewish property.[1]

In some Catholic countries, such as Italy, where the Jews were deeply woven into the fabric of society, the antisemitism of the Church had little popular resonance. Enlightened Catholic theologians such as Jacques Maritain condemned antisemitism vigorously. Progressive Catholic thinkers like those associated with the Mouvement Républicain Populaire in France called for a reassessment of attitudes towards Jews. All this moderated but did not alter the nature of the ancient antagonism of the Church to the Synagogue. Nazism had been effectively eradicated and discredited in May 1945, but for more than a decade after that date, as for the previous nineteen centuries, the foremost spiritual institution in Europe continued unashamedly to regard the inculcation of contempt for fellow humans as not merely permissible but a spiritual duty and a central element of the Christian faith. Ecumenical politeness at the end of the century should not erase this historical fact from the record.

All the more impressive, therefore, was the process by which the Church of Rome, in the post-war period, cleansed itself of this stain of exclusiveness, spiritual arrogance and inhumanity.

The Catholic Church was not unique in its perpetuation of anti-Jewish doctrines. The Orthodox Churches in Russia, Romania and Greece were also deeply imprinted with antisemitic ideas. Nor were the Protestant Churches immune from it – as the conduct of the majority branch of the Lutheran Church in Germany had demonstrated during the Nazi period.

Relations between Judaism and Christianity in the post-war period were haunted not only by traditional anti-Jewish teachings but also by Jewish memories of the conduct of the Churches during and immediately after the war. Throughout the twelve years of Nazi power, the Vatican had seemed more concerned with the danger from the extreme left than from the extreme right. Pope Pius XI had denounced racism and antisemitism in strong terms but his successor, Pius XII, who ascended the papal

throne in 1938, preserved a more diplomatic silence. In his statements on Nazi treatment of the Jews, he limited himself to a few
oracular and indirect comments.

In the immediate post-war years, several senior members of the
hierarchy, driven by anti-communist zeal or other motives, made
explicitly antisemitic public statements. The Bishop of Vienna,
interviewed by the Anglo-American Committee of Inquiry in
1946, explained 'that the Church did not fight the Jews but only
the Jewish spirit of materialism'.[2] The Polish Primate, Cardinal
Hlond, had a long record of such utterances. In 1936 he had lent
support to the economic boycott of Jews: 'One does well [he
wrote in a pastoral letter] to prefer one's own kind in commercial
dealings and to avoid Jewish stores and Jewish stalls in the mar-
kets.'[3] After the war Hlond set the tone for the Polish hierarchy's
identification of the Jews with the deeply unpopular ruling communist group. He told a visiting Jewish dignitary that the Jews in
power were 'endeavouring to enforce a system inimical to the
majority of the nation'.[4] Examples like this could be multiplied
many times. They point to a strain of prejudice which was not
merely theoretical but which also gave rise to actions and policies
that deeply injured Jews.

Among the most painful of such cases were those of Jewish
children whose lives had been saved by Catholics during the war
and whose souls were subsequently demanded, as it were as a
ransom, by the Church. Thousands of such children had been
sheltered by religious orders, by Catholic orphanages, or by families during the occupation. While in hiding, most of the children
had been brought up as Christians and some of them had no
knowledge or only a dim recollection of their Jewish origins. The
result was often to provoke a severe crisis of identity at the end of
the war. The Israeli historian Saul Friedländer has written an
evocative account of his years as such a hidden child and of his
near-embrace of Christianity as a consequence.[5] In his case the
crisis was resolved by his decision to emigrate to Palestine. In
many others the outcome was different.

Robert and Gérald Finaly, born in 1941 and 1942 respectively,
were the sons of Austrian Jewish parents who had fled to France in

1936. During the war the parents, fearful for their infant sons, had entrusted them to the care of the municipal crèche in a suburb of Grenoble. In 1944 the parents were deported and later died at Auschwitz. Their sons were hidden until the end of the war by a Catholic foster-mother, Antoinette Brun. In 1945 the boys' aunt in New Zealand and another in Israel discovered that they had survived and claimed custody. A long legal battle ensued, in the course of which Mlle Brun kidnapped the children and, with the aid of militant Catholics, had them baptized and brought up as Catholics. A court order was issued in December 1950 requiring their return to their family, but it was not obeyed. Court proceedings continued until 1953. Meanwhile, the boys were hidden in convents of the sisters of Notre-Dame de Sion. In early 1953 Mlle Brun was found guilty of kidnapping and was imprisoned, but the boys were still not produced. In fact, they had been smuggled over the border to Spain. Four Basque priests who had organized their transfer and the mother supérior of the order of Notre-Dame de Sion were arrested.

The case became a national scandal in which the Church authorities and the Jewish community were engaged. A great public outcry mobilized all the anticlerical forces of the Republic against the Church. Left-wing intellectuals signed a manifesto denouncing the attitude of the Church. François Mauriac took up the cause of those who claimed the boys for the Church (he later modified his position). The Catholic press complained of a campaign of calumny against Catholics, who, they pointed out, had after all taken great risks to save Jewish children during the war. The French Primate, Cardinal Gerlier, whose record was marked by Vichy associations, issued a statement affirming the noble motives of the Basque priests. At last, in March 1953, Church representatives reached an agreement with the acting Chief Rabbi of France, Jacob Kaplan, whereby the boys would be returned to their family. But the boys were still not produced. Kaplan issued a pained protest against the Church's blatant failure to fulfil its agreement. Gerlier reacted angrily. Only after further impassioned national debate were the boys finally handed over to their relatives in Israel in July 1953.

The episode was more than an ephemeral 'tug-of-love' sensation. For those with historic memories, the case recalled the famous Mortara case of 1858, in which a six-year-old Jewish child in Bologna had been secretly baptized by his Catholic nurse and abducted to Rome. The Church refused to permit the child to be returned to his parents lest he receive a Jewish upbringing. The affair became a worldwide *cause célèbre*. Ignoring all protests, the Church had its way: the child remained separated from his parents and was brought up as a Christian. He died a member of the Augustinian order at an abbey in Belgium in 1940. The Finaly case, occurring as it did long after the end of the temporal power of the Pope and in a secular state, had a different outcome. But the long-drawn-out controversy went to the heart of the Christian–Jewish relationship in Europe in the immediate post-war period – a relationship that remained deeply troubled, at some points poisoned.

Christians who had saved Jewish children during the war had risked their own lives in doing so. They had acted out of a profound conception of Christian love and charity. Many of them, in seeking to save, as they saw it, the souls of these children, after the war acted out of similarly generous motives.

At the same time, however, documents recently published reveal more clearly than was apparent at the time the deeply ingrained antisemitism that lay at the root of the actions of Mlle Brun and her supporters. During the boys' captivity, the elder of them, Robert, wrote a series of letters to his aunt that were evidently dictated to him by his captors (some were not in his handwriting although signed by him). They were violently antisemitic in content.[6] There is no doubt that the boys' captors saw the affair not as a simple matter of the children's welfare but as a crusade for the salvation of their souls. The boys remained in Israel; Robert became a doctor in Beersheba. The affair thus had a happy outcome from the point of view of the boys' family. But the Finalys were not the only children who had been adopted by Mlle Brun. Several of these had no relatives left to claim them at the end of the war and were automatically brought up as Catholics. About these there was no public outcry. Nor were these isolated cases: there were thousands like them all over Europe.

In the Netherlands, for example, the issue of Jewish war orphans became a matter of embittered debate in the post-war years and seriously damaged Christian–Jewish relations. About 2,000 Jewish orphans had survived in the country and of these 1,300 were under the age of fifteen in 1945. Upon the liberation they were placed under the guardianship of a government-appointed commission on which Jews were in a minority. The Jewish community urged that these children be given a Jewish upbringing in accordance with an established principle of Dutch law that an orphan should be brought up in the faith of the deceased parents. But the commission would not uphold that principle and the Jewish members withdrew for a while in protest. After a public demonstration and protests by members of the Jewish community, the commission was dissolved, but by then most of the cases had already been dealt with and the children allocated in many instances to non-Jewish homes. The issue provoked dissension not only between Jews and Christians but within the Jewish community, with some assimilationist Jews arguing that the welfare and happiness of the child must be paramount and should take precedence over the religious claim of the Jewish community. Altogether about 1,500 of the children were moved to a Jewish environment, while 500 were brought up as non-Jews (though a few of these later returned to Judaism).[7]

The case of Anneke Beekman closely mirrored that of the Finalys, but its outcome resembled that of Mortara. Anneke, born in Amsterdam in November 1940 to orthodox Jewish parents who died at the Sobibor death camp, had been hidden during the war by Dutch Catholics. A bitter post-war legal battle over her custody culminated in 1948 in a Dutch Supreme Court decision in favour of her return to a Jewish foster family. She was then hidden by her Catholic protectors and secretly baptized. In the ensuing outcry most of the secular, Protestant and Jewish press and some liberal Catholics called for respect for the court's decision, while Catholic papers complained of 'anti-Catholic McCarthyism'. Monsignor B. J. Alfrink, acting Archbishop of Utrecht, refused to intervene, arguing that the child 'voluntarily dissociates herself from the decision of the law court because, evidently, she preferred the trusted surroundings in which she grew up'. He called on the Jewish community 'to relinquish guardianship, to stop persecuting and hounding her'.[8] A number of people, including a priest and the mother superior of a convent, were prosecuted and served short prison terms for withholding the child, but she was still not produced. Public opinion gradually turned against the Jewish community. The court decision was never implemented. In 1961, when she reached her majority, Anneke returned to the Netherlands after several years in Catholic institutions in Belgium and France. She told a television interviewer: 'I am a Catholic by free choice.'[9]

Although this was a problem that primarily affected occupied Europe, similar issues also arose in Britain. On the eve of the Second World War the British government, under pressure on account of its restriction of Jewish immigration to Palestine, had permitted up to 10,000 'non-Aryan' children to be brought from Germany to England. A total of 9,354 arrived in 1938–9 under the auspices of the 'Children's Movement'; of these a little over 8,000 were Jews and the remainder so-called 'non-Aryan Christians'.* Many of the Jews were lodged with non-Jewish foster families – the exact proportion is unknown but it may well have been more than half.[10] They were generally placed in non-Jewish homes only with the consent of the parents. But such parental consent was often given under circumstances of implicit pressure, since many parents no doubt felt that the best hope of saving their children was to avoid setting any restrictive conditions on their placement.

The basic cause of the problem was that sufficient Jewish homes in England were not easily available. Children from orthodox backgrounds were almost invariably placed in orthodox homes or hostels, but not enough orthodox families could be found to take in children. As a result, some orthodox Jewish children were held back in Germany.[11] There were also other reasons. Children were

---

* Susan Groag Bell's remarkable memoir, *Between Worlds* (New York, 1991), evokes with great candour and inner truth the special difficulties and dilemmas that confronted the latter group of doubly rejected and often ignored children.

deliberately dispersed throughout the country to areas with few Jewish inhabitants in compliance with government policy that was founded on the fear that heavy densities of Jewish population would arouse antisemitism. In 1940, when large numbers of children, including many refugees, were on government advice evacuated from London and other large cities, many refugee children were moved from Jewish families to non-Jewish ones in the country.

The orthodox attitude was that Jewish children, whether orthodox or not, must remain Jewish. The Chief Rabbi specified in this connection that his responsibility was not 'limited to children of strictly orthodox parents'.[12] The policy of the Children's Movement was different. It was neither a religious body nor an exclusively Jewish one. The children for whom it held responsibility came from a variety of backgrounds, only a small minority of them orthodox. Here was a sad case of conflicting conventional assumptions: on the one hand, those of orthodox Judaism; on the other, those of a liberal society – but one that was in some senses still predominantly a Christian one. A clash was almost inevitable.

During the war some orthodox sections of the community, in particular Rabbi Solomon Schonfeld's Union of Orthodox Hebrew Congregations, launched a furious public campaign against what was termed the 'Child-Estranging Movement'.[13] There is evidence that some Christian foster families and some of the Christian bodies involved in refugee work did occasionally engage in proselytization that was not exactly frowned on by some Church authorities.[14]★ Many children were brought up as Christians and a few were baptized without their parents' consent. Exactly how many is impossible to say. A Children's Movement memorandum prepared in 1949 states that 129 children had been baptized up to July 1948, eighty-three with and forty-six without the consent of parents.[15] But this almost certainly understates the

---

★ On the other hand, some foster-parents were scrupulous in ensuring that children received a Jewish education. In one case known to the author, a German-Jewish boy, installed in the household of an English country vicar, was punctiliously instructed in preparation for the barmitzvah ceremony.

number of those who, in one way or another, moved away from Judaism. A post-war survey, based on analysis of a sample of 100 cases, found that sixteen were known to have converted to Christianity. A further thirty had emigrated and their religious affiliation was unknown. Of the remainder only twenty-seven were, as the report put it, still 'close to Jewish circles'. Whether this sample was altogether representative is open to question. Another analysis, conducted on behalf of the Chief Rabbi in 1951 by Julius Carlebach, was based on examination of 1,250 files and produced somewhat different and, from the Jewish religious viewpoint, less alarming results.[16]

This was not merely a statistical question. It was a highly distressing human problem, often a confusing and messy one. In a few instances children appear to have been receiving both Christian and Jewish religious instruction at the same time! Among the case files of refugee children, for example, is that of a young refugee girl who was lodged with a Christadelphian family in the Midlands. They sent her to Sunday school, claiming that her mother had given consent – although this point remained in dispute. Upon the intervention of refugee-organization representatives, she was visited by a Reform Jewish minister and a correspondence course in Judaism was arranged. The foster-parents resented the interference and insisted on their right to bring the girl up as a Christian. Some consideration was given to moving the girl to another family. But since she seemed to be happy where she was, she remained there. In 1943 the girl's father was miraculously liberated in Italy. In letters to England he stressed that he wished his daughter to remain Jewish. After a great deal of bureaucratic difficulty he succeeded in making his way to England in 1946. He proposed moving to Palestine with his daughter. But their reunion was a tragic encounter: she barely remembered her father and they could hardly communicate. They had become quite alien to each other both in language and in social and religious outlook. She had no interest in going to Palestine. After a short time, he left for Palestine and the girl remained in England. 'The general impression that one receives from these files [wrote Julius Carlebach in 1951] is that, probably owing to their painful experiences, many of these children became either wholly indifferent or cynically contemptuous of religion.'[17]

In Protestant Europe the atmosphere of Christian–Jewish relations began to evolve in the late 1940s and 1950s. In Germany, as early as October 1945, the leaders of the Protestant Churches, most of which had collaborated with the Nazis, issued the 'Stuttgart Declaration of Guilt', in which they apologized for the sufferings inflicted during the Nazi era. The statement did not refer directly to the Jews. But in 1950 they issued a further, more far-reaching statement: 'Through omission and silence before the God of Mercy, we were co-responsible for the wickedness which was committed against Jews by members of our own people.'[18] In Hungary the council of the Reformed (Calvinist) Church issued a unanimous resolution in 1946 in which it 'confesse[d] with deep humility the sin . . . [in that] it failed to step forward bravely to defend those who were innocently persecuted'.[19] Penitential prayers were ordered to be recited on one Sunday each year in all the Reformed Churches in Hungary. The Synod of the Czech Evangelical Brethren issued a similar statement in December 1945. The World Council of Churches, to which most Protestant Churches belonged, at its founding meeting in 1948 denounced antisemitism 'no matter what its origin, as absolutely irreconcilable with the profession and practice of the Christian faith. Anti-Semitism is a sin against God and man.'[20] In Britain the Council of Christians and Jews (boycotted for several years by the Roman Catholic Church on the instruction of the Holy Office★) worked to destroy negative stereotypes of Jews. In the late 1950s shifts of this attitude were discernible even in the Catholic Church, although the only formal sign of this was the Pope's decision to alter the wording of the Good Friday prayer from 'the perfidious Jews' to 'the unbelieving Jews'.

Sudden and dramatic change in this as in other spheres was

★ The instruction for the boycott was allegedly issued by Cardinal Alfredo Ottaviani, head of the Holy Office. It was vigorously contested by Archbishop (later Cardinal) Heenan, who went specially to Rome and pressed, with eventual success, for its reversal.[21]

inaugurated with the pontificate of John XXIII. The new Pope had an honourable record of helping Jewish refugees during his period as nuncio in Istanbul during the Second World War and took a personal interest in the cause of revising Catholic doctrine and attitudes to the Jews. This was one of the objects that he set for the Second Vatican Council, whose convocation he announced in 1959. During the preparations for the council he appointed Cardinal Augustin Bea, SJ, head of the Secretariat for Promoting Christian Unity. In June 1960 the Pope discussed Jewish–Christian relations with the French-Jewish scholar Jules Isaac. At the end of the audience the Pope told his visitor: 'Go to Cardinal Bea and everything will be all right.'[22] Bea, a German by birth, was a gentle diplomat, a vigorous octogenarian and a former rector of the Pontifical Biblical Institute. He spoke Hebrew fluently. Though a Church traditionalist, he was deeply committed to the objective of Catholic–Jewish reconciliation and became its most eloquent protagonist at the Vatican Council. At the first meeting of the members and consultors of the Secretariat for Christian Unity in November 1960, Bea announced that the body was to take up 'the question of treating Jews not on its own initiative but at the express command of Pope John XXIII'. Correctly foreseeing difficulties, however, the Pope requested that the entire matter be dealt with *sub secreto*.[23]

The question of relations with the Jews proved to be one of the most controversial issues at the Council after its opening in 1962. In presenting an initial draft schema, 'On the Jews', to the Council in November 1963, Bea reminded the assembled fathers that the Church was 'in some sense the continuation of the chosen people of Israel'. He emphasized that a declaration on the Jews was particularly necessary in the wake of Nazism, though he insisted that Nazi antisemitism should in no wise be understood as having drawn its inspiration from Christian doctrine – 'a quite false allegation'. He argued strongly in favour of a retraction of the charge of deicide: 'For the Jews of our time can hardly be accused of the crimes committed against Christ, so far removed are they from those deeds.'[24] The draft schema was largely the work of Father [later Monsignor] John Oesterreicher, a Jewish convert to

Christianity, and reflected what Archbishop Heenan of Westminster called 'his deep-seated Jewish consciousness'.[25] Heenan and others thought, with a certain naïve benevolence, that the involvement of such Jewish apostates would reassure Jews. In fact, it was by no means welcome and, in response to persistent Jewish lobbying, they were eventually eased out of high-level involvement in Catholic–Jewish relations.[26]

The proposed declaration encountered fierce resistance from conservative theologians, as well as from representatives of Catholic minorities in Arab countries, who feared that a more friendly Church attitude towards Jews might have negative repercussions on the often precarious position of their own flocks. The debates and behind-the-scenes discussions on the problem revealed the powerful residue of anti-Jewish prejudice within the hierarchy. Leading the opposition to the declaration was Bishop Luigi Carli of Segni who (as an English Catholic observer put it) 'strange as it may seem thought it necessary to champion what I may call old-fashioned biblical antisemitism – [he] really believed that it was a Christian duty to think of the Jews as an accursed race'.[27] Carli headed the 'Coetus Internationalis Patrum', a diehard group that also had the support of Cardinal Siri of Genoa and the French Archbishop Marcel Lefebvre.* The conservatives could also count on the sympathy of influential figures such as the Vatican Secretary of State, Cardinal Cicognani, and of Cardinal Ottaviani, who was said to view theology 'as a penal code to be enforced'. Ottaviani had allegedly remarked, 'Please God, let me die before this Ecumenical Council ends, so that I may die a Catholic.'[28]

Conflict over the issue attained such an intensity that by the time of the Council's third session the two texts on religious freedom and the Jews had emerged (in the words of one commentator) 'for most interested non-Catholic observers of Vatican II . . . as the touchstone of the Council's relevance and sincerity'.[29] Bea

---

* Lefebvre's continuing opposition to the decisions of Vatican II led to his excommunication in 1988. In his later years he led a small body of arch-traditionalists who continued to celebrate the Tridentine mass and were politically aligned with the antisemitic Front National.

himself considered that it was on the passage of the declaration that would 'largely hinge a favourable or unfavourable judgement on the whole Council'.[30]

Matters came to a head in October 1964, when, apparently under pressure from the conservatively inclined Curia, Bea was obliged to announce that the declaration on the Jews, originally intended to be the last section of the schema on ecumenism, was to be moved into the constitution on the Church, a more strictly theological document. Cardinal Heenan, in an address in London to the Council of Christians and Jews, explained that objections to the original proposal had come from Middle Eastern bishops, who were concerned about 'the strong feelings between Arabs and Jews'. But he stressed that the Secretariat for Christian Unity wished to include the chapter on Jews in the ecumenical schema because 'the Catholic Church, in the name of all Christians, should make some strong gesture by way of repentance for the unheard-of atrocities committed against Jews in our own time'.[31] Further discussion in the council was repeatedly postponed while Bea worked diligently to build a consensus that would satisfy conservative Curia members, Arab bishops and lobbyists for Jewish organizations. In Aleppo and other cities in the Arab world, there were demonstrations against the draft, which was regarded as a concession to Israel. At one point it was even rumoured that President Nasser of Egypt had made a direct approach on the subject to the Pope.

These deliberations took place against the background of a fierce public controversy about the conduct of Pius XII on the Jewish question during the war. The furore was ignited in 1963 by the German playwright Rolf Hochhuth (a Protestant), whose *Der Stellvertreter* became a *succès de scandale* with its depiction of a Pope silent and unconcerned about the fate of the Jews. Like many a work of art, it was marked, some said marred, by a number of historical inaccuracies. But professional historical investigations, notably Saul Friedländer's *Pius XII and the Third Reich: A Documentation*,[32] endorsed its central message. The Vatican did not open its own archives to researchers. But sensitive to such criticism of its wartime diplomacy, it began to publish a series of documents from its archives showing the measures taken and the concern expressed by the Pope and other senior churchmen for war victims.[33] Yet as a Catholic historian, Father John Morley, concluded, the overall impression left by these documents was not wholly reassuring: 'Vatican diplomacy failed the Jews during the Holocaust by not doing all that it was possible to do on their behalf. It also failed itself, because in neglecting the needs of the Jews, and pursuing a goal of reserve rather than humanitarian concern, it betrayed the ideals that it had set itself.'[34]

This controversy, which rumbled on for many years, was not merely historical. It had a vital contemporary subtext: to what extent should the Church feel obliged, particularly in the light of the events of the Hitler years, not merely to change its doctrine regarding Jews but to express humility and contrition for what were now seen as errors of omission and commission in the past? Many churchmen, wedded to the idea of the historic continuity of the Church, found such an admission difficult to stomach. Hence the peculiarly embittered atmosphere in which the conciliar debates on the Jewish issue proceeded.

The declaration *Nostra Aetate*, issued in the council's final session in 1965, after a vote of 2,221 in favour and ninety-one against,★ stated that 'the Church . . . cannot forget that she received the revelation of the Old Testament through the people with whom God in His inexpressible mercy concluded the Ancient Covenant'. It recalled that 'the Apostles, the Church's mainstay and pillars, as well as most of the early disciples who proclaimed Christ's Gospel to the world, sprang from the Jewish people'. While noting that the Jews had not accepted the Gospel, 'indeed, not a few opposed its spreading', it added: 'Nevertheless, God holds the Jews most dear for the sake of their fathers'. The declaration continued:

> Since the spiritual patrimony common to Christians and Jews is thus so great, this Council wants to foster and recommend that mutual understanding and respect which is the fruit, above all, of Biblical and theological studies as well as of fraternal dialogues.

★ Opponents of the declaration mustered somewhat larger support on certain clauses: for example, the passage stating that the Jews should no longer be presented as 'rejected by God and accursed' was carried by 1,821 to 245.

True, the Jewish authorities and those who followed their lead pressed for the death of Christ; still, what happened in His passion cannot be charged against all the Jews without distinction then alive, nor against the Jews of today. Although the Church is the new people of God, the Jews should not be presented as rejected or accursed by God, as if this followed from the Holy Scriptures. All should see to it, then, that in catechetical work or in the preaching of the word of God they do not teach anything that does not conform to the truth of the Gospel and the spirit of Christ.

Furthermore, in her rejection of every persecution against any man, the Church, mindful of the patrimony she shares with the Jews and moved not by political reasons but by the Gospel's spiritual love, decries hatred, persecutions, displays of anti-Semitism, directed against Jews at any time and by anyone.[35]

These words marked a revolution in the thinking of the Christian Church and a decisive break with the anti-Jewish doctrines of the past. The Church spoke of and to the Jews with a completely new voice. A liberal commentator noted that it 'was not important because of what it could do for the Jews but what it did, theologically and morally, for the Catholic Church'.[36]

The declaration had many limitations. As a result of opposition from the Curia and elsewhere, the original draft had been watered down. In the passage 'May Christians never present the Jewish people as one rejected, cursed, or guilty of deicide', the final phrase was deleted. Antisemitism was 'decried' rather than 'condemned'.[37] Nor did the declaration fulfil the hopes of Bea and Heenan by expressing contrition for the Church's long history of anti-Jewish utterances and persecutions. It did not refer to the Holocaust. Nor did it mention Israel. It did not even accord to Judaism the same respect that was accorded to Hinduism, Buddhism and Islam, of discussing its beliefs in its own terms, as distinct from the context of Christian doctrine. Not without irony, Bea compared the final product to

the biblical grain of mustard seed. Originally it was my intention [he continued] to make a short and simple statement on the relation between the Church and the Jewish people. But in the course of time, and particularly in the course of discussions in this Assembly [i.e. the Council], this seed, thanks to you, has almost grown into a tree in which all the birds of the air are nesting.[38]

Conservative opponents of the declaration continued rearguard sniping: in 1966 Bishop Carli published an article affirming that Judaism carried 'by its very nature . . . [the] judgement of condemnation by God'.[39] At the other end of the spectrum, radical Catholic theologians were disappointed with the result and wanted to go much further. Hans Küng, in a book published shortly afterwards, wrote:

> Only one thing is of any use now: a radical *metanoia* [change of mind], repentance and re-thinking; we must start on a new road, no longer leading away from the Jews, but towards them, towards a living dialogue, the aim of which is not the capitulation but simply the understanding of the other side; towards mutual help, which is not part of a 'mission', to an encounter in a true brotherly spirit.[40]

Pope Paul VI endorsed the emphasis on dialogue which provided a basis for further steps towards mutual understanding over the next three decades.

The initial reaction from the Jewish world to *Nostra Aetate* was tepid. Orthodox Jews, in particular, tended to remain unimpressed by the changes in Church doctrine and pointed to the continuing insistence of the Church that through it alone could souls attain salvation. In any case, most saw no useful purpose, and even some dangers, in theological dialogue with Christians. Even an open-minded, liberal Jewish participant in Christian–Jewish dialogue such as Geoffrey Wigoder noted that 'on the subject of salvation Judaism's pluralism and universalism can be contrasted with Christianity's traditional exclusivism and particularism'.[41] For this and other reasons, there remained a considerable suspicion that Christians had conversionist motives for wishing to engage in dialogue. Christian efforts at proselytism caused peculiar offence to many Jews, not only the orthodox. Some Protestant Churches, including the Lutherans, still maintained missions to the Jews, as did certain fringe cults such as 'Jews for Jesus'. The Roman Church, on the other hand, did not actively proselytize among Jews.

In the event, the initiative was taken not by religious leaders but, in the main, by secular Jewish organizations. Exploratory Catholic–Jewish discussions began in 1968 but encountered difficulties arising from Jewish insistence that Catholics acknowledge the religious bond of Jews with the Land of Israel – regarded by Vatican diplomats as a dangerous first step towards recognizing the legitimacy of the State of Israel. Nevertheless, some further progress was made. In 1970 an International Jewish Committee on Inter-religious Consultations (IJCIC) was formed by the World Jewish Congress, the Synagogue Council of America, the American Jewish Committee, B'nai B'rith International and the Israel Interfaith Committee. The following year this body established a Liaison Committee with the Roman Catholic Church. The Holy See established a Commission for Religious Relations with Judaism – balanced by one for Islam. The Commission was charged 'to develop its activities for the effectiveness and just realization of the orientations given by . . . *Nostra Aetate*'.[42]

Finally, in January 1975, ten years after the original declaration, the Vatican issued a second major document, 'Guidelines and Suggestions for Implementing the Conciliar Declaration *Nostra Aetate*'. This document, couched in respectful and friendly tones, a world apart from traditional Church utterances on Judaism, admitted at the outset: 'To tell the truth, such relations as there have been between Jew and Christian have scarcely ever risen above the level of monologue. From now on real dialogue must be established.' The statement called for a greater effort in liturgical readings 'to see that homilies based on them will not distort their meaning, especially when it is a question of passages which seem to show the Jewish people as such in an unfavourable light'. The statement recalled that 'Jesus was born of the Jewish people'. It urged that in Catholic education 'the Old Testament and the Jewish Tradition founded upon it must not be set against the New Testament in such a way that the former seems to constitute a religion of only justice, fear and legalism, with no appeal to the love of God and neighbour'. And it acknowledged that 'the history of Judaism did not end with the destruction of Jerusalem but rather went on to develop a religious tradition ... rich in religious values'.[43]

Jewish responses to this document too tended to be mixed. On the one hand, the tone and content of the guidelines for religious instruction were welcomed. On the other hand, disappointment was expressed at the continuing failure to recognize the central role of peoplehood in Jewish self-understanding. A Catholic critic noted some significant omissions:

> there is no word of the guilt of Christians in the persecution of the Jews, though their centuries-long suffering is mentioned; Judaism is here a religion only; there is no word on the link between faith and nationhood, nor of the continued validity of the Sinai covenant. The land of Israel which constitutes, now as ever, an integral part of the Jewish religious consciousness is not alluded to.[44]

A third major Vatican document was published in 1985, entitled 'Notes on the Correct Way to Present the Jews and Judaism in Preaching and Catechesis of the Catholic Church'. This statement advanced further along the road mapped out by the previous two. It reflected recent biblical scholarship in conceding that 'it cannot be ruled out that some references [in the New Testament] hostile or less than favourable to the Jews have their historical context in conflicts between the nascent Church and the Jewish community'. And it declared: 'Attentive to the same God who has spoken, hanging on the same word, we [Christians and Jews] have to witness to one same memory and one common hope in Him who is master of history.'[45] Yet as the careful analysis by Geoffrey Wigoder made clear, the document still fell short of what might have been regarded as satisfactory by Jewish participants in the dialogue. It still affirmed that salvation could be attained only through the Church; it contained only the most oblique reference to the Christian record of antisemitism; and it referred only in passing to the Holocaust.[46]

Meanwhile, a great shift in attitudes to Jews had taken place in the post-war decades among Protestants too. The distinguished Swedish Lutheran theologian Krister Stendahl, writing in 1967, made an outstanding effort to cut through some of the cant that conventionally surrounded discussion of the topic. He called for a re-evaluation of the 'facile distinction' between 'Christianity as an ideal phenomenon' and so-called 'bad "Christians"' who 'in their lack of true Christianity have committed heinous crimes':

> After 2000 years such a facile distinction becomes rather suspect. It is a striking example of the most primitive mistake in the comparative study of religions. One compares one's own religion in its ideal form with the actual form and manifestations of other faiths. We must rather ask openly and with trembling whether there are elements in the Christian tradition – at its very center – which lead Christians to an attitude towards Judaism which we must now judge and overcome.

Stendahl deplored the 'pious fraud' which led, for example, to the publication of a bowdlerized edition of the Gospel of St John in which anti-Jewish elements had been deleted or changed. He urged, instead, recognition of 'the serious fact that the Christian Bible itself contains material about the Jews which must strike the contemporary reader as offensive and hateful' and which 'functions as "divine" sanction for hatred against the Jews'.

While critical of Catholic approaches to the issue, Stendahl did not spare his own Church. In much Lutheran theology the 'whole system of thinking, with its image of the Pharisees and of the political Messianism of the Jews, treats Jewish piety as the black background which makes Christian piety the more shining'. More than changes in liturgy and catechism, more than dialogue were required. What was needed, Stendahl suggested, was for Christians to ask Jews 'whether they are willing to let us become again part of their family, a peculiar part to be true, but, even so, relatives who believe themselves to be a peculiar kind of Jews'. This extraordinary expression of Christian humility and contrition probably went too far for most Christians, but the matter was very different in the case of Stendahl's profession of a 'theology of history' in which religion would be not a matter of 'timeless truths' but rather one of 'continuous interpretation'. This idea found wider acceptance, enabling Christian theologians, both

Catholic and Protestant, to apply standard scholarly techniques of analysis to sacred writings without fear or embarrassment at what such approaches might yield and what doctrinal consequences might ensue.[47]

Protestant–Jewish dialogue took place at several levels in different countries. The World Council of Churches, to which most Protestant Churches belonged, held a series of discussions that led in 1982 to the issuing of 'Ecumenical Considerations on Jewish–Christian Dialogue'. This document went much further than any earlier Catholic statement towards satisfying Jewish interlocutors. 'It should not be surprising,' the statement declared, 'that Jews resent those Christian theologies in which they as a people are assigned to play a negative role. Tragically, such patterns of thought in Christianity have often led to overt acts of condescension, persecutions, and worse.' The document tried to correct the false images of Jews and Judaism, which, it said, had been inculcated by Christian teaching over the centuries. More than the Catholic statements, the document made a significant effort to appreciate Judaism in terms of its own self-understanding rather than within an exclusive or triumphalist Christian route to salvation. It sought to incorporate an appreciation of the link in Judaism between the people and the Land of Israel. It confessed that 'teachings of contempt for Jews and Judaism in certain Christian traditions proved a spawning ground for the evil of the Nazi Holocaust'. On the other hand, on the issue of proselytism and missionary work, on which Jews held strong feelings, the document achieved only a summary of the different positions held by various parties to the dialogue.[48]

Of course, Christian–Jewish dialogue was an activity generally conducted at a rarefied intellectual level by a handful of theologians and 'experts'. Doctrinal pronouncements and Church documents were not read by the majority of the faithful. At most, they influenced them at one remove through the homilies of the clergy and the instruction of teachers in Church schools. The real test of the revolutionary changes in Church doctrine came in everyday contact between Jews and gentiles. Overall, there is no doubt that the new attitude did filter down to the masses in the course of the post-war decades. The process was reflected in a gradual easing of public hostility towards Jews, as measured by public opinion polls in, for example, France and Poland. Nevertheless, even as the dialogue encountered obstacles over sensitive issues, such as the Holocaust, Israel and the relationship between traditional Christian teaching and antisemitism, so these very problems repeatedly emerged in new forms in daily life to provide troubling reminders of the difficulty of overcoming the past.

An example, trivial in itself but illustrative of such difficulties, was the series of rows, punctuating the post-war period, over the 'passion play' in the little Bavarian village of Oberammergau. Performed every decade since 1634, this play, in which the greater part of the population of the village acted, attracted hundreds of thousands of spectators and acquired a symbolic significance that was felt far beyond Bavaria or Germany. From 1750 to 1850 the text used for the play, although it contained some antisemitic passages, had laid chief responsibility for the Crucifixion not on the Jews but on the devil. In 1860, however, and at ten-yearly intervals thereafter, a different text, written by a local parish priest, Father Alois Daisenberger, had been performed. This version ascribed guilt for the deicide to the Jews and was strongly anti-Jewish in tone. Perhaps not coincidentally, the wider popularity of the play dated from that period in which antisemitism in Germany was formulated as a political doctrine.

The performance of such a play in post-war Germany naturally aroused criticism from both Jews and Christians, particularly after Vatican II. During the 1960s the villagers, who themselves decided on the version they wished to perform, came under pressure from Church authorities, reacting in part to Jewish complaints, to change the text that was performed. Extreme rightists in Germany sought to exploit the issue in their propaganda, complaining of attempts to 'whitewash Judas'.[49] Within the village different factions emerged championing different versions of the text, some more, some less objectionable to the outside critics. Most villagers resented the external interference: repeated votes produced majorities hostile to revision of the most offensive passages in the text.

Although some changes were made – for example, in one of the tableaux Moses was no longer depicted with horns on his head – the latest performance of the play, in 1990, still contained the so-called 'blood curse': 'His blood be upon us and upon our children' (Matthew 27: 25). Protests by Catholic theologians availed nothing.

By itself, the matter might seem of no importance: Oberammergau was a remote village populated by devout but stubborn and ill-educated country folk. More disturbing was the wider public response. That such a production could be staged in Germany in the 1990s in the manner of a major religious as well as touristic event, attracting an aggregate audience of half a million people, was a sign of how long it might take before the decisions of Vatican II percolated down to the level of the faithful.[50]

At the very summit of the Church, another sign of the slowness of the spirit of *Nostra Aetate* to take effect was the continuing reluctance of the Holy See to establish diplomatic relations with Israel. Still fearful of a reaction by Arab countries against their Christian minorities, the Vatican remained extremely reticent on the issue. In January 1964 Pope Paul VI paid a brief visit to the Holy Land but rendered only the most minimal acknowledgement of the sovereignty of his Israeli hosts. In 1973 he welcomed the Israeli Prime Minister, Golda Meir, as a visitor to the Vatican, but this was held to be purely a matter of courtesy, no more diplomatically significant than the similar audience given by Pope John Paul II to Yasir Arafat in 1982. Cardinal Doepfner of Munich went beyond customary Catholic formulations in 1974 when he declared that the Jewish people were 'entitled to a country of their own within politically secure frontiers', but he was speaking for himself and not on behalf of the Vatican.

In June 1979 Pope John Paul II visited Auschwitz and delivered a major address at the site of the wartime gas chambers at Birkenau. The first Polish Pope recalled that it was not his first visit there; the death camp lay within his former diocese of Cracow. Referring to the memorial inscriptions in many languages, the Pope said:

In particular I pause with you, dear participants in this encounter, before the inscription in Hebrew. This inscription awakens the memory of the people whose sons and daughters were intended for total extermination. This people draws its origin from Abraham, our father in faith (cf. Rm. 4:12), as was expressed by Paul of Tarsus. The very people who received from God the commandment 'Thou shalt not kill' itself experienced in a special measure what is meant by killing. It is not permissible for anyone to pass by this inscription with indifference.

To the estimated crowd of 1 million who were present and to the many more who (like the present writer) heard the live broadcast of the Pope's speech by Vatican Radio these words carried great conviction.

Yet the complete text of the homily aroused some unease among Jews. The only two victims mentioned by name were Maximilian Kolbe, a Catholic priest who had volunteered to die in place of another prisoner, and Edith Stein, a Carmelite nun. Kolbe in earlier days had been an antisemitic agitator; Stein was a convert from Judaism. The scriptural phrase that the Pope took as the peg for his remarks was: 'This is the victory that overcomes the world, our faith' (I John 5: 4). To many Jews, however, the choice of these personal models and this phrase appeared inept, perhaps even verging on the offensive. For to no Jew, and perhaps to no morally sane person, could Auschwitz be seen as anything but unmitigated defeat. The utterance, evidently well-intentioned, nevertheless seemed, at least in these passages, to echo the 'triumphalist' vocabulary of the Church towards the Jews that had supposedly been discredited by Vatican II.[51]

In the late 1980s relations between Catholics and Jews and between Poles and Jews were soured by an ugly controversy over the establishment in 1984 of a Carmelite nunnery at Auschwitz. The convent was installed in a building that had been constructed in the 1930s as a municipal theatre and was used during the war as a storehouse for poison gas. The episode was a case study in mutual miscomprehension and conflicting values. The existence of the nunnery did not become generally known until the spring of 1985, when the Pope visited Belgium and a Belgian Catholic organization, 'Aide à l'Église en détresse', issued a tract calling for contributions to support the 'convent for the Pope'. According to its supporters, the convent was intended to enable the nuns, by means of prayer and penitence, to 'construct with their own hands the sacred sign of love, of peace, and of reconciliation which will testify to the victorious power of the Cross of Jesus'.[52]

Jews, not surprisingly, objected to the introduction of Christian imagery in such a place and to the propriety of using Auschwitz as a place of testimony to the 'victorious power of the Cross'. Professor Ady Steg, president of the Alliance Israélite Universelle, a leading French Jewish organization, spoke for many when he asked: 'Is it really decent to seek to proclaim the victory of Christ in the very place where, on Christian soil, after two thousand years of Christian civilization, there was done what was done?'[53] The Chief Rabbis of Britain, France, Romania, Strasbourg and Zurich addressed a letter to the Pope, declaring unacceptable the notion of sanctifying a place that had been profaned and damned. Such Jewish demurrals were initially met with genuine incomprehension by many Catholics. Poles, it was suggested, had suffered at Auschwitz no less than Jews. Both the Pope and the Polish Primate, Cardinal Glemp, came under strong pressure to secure the convent's removal, but there was resistance among Polish Catholics to appearing to capitulate to Jewish pressure.

It fell to a Catholic and Pole, Jerzy Turowicz, to produce one of the most perceptive and sensitive analyses of the problem. Turowicz was the founder and editor of an influential Polish Catholic weekly, *Tygodnik Powszechny*, and a close friend and adviser of the Pope and of Cardinal Macharski, Archbishop of Cracow, within whose province Auschwitz was situated. In an article in his journal in June 1986, Turowicz wrote:

> We must admit that we Catholics have not apparently understood to its full extent the extreme sensitivity, justifiable and comprehensible, of the Jewish people ... Auschwitz represents for the Jews the symbol of their total abandonment, the symbol of their absolute solitude in the face of death, the symbol of the passivity of the other nations in the face of their destruction.

He pointed out that for the Jews the convent constituted a

deliberate attempt at annexation and appropriation by Catholics of the symbolism of Auschwitz. And he warned his fellow country-men not to suspect that the campaign against the convent was some sort of anti-Catholic or anti-Polish plot. While defending the sincerity of purpose of the founders of the convent, he urged the initiation of a dialogue in order to find a solution to the problem, possibly by means of the creation of an inter-confessional centre for meditation.[54] This moderate and eloquent statement pointed the way towards the solution that was eventually adopted.

After further protests, including some by Catholics and Protes-tants, a Christian–Jewish conference met at Geneva in two sessions in July 1986 and February 1987. Among those who participated were Turowicz, Macharski and Jean-Marie Lustiger, the Jewish-born Archbishop of Paris. The Jewish participants included Chief Rabbi René Sirat of France, Professor Steg, Tullia Zevi (the president of the Italian Jewish community) and Gerhart Riegner of the World Jewish Congress. The conference produced a joint declaration of which the key element was an undertaking by the Catholics that there would be no permanent Catholic place of worship at Auschwitz-Birkenau and that a centre of information, education and prayer, within which the Carmelites would be accommodated, would be established outside the area of the camp. Cardinal Macharski, who accepted overall responsibility for the project, undertook to see to its realization within a period of twenty-four months.[55]

More than two years elapsed and the nuns evinced no sign of any intention to move. To many, the Church's failure to abide by the Geneva agreement recalled its similar conduct in the Finaly case in 1953; moreover, the *non possumus* attitude of the Polish Primate seemed reminiscent of that of Cardinal Gerlier in 1953.* Renewed Jewish protests were met with vague statements about 'administrative difficulties', accompanied by an apparent hardening of attitudes in Poland. In April 1989, 1,375 inhabitants of Oświęcim (the Polish name for Auschwitz) signed a petition criticizing 'the illegal demands of the Jewish side to ruthlessly carry out an

* See above, p. 134.

unwarranted eviction of the convent of barefooted Carmelite nuns'.[56]

An ugly climax was reached in July 1989, when an American rabbi, Avraham Weiss, and seven supporters forced their way into the garden of the convent, meeting with blows from Polish workmen on the site. The incident provoked an uproar in Poland – and distress among Jews. Cardinal Macharski announced soon afterwards that in the light of the 'aggression' at Auschwitz, he no longer regarded himself as bound to fulfil the Geneva agreement. A few days later, in a homily delivered before a congregation of 100,000 pilgrims at the shrine of the Black Madonna at Czesto- chowa, the Polish Primate, Cardinal Glemp, uttered some ill- considered public remarks, accusing Jews of 'getting peasants drunk' and 'breeding communism'. He admonished Jews not to speak to Poles 'from a position of a people raised above all others' and he complained of the power of Jews over the mass media.[57] Glemp's homily, an eerie echo of traditional attitudes towards the Jews in the Polish Church, evoked a renewed storm of outrage among Jews – and others. Lech Wałęsa called the remarks 'a shame and a disgrace'.[58] Soon afterwards, Sister Teresa, mother superior of the Auschwitz convent, gave an interview in which she blamed Jews in post-war Poland for introducing atheism and closing Catholic institutions, asserted that only 30 per cent of the victims at Auschwitz had been Jews and compared the dictatorial attitude of Jews to that of Hitler. 'Why are the Jews creating such a disturbance for us?' she asked disingenuously, adding: 'You can tell the Americans that we are not moving a single inch.'[59] Glemp was eventually compelled to issue a grudging apology and, under Vatican pressure, the essentials of the Geneva agreement were reaffirmed.

It was not until April 1993, however, that the Pope himself reluctantly intervened with a public letter to the nuns, in which he declared that it was 'the wish of the Church' that they move – though the very terms of his letter indicated a certain sympathy with their spiritual intentions.[60] Nearly three more months elapsed before the small group of sweet-faced young nuns moved to a building on an 'ecumenical' site some distance away from

Auschwitz.* As a final gesture of defiance, however, the head of the nuns' religious order, without the foreknowledge of the local authorities or the bishop of the diocese, concluded an agreement to sublet the building to a supposed patriotic association of victims of the Nazi regime – in fact, a front organization controlled by a lawyer associated with the extreme political right in Poland. The large cross that had been erected on the building in 1988 was still there in 1994, drawing daily groups of Catholic worshippers and provoking renewed Jewish demonstrations.

The affair seriously damaged Catholic–Jewish relations not only in Poland but in many other countries. In France it evoked bitter controversy and produced some surprising reactions. The progressive Catholic intellectual Jean-Marie Domenach denounced what he said was the attempt of some Jews to 'arrogate to themselves a sort of exclusivity of genocide'. He denied the right of people who, he said, had not given proof of their struggle against racism to 'draw on the dividends of Auschwitz'. Challenged as to the propriety of these remarks, he added that he agreed with Glemp that three-quarters of the Western media were controlled by Jews. And he added on his own account: 'we are subject to permanent intimidation. When it's a matter of Judaism, people like me have no right to speak!'[61] These words aroused considerable concern, coming as they did not from an old-style Catholic antisemite but from a Resistance hero who, as editor of the progressive Catholic journal *Esprit*, had in the past shown sensitivity to Jewish issues.

Perhaps sensing the dangers inherent in such disputes, Pope John Paul II took a number of initiatives in the late 1980s and early 1990s to improve Catholic–Jewish relations. In April 1986 he visited the main synagogue in Rome and made a warm reference to Jews as the 'elder brothers' of Christianity.[62] In December 1990, on the twenty-fifth anniversary of *Nostra Aetate*, he endorsed the

---

* The author was one of three Jews who were the first to visit the nuns in their new home after their move in the summer of 1993. Seemingly oblivious to the long-lasting damage their enterprise had caused to Christian–Jewish relations, they affirmed their desire for peace, understanding and dialogue with Jews.

proposals of Catholic–Jewish dialoguers for a number of practical measures to advance the ideas in that landmark text. At the same time he condemned antisemitism as 'a sin against God and humanity' and said that the Church must repent its own antisemitism of thought and action in the past.[63]

By the 1990s the Jews' Christian problem had greatly diminished, even if it had not disappeared. The new Universal Catechism of the Roman Catholic Church, issued in 1992, incorporated most, though not all, of the major doctrinal statements of the previous thirty years concerning the Jews and Judaism. The establishment of diplomatic relations between Israel and the Vatican, agreed in December 1993, marked a further advance in Catholic–Jewish relations – in some ways of greater symbolic importance for the Diaspora than for Israel itself. Meanwhile, formal dialogue between Jews and the Orthodox Churches was inaugurated in 1993 with a meeting in Athens.

Such changes would have been inconceivable in 1945 and indicated the long road that the Church had walked since the end of the war. The Jewish–Christian relationship, profoundly sick in 1945, had become relatively healthy by the mid-1990s. At the same time, in the secular societies of Europe the old doctrinal disputes had come to appear almost irrelevant and disconnected from reality. Both religions were now on the defensive against similar forces of social change. Both seemed ill-equipped to confront the secularizing challenge. For the Christian Churches the process threatened decline and loss of influence. For European Jews, however, the threat was of an altogether different magnitude. They faced the prospect of dissolution and eventual extinction.

CHAPTER SEVEN

Three Germanies and the Jews

On 6 March 1945, immediately after the liberation of Cologne by US forces, a handful of Jews who had somehow survived in hiding in the city emerged into daylight. One later recalled:

> Most of the survivors met in front of the former synagogue; in the days after the liberation this was the general meeting place of any surviving Jews. An attempt was made to clear at least one of the rooms of debris. Then they went to the Jewish hostel and began to work there, clearing rubble, replacing doors and windows. Before long, it was possible to hold the first divine service. Soon afterwards the survivors held their first meeting. By this time the number had increased to fifty. A sign in German and English was hung on the door of the community centre. People started arriving, wearing the thin, striped concentration camp uniform; they came from every direction, exhausted and in need. Some had got lifts in military vehicles, others had made their way to Cologne on foot.[1]

Similarly pathos-filled scenes were enacted in most of the major cities of Germany.

On 11 May, nine days after the fall of Berlin, Jewish religious services were again held in the German capital, in a prayer-hall at the Weissensee cemetery. In the course of the following weeks more than 1,000 Jews reappeared who had survived the war concealed in the city. They were joined by 1,628 people who returned from concentration camps. In addition there were several thousand Jews who had been spared by the Nazis on the ground that they were married to non-Jewish spouses. Altogether, by the autumn of 1945, more than 7,000 Jews were living in Berlin.

As the survivors cast around for their bearings, unedifying disputes broke out over control of Jewish institutions – and of communal assets that had been plundered by the Nazis. Neither local German authorities nor the occupying powers could easily solve such problems. In Berlin the question of who exactly represented the Jewish community proved particularly hard to settle. The Russians remained in sole occupation of the city from 2 May until 4 July, when British and American forces were permitted to occupy the western districts. On their arrival, the Russians found still in shadowy legal existence the Reichsvereinigung der Juden in Deutschland, a residual organization established by the Nazis to administer Jewish properties after their sequestration and after the deportation of the Jews of the city to the death camps.

One group of surviving Jews headed by Dr Fritz Katten, Erich Nelhans and Erich Mendelsohn, purporting to constitute 'the Jewish community of Berlin', wrote to the city's Police President on 2 July, asserting that they were 'representatives of the newly appointed executive of Berlin *Mitte*'. They denounced the acting director of the Reichsvereinigung, Dr Lustig, as 'a close collaborator of the Gestapo in deporting Jews'. Katten suggested that 'the remnant of the Jews that escaped the sword should be compensated not out of the property of the impoverished German people but from the large property, lying unused, of the Jewish community in Berlin' and demanded that the police accept the appointment of a person to be nominated by his executive 'within the next forty-eight hours' as a replacement for Lustig.[2]

In the legal and administrative chaos of post-liberation Berlin, the military and civil authorities found themselves almost at a loss how to respond to such approaches. A police memorandum of 8 July noted that, as a consequence of the collapse of the Nazi regime, the Reichsvereinigung 'being an institution of Hitler–Fascism, is to be regarded as dissolved, if not de jure at least de facto'. It was accepted that former Jewish property administered by the organization all over Germany must 'be returned to the ownership of Jewish communities in the various parts of Germany from which it came'.[3] The questions remained, however, of who exactly represented such communities and how the properties should be administered in the meantime.

Conflict over these issues in the course of the following weeks exasperated the local authorities, who approached despair in the face of what the municipal official responsible for handling the matter called 'the incessant series of scandalous *affaires*'. The president of the Jewish community, Nelhans, a religious Jew who was a former member of the Mizrachi (religious Zionist) party, was said to have 'behaved in the most arrogant and provocative way' in meetings with the local authorities. In view of 'all the incidents', the official urged the replacement '*at once* of the most heavily compromised members of the executive of the Jewish community, namely Messrs. Nelhans, Katten and Mendelsohn, and their replacement by worthier Jewish gentlemen'.[4] Nelhans was later arrested by the Russians and sentenced to fifteen years' imprisonment on a charge of aiding Soviet soldiers to desert. He was never seen again.

Such wrangles were not unique to Berlin and often continued for months or years before being resolved. The occupying powers, themselves jockeying for position, took little interest in the issue, leaving it in the hands of the civil authorities. As for international Jewish organizations such as the 'Joint', they were reluctant to become involved in quasi-political issues, preferring to concentrate their efforts on the urgent immediate problems of relief.

In the eyes of the greater part of the Jewish world the idea of reconstituting Jewish communities in Germany was in any case anathema. For most European Jews, post-war Germany was a land stained with blood in which self-respecting Jews should not live. Even some of the Jews in Germany themselves felt that they were merely a 'liquidation-community' living in 'a stopping-place between the camps and the grave', as Moritz Abusch, an early post-war leader of Jews in Germany, put it.[5] A few Jews felt that it was important to participate in the rehabilitation of democracy and decency in Germany. The American-born violinist Yehudi Menuhin, for example, went to perform in Germany in 1947, but his action aroused strong feelings. Most exiled German Jews wanted nothing more to do with Germany or Germans. Robert Weltsch, former editor of the *Juedische Rundschau*, who had devised the famous 1933 headline '*Tragt ihn mit Stolz den gelben Fleck!*' ('Wear the yellow mark with pride!'), wrote after a visit there in 1946: 'We cannot assume that there are Jews who feel themselves drawn towards Germany. It reeks of corpses, gas chambers and torture cells here. There are indeed a few thousand Jews still living in Germany today ... This vestige of Jewish settlement in Germany should be dispersed with the utmost speed ... Germany is no place for Jews.'[6]

Overt antisemitism was not a major problem in the immediate aftermath of the war. During the first few months public manifestations of Nazi feeling were infrequent. A compilation of such incidents reported by the Berlin police cited only one involving Jews: '3 July 1945: Posters attached to the Levetzowstrasse Synagogue. Their contents were directed against preferential treatment of former concentration camp inmates and against friendship with the Soviet Union.'[7] Although the episode was trivial, it pointed towards the new form that antisemitic feeling was beginning to take: resentment of the apparently favoured status enjoyed by Jews under the new dispensation.

Jews and other recognized 'victims of National Socialism' were indeed issued with special identity documents, but these did not always win the bearer favour from local Germans or the occupation regimes. The survivors, feeling abandoned, ignored and isolated, began to express disillusionment and despair:

> They are bitterly disappointed because they had expected the liberation to make a much bigger difference to their lives. What they mind most is the indifference towards them of the British and American authorities. The Jewish survivors feel that little has changed in Berlin since the coming of the Russians, except that the food shortages have become worse. They remain a suffering minority; nobody cares what becomes of them and they will soon have reached the limits of human endurance ... so that if help does not arrive quickly, the problem posed by the Jewish survivors in Berlin will largely be solved by their suicide and death.[8]

By August complaints of this sort against the Allied military administration in Berlin were reaching the Foreign Office in London – though to little effect.[9]

While relatively few German Jews had survived in hiding within the Reich, larger numbers of Polish and other East European Jewish refugees gathered in the country after the liberation, most, but not all, of them in 'displaced person' camps. Even after the horrors of the Nazi period, the old antagonism between German Jews and 'Ostjuden' had not disappeared. A 'Joint' representative in Berlin in early 1946 commented:

> Strains and tensions between the Polish and German Jews [have] been apparent in Berlin. The Polish Jews, recently arrived from Poland, are wont to make constant remarks regarding the questionable Jewish character of the Gemeinde (Community) members and the Gemeinde members in turn do not miss an opportunity to remark on the high degree of black marketeering practice among the Polish Jews.[10]

In Munich, where only a few dozen members of the pre-war 11,000-strong Jewish community had survived, the German Jews tried to prevent DPs from settling in the city or, when they did so, from joining the community.

Jews nevertheless moved from the DP camps into nearby cities, where they set up small-scale businesses. Rumours soon spread that the DP camps were black-market centres, trading in goods from American army stocks or from charitable donations. The privileges that had been accorded to Jewish DPs did not increase their popularity among the surrounding German populations, among other DPs or with the occupying armies, some of whom came to see the Jews as parasites or worse. The fact that German police were forbidden entry into the camps, some of which had their own Jewish police units, seemed to place the DPs beyond the law.

The allegations had a substratum of truth. An official of the 'Joint' commented in 1949: 'The Jewish DPs are amongst the most conspicuous black market offenders ... and the brazen form of their operations has had a substantial bearing on the growth of anti-Semitism ... The most prominent element behind the recently uncovered smuggling ring ... were Jewish DPs.'[11] Möhlstrasse in Munich became notorious as a centre of the black market. Some of the DPs who returned to Germany from Israel after 1948 resumed black-marketeering and a few opened brothels. 'If there is a God [wrote one Jewish witness], why, after making us suffer so terribly much in the past, has he punished us with the Möhlstrasse, which is a disgrace to us before all the world and which must make every decent Jew blush with shame?'[12]

The problem became serious enough to warrant controversy in provincial politics. In June 1947 it was discussed in the Bavarian ministerial council. One participant said that the involvement of Jews in the black market had produced 'a hatred of Jews which was previously completely unknown'.[13] By early 1948 the matter had moved from such closed circles to open public debate in the Bavarian Landtag (state assembly), where there was talk of a 'spontaneously increasing wave of antisemitism'.[14]

Black-marketeering was not the only such problem, nor were DPs the only offenders. Some German Jews too had been contaminated by the moral climate of the Nazi years. In 1952 Dr Philip Auerbach, President of the Bavarian Landesentschädigungsamt (compensation office) and Rabbi Aaron Ohrenstein, the Bavarian Landesrabbiner (provincial chief rabbi), were placed on trial, accused of bribery and blackmail. Although some of the most serious charges were dismissed, others were upheld and Auerbach was found guilty. He committed suicide three days later, protesting his innocence and asserting that he was a second Dreyfus. There is some evidence of political motivation for the institution of these proceedings.[15] But sufficient proofs of malfeasance came to light to lead 'Joint' officials to take a dim view of both defendants.[16] The case was unfortunately symptomatic of a leadership vacuum in a community that was regarded by many Jews in other countries as beyond the pale, morally suspect by the very fact of its members having chosen to live in an accursed land.

A Jewish community nevertheless continued to exist in Germany and was gradually reinforced by the return of many exiles of the Nazi period. The earliest to do so were a small number of politicians and intellectuals who began, quite early, to play a part in the reconstruction of the country. The majority of the politicians were Social Democrats such as Herbert Weichmann (later Mayor of Hamburg), Joseph Neuberger and Rudolf Katz. Returning intellectuals included two leading figures of the 'Frankfurt School' of social philosophers, Max Horkheimer and Theodor Adorno, the political scientist Richard Loewenthal, who took up a chair at the Free University of Berlin, the poet and novelist Alfred Döblin, who had converted to Christianity while in exile, and the religious thinker and ardent German patriot Hans Joachim Schoeps, who took up a chair at the University of Erlangen.

On the other hand, the majority of Jewish intellectuals, writers and artists who had gone into exile did not return. Figures such as Kurt Weill, Arthur Schnabel and Richard Tauber, who had made Berlin and Vienna world-class centres of musical life, remained in the USA or Britain. The leaders of German Jewish scholarship settled in Israel (Gershom Scholem, Martin Buber) or the United States (Alexander Altmann, Nahum Glatzer). Cinematic directors and writers such as Fritz Lang, Ernst Lubitsch and Billy Wilder were permanently lost to Hollywood. The most poignant professional difficulties were encountered by German Jewish writers who found themselves cut off from the living source of their language. Some continued to write in German but lived abroad: Lion Feuchtwanger in the United States, Nelly Sachs, the 1966 Nobel literature laureate, in Sweden. The absence not only of the dead but also of these exiles impoverished German cultural life and irreparably changed its character.

The only large organized group of German Jews who returned came in the late 1940s from Shanghai. About 18,000 German and Austrian Jews had emigrated there in the late 1930s, the Shanghai International Settlement being practically the only place on earth at that time for which immigrants did not have to obtain entry visas. The refugees created a miniature German colony in these exotic surroundings, with German newspapers, cafés and cultural life. The Japanese, who occupied the whole of the city from December 1941 to September 1945, confined them to Hongkew, an insalubrious and crowded quarter, but did not otherwise molest them. Between 1945 and 1946 most settled in Israel, the USA or Australia, but about 2,500 returned to West Germany.

From the outset of the establishment of the Federal Republic in

1949, Chancellor Adenauer determined to tackle the Jewish question in a forthright manner. In a conversation with the British and United States High Commissioners in late 1949 he gave it as his impression that the Nazi tradition in Germany was still alive in regard to the Jewish question and made it clear that he intended to take measures to overcome this. He proposed establishing a special section for Jewish affairs in the Interior Ministry. It would be headed by a German Jew nominated by the Jewish community and would be responsible for the protection of Jews throughout the country.[17] Nothing seems to have come of this idea but it exemplified Adenauer's activist approach to the Jewish question which found fulfilment in the Luxemburg reparations agreement.

On the other hand, the retention in office of large parts of the Nazi bureaucratic, military and judicial apparatus troubled both Jews and non-Jews. The most notorious such case was that of the head of Adenauer's Chancellery from 1953 onwards, Dr Hans Globke, who, as an official in 1936, had helped draft the authoritative commentary on the Nuremberg racial laws of 1936.* More than 3 million Germans were screened in the so-called 'denazifications' conducted by the Allies during the occupation, but many of the investigations were perfunctory and the process was widely acknowledged to have been unsatisfactory.

The government of the new state well understood, however, that its conduct towards the Jews would be a touchstone of its rehabilitation in the world. It therefore took energetic measures to help provide a legal and financial basis for the reconstitution of Jewish communities throughout Germany. Although the post-war German Jewish communities were not in the end recognized as the legal successors of those that had been destroyed by the Nazis, they generally received a share of the communal assets (the bulk being distributed to Israel and world Jewry). Some reparations

---

* The Globke case was complicated. Apart from Adenauer, other anti-Nazis, including Cardinal Preysing, maintained that he had been hostile to Nazism and had helped Jews. Terence Prittie, a fair-minded outside observer, offers a balanced semi-defence of Globke in his biography *Konrad Adenauer 1876–1967* (London 1972), 217–19.

funds were channelled to Germany through the Memorial Foundation for Jewish Culture to help reconstruct Jewish educational and other institutions to replace those destroyed by the Nazis. The West German government and the governments of the *Länder* also provided funds directly to Jewish institutions in Germany – in part from the religious taxes collected from members of the Jewish community. But the tax base of the community was so small – there were only 16,186 registered Jews (including 4,568 in Berlin) in 1956 – that much larger amounts had to be provided from general taxation. The West Berlin Senate provided 2.5 million marks to fund the building of a Jewish cultural centre on the site of the former synagogue in Fasanenstrasse.

Following the restoration of full independence to West Germany in 1955, a law was passed offering the sum of 6,000 marks to any returning Jew who had left the country because of persecution under the Nazis. A few thousand more German Jews, as a result, returned from Israel. The Jewish population of West Germany consequently began to climb – to 21,499 by 1959. Even after the return of these exiles, however, German-born Jews remained a minority in the community.

The German Jewish community in the 1950s and 1960s differed from every other Jewish community in Western Europe (except that of Austria) in its demographic make-up, which seemed to offer little hope of group survival. The returning Jews were predominantly old people. The annual death-rate was seven times as high as the birth-rate. These unpromising statistics were, however, balanced by a small flow of continued Jewish immigration: in the 1950s and 1960s from Hungary and Poland, in the 1970s and 1980s from the Soviet Union, Israel and Iran (the latter particularly in Hamburg). By 1965 official membership of the community stood at 25,594 and by 1985 at 28,000. Nine thousand Israeli citizens, most of whom did not join the Jewish community, were living in the country in the mid-1980s – although probably only a minority intended to settle there permanently.

Public opinion polls showed that although antisemitic attitudes gradually declined in the post-war period, a residue of prejudice remained. In 1952, 37 per cent of West Germans questioned thought that there were too many Jews in the country; the percentage had fallen to 18 per cent by 1962. Whereas 70 per cent stated in 1949 that they would not marry a Jew, only 29 per cent said the same twenty years later. Nevertheless, in 1974 (a decade after Vatican II), 28 per cent still believed that Jews were 'being punished today by God for killing Jesus' and 60 per cent thought that Jews had 'too much power in business'. In comparison with similar surveys in France and the USA, Germany (and Austria) in 1970 remained significantly more antisemitic.[18] Popular attitudes towards the Nazi past remained defensive and self-exculpatory. A poll in 1961 found that 34 per cent of those questioned thought it was good 'to remind the world about the terrors of the concentration camps', whereas 45 per cent thought it was bad.

Such attitudes, even if those of a declining minority, translated into some distressing events. In 1958 the synagogue in Düsseldorf was desecrated. On Christmas Eve the following year swastikas and anti-Jewish slogans were scrawled on the walls of the new synagogue in Cologne, inaugurating a wave of swastika-daubings on Jewish buildings and cemeteries all over the country. Adenauer broadcast to the people urging them to give the malefactors 'eine Tracht Prügel' (a good hiding), but the incidents continued. In the course of the following month there were more than 600 such episodes. Juvenile hooliganism rather than an organized antisemitic movement was generally reckoned to be behind the attacks, which eventually dwindled in number.

In the political arena right-wing and neo-Nazi groups made little headway. The extreme-right NPD scored some minor successes in provincial elections in the 1960s but failed to win any seats in the Bundestag. After 1969 it gained fewer than 1 per cent of votes in four successive elections.

On the left and among younger Germans, as well as in the Protestant Churches, a very different mood prevailed. From the 1960s onwards many young Germans visited Israel as guest workers in kibbutzim and returned home with a transformed image of the Jew. Nevertheless, 'this atmosphere – a strange mixture of bad conscience and good intentions', as one German Jew called it,[19] was often stifling in its very benevolence.

The relationship between Germans and Jews remained an abnormal one and Jews seldom integrated fully into German society. One small sign of the continuing constraints in the relationship was the fact that, notwithstanding the conscription laws, Jewish citizens in the Federal Republic were not compelled to serve in the armed forces if they did not wish to do so.

A survey of an 'élite sample' of German Jews in 1977 demonstrated their rootlessness: 60 per cent of those questioned said they felt no 'sense of home' (*Heimatgefühl*) in Germany; the same proportion said they had no 'ties of friendship with the Gentile world'; and 80 per cent said they had no 'sense of belonging'.[20] Even young Jews in Germany and Austria, according to the editor of an anthology of their views in 1985, 'put on a mask when dealing with others; only when they are among themselves do they allow themselves to remove that mask'.[21] A Jewish policeman, for example, said: 'The decision whether to be a Jew or a German is one that all of us living in Germany have to make. I know of no German Jew in whom the two identities blend.'[22] Such attitudes were in startling contrast both with those of pre-war German Jewry and with the strong sense of rootedness expressed by Jews in nearly all other West European societies.

The gradual disappearance of the wartime generation brought some changes by the 1980s. In particular, immigration from the USSR brought new life to the community. By the end of the decade more than half of the Jews in Berlin were Russian immigrants. They also brought a more normal age structure. In 1986 a Jewish school, the first since the war, opened in Berlin and proved an immediate success. By 1989 it had attracted 150 pupils in four grades, an estimated 65 per cent of the age cohort.[23] But against the background of heightened fears of terrorism, the school, like every Jewish institution in Berlin, and most in Germany, operated with prominently positioned, round-the-clock, armed guards. If some sort of Jewish communal life had been re-established in Germany, it could still not be said to have resumed a place of normality and ease within German society.

Nor had the leadership of German Jewry surmounted the

problems of morale that had afflicted it since the war. A major
scandal in 1988 raised such issues anew. Shortly after the death of
Werner Nachman, head for the previous nineteen years of the
Jewish Central Council, the main representative body of West
German Jewry, it was discovered that he had embezzled several
million marks from reparations funds in his care. Both the government and the Jewish community were deeply embarrassed. Only a
few weeks before the disclosures, the West German Chancellor,
Helmut Kohl, had eulogized Nachman at his funeral. Nachman's
successor as head of the community, Heinz Galinski, called the
affair 'one of the darkest hours for the community since 1945'.[24]
The German press treated the matter with discernible restraint and
it soon disappeared from the headlines.[25] But the affair reinforced a
semi-submerged feeling in much of the Jewish world that the very
existence of a Jewish community in Germany was somehow
disreputable.

Even a generation after the war everything Jewish in West
Germany was haunted by the ghosts of the past. Adenauer's visit
to Israel in 1966 and the establishment of diplomatic relations
between Bonn and Tel Aviv brought close political contact but
not normalization. When the first Social Democrat Federal Chancellor, Willy Brandt, visited Poland in 1970, he made the symbolic
gesture of kneeling in silent homage at the Warsaw ghetto memorial, but his action produced criticism from some nationalist elements at home.

German leaders, at all levels of government and society, continued to make gestures of sorrow and repentance towards Jews and
towards Israel. Sometimes, however, the effect was blotted out by
instances of crass insensitivity. The most astonishing example of
such behaviour occurred in May 1985, during an official visit by
President Reagan to West Germany. At the insistence of Chancellor Kohl, and ignoring warnings from many of his advisers,
Reagan went to a cemetery of Waffen SS war dead at Bitburg.
The incident provoked indignation – not only among Jews. The
critics complained that Reagan appeared to be offering not so
much reconciliation but retrospective absolution to the perpetrators
of war crimes. Elie Wiesel took the opportunity, in the course of

an award ceremony in Washington, to deliver a dignified but pointed rebuke to Reagan.

Three years later, another embarrassing incident occurred at the official commemoration of the fiftieth anniversary of the *Kristallnacht* pogrom of November 1938. The President of the Bundestag, Philipp Jenninger, the second-ranking official in the Republic, delivered a formal address to the parliament and assembled guests that seemed to blame the Jews for their own fate. Poor judgement rather than ill-feeling was probably the cause of this astonishing *faux pas* – which led almost immediately to Jenninger's resignation. Jarring episodes such as Bitburg and the Jenninger affair raised anew the question of how genuine was the remorse and how deep the change in German attitudes to the Nazi past.

It had meanwhile fallen to the Federal President, Richard von Weizsäcker, son of a convicted war criminal, to address these issues in a much-admired speech in May 1986. Weizsäcker invited his fellow countrymen to 'look truth straight in the eye – without embellishment and without distortion'. Rejecting the frequently heard apologia that the German people had not known what was being done to the Jews, Weizsäcker pointed out: 'There were many ways of not burdening one's conscience, of shunning responsibility, looking away, keeping silent.' He urged that 'everyone who directly experienced that era should today quietly ask himself about his involvement . . . There can be no reconciliation without remembrance.'

Statements such as this indicated that West German society had by the late 1980s achieved a capacity for mature self-examination and self-criticism in relation to the Nazi past that enabled Jews to feel relatively secure even if not altogether at ease or at home in the Federal Republic. In this, at any rate, the Federal Republic had advanced further than the other two German states in the post-war period.

East Germany, ruled between 1949 and 1989 by men who had in many cases suffered imprisonment or persecution as communists under Hitler, was a state that outlawed antisemitism and any form of fascist activity; yet unlike its western neighbour, it became virtually *Judenrein* within a few years of its establishment.

This was in spite of the fact that some Jews in the late 1940s saw in East Germany a place where they could help build a decent existence. In the early post-war years, several exiled Jewish communists and fellow-travellers returned to live there. They included the philosopher Ernst Bloch (who later moved to West Germany), the satirical artist John Heartfield and the writer Arnold Zweig, who returned from Palestine. A few German communists of Jewish origin became prominent figures in the East German regime. The total number of Jews in East Germany, however, even at the outset, was small. The intensification of the Cold War soon brought this tiny remnant to the verge of disappearance.

Until 1952 the Berlin Jewish community remained united under the leadership of a Berlin-born, American-trained rabbi, Peter Levinson. Even before the erection of the Berlin wall, however, a schism became inevitable. In early 1953, with Stalin's anti-Jewish campaign at its height, many of the remaining Jews in both East Berlin and other East German cities began to feel uneasy. About 500 decided to heed a public appeal by Levinson and flee to West Berlin. Among them was the head of the East German community, Julius Meyer.

These departures took place against the background of an affair which, like the Slánský trial in Czechoslovakia, showed that communism and antisemitism were, in practice, not incompatible. Yet, as Jeffrey Herf has recently shown, the case of Paul Merker also displayed, in the personality of at least this one communist, a stubborn strain of humanist resistance to the exploitation of racial feeling. Merker, a non-Jew, was a leading member of the German Communist Party in the Weimar period and had spent the war years in exile in France and Mexico. He was the only member of the German communist leadership who devoted serious attention to Nazi antisemitism and attempted to deal with it at an ideological level. In published works from exile he declared that resistance to antisemitism must be central to the antifascist struggle. He called for restitution to be made to the Jews and he even expressed sympathy for Jewish nationalism. On his return from exile in

1946, he became a member of the Central Committee of the SED (Communist Party) and, while occupying official positions in Berlin, pressed for compensation to German Jewish survivors. He also praised the Zionist struggle against British imperialism.

Merker's official career ended abruptly in August 1950, when he was disgraced and expelled from the party. In December 1952 he was arrested and gaoled. His interrogation was conducted in the usual crude Stalinist vein, with a coarse overlay of undisguised antisemitism. His inquisitors jeered at him as 'king of the Jews' and charged that he intended to 'sell the DDR [German Democratic Republic] off to the Jews'. Although released and partially rehabilitated in 1956, he lived only a shadow existence as a non-person until his death in 1969. Remarkably, he held throughout to his earlier positions regarding the Jews and Zionism.

East German secret police files released after 1989 show that Merker's unique engagement in the Jewish question was at the heart of the regime's quarrel with him. His enemies accused him in secret party documents of having worked in 'the interests of Zionist monopoly capitalists' and charged that he had been a pawn of 'the USA financial oligarchy who called for the indemnification of Jewish property only to facilitate the penetration of USA finance capital into Germany'.[26] Prominent Jewish communists who had been associated with Merker in Mexico were also attacked. One, Alexander Abusch, fell under a cloud for a while but later gained rehabilitation and served as East German Minister of Culture from 1958 to 1961. Another, Leo Zuckerman, fled to West Berlin in January 1953.

In the 1950s and 1960s several thousand people of Jewish extraction still lived in East Germany, though most did not choose to register as members of the Jewish community – whether for reasons of conviction or prudence. In East Berlin the spiritual leader of the community was Martin Riesenburger, who had survived the war in Berlin because of his gentile wife and as a burier of Jewish dead. He was known as the 'red rabbi' (he had never, in fact, been ordained a rabbi, although he had studied before the war at a rabbinical seminary). By the time the Berlin wall was erected in August 1961, official community membership in East Germany had fallen to 1,800. Most lived in Berlin and most were old. The East German regime did not maltreat them – although it refused to pay reparations for Nazi crimes or to restore Jewish property confiscated by the Nazis.

After 1967 East Berlin radio and other organs of propaganda broadcast sharp denunciations of Zionism and Israel, among the most harsh issued by any communist country. Even the tame official Jewish leadership protested from time to time, warning of 'the extremely close relationship between this anti-Israel attitude and traditional antisemitism'.[27] The government did not prevent religious worship, but between 1969 and 1987 there was no rabbi at all in the country and by the 1980s only 650 people were formally registered as members of the country's eight Jewish communities. Membership of the largest, East Berlin, fell from 450 in 1971 to a mere 200 by 1986; more than half of these were over sixty years old.

In the mid-1980s the East German leadership undertook a number of gestures of reconciliation towards Jews. They announced plans to restore the great Oranienburgerstrasse synagogue in Berlin, which had lain half-derelict since being attacked by arsonists on *Kristallnacht* in November 1938. The president of the World Jewish Congress, the Canadian businessman Edgar Bronfmann, visited East Berlin and was received by high dignitaries, including the communist leader, Erich Honecker. Hints were dropped of concessions in the sphere of reparations and confiscated Jewish property. The motive for these overtures was unclear: the most plausible analysis is that the regime hoped for Jewish help in securing 'most-favoured nation' trading status from the United States.[28] By the time of East Germany's collapse in 1990, however, its Jewish community was on the brink of dissolution.

If the Federal Republic made substantial efforts to acknowledge and deal with the legacy of Nazism, and if the East Germans at least paid lip service to doing so, the third German state behaved very differently. The convenient myth of Austria as Hitler's 'first victim' enabled successive governments after the war to avoid any serious confrontation at all with the past. Nor was there, at first, any official or public readiness to accept the return of substantial numbers of Jews as fellow citizens.

When the Anglo-American Committee of Inquiry visited Vienna in February 1946 the socialist president of Austria, Karl Renner, told its members that there was no longer any room in the country for Jewish businessmen – 'and even if there were room . . . I do not think that Austria in its present mood would allow Jews once again to build up these family monopolies. Certainly we would not allow a new Jewish community to come in from Eastern Europe and establish itself here when our own people need work.'[29] Austria paid no reparations to Austrian Jews who had been victims of Nazi persecution and restored sequestered Jewish real estate and other property to its owners only partially and with reluctance. Why could the Jews not 'earn their own living like everybody else in Austria?' asked the Interior Minister, Oskar Helmer, in 1948.[30]

As in Germany, the presence of DP camps and the favourable treatment accorded to their residents in such matters as rations heightened latent popular antisemitism. At Bad Ischl in the American occupation zone, Austrian police had to intervene to put down a riot outside a hostel for Jewish refugees. There were shouts of 'Out with the tourists!' and 'The Jews are getting fat!' and stones were thrown at the hostel's windows. When the organizers, allegedly communists, were put on trial by the American authorities, they enjoyed widespread support from most political parties in the country.[31]

In these unpromising circumstances a small Jewish community was nevertheless resuscitated in Austria. At first it faced problems of adjustment that resembled those in Germany. In Vienna, as in Berlin, a handful of the few surviving Jews were accused of collaboration with the Nazis. Dr Emil Tuchmann, head of the Jewish hospital, was investigated by the Vienna police on charges of having used violence against fellow Jews and selecting people for deportation to concentration camps. Some Jews claimed in his defence, however, that he had helped save lives in impossible circumstances. Tuchmann retained charge of the hospital during the early months of liberation but in August 1945 he was forced out of office, arrested and later disappeared.[32]

In the early 1980s about 12,000 Jews lived in Austria, half of them in the capital – all that remained of the great cultural hothouse of Viennese Jewry. The dominant figure in post-war Austrian politics, Bruno Kreisky, was a Jew (though a non-believer); but he angered many fellow Jews by his efforts to resolve the Middle East conflict through idiosyncratic personal diplomacy. Throughout his long tenure of office as Chancellor in the 1970s, Kreisky served, in a way, as a legitimation for Austria in its relationship to Jews. His presence helped deflect criticism of the signal failure of Austrian government or society to acknowledge Austria's role, as a part of the Third Reich, in the slaughter of European Jewry. A turning point came only in the late 1980s as a result of the Waldheim affair.

Throughout his years as UN Secretary-General between 1972 and 1982, Kurt Waldheim had seemed a model international civil servant – discreet, patient and non-partisan. Waldheim had served as an intelligence officer in the German army during the war and had been listed by the United Nations War Crimes Commission as a potential war criminal. He was accused of involvement in the execution of hostages during the vicious fighting between the German army and partisans in the Balkans in the last year of the war. The investigation was never concluded one way or another. Extraordinarily, the accusations remained secret, apparently unknown to Waldheim himself, for the next forty years. They resurfaced (nobody knew whence) only in 1986, when he was campaigning for the presidency of Austria. In the course of the ensuing controversy, it emerged that Waldheim had concealed crucial parts of his war record and lied about others. Waldheim called the accusations 'a defamation campaign'.[33] The affair did not, in the event, seem to affect his popularity in his homeland. Indeed, the attacks on Waldheim backfired politically, producing a fierce nationalist reaction with disturbing antisemitic overtones. In June 1986 Waldheim was elected to the Austrian presidency.

The angry debate continued, particularly in the United States, and in April 1987 the US Justice Department took the un-

precedented step of placing the head of this friendly state on its
'watch list' of people barred from entering the USA because of
'prima facie evidence that [he] . . . participated in the persecution
of persons because of race, religion, national origin or political
opinion'.[34]

Waldheim enjoyed support from some oddly assorted quarters,
among them former Chancellor Kreisky, the British publisher
Lord Weidenfeld (of Austrian Jewish origin), the Soviet news
agency TASS, Churchill's former private secretary Sir John Colville,
and the Vienna-based 'Nazi-hunter' Simon Wiesenthal. Even
more surprising was the demonstrative support Waldheim received from the Vatican and, indeed, the Pope personally. In
June 1987, when Waldheim was *persona non grata* in virtually
every civilized state, the Pope received him as a guest in Rome.
The US, Dutch, Italian and other ambassadors boycotted the
welcoming ceremony as a gesture of disapproval. Italian Jewish
students were joined by some leftists in demonstrating near St
Peter's. Bizarrely, the Pope was almost the only head of state to
welcome Waldheim as a visitor during his tenure of office. In
the following year the Pope paid a return visit to Austria. And
in July 1994 the nuncio in Vienna, acting in the name of the
Pope, awarded Waldheim, by this time retired from the Austrian
presidency, an honorary knighthood (Cavaliere di Collare dell'
Ordine Piano) in recognition of his work 'in the service of
peace'.

Meanwhile, in an effort to put the controversy to rest, Waldheim had reluctantly agreed to cooperate with an international
commission of six military historians who examined all available
records concerning his past. The group was headed by Hans
Rudolf Kurz, a Swiss, and included several eminent experts on the
Second World War. As the commission deliberated, public support
for Waldheim in Austria increased well beyond the level of voting
that had been registered on his behalf in the presidential election.
The Jewish community in Vienna received an avalanche of hate
mail. Some of Waldheim's supporters stepped over the line into
crude antisemitism. The general-secretary of the conservative
People's Party, Michael Graff, was compelled to resign after

telling a French reporter that Waldheim was innocent 'so long as it's not proved that he strangled six Jews with his own hands'.[35]

The historians' commission finally reported in February 1988. Its findings brought little comfort to the Austrian president. While the historians stated that evidence regarding Waldheim's actions during the war was inconclusive, they showed that he was much more knowledgeable about war crimes committed in his area of service than he had admitted. His 'representation of his military past,' they concluded, 'is not in harmony with the results of the work of the commission'.[36] Even some of Waldheim's hitherto most vocal supporters, notably Kreisky and Wiesenthal, now abandoned him and urged resignation, as did thousands of demonstrators in the centre of Vienna. Waldheim's response was once again to dismiss all accusations against him as 'manipulations, lies and forgeries'.[37] By this stage his presidency had become a heavy diplomatic and political burden for Austria. He insisted, all the same, on remaining in office for the duration of his term.

The affair rumbled on, casting an ugly shadow over the official commemoration, in March 1988, of the Anschluss fifty years earlier. Waldheim was excluded from most of the ceremonies. The anniversary was the occasion for another demonstration outside the presidential office, on which the Associated Press reported:

> Rosa Jochman, a former concentration camp inmate and resistance fighter, gave an emotional speech that left many spectators weeping. She recalled that even people who were not directly responsible for Nazi atrocities 'simply walked by' acts of violence. 'It is not true that one should not mourn, one must,' she said. 'All those who lived through it must speak. I will never be silent.' The organizers appealed for a minute of silence after the speech and the entire square fell silent.[38]

After that the affair slowly faded from the headlines. Waldheim served out the remainder of his term miserably and then crept unlamented into retirement. It remained to his successor, on a visit to Israel in 1994, to begin to make amends by offering, on behalf of the Austrian state, an explicit recognition of its role in the Holocaust.

'What are you and where are you going as a Jew in Germany? Sooner or later this question presents itself to every Jew in repeated connections [*mehrfacher Beziehung*].'[39] Thus a German-Jewish journalist in the late 1970s. As the three Germanies moved in the 1990s into the common framework of the European Union, the question remained alive in all of them. Indeed, it became more pertinent as Germany became, with the continuation of Russian-Jewish immigration, the only country in Europe where the Jewish population was increasing. Could it be that, by the end of Hitler's century, some sort of Jewish future, so hard to descry in the rest of Europe, would be visible in Germany?

CHAPTER EIGHT

The Soviet Jewish Revolt

By many standards of measurement the Jews were the most successful ethnic group in post-Stalin Russia: the best educated, most urbanized, most professionalized. They were also (perhaps partly as a result) among the least liked. In spite of their success, they became one of the most discontented elements in Soviet society, so much so that they formed in the 1970s and 1980s a movement of peaceful resistance which generated what was in effect a revolt. The movement achieved its central objective; yet in doing so, it helped bring about the disappearance of the greater part of Soviet Jewry itself.

The exact number of Jews who remained in the USSR after 1945 is not known precisely, although the generally accepted figure of 3 million is almost certainly an exaggeration. The first post-war Soviet census did not take place until 1959 and returned a total of 2,267,000 Jews.★ The changes in Soviet borders during and after the war, as well as the repatriation of significant numbers of Polish and Czechoslovak Jews, complicate the picture. Later demographic estimates, however, confirmed that the Soviet Jewish population after the war entered a period of steep and continuous decline.[3]

★ For a long time Soviet census counts of Jews were held to be at least 10 per cent too low, since many Jews were believed to have concealed their true ethnicity from census enumerators. Some experts held that the total number of crypto-Jews and half-Jews in the USSR might be as many as 1.5 million.[1] Recent research, however, has vindicated the accuracy of the Soviet figures.[2]

By the late 1960s the demographic patterns of Soviet Jewry closely resembled those of Jews in Western Europe and the United States. Jewish births had fallen far behind the already low rate for the general population. In 1969 the Jewish birth-rate in the Russian Federation was 6.7 per 1,000; for the general population the rate was 14.7 per 1,000. One reason for the low birth-rate was the destruction of a large part of the potential parental generation in the war. Moreover, Jews married later and from an early stage tended, like the Jewish middle class in the West, to limit their families by artificial birth control. The Jewish age profile was significantly older than the rest of the population: according to the 1970 census, 26.5 per cent of Soviet Jews were sixty or older. Ageing was particularly noticeable in the European republics: 43 per cent of Jews in the Russian Federation were over the age of fifty. As a result, Jews had an unusually high death-rate. The combined effects of a low birth-rate and a high death-rate produced an annual natural *de*crease in population that has been calculated at 0.46 per cent for the USSR as a whole between 1959 and 1970 (probably somewhat higher for the European republics). As a result of these processes, the Jewish population of the USSR declined even faster than that of Western Europe – to only 2.15 million, according to the 1970 census.

By almost every measure the Jews were becoming less distinctly Jewish and more assimilated into Soviet society. Yiddish was no longer the lingua franca of Soviet Jews. In 1959 fewer than a fifth of them (410,000) declared it their mother tongue. Only in Soviet Moldavia and Lithuania did half or more of all Jews still do so. By 1979 only 14.2 per cent of Soviet Jews declared Yiddish their first language. Many customs central to Jewish tradition faded away, among them circumcision, barmitzvah and immersion in *mikvaot* (ritual baths). Jews became the most acculturated and assimilated national minority in the Soviet Union. As in the West, the rate of intermarriage with non-Jews increased rapidly. In the Russian Federation by 1979 a third of marriages contracted by Jews were estimated to be with non-Jewish spouses.

Yet in spite of these indicators, Jews were not absorbed as an invisible element in Soviet society. As in the case of Jews in

Britain, survey information suggested that the social circles of Jews in the Soviet Union were heavily Jewish. A study in 1976 found that, on average, more than 3.5 out of the five best friends of Jewish respondents were Jews[4] – particularly striking given the fact that the Jews were the most dispersed of any Soviet nationality, forming a majority of the population in no single region. Several other features marked them out from the rest of the population. They were much more urbanized: more than 95 per cent of them lived in towns, according to the 1959 census. Jews were to be found particularly in major cities such as Moscow (239,000 Jews in 1959), Leningrad (169,000) and Kiev (153,000), though in all of these they formed only a small minority of the population. The process of urbanization continued during the 1960s and 1970s: by 1979 only 1.5 per cent of Soviet Jews lived in rural areas – the lowest percentage for any Soviet national group. Even those Jews who lived in the countryside tended to be professionals, such as engineers or doctors, who constituted a quasi-urban element in rural society.

In spite of considerable evidence of anti-Jewish discrimination in admissions to higher education, Jews were much better educated than the general population. According to the 1970 census, 47 per cent of adult Jews in the Russian Federation had had some form of higher education. In other Soviet republics the percentage was less impressive but still much higher than the general population: 28 per cent in the Ukraine, 25 per cent in Byelorussia, 29 per cent in Latvia and 18 per cent in Moldavia. The Jews were also heavily concentrated in the professions. This characteristic was even more marked in the USSR than in Western Europe or the USA, where a large part of the Jewish population was involved in business. In 1960 more than one in three physicians and two-fifths of lawyers in Moscow were said to be Jews. Soviet Jews were particularly numerous in the arts, above all in music, and in scientific research. In 1947, 18 per cent of all scientists in the USSR were Jews. The percentage gradually fell – to 7 per cent by 1970. Nevertheless, in some fields regarded by the Soviet government as of key importance, such as physics and mathematics, Jews remained disproportionately important, especially in the senior ranks of the most prestigious research institutions. In the early 1970s Jews constituted 14 per cent of all holders of the *Doktor nauk* degree, the highest science qualification in the USSR. They were also specially prominent in the capital: 14 per cent of all scientists in Moscow were Jews.

The Jews were thus a peculiar and peculiarly important group in Soviet society. It had always been so. Their participation in politics, however, had declined. In the early years of Soviet power, Jews had been disproportionately over-represented among the political élite. By the 1950s few Jews remained in prominent positions. Of 1,443 members of the Supreme Soviet in 1964, only eight were Jews. The last Jew to occupy a top-level position in the Soviet hierarchy, Lazar Kaganovich, was ousted in 1957 and denounced as a member of an 'anti-party group' that allegedly sought to depose Khrushchev. At the republic, regional and local levels, Jews were hardly to be found among parliamentary representatives or party officials. Their increasing exclusion from such positions was the more striking when set beside their disproportionately high representation among members of the Communist Party. Indeed, as late as 1976, the ratio of party members to the Jewish population was higher than for any other nationality group in the Soviet Union.[5]

The official Soviet line in the post-Stalin years was that no Jewish problem existed in Russia. The Jews had been successfully assimilated in Soviet society. Antisemitism was a thing of the past. Episodes such as the 'Doctors' Plot' were disowned and regretted. The accused doctors were released almost immediately after Stalin's death in March 1953. In the following years Jewish writers and cultural activists were released from prison camps. Beginning in 1956, those who had been the victims of purges and were executed or died in captivity were 'rehabilitated'. The Jews shared with the rest of the population in the relaxation of the political atmosphere under Malenkov and Khrushchev in the mid-1950s and the terror of the period 1948–53 dissipated.

On the other hand, in his famous 'secret speech' to the twentieth party congress in 1956, Khrushchev skirted around the anti-Jewish aspects of the dictator's crimes. The Yiddish schools, newspapers, theatres and publishing houses that had been closed under Stalin were not reopened under his successors. In spite of the official recognition of the Jews as a nationality and of Yiddish as a Jewish national language, specifically Jewish literary expression was held to be no longer necessary since, as the Soviet ideological chief Mikhail Suslov put it in 1956, there was no point in reviving a 'dead culture'.[6]

A revealing glimpse of the thinking of the inner group of Soviet leadership on the Jewish issue is afforded by the minutes of a discussion in May 1956 between visiting French socialists and the chief Soviet leaders. Khrushchev admitted that the 'Doctors' Plot' had been 'utter nonsense'. In response to a query about Jewish cultural freedom, however, he remarked that 'if one created Jewish schools, there would be very few who would favour going there . . . The Yiddish theatre has declined for lack of spectators.' He conceded that 'there exist in our country anti-Semitic feelings'. These, he said, were 'survivals of a reactionary past'. He explained that at the time of the revolution many Jews, who were 'better educated, perhaps more revolutionary than the average Russian', had participated in senior posts in the party and state. But

> if now the Jews wanted to occupy the top jobs in our republics, they would obviously be looked upon unfavourably by the in-digenous peoples. The latter would ill receive these claims . . . For example, in the Ukraine, if a Jew is appointed to an important job and if he surrounds himself with Jewish fellow-workers, it is understandable that there may be jealousy and hostility towards the Jews.[7]

In another conversation with a French journalist in 1958, Khrush-chev expressed himself more pungently. He recounted how he had visited Birobidzhan, which he depicted as a veritable promised land, flowing with milk and honey: 'There is water and sun. There are vast forests, fertile lands, minerals in abundance.' The only problem, he said, was that Jews did not like to go there. 'How can one explain this disagreeable phenomenon? In my opinion by historical conditions. The Jews have always preferred the trades of craftsmen . . . They do not like collective work, group discipline. They have always preferred to be dispersed. They are individualists.'[8] Behind the defensive bluster one can detect in such statements a note of irritation and perplexity with a problem that would not go away.

After 1957 some loosening of the cultural limitations on Jews was allowed, apparently in response to overseas pressure that included awkward questions from West European communists such as Louis Aragon. In 1957 a yeshiva was permitted to open in Moscow, although few students enrolled and the authorities placed numerous obstacles in the way of the institution's functioning. Occasional Yiddish theatrical performances were again permitted. From 1959 some Yiddish books were published, but in small editions with many copies reserved for overseas customers. Almost the only other permitted form of Jewish cultural expression was concerts of Yiddish songs, which were very popular and drew large audiences. In May 1963 the New York Metropolitan Opera tenor Jan Peerce was invited to perform in the USSR and received a rapturous reception for his renderings of Hebrew and Yiddish songs.

Permission was given in 1961 for the publication of a bi-monthly (later a monthly) Yiddish literary journal, *Sovyetish Heymland*. Apart from the *Birobidzhaner Shtern*, a local newspaper in the 'autonomous region' that printed translations of official news releases and had a circulation of only 1,500, this was the first Yiddish periodical to appear since the 1940s. The editor, Aron Vergelis, the only Yiddish writer permitted to travel freely overseas, was a party-liner who ensured that the magazine faithfully echoed official thinking.* Circulation was limited to 25,000 (later reduced), a large part of which was sent abroad for propaganda purposes.

The atmosphere for Jews began to sour again in the last years of

---

* Sometimes, however, even this apparatchik revealed a sentimental regard for Jewish historic continuity. In 1966 he interceded (unsuccessfully) to prevent the closure of a Yiddish dramatic society and choir in Riga. On another occasion he broke down in tears at a Yiddish theatre show in Vilna, excusing himself with the words 'My childish dreams . . . my silly dreams'.[9]

Khrushchev's rule and even more so after his deposition in October 1964. To some extent this was part of the general move towards cultural frigidity after the short-lived 'thaw'. Yuli Daniel, defendant with Andrei Sinyavsky in a famous trial on a charge of defaming the Soviet Union, was not, so far as is known, attacked *qua* Jew. At the same time, however, other actions were taken specifically against Jews. Writers such as Vasily Grossman were forbidden to publish works dealing with Jewish themes. Moscow Jews were warned against having any contact with Israeli diplomats or tourists from abroad. Jews who attended synagogue services were told to avoid even shaking hands with such visitors. Most extraordinarily, the antisemitic blood libel was revived in 1963 in a publication issued by the Ukrainian Academy of Sciences: T. K. Kychko's primitive *Judaism without Embellishment* was distributed under official imprimatur in an edition of 100,000 copies.

A spate of prosecutions of Jews for 'economic crimes' in the early 1960s resulted in the execution of several of those found guilty. Some Sovietologists believed that the matter should be seen in the context of a general anti-religious campaign. In several cases, however, the accompanying publicity was undeniably inspired by antisemitism. In Lvov, for example, five Jews were accused of having formed 'a band of profiteers trading in gold and valuables, who nested snugly beneath the vaults of the Lvov synagogue'. The synagogue was said to have been a 'screen' for criminal activities in which religious officials in particular had participated.[10] The Lvov synagogue was closed shortly afterwards, as were many others throughout the country – part of a general anti-religious campaign throughout the USSR. By 1963 the number of functioning synagogues in the USSR had declined to ninety-six.

The executions evoked protests in the West. In response to a plea from Bertrand Russell, then at the height of his anti-nuclear civil disobedience campaign, Khrushchev took the opportunity to write a long defence of the Soviet position. His statement contained nothing new but its length demonstrated the sensitivity of Soviet leaders to such criticisms and their realization that such episodes damaged public support in the West for the efforts towards the 'peaceful coexistence' that the USSR was trying to promote.

The most controversial issue remained emigration. With the exception of Polish and Czechoslovak Jews repatriated in the late 1940s, the departure of Jews, like that of every other citizen, was almost completely banned in the USSR until the 1970s. The Soviet government's fear of a 'brain drain' of highly qualified professionals, particularly scientists, was one of the main reasons for official reluctance to sanction Jewish emigration.

Nevertheless, here too a glimmer of change first began to be discernible under Khrushchev when a small number of Jews were allowed to leave each year – mainly cases of so-called 'family reunification'. Such emigrants were predominantly elderly or infirm persons whom the Soviet authorities regarded as a burden rather than an asset. In what in retrospect appears as an interesting foretaste of its policy in the 1970s, the Soviet Union began in 1965 to permit a trickle of Jewish emigration to Israel. Although the numbers were small, the breach of a taboo that had existed since the early 1920s was significant. In 1966 more than 2,000 were allowed to leave. The change in policy was one of several signs of a warming in Soviet–Israeli relations at this period. The Soviet government apparently wished, by this slight opening of the tap, to give the Israelis the impression that further, perhaps more substantial, rewards might be forthcoming in return for good behaviour.

The 1967 Arab–Israeli war, in this as in many other spheres, marked a historic turning point. In the USSR as elsewhere the Israeli victory over its Soviet-armed enemies evoked enormous pride among Jews and stimulated Jewish identification and self-confidence. The warming trend in Soviet–Israeli relations of the previous two years suddenly ended. Jewish emigration was abruptly halted for more than a year.* Soviet propaganda turned full-blast against Israel. Zionism was equated with fascism and

* Emigration of ethnic Germans was also greatly reduced between 1967 and 1971, suggesting that there may have been other, more general reasons for the reduction in Jewish emigration.

racism. Soviet Jews were required to join in the anti-Israeli chorus. The supposedly literary journal *Sovyetish Heymland*, for example, in its issue of July 1967, parroted the official line: 'Occupation and annexation are the path of adventurers who are the pawn of imperialists.'

In several cities small nuclei of Jewish activists began to meet and concert their thinking. Pressure for emigration became open. The story went round at this time that when the question 'How many Soviet Jews would want to emigrate?' was asked, the answer was given, 'One hundred and twenty per cent: all the Jews plus another 20 per cent who would say they were Jews in order to be able to leave.' In the late 1960s this appeared highly exaggerated – though from the vantage point of the 1990s, it seems not too far from reality.

One of the earliest public manifestations of the new assertiveness among Soviet Jews was a petition in February 1968 by twenty-six Jewish intellectuals in Lithuania who complained of a 'rising tide of antisemitism'.[11] In September 1968 several thousand people gathered at Babi Yar to commemorate the wartime massacre there of the Jews of Kiev. The following April a Jewish student, Ilya Ripps, attempted to immolate himself in Riga, after the manner of Buddhist protesters in South Vietnam, in order to draw attention to the refusal of the Soviet authorities to permit Jewish emigration. Such spectacular acts of defiance were evidence of what, it soon became clear, was a widespread Zionist emigration movement that had welled up among Soviet Jewry.

The Soviet authorities sought to handle these surprising manifestations of opposition with a characteristic mix of carrot and stick, propaganda bombast and repressive police action. As a concession, they resumed issuing small numbers of exit visas in October 1968. As soon as this became generally known, however, they found themselves bombarded with thousands of applications to leave. In an effort to rein in the emigration movement, the government broadened its anti-Zionist campaign from an attack on Israeli policies to a portrayal of Israel as an ugly and unattractive society:

No, gentlemen Zionists [announced an article in *Izvestiia* in December 1969], it is not that anyone is forbidden to leave or hindered in leaving for Israel. All that is imagined by you. They don't want to go to you because, firstly, who would want to move backwards, from a country of the advanced social structure of socialism to a country that is typically bourgeois, capitalist, with its crying contrasts and contradictions, its wolfish laws, social order and morality?[12]

The Chief Rabbi of Moscow and other prominent Jews were induced to make broadcasts and write articles along similar lines.

The Jewish opposition quickly mastered the arts of conducting counter-propaganda in the special conditions of Brezhnev's USSR. Eventually they succeeded in using it much more skilfully than the government's blatantly 'inspired' spokesmen. Many of the Jewish activists' techniques were similar to those used by other Soviet dissidents to promote their cause. Prominent among these was the publication of underground *samizdat* literature – often painstakingly typed in multiple carbon copies, since duplicating and photocopying machines and, of course, printing presses were rigorously controlled by the authorities.

The first such document produced by Soviet Jews appeared in May 1968 in the form of an appeal to the United Nations by eighteen Jewish families in Georgia who, 'unconquered and eternally alive, and having transmitted to us the tradition of struggle and faith', demanded the right to emigrate to Israel.[13] In February 1970 an underground Zionist magazine, *Iton*, appeared in Riga. In April that year the first issue of *Iskhod* (Exodus) appeared in Moscow, containing thirty-eight pages; a second followed two months later. The characteristic feature of these publications was a series of collective petitions, fifty-two in these two issues of *Iskhod* alone. Most appealed against restrictions on Jewish religious and cultural expression in the USSR and demanded the lifting of barriers to emigration.

A letter to the UN Secretary-General, U Thant, from a group in Vilnius (Vilna), recalled:

Before the Second World War there was a large Jewish community in Lithuania with great Jewish cultural traditions . . . At the present moment there is no trace of the former Jewish culture in our area. There are no Jewish schools, no professional theatres, no publishing houses, there are not even any Jewish newspapers, and there is no reason to expect all these to be reborn.

We are cut off from our long history, from our traditions and from the spiritual heritage of our ancestors. We have absorbed Lithuanian and Russian culture but we have not become Lithuanians and Russians. We remain Jewish, although we are deprived of everything that the other peoples of the USSR have.

Another such letter, addressed to President Shazar of Israel by a group of Jews in Minsk, declared:

Our wish to live in Israel is explained by the natural human desire to speak one's own language, to live in close contact with Jewish national culture and to acquaint one's children with this culture of which we are now deprived. We cannot imagine how we can continue to live far from Israel. All our thoughts and all our actions are aimed at the fulfilment of our main dream, the return to Israel. No obstacles will stop us.[14]

Altogether the petitions in these two issues were signed by 600 people, who, with extraordinary boldness, gave their full names and addresses – a direct challenge to the Soviet authorities. Several of the signatories were arrested shortly after signing. In addition to such appeals, activists also published clandestine translations of works on Jewish history by Heinrich Graetz, Simon Dubnow and Cecil Roth, novels such as *Exodus* by Leon Uris, Sartre's *Réflexions sur la question juive* and Hebrew language primers. Notably absent were books or articles on religious themes; with rare exceptions, the Jewish activists were inspired by politico-national rather than religious convictions.

Like other dissidents, the Jewish activists did not rely on the circulation of dog-eared carbon copies alone. They quickly learned how to use the foreign media to achieve a much wider audience for their ideas. They made contact with foreign journalists stationed in the Soviet Union. They ensured that their messages reached Israel Radio (broadcasting in Russian, Yiddish, Georgian and Hebrew) and American radio stations in Europe, which then broadcast them back to listeners in the Soviet Union. Although no listening figures are available, there is evidence that Israel Radio, which (when not jammed) was clearly audible, particularly in the southern areas of the USSR, attracted a large and faithful audience. Many later immigrants to Israel owed their knowledge of Hebrew to this source. The Soviet authorities sought to curtail contacts between the dissidents and foreign journalists in Moscow, whose movements and meetings were closely monitored. But short of expelling the journalists, which would have impaired the atmosphere of international *détente*, they could not altogether prevent such contacts. No doubt, also, the secret police regarded such encounters as a useful means of identifying activists.

In June 1970, in an effort to escape to Israel, ten men and a woman attempted to hijack a twelve-seat passenger plane from Leningrad to Sweden. The three leading conspirators in the hijacking were Sil'va Zalmanson, aged twenty-seven, an engineer from Riga; her husband, Eduard Kuznetsov, who was two years older, a former philosophy student at Moscow University, who had been imprisoned between 1961 and 1968 on charges of anti-Soviet propaganda; and Mark Dymshits, aged thirty-three, a former military and civilian pilot. The would-be escapers were all arrested and in December 1970 were placed on trial in Leningrad. In the Stalin period such a trial, if it had taken place at all, would either have been held in secret or, if the authorities could be sure of wringing abject confessions of guilt from the accused, might have taken the form of a show trial. It was typical of the quasi-legal procedures of the Brezhnev period, however, that the Leningrad trial was neither secret nor fully open to the public. Relatives of the accused and others with special passes were admitted, with the result that accounts of the proceedings were published in *samizdat* form in the Soviet Union and thence leaked out to the West.

Most of the defendants admitted that they had intended to seize the aircraft in order to try to get to Israel because their efforts to emigrate legally had repeatedly been thwarted. Dymshits told the court that he had wanted to emigrate because he could not give his children a Jewish upbringing in the USSR. Sil'va Zalmanson admitted that she had typed out the first issue of *Iton*. Another defendant, Ara (Leiba) Knoch, said that he regarded Israel as his fatherland whereas in the USSR he had the rights only of a prisoner. The prosecutor told the court: 'There are those who say that this trial is against the Jews but that is untrue. This trial is not about Jews. It is a criminal trial in which the majority of the criminals are Jews. But I do not consider Kuznetsov to be a Jew. I consider that Kuznetsov is a Russian.' He demanded the death penalty for Kuznetsov and Dymshits and harsh prison sentences for the rest. As was common in the USSR, the KGB had tried to demoralize the accused by turning them against one another but the ploy failed. Dymshits told the court: '. . . it is gratifying that even here we have not lost our humanity and started to eat each other like spiders in a jam-jar.' Several of the group made altruistic pleas in their final statements to the court, urging leniency for their fellow accused who were threatened with death. Some made passionately Zionist speeches. Sil'va Zalmanson said: 'Israel is a country with which we Jews are linked spiritually and historically . . . Even now I do not doubt that one day I shall live in Israel. This dream, sanctified by two thousand years of hope, will never leave me. Next year in Jerusalem! Even now I repeat: "If I forget thee, Jerusalem, let my right hand forget its cunning."' When she repeated these words in Hebrew, the procurator of the court cut her off.

The court handed down death sentences against Dymshits and Kuznetsov and imposed long terms of imprisonment in 'strict-regime' camps on the rest.[15] The death sentences were later commuted, perhaps as a result of Western protests.

In the spring of 1971 the Soviet government performed a remarkable volte-face: for the first time Jewish emigration to Israel was permitted on a large scale. Over the next decade a quarter of a million Jews left the country. The reasons for this dramatic change remain obscure but were probably linked to the desire of the Soviet leadership to secure a more harmonious relationship with the United States and Western Europe. It is noteworthy in this connection that similar large-scale emigration of ethnic Germans to West Germany began shortly afterwards. The long campaign in the West for Soviet Jewish emigration and the support it had secured across the political spectrum helped to persuade the Brezhnev regime that a concession on this point would earn political credit that would help secure the diplomatic and economic agreements that it sought from NATO member countries.

In spite of this half-opening of the door, the process of emigration remained difficult. The application procedure for exit visas was a bureaucratic obstacle course. Applicants first had to obtain an affidavit from a family member in Israel containing an 'invitation' to emigrate. The period between initial application and departure was often lengthy and generally uncomfortable since the fact of application ordinarily led to dismissal from jobs or educational institutions. Those who failed to gain permission to leave were often unable to resume work and thus remained in an unviable limbo. The procedure was complicated by the absence of diplomatic relations or direct travel connections between the USSR and Israel. Israeli visas were issued by the Finnish or Dutch embassies in Moscow, which represented Israeli interests there. Those who finally received permission to leave travelled first by train to Vienna, where they were met by representatives of the Jewish Agency (the quasi-governmental body responsible for immigration to Israel). From there the Agency arranged their onward travel.

What was, no doubt, seen by the Soviet authorities as a safety valve that might ease internal and external pressures, incidentally ridding them of the most irksome troublemakers among Soviet Jewish activists, turned out to be something very different: a slow-burning fuse that threatened to ignite an explosion. To some extent the Soviets' difficulties arose from the internal contradictions (to use a Marxist phrase) of their own policy. Having decided to permit troublemakers to leave, they thereby implicitly encouraged would-be emigrants to cause trouble. Having then conceded large-scale emigration, they were reluctant to witness a 'brain drain' of a significant proportion of their scientific and technical élites. In the hope of preventing that, the Soviet government issued a decree in August 1972 obliging emigrants 'to compensate state expenditures for training in an institution of higher education'.[16] This exit tax provoked strong criticism in the West, as a result of which the Soviet government officially withdrew the impost. At the same time, however, other bureaucratic restrictions were imposed to limit the emigration of highly qualified people. Zionist activists, meanwhile, continued to be dismissed from their jobs, expelled from academies, arrested and sentenced to prison or labour camp terms on charges of espionage, hooliganism or defamation of the Soviet state.

In the West, particularly in Britain, France and the United States, a public movement, drawing in many non-Jews as well as Jews, developed a sophisticated public-relations campaign demanding the right of emigration for Soviet Jews. It attracted support from politicians and eventually from governments. The campaigners bombarded Soviet officials with letters and petitions and persuaded Western politicians, including some 'Euro-Communists' in France and Italy, to take up the cause with the Soviet authorities. The issue was kept constantly in the public eye through demonstrations, advertisements and publicity gimmicks. Militants disrupted performances by visiting Soviet artists and even threatened violence. In one case in New York a bomb was set off in the office of an impresario, killing a Jewish woman secretary. In Western Europe, however, the movement remained generally peaceful.

The Soviet reaction to this internal and external challenge was ham-fisted and counter-productive. A half-hearted effort was made to revive interest in Birobidzhan, where the frequency of publication of the local Yiddish paper was increased from three to five times a week. Tired propaganda themes were recycled, such as the film shown on Moscow television on 5 May 1973 in which an elderly Jew appeared and said that he had been born in Poland, had emigrated to Israel, but had now found his true homeland – Birobidzhan! Copies of samizdat publications were seized and their editors arrested. Activists' telephones were tapped or disconnected to prevent their communicating with one another or with foreign supporters; but the introduction of direct-dialling between major Soviet cities and the West made it technically more difficult for the secret police to block calls to and from overseas.

Many dissidents were harassed or arrested. The cases of these 'prisoners of Zion', as they were known, provided more fodder for protest. The ballet dancers Valery and Galina Panov were summoned to KGB offices and accused of having unauthorized contacts with foreigners and of spreading information that 'blackens the name of the Soviet Union'.[17] Their cases were among the many that soon became *causes célèbres* in the West.

President Nixon's visit to Moscow in June–July 1974 was the occasion of a major effort by Jewish activists to publicize their cause. The hope was that such publicity, magnified by sympathizers in the West, would compel the American President to raise the Jewish emigration issue with his hosts, linking it with the broader effort for East–West *détente*. As part of this strategy, a group of Soviet Jewish scientists announced the convening of an international scientific seminar to coincide with Nixon's visit. The seminar never took place because most of the organizers were imprisoned; invited Western guests, who included fifteen Nobel Prize winners, were refused visas to travel to the USSR. When the wives of three of the arrested organizers visited KGB headquarters to inquire about their husbands, they were told that the seminar was 'a sly anti-Soviet action'.

The ensuing conversation cast a lurid light on the attitudes of middle-ranking Soviet officials:

KGB official: Why do you need an international seminar? You could have given lectures to one another. What do you need guests from England and America for?
[. . .]
Irina Brailovskaya: But we are living in the same world and scientists from capitalist countries often come to Moscow to congresses. Do you suggest that scientific contacts should be discontinued?
KGB official: No, we are living in different worlds. We will not let you gather for the seminar. All who try to come will be arrested. Nobody will get there.
Irina Brailovskaya: Will you arrest our foreign colleagues too?
KGB official: Your foreign colleagues will get a kick in the pants. If you open the door to those who come to your apartment to carry

out an anti-Soviet action, you will have to answer for it before the law.

Nina Voronel: According to what law is a Soviet citizen forbidden to open the door to someone who is ringing the doorbell?

KGB official: Open it, open it. You may find there a murderer or a robber. We are not responsible for anything.

Nina Voronel: Does that mean I should be afraid of anyone who comes into my apartment?

KGB official: We warned your neighbours that an anti-Soviet action is being planned in your apartment. They will gather for a meeting and the apartment may stop being yours.[18]

The mixture of quasi-legalism and crude threat was typical of KGB tactics.

The boldness of the activists' conduct was explicable not only in terms of personal bravery but also on the basis of the shared understanding of officialdom and citizens in the Soviet Union that, in the post-Stalin era, there were limits to the sanctions available to the regime in dealing with dissent. Protesters might be harassed, lose their jobs or, in extreme cases, be sent to labour camps or locked in mental institutions; but the price of protest was no longer death. Experience had taught dissidents that each act of repression was itself a propaganda victory for their cause. Short-term suffering frequently proved to be the passport to long-term success, since most diehard protesters eventually received exit permits.

The case of Anatoly Shcharansky became the most notorious example of Soviet use of quasi-legal mechanisms to seek to damp down the Jewish emigration movement. Shcharansky was unusual in playing a significant role in both the Jewish emigration movement and the general human rights movement in the USSR. Perhaps for this reason he was singled out for specially vindictive treatment by the Soviet authorities. In 1978 he was tried on charges of spying for the USA. The prosecutor accused him of 'illegal behaviour, ideological error, and political thoughtlessness'.[19] He was found guilty and sentenced to three years in prison plus ten in a hard-labour camp. Protests, including one from President Carter, who denied that Shcharansky was an American spy, availed him nothing. A man of outstanding moral courage, Shcharansky became a martyr figure for the Soviet Zionist cause. His ordeal forced the Soviet Jewish issue on to the agenda of East–West diplomacy and kept public interest in it alive at a time when the campaign for Soviet Jews was flagging. He was not released until February 1986, when, as part of a complicated East–West deal, he was exchanged at the Glienicke Bridge at the border between West Berlin and East Germany. He then emigrated to Israel, where, as Natan Sharansky, he became a leader of Soviet Jewish immigrants.

As it became clear in the course of the 1970s that militancy produced results, the activists became bolder. They held picnics celebrating Israeli Independence Day. They went on hunger strike. On Jewish festivals thousands gathered outside the main Moscow synagogue and danced in the street to Israeli music. Hebrew classes were established. Some were suppressed by the police but continued in private apartments, making use of photocopies of elementary Hebrew textbooks such as *Elef Milim*.

How can this extraordinary welling up of Jewish consciousness be explained? It does not seem to have been, in the case of the majority of Jews, a religious revival. Semi-official figures in 1976 indicated that there were no more than 60,000 observant Jews in the entire country. This roughly tallied with the findings of an unofficial survey of Soviet Jews in that year, which found that only 7 per cent of respondents declared themselves believers. The largest group, 53 per cent, approved the statement: 'I don't believe but I have respect.' Only 3 per cent declared: 'I consider it necessary actively to struggle against religion'; remarkably, an appreciable number even of this last group expressed interest in Jewish culture and even in attending synagogue![20] About 85 per cent of those questioned said they wanted their children to know a Jewish language, generally Hebrew rather than Yiddish, and most expressed the desire for some form of Jewish education for their children.[21]★

★ These figures cannot be regarded as more than broadly indicative since the organizers of the survey, in spite of considerable efforts, could not question a representative sample. The survey was conducted openly and officials did not,

The awkward and increasingly undeniable fact was that half a century of 'Soviet reality' had not solved the Jewish problem in the USSR. In some ways the Jews had succeeded in assimilating into Soviet society, as the rising figures for mixed marriages indicated. In others, however, they found themselves subject to irksome new restrictions: an effective *numerus clausus* in many institutions of higher education and virtual exclusion from positions of political power in dramatic contrast with the early revolutionary years. An analysis of the ethnic composition of Soviet elected political organs in 1978 showed a complete reversal of the position in the early years after 1917: Jews were now 'relatively the most under-represented nationality in the USSR'.[22]

Western supporters of the Jewish emigration movement included not only Jews, Zionists and champions of civil liberties, but also anti-communist Cold Warriors who regarded the Jewish issue as a useful device for discrediting the Soviet system. The aims of these groups sometimes diverged, particularly over the question of *détente*, which many anti-communists opposed as a form of appeasement. Some feared that a relaxation of East–West relations would render Western governments less ready to become involved in the contentious issue of Soviet Jewry. Others believed that they were most likely to achieve results within a context of improved East–West relations. Most of the Russian Jewish movement's leaders themselves displayed no such comprehension of the significance of *détente*. The ever more aggressive tactics that they urged upon their Western supporters in the end proved counter-productive.

A case in point was the attempt to tie the issue of free Jewish emigration to that of American–Soviet trade. In 1972 the USA and USSR had signed an agreement under which the Soviet Union was granted 'most-favoured-nation' status. Two years later, however, as a result of pressure by lobbyists on behalf of the Soviet Jewry movement, Congress passed the Jackson–Vanik

---

at first, interfere with it. Later, however, they seized the data that had been collected. Hidden copies were subsequently smuggled out of the Soviet Union. The published results were based on a set of 1,215 interviews conducted in various parts of the USSR.

Amendment (named, respectively, after its sponsors in the Senate and House of Representatives), which linked the grant of MFN trading status to freedom of emigration. At the same time, other changes were made rendering the trade treaty only marginally advantageous to the USSR. As a result the Russians had little economic incentive to adhere to the agreement and felt free to resist what *Izvestiia* termed 'an effort at inadmissible interference in the internal affairs of our country'.[23] Accordingly, in January 1975, the Soviet government repudiated the trade treaty.

The agitation in the West focused primarily on the right of Soviet Jews to emigrate to Israel but in general slurred over the question of whether they should have the right to emigrate also to other countries. On this issue a tacit unholy alliance developed between Moscow and Jerusalem, each of which for its own reasons wished to prevent emigration to countries other than Israel. The Israelis, particularly after the October 1973 war, when immigration from elsewhere dipped, saw Soviet Jewry as a major reservoir of potential new citizens. The Soviets, for their part, wished to avoid any broadening of the demand for emigration among the general population, and therefore rationalized the exceptions dictated mainly by foreign-policy considerations (Jews emigrating to Israel, ethnic Germans to West Germany and a few other smaller groups) under the rubric of 'family reunification' or similar schemes.

Lost in all this were the real desires of the Soviet Jewish emigrants themselves. As the emigration gathered pace, it became clear that while the main thrust of the activists, both within the USSR and abroad, was Zionist, many emigrants themselves were more interested in going to the United States, Canada, West Germany, Australia or New Zealand than to Israel. In 1971 more than 99 per cent of the emigrants had settled in Israel. The 1973 Middle East war and the ensuing economic crisis in Israel rendered it a much less attractive destination than hitherto. By 1975 nearly half of the emigrants consequently sought other destinations. Only 31 per cent of the emigrants between 1977 and 1989 chose to settle in Israel: a total of 79,067 out of 252,887 Jewish emigrants. The great majority of the remaining 69 per cent sought entry to the United States (see Table 3, p. 200). Jews from European Russia, as

Table 3: Jewish Emigration from the USSR and CIS, 1948–94

Year	To Israel	To USA	Elsewhere	TOTAL
1948–53	18*			18*
1954–64	1,452*			1,452*
1965	891	12		903
1966	2,047	36		2,083
1967	1,390	72		1,462
1968	223	92		315
1969	2,979	156		3,135
1970	1,027	135		1,162
1971	12,966	214		13,180
1972	31,432	453		31,885
1973	33,283	1,449		34,732
1974	17,065	3,490	389	20,944
1975	8,293	5,250	1,000†	14,543
1976	7,258	5,512	1,491	14,261
1977	8,253	6,842	1,641	16,736
1978	11,998	12,265	4,602	28,865
1979	17,277	28,794	5,262	51,333
1980	7,393	15,461	1,000†	23,854
1981	1,806	6,980	711	9,497
1982	756	1,327	594	2,677
1983	390	887	40	1,317
1984	350	489	71	910
1985	348	570	222	1,140
1986	206	641	67	914
1987	2,069	3,811	2,272	8,152
1988	2,173	10,576	9,654	22,403
1989	26,048	36,738	22,303	85,089
1990	185,227	31,283	13,000	229,510
1991	148,000	34,715	12,000†	194,715
1992	64,441	45,888	5,000†	115,329
1993	69,191	35,581	16,000†	120,772
1994	68,100	32,835	5,000†	105,935
Total	**734,350**	**322,554**	**102,319**	**1,159,223**

* Not including Jewish repatriates to Poland and Czechoslovakia, most of whom continued on to the USA or Israel. They are estimated to have numbered at least 175,000.
† Conjectural figures.

distinct from the more traditionalist Jews of Georgia, Daghestan and elsewhere, seemed particularly affected by this trend. Among the Europeans, the propensity to seek destinations other than Israel was greatest among emigrants from the heartland of Russia, eastern Ukraine and Byelorussia as opposed to areas annexed by the USSR during and after the Second World War such as Moldavia, Bukovina and the Baltic states.[24] The higher level of assimilation among Jews in areas held by the Bolsheviks since the end of the civil war evidently diminished their degree of Jewish consciousness and their interest in settling in Israel.

The emigrants from areas such as Georgia and Soviet Moldavia were often poorer and generally much less well educated than those from the heartland. As in earlier Jewish migrations, such as that from North Africa in the 1950s, Israel was thus confronted with the awkward fact that the best-qualified emigrants were creamed off to other countries, leaving Israel with an exceptionally difficult task of social absorption. Israeli officials wrung their hands but could do little to change this trend. A Jewish Agency spokesman commented lamely that the large number of emigrants choosing destinations other than Israel was the result of a deliberate Soviet policy of granting visas to persons 'of lesser Jewish and Zionist convictions' in order to inflate the 'drop-out' rate.[25]

The United States government recognized Soviet Jewish emigrants as 'refugees' only so long as they had not been admitted for settlement to another country. Those who resided, even for a short time, in Israel automatically lost that status. Many Soviet

---

Note: Figures for immigration to Israel are derived from official sources; those for immigration to the USA are computed by the Hebrew Immigrant Aid Society (HIAS). Figures for Soviet Jewish emigration to countries other than Israel and the USA are difficult to establish with precision. Use has been made of figures compiled by Professor Sidney Heitman of Colorado State University and of a number of other sources. Minor discrepancies in published figures arise from cases of re-emigration, from cases of tourists who subsequently decided to settle in Israel and from the inclusion of non-Jewish family members. In recent years these have constituted a rising proportion of the emigrants – since 1992 perhaps as many as a quarter of the total. Figures in the table have been adjusted to include all accompanying family members.

Jews therefore adamantly resisted the blandishments of Jewish Agency representatives in Vienna and Rome, fearing, with some reason, that if they so much as set foot in Israel they would lose any hope of admission to the United States. Some of those who were unable to secure US visas lingered on in Europe, congregating in small Italian ports or other byways, caught in a strange limbo. Alarmed by this development, the Israelis pressed American Jewish voluntary organizations to refuse financial assistance to Jews who decided not to go to Israel. Bodies such as HIAS were anxious to avoid a damaging public controversy over the issue but at the same time felt bound to respect the principle of freedom of choice and refused to comply with Israeli wishes.

The emigration wave reached a peak in 1979, when 51,333 Jews left the USSR. Thereafter the Soviet government slowly closed the emigration tap. In 1980 there were only 23,854 emigrants (most of whom had received permission to leave the previous year) and in 1981 only 9,497. For the next six years the exodus slowed to a trickle. The sudden halt to large-scale Jewish emigration in late 1979 was clearly connected with the end of the period of East–West *détente* following the Soviet invasion of Afghanistan. Shortly afterwards German and Armenian departures were cut too. The Russians also continued to complain about the Jackson–Vanik Amendment. In addition, the Soviet government may also have had domestic political reasons for limiting all emigration.[26]

The change in government policy did not reduce Jewish pressure for the right to leave. As of March 1983 more than 382,000 Jews in the USSR were said to have 'requested and received notarized invitations from relatives in Israel', the first stage in the emigration application process, but were still awaiting exit permits. Meanwhile, on a conservative estimate, 2,906 families had been formally denied exit permits and were thus in the category of so-called 'refuseniks' – unable to leave the Soviet Union but also unable to live there. Most had been dismissed from their jobs or expelled from universities and were liable to prosecution as 'parasites'.[27] A list of all known refuseniks, published in the West in 1986, included 3,193 households, comprising altogether over 11,000 individuals. The majority were people of working age and the average length of time they had lived under the shadow of official refusal of permission to emigrate was nearly nine years. More than two-thirds of the heads of families had been employed as scientists, engineers or technologists.[28]

The Soviet authorities' actions seemed to demonstrate that they had no new concept for dealing with the Jewish problem. By and large they relied on the techniques that had been tried and had failed in the past. Harassment and arrests of dissidents were stepped up, but predictably produced a hostile counter-reaction rather than cowing the movement. New life, of a sort, was breathed into official propaganda with the creation of an 'anti-Zionist commit-tee' of Russian Jews who were wheeled out to affirm their support for the official line. As in the past, repression was combined with conciliatory gestures. In 1983 the Soviet government pledged to deal favourably with applications for 'family reunion' – the semi-fictional basis on which the Soviets had permitted all Jewish emigration hitherto. Applications would henceforth be answered within six months and persons who were refused permission to leave would be permitted 'to renew applications after reasonably short intervals'.[29] These apparent concessions were not, however, translated into discernible changes in bureaucratic practice.

The large-scale emigration of the 1970s accentuated the process of demographic decline already in train among Soviet Jewry. In the 1970s the natural rate of decline is estimated to have increased to about 1 per cent per annum, and in the 1980s to perhaps as much as 1.5 per cent. This downward spiral, particularly when heightened by large-scale emigration in the 1970s, spelt demo-graphic oblivion for Soviet Jewry. The 1979 census counted only 1.81 million Jews in the USSR. The departure of many young people left behind an ageing community. By 1986 the median age of Jews in the Russian Federation was estimated as fifty. The emigration also drew off the most politically dynamic Jewish dissidents, as well as many of the culturally and religiously most active elements in Soviet Jewry.

As a result Jewish life in the USSR in the early 1980s presented an anaemic appearance. In the whole of the Soviet Union there were not more than thirty to thirty-five qualified rabbis and fifty functioning synagogues. Byelorussia had no rabbis at all and only four synagogues. In Minsk, which had a Jewish population of 30,000, barely 100 attended synagogue services regularly. A touring troupe, the Jewish Musical Chamber Theatre, was formed in 1978 and some amateur dramatic groups performed from time to time. A Russian–Yiddish dictionary was published in 1984 but otherwise few Yiddish books appeared. Attempts by Western visitors to smuggle in forbidden Hebrew and other literature continued to be repressed; even Hebrew translations of such works as *Pinocchio* and *Snow White and the Seven Dwarfs* were confiscated.

The virtual ban on Jewish emigration lasted for a decade. In spite of the reforms of the *perestroika* period under Mikhail Gorbachev between 1985 and 1991, the exit doors were reopened only gradually and reluctantly. During his early months in power, Gorbachev's public reactions to efforts by Western politicians and journalists to raise the issue fell into the standard Soviet mould. Meeting the American black politician Reverend Jesse Jackson in Geneva in 1985, Gorbachev protested: 'Jews are a part of the Soviet people. They are fine people. They contribute a lot to the development of our country. They are very talented people. Therefore the so-called problem of Jews in the Soviet Union does not exist.' . . . Or if it did exist, he added, it was only 'with those who like to mar relations'.[30] In the spring of 1987 the American Secretary of State, George Shultz, participated in a Passover *seder* at the US Embassy in Moscow to which fifty refuseniks were invited, among them well-known figures such as Aleksander Lerner, Vladimir Slepak, Ida Nudel and Iosif Begun. Gorbachev commented acidly to visiting American congressmen: 'Not a single normal person was there, only people who complained.'[31] Typically, however, while grumbling publicly, he gave private signals indicating readiness to make concessions to Western pressure. The number of Jewish emigrants, only 914 in 1986, multiplied ninefold in 1987. In 1988 the number leaving reached 22,403 – of whom under 10 per cent chose to go to Israel.

The liberalized social and cultural atmosphere under Gorbachev's rule significantly expanded the opportunities for Jewish self-expression within the Soviet Union. *Ulpanim* (Hebrew language classes) were established for intending emigrants. Zionist activity, no longer routinely suppressed by the authorities, moved into the open. In Minsk, for example, a Zionist group was formed with the title 'Ha-Tiqvah' ('the hope' – also the title of the Israeli national anthem). In Moscow in 1988 a Hebrew Teachers' Association was set up, with participants from cities in many parts of the USSR. Religious Sunday schools, once illegal, sprouted. Old synagogues that had been used for other purposes were restored to the Jewish community and reopened for worship. In 1989 the Soviet media officially announced the complete rehabilitation of the Yiddish writers and intellectuals executed by Stalin in 1952. Contacts with Jewish communities overseas resumed and Jewish organizations in Western Europe and North America sent money, books, visitors, teachers and rabbis to help the process of revival. The Joint Distribution Committee was allowed to resume activity in the country for the first time since 1938.

Glasnost also opened the door to the public expression of antisemitism in ways which had hitherto been unusual. Pamiat', a vehemently nationalist organization, held a public meeting in Moscow in May 1987. Its leaders were formally received by the Moscow party boss, Boris Yeltsin, and it spread antisemitic propaganda openly in Moscow and Leningrad. In Ukraine and Byelorussia local nationalist groups of a similar type appeared.

Soviet Jews, like Soviet society as a whole, thus faced bewildering cross-cutting pressures in the late 1980s. As the planned economy foundered and as the entire Soviet political edifice began to totter, a sense of disorientation and anxiety spread throughout the population. Jews, however, felt a special sense of insecurity, heightened by reflection on the Jewish experience in previous times of trouble in Russian history. The result, beginning in October 1989, was to be mass emigration on a scale that placed a question mark against the very survival of Russian Jewry.

CHAPTER NINE

East European Shadows, 1953–89

In Eastern Europe, as elsewhere, the social patterns of Jews diverged significantly from those of the general population. More than before the Second World War the Jews were overwhelmingly an urban people. Yet even if compared with the urban population alone, the Jews were different. The old Jewish proletariat of cities such as Lodz and Warsaw had been destroyed. After 1945 the remaining Jews in Eastern as in Western Europe were moving into professional occupations: doctors, scientists, teachers, musicians, journalists, engineers. A survey in Yugoslavia in 1971 showed that nearly half the Jews in Belgrade and Zagreb and 56 per cent in Sarajevo were professionals.[1] Even in a country such as Romania, whose Jewish community was one of the most backward culturally and economically in Europe, Jews were significantly better educated than their fellow countrymen: 8.2 per cent of Jews in 1956 had had a higher education, as against only 1.6 per cent of the general population.[2]

Demographic trends among Jews in Eastern Europe resembled those in the USSR and Western Europe. Deaths outnumbered births. Emigration steadily depleted Jewish communities. Jewish out-marriage grew, particularly in smaller centres, where potential Jewish marriage partners were scarce. In Wrocław (formerly Breslau) in Poland, where about 1,200 Jewish families lived until the 1960s, it was estimated that 43 per cent of marriages contracted by Jews between 1946 and 1965 were with non-Jews.[3]

Although the death of Stalin brought about a winding down of the official antisemitic campaign in Eastern Europe as well as in the USSR, the general position of Jewish communities in the region underwent only a gradual easing. Atheism remained official policy and religious instruction and, in some cases, religious worship continued to be discountenanced. Contacts with Israel or with Jewish communities in the West were severely discouraged. The 'Joint', unable to resume welfare activities except in Yugoslavia, reduced its spending in Europe by the mid-1950s to only about $8 million per annum, amounting to 28 per cent of its budget – as against 80 per cent in 1946. Communist suspicions of the 'Joint' were still acute.

The only country in Eastern Europe in which Jews eventually achieved a modicum of security and social integration was Hungary. In the first period of modern Hungarian independence, between 1867 and 1918, Hungarian society had been relatively open to permeation by Jews; many converted to Christianity and some were ennobled. The pressures of war and revolution between 1914 and 1956 had brought a powerful strain of anti-Jewish feeling to the surface. During the first Hungarian Soviet Republic, which held power for 133 days in 1919, 161 out of the 203 highest officials had been Jews. In the ensuing White Terror of 1919–20, large numbers of Jews, many of whom had nothing to do with communism, had been murdered. Throughout the inter-war period and during the Second World War right-wing groups had combined militant anti-communism with rabid antisemitism. At the same time Jews remained prominent among the active cadres of the banned communist party. Rákosi, the post-war Stalinist boss in Hungary, like many of his chief lieutenants, was a Jew.

The Hungarian revolution of 1956, led by the communist Imre Nagy, produced a resurgence of nationalist xenophobia which found a target not only in the Russian overlords but also in the Jews. That antisemitism should reappear in 1956 was hardly surprising. By historical standards, however, the phenomenon was relatively small-scale. The leaders of the revolution took care to contain expressions of anti-Jewish feeling. Yet although the number of recorded antisemitic incidents was small, many Jews chose not to wait for more. Among the tens of thousands of Hungarians who fled, mostly on foot, across the frontier to

Austria were not only anti-communist revolutionaries fleeing revenge at the hands of the Soviets and their puppets but also nearly
20,000 Jews in flight, as many feared, for their lives. Nearly 9,000
went to Israel. A similar number settled in the United States and
Canada, and about 2,000 in Britain.*

In the event, the regime of János Kádár, which took power
under the Soviet aegis, maintained a scrupulously tolerant policy
towards Jews. Religious practice remained free and as the
political-cultural climate eased after 1960 some forms of Jewish
cultural expression were permitted. In the 1970s thirty synagogues
were functioning in Budapest. There were ten kosher butcher-
shops, a Jewish high school, a hospital, an orphanage and a
museum. The state-controlled radio broadcast Jewish religious
services once a month. Jews remained disproportionately represented in the Hungarian, unlike the Russian, political élite: a
quarter of the Central Committee members elected in 1970 and
two of the thirteen politburo members were Jewish. Emigration
to Israel was permitted for a brief period in 1957, then prohibited
for many years. Zionist activity remained taboo, although in 1960
the government gave a signal of moderation on the issue by
permitting commemoration of the centenary of the birth of Theodor Herzl. In 1967 Hungary was the last of the East European
satellites to break off relations with Israel. Anti-Zionist propaganda
in the ensuing years remained mild by comparison with the fierce
denunciations emanating from Moscow, Warsaw and East Berlin.
'For the first time in our history,' the Hungarian Chief Rabbi told
an interviewer in 1977, 'we feel this is our country. We are not
Marxists. But the state has demonstrated its respect for our religious
rights.'[4]

By the 1980s Hungary was the only country in East–Central
Europe that still harboured a substantial Jewish population. Alone
in the region, Hungarian Jewry was allowed to maintain a rabbinical seminary, headed for many years by the distinguished scholar

---

* The author recalls, in early 1957, going to Central Station, Glasgow, to
welcome the family of his mother's cousin, who had fled Budapest in November
1956 after seeing antisemitic slogans appear again on the walls of the city.

Alexander Scheiber. The seminary boasted one of the finest libraries of Judaica in Eastern Europe, although a foreign visitor there in 1983 found it in a state of considerable disorder and decay: 'There was a general air of fustiness, stressed whenever the sun came in by the dust that showed in the sunbeams . . . One felt a certain sadness at the encounter with what was an impressive monument to a great past but not a vital center for an active future.'[5]

In Hungary, as elsewhere, there were limits to official communist tolerance. In 1985 the authorities banned publication of the intellectual journal *Medvetánc* after it devoted a special issue to an analysis of Jewish identity in post-war Hungary. The magazine's extracts from interviews with Jews in Budapest revealed an undercurrent of Jewish unease even in the relatively liberal climate of late communist Hungary. One interviewee, the child of high-level functionaries, recalled:

> About being Jewish – we never talked about it at home. We were communists not Jews . . . My brother came home one day from the work camp saying they'd told him he was a Jew. I can still see him now, standing there in the middle of the front room with his bags and shouting that they'd abused him by accusing him of being a Jew. My older sister said: Of course, because you *are* a Jew. My brother denied it flatly. Yes, you are, she said, just like Mum and Dad. So then he said that everyone else might be Jewish but he was not. Well, my brother became an antisemite. He suffered terribly from having been born a Jew – the Jews made him sick.

Other interviewees confessed to feelings of confusion at discovering they were Jewish and to a general tendency to keep the matter secret. The very word 'Jew' was often a source of embarrassment, so that Jewish death notices in the newspapers would not announce that burial would take place at the Jewish cemetery but would merely give the address.[6]

The experience of Jews in Romania offered one of the most paradoxical mixtures of tolerance and repression in Eastern Europe. Ever since its emergence as an independent state in the course of the nineteenth century, Romania had been a classic home of antisemitism. The Romanian Orthodox Church, no less than the

Russian, was deeply imbued with anti-Jewish doctrine. Here, as elsewhere in Eastern Europe, the role of the Jews as pioneers in the development of industry and commerce, and in the arts, journalism and the professions, aroused nationalist, rural and anti-modernist resentments against them. In the 1930s Romanian fascists, including some rabble-rousing priests, called for stern action against Jews. During the Second World War the Romanian government persecuted and deported large numbers of Jews to an area known as 'Transnistria', where thousands died of starvation, cold or disease. The Germans deported many more to death camps. By the end of the war the community had shrunk to 420,000, half its pre-war size. The purges of the late 1940s appeared to render antisemitism once again respectable and heightened the fears of surviving Jews. Of all countries in Eastern Europe, Romania appeared to offer the dimmest prospects for Jewish revival.

Yet, against this bleak historical backcloth, Romania distinguished itself from the rest of the communist bloc in the post-Stalin period in the special solicitude that it seemed to show towards its Jews. The country threw up one of the few authentic Jewish leaders to emerge anywhere under communist rule: Moshe Rosen (1912–94), who served as Chief Rabbi of Romania from 1948 until his death, was the undisputed ethnarch of Romanian Jewry for most of his period of office. From 1957 he held a seat in the Romanian parliament and from 1964 he assumed the additional office (almost unheard-of for a rabbi anywhere in the world) of president of the Jewish community.

Rosen was a canny and gifted negotiator who established a mutual understanding with the idiosyncratic communist dictator Nicolae Ceauşescu. Rosen played on Ceauşescu's greatest weaknesses, his megalomania and greed, to carve out some patches of freedom for Romanian Jews. Even before Ceauşescu's ascent to power, Romanian Jews were permitted in 1958 to emigrate to Israel and tens of thousands immediately seized the opportunity to leave. Later, an extraordinary system of state-to-state bribery was instituted whereby Israel paid what was in effect a head tax for each Jew who emigrated. The charge varied but a typical payment was $3,000 per person; the price was much higher, however, for individuals with higher education or special skills. Those Jews who remained behind shared the general suffering of the rest of the population, particularly during the harsh later years of Ceauşescu's rule. But religious life was free, synagogues operated throughout the country and in some small towns in Moldavia the last remnants of Yiddish-speaking *shtetl* life, characteristic of the pre-1914 period, could still be dimly glimpsed.

In March 1967 the 'Joint' was permitted to resume activities in Romania for the first time since 1950. The following June, when the Soviet Union and its satellites broke off relations with Israel, Romania became conspicuous by maintaining its embassy in Tel Aviv and even cultivating closer relations with the Jewish state. In the 1970s and 1980s Ceauşescu repeatedly played a behind-the-scenes role in Arab–Israeli contacts, seeking to establish himself as a kind of honest broker, no doubt hoping thereby to enhance his standing as an international statesman. Rosen justified his readiness to play Ceauşescu's game by pointing to the undoubted results that he achieved in Jewish emigration and religious freedom. Some anti-communists, including his predecessor as Chief Rabbi, Alexander Safran, criticized him as a collaborator. Yet by 1989, when the Jewish population had dwindled to fewer than 30,000, mostly old people, the leader of Romania's Jews could justifiably claim to have achieved his main goal of emulating his namesake by leading his people towards the Promised Land.

The Hungarian and Romanian Jewish experiences contrasted dramatically with those of Jews in the rest of Eastern Europe – nowhere more so than in the case of Poland. In the early post-Stalin period the role of Jews in Polish politics became an issue in complex intra-party feuds. Although Jews were represented in both Stalinist and reformist camps in the party, a conservative group, the 'Natolin faction', sought to utilize antisemitism as a weapon against party rivals. During this struggle, which culminated in the so-called 'Polish October' in 1956, Soviet party officials expressed support for the elimination of Jews from senior positions in the party, government and press. 'You already have too many

Abramoviches' was the remark widely (and, it is now known, correctly) attributed to Khrushchev.[7]

Under the rule of Władisław Gomułka in the years after the 1956 crisis, Jews were steadily eliminated from the most senior posts, particularly in the security apparatus. From about 1959 Jews were accorded special attention by Polish counter-intelligence as a group 'from which Zionists may originate'.[8] Roman Zambrowski, the last Jew in the politburo, was dropped in 1963. Meanwhile, a special card index of Polish Jews was prepared and in 1965 the politburo, acting on advice from the USSR, endorsed a plan for a wholesale purge of Jews from official positions. A beginning was made in July 1966, when all Jews remaining in the security services were dismissed. Apparently the card index was judged insufficiently reliable, since, according to one source, 'the security men went in threes to the toilet and showed each other their penises as proof of not being Jewish (circumcision on purely hygienic grounds is not practised in Poland)'.[9]

Following the Six Day War a sudden deterioration in the position of Jews in Poland became evident. Israel's victory over the Soviet-backed Egyptians and Syrians was openly welcomed by many Polish nationalists, including even some antisemites, who saw in the event an opportunity to cock a snook at their Russian overlords. In an apparent effort to divert the nationalist current by exploiting antisemitism, Gomułka, in a speech on 19 June 1967, warned against the danger of a 'fifth column', assailed 'dual loyalty' and declared that 'every Polish citizen must have only one country – the People's Poland'.[10] Gomułka's wife was Jewish but, if anything, this seems to have intensified his expression of anti-Zionism – perhaps out of fear that he might otherwise himself be suspected of heretical leanings on this issue.

In early 1968, following student riots that had a destabilizing effect on the regime, Gomułka complained that 'an active part was played by university students of Jewish origin or nationality'. Some Polish Jews, he said, 'are linked in their hearts not with Poland but with Israel'.[11] These comments were an eerie foretaste of the complaints heard in Paris a few weeks later, from the opposite end of the political spectrum, about the revolutionary activities of the 'German Jew', Daniel Cohn-Bendit. But whereas in republican France such language produced a general sense of repugnance, the reaction in Poland was different. There, anti-semitism developed into a political force that had devastating effects on the small surviving community of Jews.

The leader of the antisemitic movement was the minister of the interior, General Mieczysław Moczar, a representative of the 'parti-san' group of 'internal' communists. Oddly, Moczar was not a Pole but a Byelorussian; hence, perhaps, his exaggeration of his Polish nationalism. Moczar's antisemitism dated back at least to the wartime period, when he was said to have felt resentment at having to take orders from Jewish communist political commissars from the USSR. In the 1950s he had backed the anti-Jewish 'Natolinite' faction of the party. In the late 1960s, perhaps ambi-tious to replace Gomułka, he sought to build popular support by resort to nationalistic and antisemitic rhetoric, for which Gom-ułka's speeches had given *carte blanche*. In a broadcast on Warsaw radio on 7 October 1967 he equated Israeli attitudes to Arabs with those of Nazis to Poles and Polish Jews. Moczar warned: 'Only the blind Zionists, and among them also ours in Poland [*sic*] simply do not want to see this.'[12] In another speech, on 4 May 1968, Moczar answered critics who accused the party of antisemitism: 'In return for big reparations from the West German government, certain representatives of Zionism are trying to absolve the Ger-mans of the crimes committed against Jews, perfidiously represent-ing the Poles as accomplices [of the Nazis]. By means of the bogy of antisemitism these forces endeavour to compel us to leave trouble-makers and enemies of People's Poland unpunished.'[13]

Some articles in the Polish press at this time pushed the Nazi–Jewish parallel further, accusing Jews of having collaborated with the Nazis, referring to the Nazi-appointed 'Jewish Councils', stress-ing the role of the wartime 'Jewish police' and so forth. Moczar's 'partisans' were given vocal support by the government-sponsored Catholic lay organization Pax, which was headed by an ex-fascist, Bolesław Piasecki, reputedly a senior Soviet intelligence agent.

Although the campaign purported to be 'anti-Zionist' as distinct from anti-Jewish, the victims were Jews without distinction, many of them faithful communists, most without any Zionist connections. Many received threatening letters and telephone calls. Jewish pupils were ordered to leave schools and universities. Girls with Jewish boyfriends were subjected to vulgar insults. The security service, meanwhile, was rumoured to be discussing plans for radical anti-Jewish measures, such as sending all Jews to camps.

One of the fullest and most candid expressions of the anti-Jewish party line appeared in the form of a 9,000-word ideological article in the journal *Miesiecznik Literacki* by Andrzej Werblan, head of the education department of the communist party's central committee. Werblan did not bother with euphemisms about 'Zionism'. He wrote directly about the need for a 'correction of the irregular ethnic composition of the central institutions [of the party]'. 'No society,' he suggested, 'can tolerate excessive participation of a national minority in the supreme organs of power' – an interesting echo of the pre-war Polish *numerus clausus* directed against Jews. The Jews who had joined the Polish party, he claimed, were not true proletarians but came from 'well-to-do milieux of the middle class and bourgeoisie'. They had joined not out of social convictions but as a 'protest against national discrimination'. Now it was necessary to root out 'a group of activists with sectarian, cosmopolitan tendencies . . . A specifically bad atmosphere [he continued] was created in the institutions in which there was a concentration of many groups of people of Jewish origin.' In common with other regime apologists at this time, Werblan suggested that these Jews were seeking immunity on account of their Jewishness: 'Activists of Jewish extraction often branded all criticism of themselves as antisemitism.'[14] That this was no fringe outburst but, on the contrary, a faithful reflection of official thinking was indicated by the fact that extracts from the article were printed in the party daily *Trybuna Ludu*.

Some communists abstained from or even resisted the campaign. The weekly newspaper *Polityka*, edited by Mieczysław Rakowski, refused to publish antisemitic material. One member of the politburo, Edward Ochab, wrote to Gomułka: 'As a Pole and a Communist, I protest with the most profound indignation against the antisemitic uproar organized in Poland by various dark forces.'[15] Ochab resigned all his offices; his letter, however, was not published until 1981. (Neither Rakowski nor Ochab was Jewish.)

The campaign evoked expressions of outrage from abroad but these were rejected by the Polish authorities, whose propagandists went so far as to accuse 'Zionists' of themselves sticking up swastikas as evidence of antisemitism in Poland. The Prime Minister, Jozef Cyrankiewicz (a former prisoner at Auschwitz), complained of a 'Pole-baiting campaign which has probably had no parallel since the times of Bismarck'.[16]

The few Jews who still occupied prominent political positions were dismissed, among them the editor of *Trybuna Ludu*, Leon Kasman, and his deputy, Wiktor Borowski. Intellectuals were also prime targets. Although some non-Jews, such as the philosopher Leszek Kołakowski, also came under attack, the great majority of the academic victims were Jews. Among those who lost their jobs were the sociologist Zygmunt Baumann (he later moved to the University of Leeds), L. D. Blaszczyk, Director of the Institute of History at Lodz University, Julius Katz-Suchy, Professor of International Relations at Warsaw University and former Polish Ambassador to India, and Adam Schaff, Director of the Institute of Philosophy in the Academy of Sciences and author of *Marxism and the Human Individual*.

Continued operation became virtually impossible for the last remaining Jewish institutions in Poland. Hersch Smolar, editor of the Yiddish newspaper *Folksshtime*, was dismissed. Ida Kaminska, head of the State Yiddish theatre and last of a great family of Yiddish theatrical troupers, was forced into exile. Although the theatre subsequently reopened, most of its actors, as well as its audiences, were henceforth non-Jewish. The Jewish Historical Institute in Warsaw too was closed for a time. Other measures taken in this period included a renewed prohibition of activities by Western Jewish welfare organizations such as the 'Joint' and the Organization for Rehabilitation and Training (ORT).

The result of all this was another, this time final, wave of Jewish departures from Poland. Between 1968 and 1972 more than 10,000 Polish Jews were assisted by HIAS to go to North America,

Australia, Western Europe and Scandinavia. Another 4,000 went to Israel. The total number of Jews who left Poland in this period was probably about 20,000. By the early 1970s the country's Jewish population, which had been over 200,000 even after the war, was reduced to no more than 6,000 elderly people, mainly in Warsaw and Cracow.

The enduring strength of negative Jewish stereotypes in Poland was confirmed by a survey of attitudes among students conducted between 1975 and 1982. While respondents often stressed the supposedly positive attitude that Poland had historically adopted towards the Jews, manifested in the writings of Mickiewicz and in the aid allegedly given to Jews by Poles during the Second World War, the common image of the Jew continued to be that of an avaricious, untrustworthy, opportunistic, money-worshipping liar. The negative stereotype seemed, in most cases, to have been transmitted from the previous generation by word of mouth. Only 25 per cent of those questioned had actually met a Jew.[17]

That antisemitism served some dark function deeply entrenched in Polish political culture was again demonstrated during the struggle between the communist government and the Solidarity movement in Poland in 1980–81. During this period 'antisemitism without Jews', as it came to be called by Western observers, became a weapon used by government supporters against its opponents. Efforts were made to discredit Solidarity activists in the eyes of the population by charging that they were Jewish or controlled by Jews. A few Jews, such as Bronisław Geremek and Adam Michnik, did indeed play significant roles in the movement. They were almost all non-practising and far from whatever re-mained of organized Jewish life in Poland.

The orchestrators of the renewed antisemitic movement were nationalist intellectuals who appeared to have the backing of the Ministry of the Interior. The extremist anti-Solidarity Grunwald Patriotic Union, formed in 1981, promoted the anti-Jewish theme with greatest vigour. The organization was said to enjoy the protection of Stefan Olszowski, an ambitious member of the politburo. In March 1981 a repetition of the antisemitic campaign of 1968 seemed to be in the offing. Leaflets and posters appeared on the streets of Warsaw denouncing 'Jewish chauvinists' who were attempting to 'usurp power' through Solidarity.[18] A demonstration was called to honour Poles who had been 'tortured, sentenced and executed' by the 'Zionist clique' – an apparent reference to the communist government of the Stalinist period.[19]

That support, if not inspiration, for the renewal of the anti-Zionist propaganda theme may have come from a higher, non-Polish source was suggested by the appearance in a Soviet newspaper of an article claiming that Zionist organizations were engaged in a 'massive campaign to undermine the socialist foundations of Poland'.[20] Among the alleged perpetrators named in the article were the World Jewish Congress and *Commentary* magazine, published by the American Jewish Committee. Neither organization was, in fact, 'Zionist' but on this occasion, as in 1968, 'Zionist' was an open code word, clearly intended to be understood as meaning 'Jewish'.

Reformist elements in Poland, meanwhile, sought to turn the flank of the campaign by seeking the rehabilitation of the victims of the 1968 repression and by other symbolic gestures. Only a few hundred people turned up for the Warsaw demonstration and Solidarity issued a strong denunciation of the attempt to revive antisemitic feeling, as did some former members of the Home Army resistance movement, liberal intellectuals and others. Perhaps conscious that antisemitism was no longer quite so effective a recruiting device as in the past, some leaders of the Communist Party too repudiated the Grunwald movement. The influential weekly *Polityka*, associated with the liberal wing of the party, condemned attempts by hardliners to use antisemitism in intra-party struggles. Even General Moczar declared: 'I do not think it possible to incite antisemitic attitudes in Poland. We simply will not permit it.'[21] But his remarkable change of tune was regarded with suspicion and he failed to gain re-election to the party's central committee in July 1981.

A new spirit was evidently also abroad in some sections of the Polish Catholic Church. Many Catholic intellectuals joined in the condemnation of antisemitism. On 4 July 1981 a commemorative mass was celebrated in churches in Kielce and elsewhere in memory

of the victims of the pogrom of 1946. The Catholic lay organization Pax, which had been in the forefront of the antisemitic
campaign of 1968, held aloof from it on this occasion. The Polish
Primate, Cardinal Wyszyński, in a homily on 1 March 1981,
pointedly quoted from a work by Julian Tuwim, one of the
greatest of modern Polish poets, who had frequently been a target
of antisemitic attack. The secretary of the Polish PEN Club,
Władysław Bartoszewski, a prominent Catholic, who had participated during the war in underground efforts to save Jews, denounced the distortions of history by antisemites, some of whom
went so far as to claim that Jews themselves had participated in the
mass murder of fellow Jews during the war: 'If we take such ideas
seriously, and not as a symptom of mental disorder, we should not
be surprised that voices are heard in circles hostile to Poland and
the Poles attributing to us savage nationalism and moral co-respon-
sibility for the anti-Jewish attitude during the occupation.'[22]

Some parts of the ruling communist apparatus nevertheless
continued to believe that antisemitism could have a political
utility. In a series of lectures, broadcast over state-controlled
Polish Radio from 15 December onwards, Dr Jozef Kossecki of
the Higher Pedagogic College at Kielce declared: 'The Soviet
camp, whatever we may think about their system, is a barrier to
Jewish chauvinism in its plans to dominate the world.'[23] Kossecki
accused Bronisław Geremek of having sought to 'ruin every
scholar who showed any sign of sympathy for Polishness'.[24] The
broadcasts appear to have been ordered as part of the government's propaganda effort to prepare the way psychologically for
the imposition of martial law a week later. As in the previous
spring, however, the public response was cool, leading one wit to
remark, 'These people are going to compromise anti-Semitism in
Poland. If they go on, they'll make "international Zionism"
popular!'[25]

With the institution of martial law and the suppression of
Solidarity in December 1981, the Jewish issue re-emerged. Official
media laid renewed stress on the Jewishness of several Solidarity
leaders, including some who were not, in fact, Jews. Antisemitic
graffiti appeared on walls in Warsaw and anti-Jewish leaflets were

circulated. Jewish names were prominent among pro-Solidarity intellectuals arrested.

Suddenly, in early 1982, the wheel turned again. As the regime sought to improve its image (and restore Polish credit) in the West, the antisemitic campaign came to an abrupt halt – reportedly on the direct orders of the military dictator, General Jaruzelski. Over the next few months a number of demonstratively pro-Jewish actions were taken by the government. The Joint Distribution Committee was permitted to resume operations in Poland for the first time since 1967. The Warsaw synagogue was repaired. The Deputy Prime Minister, Mieczysław Rakowski, met Jewish leaders and promised that the government would combat anti-semitism. A few months later the Grunwald Union's chief patron, Stefan Olszowski, was demoted in the party apparatus; and in the spring of 1983 General Moczar was removed from his position as head of the Polish army veterans' organization.

The Polish authorities' strangely conflicting and contradictory attitudes on the Jewish issue were exhibited anew in April 1983 on the occasion of a ceremony commemorating the Warsaw ghetto uprising forty years earlier. Seeking to bolster its international legitimacy, the government organized an elaborate eight-day series of events and invited a large number of foreign guests. The organizers soon found that they had opened a Pandora's box. Dr Marek Edelman, a prominent supporter of Solidarity and the only survivor of the ghetto rising who still lived in Poland, called for a boycott of the official events and circulated a letter declaring:

> Forty years ago we not only fought for our lives, but for life in dignity and freedom. Observance of our anniversary here, where social life in its entirety is overshadowed by degradation and oppression, where words and gestures have been completely falsi-fied, is a betrayal of our struggle, is participating in something completely contradicting it. It is an act of cynicism and contempt.[26]

An unofficial meeting, in which many Solidarity supporters par-ticipated, was disbanded by the police. The official ceremonies were disrupted by the withdrawal of the Israeli delegation, as well as of Jewish groups from the West. They were incensed by a programme broadcast by Polish television a few days earlier that had compared the massacre of Palestinians in refugee camps in Beirut in September 1982 with Nazi mass murder of the Jews. The Israelis also objected to the participation of a representative of the Palestine Liberation Organization, who laid a wreath at the ghetto memorial.

Remarkably, in March 1988 the Polish government courted a repetition of its earlier embarrassment by sponsoring a commemoration of the forty-fifth anniversary of the ghetto revolt. Again Edelman called for a boycott. Again overseas guests were invited. Again the official events were overshadowed by an unofficial ceremony, on this occasion the dedication of a memorial to Henryk Erlich and Wyktor Alter, two Polish Jewish socialists, leaders of the Jewish autonomist Bund, who had died in Soviet prisons during the Second World War. One sign of change was the Polish Communist Party's acknowledgement in March 1988 that the antisemitic campaign twenty years earlier had 'brought harm to many people'. But even now it insisted that 'the party as a whole and its leadership – although not always effective or timely – nonetheless tried to discourage an atmosphere of anti-Semitism'.[27]

Such episodes indicated that the Jewish issue remained a central and unresolved problem in the Polish national consciousness. In the late 1980s, as intellectual freedom slowly returned, the matter came to occupy a significant place in public discourse. Discussion took place at several levels, some sophisticated, others descending to gutter invective. The debate was fuelled by the Auschwitz convent dispute, as well as by perceived slights such as the remark of the Israeli Prime Minister (of Polish origin), Yitzhak Shamir, that the Poles imbibed antisemitism with their mother's milk. Many Poles deeply resented the imputation of a national predisposition to antisemitism and reacted with a vehemence that sometimes bordered on self-contradiction.

After 1987, with a return to political and intellectual pluralism, a new spirit of candour and self-criticism seemed to enter Polish thinking. In particular, an article in *Tygodnik Powszechny* by Jan Błoński entitled 'The Poor Poles Look at the Ghetto', attracted much attention. Błoński, a professor of Polish Literature at the Jagiellonian University in Cracow, struggled 'to understand why we are still unable to come to terms with the whole of the Polish–Jewish past'. He took his title from a poem ('A Poor Christian Looks at the Ghetto') by Czesław Miłosz, the Nobel Prize winning Polish Lithuanian writer who wrote with great insight and humanity about the savagery enacted on his native soil in the course of his lifetime. Drawing on what he argued was the moral example of the Vatican II documents on the Jews, Błoński urged his fellow countrymen

> to stop haggling, trying to defend and justify ourselves. We must stop arguing about the things that were beyond our power to do during the occupation and beforehand. Nor must we place blame on political, social and economic conditions. We must say first of all, 'yes, we are guilty.' . . . The desecration of Polish soil has taken place and we have not yet discharged our duty of seeking expiation. In this graveyard, the only way to achieve this is to face up to our duty of viewing our past truthfully.[28]

This morally courageous article reflected the thinking of a number of Catholic intellectuals in Poland, particularly of the younger generation. For more old-fashioned Polish nationalists, however, the notion of 'guilt' was too much to stomach. Władysław Siła-Nowicki, in his contribution to the angry debate to which Błoński's article gave rise, defended the pre-war Polish *numerus clausus*: 'For me it is natural that society defends itself against the numerical domination of its intelligentsia.'[29]

Post-war Poland's miserable record on the Jewish issue might be explained as a product not of communism but of the country's long tradition of political antisemitism. No doubt there is considerable truth in this interpretation. Communist apologists sometimes even seemed to try to excuse manifestations of antisemitism on this account. Yet successive incarnations of the communist system, which claimed, after all, to be able to overcome examples of 'false consciousness' such as antisemitism, not only failed to counter it but resorted again and again – in 1945–53, in 1967–8, in 1981–2 – to naked appeals to racial animosity.

★

And not only in Poland. Communist Czechoslovakia too, a country where antisemitic traditions were comparatively weak (at any rate in its dominant western regions) and whose political culture was close to that of liberal Western Europe, followed a path on the Jewish issue that ran parallel to that taken by Poland.

Czechoslovak Jewry, like Polish Jewry, suffered almost total obliteration under Nazi rule. At the end of the war just 55,000 Jews remained in the country out of a pre-war Jewish population of 357,000. Prague, which in the eighteenth century had boasted the largest Jewish community of any city in Europe, and where Jewish symbiosis with both German and emergent Czech cultures had flourished in the nineteenth and early twentieth centuries, had only a few thousand Jews left in 1945. The Slánský trials had extinguished any hope of a revival of Jewish life in Czechoslovakia and by the mid-1950s most of the Jews had left for Israel or the United States. Indeed, it seemed as if the pitiful remnant, which had shrunk to only 15,000 by 1967, would fade out of existence as an organized entity.

An ugly episode in that year cast a sudden, harsh spotlight on the ruthlessness with which the communist regime still treated those it regarded as enemies. In August 1967 Charles Jordan, European director of operations for the American Jewish Joint Distribution Committee, was arrested in Prague by the secret police. Shortly afterwards his dead body was found floating in the river. Jordan, an American citizen whose work had probably contributed more than that of any other individual to the rehabilitation of the Jewish communities in post-war Europe, had long experience of dealing with communist governments. The 'Joint' had often been accused by communist governments of links with the CIA and with 'international Zionism'. There seems little doubt that Jordan was murdered while in police custody, although the exact circumstances of his death and the authorities' reason for doing away with him remain a mystery. The incident seemed to show, at any rate, the difficulty of establishing any sort of normal relationship between communist regimes and international Jewish organizations.

Then came the Prague Spring. The Jewish issue played a subsidiary but significant role at this critical juncture in the history of communism – and of the humane consciousness in Europe. In May 1968 the liberalizing Dubček regime fully rehabilitated Slánský and his fellow victims of the Stalin-era trials (they had been partially rehabilitated in 1963). Reformist communists in Czechoslovakia protested vigorously against the antisemitic campaign proceeding at that time in Poland. The Slovak communist leader and president of the Czechoslovak parliament, Josef Smrkovsky, called the Polish campaign 'scandalous' and declared that the struggle against antisemitism was the most sacred duty of socialists. The Polish government seems to have been considerably unsettled by this criticism from a fraternal party. On 6 May 1968 its ambassador in Prague delivered a protest note 'described as being so sharp that its text was not published'.[30]

In spite of their small numbers, several Czechoslovak Jews played a prominent part in the reform communist movement. Eduard Goldstuecker, who had served as first Czechoslovak Minister to Israel in 1948–50, was president of the Writers' Union from January 1968 and one of the most influential advocates of reform. Another Jew, Frantisek Kriegel, was one of the most fervently reform-minded members of the leading group and accordingly incurred the most vehement Soviet denunciation. Both Goldstuecker and Kriegel found themselves the targets of antisemitic hostility from opponents of the new government. Kriegel came under particularly venomous attack, which was plainly inspired not only by resentment of his militant reformism but by hatred of him as a Jew.

This was manifested in two incidents of high drama in which his colleagues among the Czechoslovak party leadership by their conduct vindicated their claim to represent a humane form of socialism. The first such incident took place during a meeting in late July between Czechoslovak and Soviet leaders at the small town of Čierna nad Tisou, near the Soviet border. The encounter occurred at the height of the crisis in relations between Czechoslovakia and the Soviet Union, whose leaders accused the Czechoslovaks of straying from the path of socialist rectitude. Violent arguments broke out, in the course of which the Ukrainian party boss, P. E. Shelest, let fly with blatantly antisemitic insults directed at Kriegel. At that point Dubček got up and walked out, accompanied by the other Czechoslovak negotiators.

The second incident took place shortly after the Warsaw Pact occupation of Czechoslovakia on 21 August. Kriegel was a member of the group that was flown to Moscow for discussions in the Kremlin, during which the Soviets berated the Czechoslovaks and persuaded them to sign a treaty of friendship legitimizing the invasion. Kriegel was the only member of the Czechoslovak team to refuse to sign the imposed agreement. When the Czechoslovak leaders were taken to the airport at the conclusion of the discussions in the Kremlin, they noticed that Kriegel was absent. Suspecting that he had been held back for possible trial and punishment, they refused to board their plane until Kriegel was produced and allowed to fly home with them.

After the invasion, the Czechoslovak media, again under orthodox pro-Soviet control, resumed 'anti-Zionist' themes, often as a device for attacking Jews who had participated in the Prague Spring. A striking example was a series of articles in April 1970 in the party organ, *Rude Pravo*. The author was F. J. Kolar, a Jewish journalist who had been imprisoned in the early 1950s, rehabilitated under Novotny, removed from his post as deputy editor of the newspaper during the Dubček period and appointed its Moscow correspondent after August 1968. In the articles Kolar condemned 'Zionist and imperialist propaganda', which, he said, had been 'spreading horrific tales about antisemitism in the countries of the socialist camp'. He explained that in the 1950s, as a result of the Slánský trials, 'intellectuals who up to then had been convinced that they were communists and Czechs or Slovaks by nationality suddenly began to discover their "Jewish fate"':

> There began the notorious Jewish exaggeration and self-pity. Zionist pseudo-humanism became an integral part of our literature . . .
>
> Deformations of Marxism–Leninism enabled these people to occupy a disproportionate number of positions in our cultural life. (Naturally, I have in mind the propagators of Zionist ideas – alien to Marxism and the Party, and not Communists of Jewish origin whose 'Jewishness' was as a rule unknown and did not bother

anyone in our country.) There began true orgies of 'Kafkaism' which had been dragged into our country by Prof. E. Goldstuecker and which is in fact an ideology of alienation, weakness, cowardice, defeatism . . .

[In 1968] the communications media turned the attitude towards the Jews and Israel into a curious kind of principal criterion of progressiveness and sincerity regarding the post-January policy [i.e. the reformist policy of the Dubček regime]. Once again they inflated artificially the so-called Jewish problem and used it for their policy, particularly in connection with the so-called anti-Jewish, antisemitic anonymous letters which were received or written to himself by Goldstuecker and other intellectuals and certain editorial offices. The so-called 'conservatives and traitors' were being branded with the dunce's hat of primitive antisemites. By these means Goldstuecker and other Jewish intellectuals tried to secure immunity. Whoever criticized them was at once labelled 'antisemite'.[31]

Kolar's articles were later expanded into a book and also used as the basis for a series of talks on the state radio. Although the 'anti-Zionist' campaign was regarded with the utmost distaste by nearly all Czech intellectuals and did not elicit any significant favourable response in the general public, the state-controlled media continued to churn out such propaganda for several years after 1968.

The campaign led, as in Poland though on a lesser scale, to a wave of Jewish emigration. The Jewish community shrank by some 50 per cent over the next two decades to under 8,000 by the late 1980s (though, as in Poland and East Germany, many crypto-Jews did not register with the community for fear of untoward consequences). Czechoslovak Jewry, like Polish Jewry, thus approached the verge of total dissolution. After the death in 1978 of Isidor Katz, Chief Rabbi of Slovakia, the country was left without any rabbi at all until 1983. In the 1980s a bare *minyan* (prayer quorum of ten men) regularly attended services at Prague's two remaining synagogues; the most indefatigable attender (if not worshipper) at the Altneuschul was a secret policeman.

Pathetically, the most widespread and tangible evidences of former Jewish life in the country, as throughout Central and

Eastern Europe, were cemeteries, an estimated 500 in Slovakia and another 345 in the Czech lands, among them the famous and beautiful burial-ground near the Altneuschul in Prague. In 1977 a representative of the community announced that even many of these cemeteries were in the process of being 'liquidated'.[32] A protest document issued in April 1989 by the opposition Charter 77 group named five in Prague alone that had been 'arbitrarily destroyed'.[33]

In these sepulchral conditions, a few live shoots of Jewish tradition sprouted up: *samizdat* editions of novels by Isaac Bashevis Singer circulated in Prague, as did Czech translations of religious texts such as the *Pirkei Avot* (Aphorisms of the Fathers). But by the late 1980s Czechoslovakia, like most of Eastern Europe, had become for Jews not much more than a graveyard.

CHAPTER TEN

West European Dilemmas, 1973–89

Many of the assumptions on which Jews in Europe had based their collective existence since the Second World War were shattered by the Arab–Israel war of October 1973. Israel emerged from the war in a chastened and demoralized condition. The ensuing international energy crisis, which threw the industrialized world into a state of panic and inaugurated a period of prolonged 'stagflation' in Europe, suddenly transformed the Middle Eastern oil-producing states into the arbiters of world events. The UN General Assembly's adoption in 1975 of a resolution asserting that Zionism was 'a form of racism and racial discrimination' testified to the diplomatic weakening and virtual isolation of Israel and the success of her enemies in delegitimizing the ideological basis of her existence in the eyes of much of the world. The vote in the assembly was seventy-five to thirty-five, with thirty-two abstentions.

The oil crisis led European leaders to adopt a suddenly humble attitude towards the Middle East oil-producing states. This was reflected in a shift in policy regarding the Arab–Israeli conflict. A joint statement issued by European Community foreign ministers on 6 November 1973 stressed the 'need for Israel to end the territorial occupation which it has maintained since the conflict of 1967'. It also referred for the first time to 'the legitimate rights of the Palestinians'.[1] The transparent intention of the statement's authors to curry Arab favour incurred some criticism. A Belgian member of the European Commission commented: 'Most Europeans could not hide a feeling of deep uneasiness, not so much about the tenor of this statement as about its timing. It conveyed the implication that, when faced with economic, social, and political consequences of a sustained oil embargo, the Nine had chosen the path of appeasement at any price.'[2]

In the course of the next few years, and particularly after the fall of the Shah of Iran (the one important Middle East oil-producing leader who was not hostile to Israel) in 1979, European leaders continued to abase themselves before the members of the oil cartel and to edge closer to the Arab position in the Middle East conflict. This shift in European attitudes was reflected in a further statement issued by a summit of European Community leaders at Venice in 1980.

The defeat of the Israeli Labour Party in the 1977 general election, after three decades of power, and its replacement by the right-wing government of Menahem Begin rendered Israel less attractive in many European eyes; Israel was now seen as too big for its boots and as a persecutor rather than a victim. The European left, most of which, except for the communists, had hitherto been generally friendly towards Israel, aligned itself increasingly with the Palestinian cause. Communists, 'new left' members of the 1968 generation, as well as parts of the respectable parliamentary social-democratic parties in Britain, France and elsewhere, now tended to view the Palestinians (in a phrase that became current especially in Germany) as 'victims of the victims'. Groups such as the British Anti-Zionist Organization worked together with Arab propaganda organs to promote opposition to 'the Zionist policy of "Lebens-raum" in occupied Palestine'.[3] Such groups were often accused of blurring the distinction between anti-Zionism and antisemitism. They responded by recruiting left-wing Jews to sign public state-ments repudiating 'racist Zionism'.[4]

The dramatic change in Israel's standing and image in the world hit the Diaspora hard. The Jews of Western Europe, who had grown used since 1967 to basking in the reflected glory of Israel's successes, suddenly faced a new and disturbing situation in which Israel was transformed from an object of pride into a worrying source of insecurity.

The most alarming consequence of these changes was the rise of international terrorism, of which Jews were particular targets and from which they suffered disproportionately. Palestinian terrorists, sometimes assisted by European ultra-leftists, hijacked aircraft and attacked airports and airline offices, particularly those of the Israeli airline El Al. Israeli passengers and in some cases Jews of other nationalities were specially targeted – as in the case of the hijacking in the summer of 1976 of an Air France plane to Entebbe, Uganda. In that incident a German terrorist ordered the separation of Jewish from non-Jewish hostages. Israeli special forces stormed the airport and secured the release of the passengers, but one, an elderly British Jewish woman who was in a nearby hospital, was murdered by terrorists in her hospital bed.

Airline security eventually reduced the hijacking threat, but in the meantime terrorists had begun to turn to other modes of attack. In December 1973 J. Edward Sieff, head of the Marks and Spencer chain of stores and a prominent supporter of Zionism in Britain, was shot and seriously wounded by a masked man. Responsibility for the attack was later claimed by the notorious Venezuelan terrorist Illitch Ramirez Sanchez, popularly known as 'Carlos'. In August 1974 'Carlos' organized attacks on the offices of three French publications, one of them the Jewish monthly L'Arche.

The threat to Jews from Palestinian and ultra-left terrorism was compounded by similar violence from the far right. In 1976 a series of bombings of Jewish institutions, attributed to the extreme right, began in France. Synagogues, schools, kosher butcher-shops, memorials, communal buildings, Jewish-owned businesses and even a day nursery were among the targets. In 1978 the neo-fascist 'French National Liberation Front' claimed responsibility for three explosions at the Paris offices of the Club Méditerranée, whose head was a well-known Jewish businessman. In March 1979 a bomb in a kosher canteen in Paris injured thirty-three students, several seriously.

Jewish institutions of all kinds throughout the Continent were compelled to take elaborate and expensive security precautions. In Belfast and Dublin, where Protestant and Catholic Churches were recognized by the warring Irish factions as inviolable sanctuaries, worshippers at local synagogues had to undergo searches before being allowed to pray.

The threat to Jews was intellectual as well as physical. In France the far right acquired a tinge of intellectual respectability through the ideas disseminated by the Groupement de recherche et d'études pour la civilisation européenne (GRECE). This body attracted significant support among students and young professionals and propagated an élitist, racist philosophy based on 'sociobiology'. Its leaders denied they were antisemites, but as one observer noted, 'consciously or unconsciously, GRECE carries a lot of Nazi ideas in its ideological baggage'.[5]

In spite of the economic crisis of the mid-1970s, however, right-wing parties made little electoral headway in Western Europe. In Britain the National Front fielded 303 candidates in the 1979 general election but failed to win a single seat. In Italy support for the neo-fascist Movimento Sociale Italiano fell from 8.6 per cent in the 1972 general election to 5.3 per cent in 1979. In Germany the neo-Nazi National Democratic Party virtually disappeared.

As in earlier periods, splits developed within Jewish communities over the most effective defence against terrorist threats. In Paris, right-wing Jewish militants, emulating the Jewish Defense League established in New York by the racist fanatic Rabbi Meir Kahane, set up vigilante patrols and threatened counter-violence against Arab targets. In Britain the quiet, diplomatic approach of the Board of Deputies was criticized by activist elements, some of whom joined in 1977 with elements of the left in forming the Anti-Nazi League. Among signatories of the League's founding statement were well-known Jewish theatrical figures such as Lionel Bart, Alfie Bass, Claire Bloom, Miriam Karlin, Wolf Mankowitz, Frederic Raphael, Janet Suzman and Arnold Wesker. Representatives of the official Jewish establishment refused to participate, suspecting the League of being a front organization for Trotskyists bent on street confrontations with National Front supporters. The involvement of far-left anti-Zionists and of figures such as the playwright Jim Allen (author of the play *Perfidy*, which accused Zionists of collaboration with the Nazis) compounded the hostility of mainstream Jewish organizations. Some Jews withdrew their support, but others, such as Miriam Karlin, affirmed it all the more vigorously, leading to further controversies within the Jewish community.

In France the organization SOS Racisme was formed in 1985 by Jewish intellectuals and others. Its objective was to form a common front, particularly with North African Muslims targeted by the extreme right. There were objections from various quarters, including the ex-communist turned militant Zionist Annie Kriegel, who considered such an attempt to form a Muslim–Jewish alliance dangerous (her fear was that the Jews involved would be seduced to support the Arab position in the Middle East conflict).

The renewed oil crisis of 1979–80, after the fall of the Shah, was accompanied by a resurgence of anti-Jewish terrorism in Europe. In January 1980 an explosion in a Jewish-owned restaurant in Berlin killed a nineteenth-month-old baby and injured twenty-four people. In July hand-grenades were thrown at a group of Jewish children near the Antwerp office of the Agudas Yisroel; one was killed and several wounded. In October a bomb at the Liberal Jewish synagogue on the rue Copernic in Paris on the festival of Simhat Tora killed four people and injured fifteen. The attackers were never discovered. Immediately after the attack the French Prime Minister, Raymond Barre, denounced it as an 'odious crime that was aimed at Jews going to synagogue and made victims of innocent Frenchmen walking along rue Copernic'.[6] The thoughtless remark was interpreted by unkind critics as a Freudian slip. It was also noted that President Giscard d'Estaing issued no immediate statement and did not visit the scene of the crime. Some other responses were also less than reassuring. Neighbouring shopkeepers in the rue Copernic visited the rabbi of the synagogue after the attack and demanded payment for damage caused to their premises. The landlord of the building next door to the synagogue, whose concierge was killed, similarly called for reimbursement of the costs of the funeral.

In August 1981 Palestinian terrorists using hand-grenades and sub-machine-guns attacked the main synagogue in Vienna, killing two people and injuring eighteen. Two months later a car bomb at a synagogue near the diamond exchange in Antwerp (where 70 per cent of the dealers were Jews, mostly ultra-orthodox Hasidim) caused three deaths and 106 injuries. As in Paris a year earlier, the attackers deliberately chose the Jewish holiday of Simhat Tora in order to cause maximum injury.

The Israeli invasion of Lebanon in June 1982 and the massacres perpetrated by Israel's Christian Lebanese allies shortly afterwards in the Palestinian refugee camps of Sabra and Shatila marked the high point of anti-Israel feeling in Western Europe. A new series of terrorist attacks broke out. Although the perpetrators seem to have been mainly Arabs and their motives connected with the Middle East conflict, the targets were often Jewish as distinct from Israeli. On 9 August 1982 a machine-gun attack on Jo Goldenberg's kosher restaurant on the rue des Rosiers in the Marais, heart of the old Jewish district of Paris, killed six people and injured twenty-two. Responsibility was initially claimed by Action Directe, a right-wing French terrorist organization, but nobody was ever brought to trial and the true source of the attack remained a mystery. Unlike his predecessor at the time of the rue Copernic attack, President Mitterrand went immediately to the scene and expressed his sympathy and outrage. The gesture was not universally appreciated: Mitterrand found himself jeered by North African Jewish critics of his Middle East policy. Further terrorist incidents took place elsewhere in Europe. An attack on the main Rome synagogue in October 1982 killed one child and caused many injuries. In September 1986 a Palestinian onslaught on the main synagogue in Istanbul killed 24 worshippers as they prayed.

Whatever semantic distinction might be drawn between anti-Zionism and antisemitism, such incidents showed that Jews all over non-communist Europe were now seen by Palestinian and other terrorists as fair game. The terrorism was psychological as well as physical. In the atmosphere of hostility to Israel, a wave of antisemitic incidents spread across Europe. Throughout the second half of 1982 and early 1983, from Greece to Norway, synagogues were daubed, prominent Jews threatened, antisemitic letters, articles and cartoons published, cemeteries desecrated.

In spite of everything, however, liberal Europe by and large showed impressive solidarity with Jews as victims of terrorism. A demonstration after the rue Copernic explosion attracted more than 100,000 participants from all parts of the political spectrum. Lord Beloff, a leading British Jew, pointed out in 1982 that 'the primary effect of the Holocaust, as we can increasingly see, was psychologically to deepen the sense of Jewish isolation and to induce Jews to judge all subsequent relations between the Jewish and non-Jewish worlds in the light of events too ghastly to recollect or communicate'.[7] Against that background, the solidarity shown by much of the general public in reaction to terrorist attacks carried some reassurance. As the former West German Chancellor Willy Brandt put it: 'Terrorism cannot engender anti-semitism. Violence today will not succeed but, on the contrary, bring about solidarity with the groups and institutions attacked.'[8]

The attacks on Jews *qua* Jews compelled even some hitherto alienated, assimilated or anti-Zionist Jews to re-examine their relationship to Jewry, Israel and Judaism. A case in point was the distinguished orientalist Maxime Rodinson, a Marxist whose writings included some of the most effective presentations of the Palestinian Arab nationalist case against Israel. In 1975 he told a Beirut newspaper that he had lately acquired

> more understanding of the nationalism of the Jewish entity in Israel ... I continue to regard my Judaism as a genealogical accident. Still, because my family was murdered on account of their Jewish origin, despite the fact that they were never religious or Zionist, because many people regard me as a Jew no matter what I say or do, and because the State of Israel claims to represent me while I do not recognize its right to do so, I am compelled to show a certain measure of solidarity ... in spite of the fact that I am forced to remain a Jew against my will.[9]

Some Jews drew pessimistic and even apocalyptic conclusions from these events. Shmuel Trigano, a French Jewish writer whose faddish and sometimes vacuous phraseology did not prevent his being hailed as a rising star in the intellectual firmament, saw the rue Copernic explosion as the latest link in a long chain stretching from the Dreyfus Affair, through Vichy and de Gaulle's 1967 press conference. Here was yet another sign that Jewish existence in the full sense was virtually impossible in France. The republican system, he argued, with its pressures towards uniformity and centralization, did not allow the Jew sufficient space to create a life in which Judaism could breathe. As against this view, the attorney Daniel Amson pointed out that terrorism was a weapon used by many groups and attacked not only Jews but French society as a whole. Jews, he argued, were in fact better integrated into French society than ever before. Isolating what he and others saw as the essential flaw in Trigano's logic, Amson asked:

> Can one . . . affirm incessantly to other people that one is different and then complain when they say the same thing? If the Jewish citizen renounces any form of particularism, the Republic integrates him without any difficulty. If he does not renounce it, he necessarily admits that he should not be like other people, and in the school, the university, or the army, the Republic allows him that too. The Republic assimilates those who identify themselves with the majority of its citizens and it does not assimilate, while at the same time protecting, those who, out of conviction or tradition, wish to be different.[10]

Chief Rabbi Jakobovits of Great Britain warned against too facile a lumping together of anti-Zionists with antisemites:

> By charging [critics of Israel] with antisemitism, you help to breed antisemitism. You give aid and comfort to the real antisemites and their movements, and you alienate true friends . . . That intense hostility to Israel spills over into antipathy against Jews is manifestly obvious. Anti-Zionism is certainly a cause of antisemitism. But the reverse is much more questionable, and often plainly untenable as a fact.[11]

The special vulnerability of Jews and Jewish institutions in Western societies in the 1970s and 1980s raised in a new form the question of whether there was a distinctively Jewish interest in politics and if so how this should be expressed. In most West European societies Jews had tended to resist the creation of a Jewish ethnic lobby on the American pattern, sensing that it was alien to European political traditions, although there were, in fact, plenty of historical examples to the contrary – for example, the

Irish vote in Britain. But in the 1970s and 1980s Jewish political behaviour in much of Western Europe began to change.

In 1977 the French Jewish representative body, CRIF, took the unprecedented action of adopting a 'Charter', the first time that it enunciated what amounted to an undisguised effort at a comprehensive political statement. The charter set out what were considered to be basic principles that formed a common denominator for the Jewish community:

● full participation of Jews in French society;
● social justice;
● condemnation of all forms of persecution;
● struggle against antisemitism;
● unconditional attachment to Israel.[12]

Most of these were obviously unexceptionable general statements to which all Jews could adhere; the last, however, fell into a different category since there were many Jews whose attachment to Israel, while real and sometimes deep, was by no means 'unconditional' – particularly after the installation of the Begin government in that year.

The pattern of Jewish political commitments in France was, meanwhile, changing. A number of young Jewish intellectuals, of whom the most prominent was Bernard-Henri Lévy, turned against Marxism and revolution; at the same time, they defined themselves strongly, at times vehemently, as Jews. Lévy's denunciation of 'l'idéologie française', which he defined as Vichyite and racist, evoked passionate debate. The political scientist Pierre Birnbaum drew renewed attention to the significant antisemitic elements in the political traditions of left as well as right in France. The historian Henry Rousso argued that strong Vichyite strains remained in the post-war French political consciousness. Shmuel Trigano argued that the centralizing Jacobin tradition had sought to stamp out any competing subcultures. What struck a new note in all these cases was the writers' failure to make ritual obeisance to the French political tradition and its values; on the contrary, their works amounted to a collective critique of the failure of that tradition to realize many of its own purported values.

A recurrent theme of controversy at each presidential or parliamentary election in France in this period was the issue of the 'Jewish vote'. Did it exist? Should it exist? How important was it? The traditional answers to these questions in republican France had been no, no and not at all. So long as the assimilationist consensus prevailed, these remained the answers given by most French Jews. Attitudes began to change under the weight of the North African Jewish influx in the early 1960s and as a result of the passions aroused by the 1967 war and de Gaulle's notorious press conference of November 1967. By the early 1970s a Jewish dimension in French politics had emerged whether the communal leadership liked it or not.

Representatives of the Jewish establishment, such as Alain de Rothschild, president of the Consistoire Central, did not like it. Rothschild emphasized at the time of the 1973 elections that 'aucune consigne de vote n'est donnée'.[13] Similarly a writer in the official organ of the Consistoire warned that talk of a 'Jewish vote' 'would be a matter of a state within a state – which is inadmissible and false'.[14] This was the voice of French Jewish traditionalism.

The communist-leaning Presse Nouvelle Hebdo agreed that 'the past history of the Jews in France leads us to reject any sort of "Jewish vote" '. This was the voice of socialist internationalism. At the same time, recalling its primary role of propagandizing for the party among the Jewish 'masses', the paper added: 'There nevertheless exists a Jewish electorate in whose eyes certain rights and guarantees seem legitimately essential.'[15] This was the voice of electoral pragmatism.

Less equivocally, Jean Kling, Chief Rabbi of Lyons, thought it an encouraging sign of the 'moral health of our democracy' that the idea of a Jewish vote was starting to be accepted as legitimate.[16] As for the French electorate in general, most seemed untroubled by the idea that French Jews might have specific interests and concerns: a poll in 1970 showed that 69 per cent of those questioned agreed that it was 'quite normal' for Jewish citizens to have a special preoccupation with Israel.

Whatever the anxieties or preferences of Jews themselves, the behaviour of the various political parties suggested that they believed in the existence of such a voting bloc and thought it worth courting. Although the Jews were estimated to constitute under 1 per cent of the electorate as a whole, there were thought to be at least twenty marginal constituencies in which Jewish voters numbered 7–10 per cent of the electorate or more and might therefore influence the result. Among these were the second, third, eighth, tenth, twelfth and nineteenth *arrondissements* in Paris, the Paris suburbs of Créteil and Sarcelles, the Lyons suburb of Villeurbanne, the second *circonscription* of Toulouse and two seats in Marseilles, one of which was occupied by the outspokenly pro-Israeli mayor, Gaston Defferre.

The legislative elections of 1973 marked a turning point in perceptions of the Jewish vote. 'For the first time in French electoral history [wrote one observer] the Jews of this country are considered as an electoral force.'[17] Representatives of all the major parties issued special statements directed to Jewish voters. The Socialist leader, François Mitterrand, for example, affirmed support for Israel and protested against restrictions on Jewish emigration from the USSR.[18] The latter was a sensitive point in view of the Socialists' electoral alliance with the French Communist Party, whose leader, Georges Marchais, singled out Israel as 'a reactionary state' in his introduction to the left-wing parties' 'common programme'. When a Communist politician, Pierre Juquin, was taxed with refusing to comment on the Soviet emigration issue, he retorted, 'This is a *French* election.'[19] Similarly, when the Jewish Gaullist deputy, Claude-Gérard Marcus, an art dealer who was a noted supporter of Israel, was reminded of his party's ambiguous attitude towards Israel since 1967, his answer was: 'This is not a vote for the Knesset.'[20]

Although many Jewish intellectuals and old-style leftists continued to vote Communist, some Jewish socialists baulked at supporting a Communist in the second round of the election – as required by the pact in seats where the Communist led the candidates of the left on the first round. The Socialist Zionist Movement of France (a grand name for a not very influential pressure group) called on Jewish voters to vote on the second round 'for the socialists and for the friends of Israel, against the outgoing [right-wing] majority and against all enemies of Israel and of the Jews of the USSR' – a coded but clear statement of hostility to the Communist Party.[21]

A distinctive Jewish vote did become visible in a few constituencies – for example, in Sarcelles, where the Communist mayor, Henry Canacos, was challenging the Gaullist deputy, Mme Solange Troisier. In municipal elections in 1972 Canacos had won a striking victory with the help of many votes from the large North African Jewish population, who were estimated to constitute more than a third of the population of the town. Canacos had included leaders of the Jewish community on his municipal list and his victory in the mayoral election was attributed at the time to Jewish hostility to Gaullist foreign policy. Sarcelles boasted a Jewish community of pronounced cohesion and self-consciousness. In a survey of Jews in the town in 1970, 77 per cent had declared that they attached 'un intérêt primordial' to Israel and its problems.[22] Troisier, like Canacos, worked hard to court the Jewish vote. She proclaimed herself 'one of the four or five UDR [Gaullist] deputies who have always been favourably disposed towards Israel'.[23] And she was prominent in protests against persecution of Jews in Iraq and Syria. Canacos's victory was nevertheless attributed to heavy support from Jewish voters.

During the 1970s and 1980s the Socialists seemed to become the party most in tune with Jewish thinking in France. In the 1973 election, two young Jewish Socialist candidates, Maurice Benassayag and Georges Bender, campaigned vigorously for the Jewish vote in the first and second circonscriptions of Paris, areas with a strong Jewish left-wing tradition. Benassayag, aged thirty-one, was a rapatrié from Algeria and a university lecturer. Bender, aged forty-two, had joined the socialists at the time of the 1968 troubles and was closely associated with Israel and with various left-wing Zionist circles. Although neither was elected, both seem to have profited at the polls from their identification with Jewish interests. In 1978 the Socialist Party created a special group, Socialisme et Judaïsme, headed by Robert Badinter, Jacques Attali and others, with the specific purpose of attracting Jewish voters. A poll of 400 Jewish voters in early 1978, before the legislative elections that spring, showed that 56 per cent intended to vote for the left and only 33 per cent for the centre-right majority. The single party with the most support was the Socialists with 49 per cent. In 1981, according to impressionistic but generally convincing accounts, Jews voted heavily in the presidential election for the successful candidacy of François Mitterrand; according to one estimate, he won as much as 70 per cent of the Jewish vote. In 1988 he again received about two-thirds of the Jewish vote in the second round against Jacques Chirac.

The existence of a Jewish vote could no longer be denied. In several constituencies where there were heavy concentrations of Jewish voters and where Jews voted strongly for a particular candidate, they could decide an election. At the same time, the importance of the Jewish vote should not be exaggerated. The number of constituencies where it counted was small. Jewish voters in France, as in other countries, often voted heavily for one particular party, but they seldom did so on the basis of perceived Jewish particularist issues. Moreover, even allowing for the high Jewish electoral turn-out in France, as in other Western democracies, the total size of the Jewish electorate in France was too small to be of major significance. Indeed, the Jewish electorate from the 1970s onwards was greatly outweighed by the votes of French Muslims, who were not only more numerous but also voted even more disproportionately than Jews for the left: an estimated 86 per cent of Muslims cast votes for Mitterrand in the first round in 1988.

Jewish politicians, therefore, even had they wished to, could not base their fortunes on an appeal to a specifically Jewish electorate. As in earlier periods, they prospered none the less, and some achieved senior political positions in this period. Jack Lang was a flamboyant socialist Minister of Culture. Pierre Dreyfus, former head of the state-owned Renault motor company, served as Minister for Industry under Mitterrand. Jacques Attali exercised backstairs influence as 'sherpa' to Mitterrand in the Elysée. Simone Veil served as Minister of Health under President Giscard d'Estaing. She encountered fierce Catholic hostility, which occasionally crossed the line into expressions of antisemitism, on account of her successful steering through parliament of a law permitting

abortion. Robert Badinter, Minister of Justice in the Socialist
government in 1981 to 1986, attracted fury from the pro-death
rather than the 'pro-life' lobby (often the same people) when he
won passage of a law abolishing capital punishment. In spite of the
decline in Jewish support for the Communist Party, a number of
Jews still played significant roles in its affairs. Henri Krasucki
became secretary-general of the CGT, the powerful communist
trade union. Jean Elleinstein led an unsuccessful attempt to reform
the Communist Party, then left it, and by 1990 was involved in
the establishment of a centre for secular Jews.

In Britain, as in France, Jews often took a more assertive stance
in the 1970s and 1980s in defending specifically Jewish political
interests. During the 1973 Middle East crisis, for example, Jewish
Conservative MPs in Britain displayed more independence from
the party whips than their Labour co-religionists had at the time
of the Suez crisis. Only two of the nine Jewish Conservatives
supported the government in the parliamentary vote on the Heath
government's embargo on shipments of arms (including gas masks)
to the belligerents.

In Britain, unlike France, there was little public debate over the
existence or desirability of a distinctive Jewish vote. The declining
size of the community in any case restricted its possible significance
to a handful of constituencies. As in France, Jewish electors rarely
decided their votes on the basis of specific Jewish interests or
issues.

A clear Jewish voting trend to the right nevertheless emerged in
this period. In a few areas (for example, Hendon and Ilford in
London and Cheadle near Manchester) a distinctive Jewish vote
was detected by psephologists. Mrs Thatcher's record as an outspoken supporter of Israel certainly helped her in her constituency
of Finchley, where 16 per cent of the voters were estimated to be
Jewish. Conversely, the outspoken hostility to Israel of some
Labour Party figures, particularly the leftist leader of the Greater
London Council, Ken Livingstone, alienated many Jews. It remains
an open question, however, whether the Jewish shift to the right
was prompted more by specifically Jewish concerns or whether
the primary explanation was an assimilatory process in which Jews

were now, like the rest of the population, voting chiefly with their pockets. In many cases, probably, socio-economic interest and a changing cultural outlook walked hand in hand.

The Jewish shift to the right was reflected in their participation in the new political élite. Jews were among the leading ideological formulators of the new conservatism. Sir Keith Joseph was regarded as Mrs Thatcher's ideological guru. Sir Alfred Sherman, a former communist, shifted to the right and became a leader-writer for the arch-conservative *Daily Telegraph*, adviser to Joseph and head of an influential Thatcherite think-tank. Chief Rabbi Jakobovits, whom Mrs Thatcher raised to the peerage, was held to embody many of the Smilesian, self-help ideals of the Thatcherite Conservative Party – more so, indeed, than many bishops of the established Church.

The number of Conservative Jewish MPs in Britain increased from twelve in the February 1974 general election to sixteen in 1987; over the same period the number of Jewish Labour MPs shrank from thirty-three to seven. The turning point was the 1983 election, when for the first time in modern electoral history there were more Jewish Conservative than Labour supporters in the House of Commons (seventeen to eleven). The Conservative Party, which had seemed unwelcoming to some Jews a generation earlier, now positively embraced them. At one point Mrs Thatcher's Cabinet had five Jewish ministers.

These changes in the political behaviour of British and French Jewries reflected the intensification of the processes of social change that had been gathering momentum since the war. Jewish population decline, already evident in the 1950s and 1960s, continued over the following two decades. In Britain the number of Jews shrank from its peak of 410,000 in the early 1950s to barely 300,000 by 1989. Jewish fertility in Britain continued to be markedly lower than that for the general population, presaging further numerical decline. Similar trends were noticeable almost everywhere else in Europe. In France, the demographic spurt resulting from North African immigration in the 1960s slowed down as the fertility rate of the immigrants began to converge with that of the established community. By the mid-1980s the average Jewish woman in France had 2.4 children; but for French-*born* Jewish women the rate was much lower: only 1.7 children.

Occupational patterns of Jews throughout Western Europe in the 1970s and 1980s continued in the same directions as in the previous two decades – principally towards the 'caring professions': medicine, teaching, social work and also law and journalism. But Jews remained disproportionately represented in small businesses. A study of Jews in Sheffield, for example, showed that in the mid-1970s, 47 per cent of those who were economically active were self-employed; the proportion for the city as a whole was only 5 per cent.[24] The old London Jewish working class, associated with industries such as tailoring, furs and cabinet-making, was rapidly dying out. One characteristically Jewish occupation, however, remained: in the early 1980s a third of all London taxi drivers were still estimated to be Jews.

The pattern in France was similar. By 1988 no fewer than 42 per cent of economically active Jews in France were estimated to belong to 'upper cadres' (professional and managerial groups).[25] Many of the North African Jews, particularly the Algerians, moved swiftly up the social ladder, some attaining positions of importance. Jean-Pierre Elkabbach, a native of Oran, became head of French state television. Jean Daniel, an Algerian Jew who had arrived in Paris in the late 1940s, was chief animator of the influential left-wing weekly *Le Nouvel Observateur*. Gilbert Trigano created the Club Méditerranée. The Algerian-born Bernard-Henri Lévy was the *enfant terrible* of the Left Bank intellectual set.

North African integration accelerated the democratization of the French Jewish community. The reign of the notables was challenged in May 1968, when, in a miniature version of the larger social conflict of the time, young Jewish radicals occupied the premises of the two most important French Jewish organizations, the Paris Consistoire and the FSJU (the main French Jewish welfare organization). As in the case of some of the other student occupations, the precise aims of the occupiers were far from clear. The demand made of the Consistoire, to permit the use of an organ in the central Paris synagogue in the rue de la Victoire, while inconsistent with Jewish tradition, was hardly revolutionary. Over the next two or three years, demands by a group of young Jewish professionals, among them the socialist politician Jacques Attali, for a greater say in the administration of the FSJU led eventually to the adoption of a new, more democratic constitution. Sephardim gradually began to play a greater role in the leadership of this and other Jewish organizations. The patrician age nevertheless lasted into the 1970s. As late as 1979, Rothschilds monopolized the three most important posts in the community: Baron Guy de Rothschild, head of the French branch of the clan, served as president of the FSJU; his cousins Élie and Alain headed the Consistoire and the CRIF.

Meanwhile, however, new organizations emerged of a more assertively Jewish and Zionist character, notably Renouveau juif, headed by a young Ashkenazi lawyer, Henri Hajdenberg, which attracted a large, mainly Sephardi following. The explicit – and, to the old guard, heretical – objective of this group was to create a Jewish ethnic lobby on the American pattern and to assert the alleged power of the 'Jewish vote'. In April 1980 Hajdenberg organized a mass pro-Israeli rally, 'twelve hours for Israel', in Paris, attracting 150,000 participants.

The growing integration of the North African Jews was also indicated by the increase in intermarriage between Ashkenazim and Sephardim. The assimilation of both into French society was indicated by the steady rise in intermarriage between Jews and non-Jews – an increasingly common phenomenon throughout Europe and one that posed a further question mark over the survival of a distinctive Jewish community. An estimated 62 per cent of French-born Jews who married between 1966 and 1975 had non-Jewish spouses. For French Jews born in North Africa, the rate was much lower: only 20 per cent. On the other hand, the rate among the predominantly secular community of Jews born in other European countries was even higher than for the French-born: 64 per cent. Except in Strasbourg, North African Jews exhibited greater resistance than natives to intermarriage with non-Jews. Overall, one in three of all Jews who married in France between 1966 and 1975 did so with a non-Jewish partner. By the mid-1980s the intermarriage rate had risen to between 55 and 60 per cent.

Interesting variations were registered not only between native-born and immigrants but between Jews hailing from different regions of the Maghreb. Only 5 per cent of marriages contracted in Paris by Moroccan or Tunisian Jews between 1966 and 1975 were with non-Jews; in the case of Algerian Jews, the proportion was 48 per cent. The difference might be considered surprising given the fact that Algerian Jews had tended to arrive in France later than the others, but is explicable by their greater sense of integration to French society and culture. Even before their departure for France, Algerian Jews had tended to marry more heavily outside the faith than Moroccans and Tunisians: the intermarriage rate for Jews in Algeria in the late 1950s was estimated at more than 20 per cent.[26]

The trend towards out-marriage troubled many Jews – not only the orthodox. In a survey of Jews in the London suburb of Wembley, for example, 63.9 per cent of parents interviewed said they would be unhappy if their children married out of the faith. A further 25 per cent said they would 'prefer them to marry someone who is Jewish'. Only 16.7 per cent expressed no reservation at all towards intermarriage.[27] By the 1970s few Jewish parents would any longer adopt the traditional extreme sanction of regarding children who married out of the faith as if they were dead.*

Throughout Western Europe the Jewish migration towards the outer suburbs of major cities continued. In London the more prosperous continued to move north-west, along a corridor stretching from St John's Wood out through Edgware into Hertfordshire. Another, less affluent stream flowed east to areas such as Ilford and Redbridge. An ultra-orthodox redoubt remained in Stamford Hill, but otherwise the old areas of Jewish settlement were abandoned. In the former Jewish East End districts of Whitechapel and Stepney, only a handful of the very poor and very old remained.

---

* Though some did: for example, the father of the British Conservative politician Edwina Currie, née Cohen.

In 1955 the E1 postal district alone had had forty-four synagogues; only eight remained in 1982 – and most of those disappeared soon afterwards.

Whereas in France provincial Jewries blossomed thanks to the arrival of the North African Jews, in England they shrivelled and in some cases died. Leeds Jewry dwindled from about 20,000 in 1952 to 16,500 thirty years later; Liverpool from 7,500 to under 6,000. Among major provincial communities only Manchester, with a Jewish population of over 30,000, seemed able to hold its own.

The decline was particularly marked around Britain's Celtic fringe. In Cardiff, once a significant Jewish centre, the remaining Jews found they could no longer maintain the central synagogue in Cathedral Road. As in many cities in England, the reduced community now gathered for prayer at a single suburban site. In many places once thriving Jewish communities disappeared altogether: the small towns of South Wales, such as Tredegar, Pontypridd and Merthyr Tydfil, where at the turn of the century Jewish pedlars had trudged up and down the valleys selling their wares in mining villages, lost almost all their Jews. 'In 1984 [a historian of Welsh Jewry writes] the ark from Pontypridd synagogue was stacked against the wall of a small disused chapel near Aberystwyth, now part of the National Museum of Wales, housing a collection of figurines of preachers and other relics of Welsh Nonconformity.'[28]

The Jews in Scotland too seemed to prefer the high road to London. Glasgow's Jewish population declined from 15,000 in the 1950s to half that number by the 1990s. The reduced community could no longer support the publication of Scotland's only Jewish newspaper, the *Jewish Echo*.

Irish Jewry, like those of Scotland and Wales, declined to the verge of dissolution. The community had a glorious history: it had produced a Chief Rabbi of Israel (Herzog), another of Britain (Jakobovits), a President of Israel (Chaim Herzog) and a Lord Mayor of Dublin (Robert Briscoe), not to mention one of the seminal characters in modern European fiction in Leopold Bloom. By the late 1980s there was much talk of 'rationalization' (i.e. amalgamation) of Dublin's five remaining synagogues, but local rivalries and ancestral loyalties prevented decisive action. The number of kosher butcher-shops declined between 1961 and 1981 from seven to two. A typical item in the *Dublin Jewish News* was a report that the managers of the Greenville synagogue, which had 'no minister, only 59 members, an attendance of 12–14 on Shabbat and 35–40 on Yomtov [festivals]', had decided to soldier on. 'Nothing,' the paper commented in a fine Irishism, 'is more emotive than emotion – and the old lady stays where she is for the moment, gazing across the road at her new Moslem neighbour.'[29] The community seemed increasingly to be living on the remains of its heritage, with the only new institution an Irish Jewish Museum, opened in 1987, and the best-celebrated festival 'Bloomsday'.

In Paris in the 1970s and 1980s, as in London, the Jewish population showed a marked tendency to move from the old inner-city areas towards the outer suburbs, particularly those to the south-west. By the early 1990s, out of 310,000 Jews in the Paris metropolitan area, only 145,000 lived within the boundaries of the City of Paris; 113,000 lived in the inner suburban belt and 52,000 in the outer suburbs. In Belleville, only occasional old people could be heard muttering to each other in Yiddish. The North African Jewish imprint remained visible (although now largely Tunisian, the more prosperous Algerians having moved elsewhere); but the area was slowly losing its former Jewish character as a result of heavy redevelopment and the arrival of new waves of immigrants from China, Vietnam and North and West Africa.

In most of the Jewish communities of Western Europe, religious observance continued to decline steadily in this period. A survey of French Jews in the 1970s showed that about a third characterized themselves as 'religious', about another third as '*communautaire*' or traditional, and most of the remainder as Jewish but not religious. Only 4 per cent, however, said that they attached no significance at all to being Jewish. Figures for attendance at synagogue followed a similar pattern. Nearly a third never attended at all. Another third did so only on Yom Kippur. Most of the remainder attended 'irregularly'; only 10.5 per cent attended regularly (i.e. on the

Sabbath and principal festivals). As is usual among Jews, men attended religious services more frequently than women. Among women born in France, only 4.2 per cent were 'regular' synagogue-goers. Among the highly secularized community of Jews born in Eastern Europe, the figure was even lower: 2.1 per cent of the women and 5 per cent of the men.[30] These patterns were reflected by other measures of religiosity, such as observance of *kashrut* or the Sabbath. Under 10 per cent of Jews born in Central or Eastern Europe followed these practices, whereas about three-quarters of those born in Morocco and Tunisia did so. As in most West European communities, the most widely practised Jewish rite apart from burial was circumcision, which persisted to a considerable degree even among families where the parents had not celebrated Jewish religious marriages and even in families where one of the parents was not Jewish. Overall, more than 80 per cent of males born to at least one Jewish parent were circumcised.[31]

Efforts to revive Jewish religious practice did not make much headway. René-Samuel Sirat, who in 1980 became the first non-Ashkenazi to be elected French Chief Rabbi, tried to move the French religious establishment back into line with general orthodox practice, opposing batmitzvah (female confirmation), banning use of the organ in synagogues on Sabbaths and festivals, and making conversion to Judaism more difficult. Such strict constructionism, however, tended to make orthodoxy less, not more attractive to most Jews. Rabbi Sirat himself admitted to a sense of failure when he deplored what he termed the 'slow but dramatic dejudaization' of his community.[32]

In Britain the quarter-century-long Chief Rabbinate of Immanuel Jakobovits, which began in 1967, followed a somewhat different pattern. The fury of the orthodox reaction against its religious competitors in the early 1960s was replaced by a more dignified restraint. Although no less strict in his orthodoxy than his predecessor, Jakobovits was a more sophisticated figure and his period as a rabbi in New York City had accustomed him to the necessity for acknowledging the existence, if not accepting the claims, of different religious streams within Judaism. In the 1980s the 'Masorti' (traditionalist) movement, headed by Louis Jacobs, at last succeeded in moving out from its bastion in St John's Wood and establishing a number of other synagogues. Jacobs was careful, however, not to challenge the authority of the Chief Rabbi at its most sensitive point, marriage: unlike Liberal and Reform rabbis, he would not conduct marriages (for example, between Jews and non-Jews) that were prohibited by Jewish law.

As religious observance declined, so did other forms of Jewish identification. Jewish languages almost disappeared. Only 15 per cent of the Jews in Paris by the mid-1970s spoke Yiddish. These were almost exclusively old people. A slightly smaller percentage spoke Judaeo-Arabic, but in spite of the more recent vintage of the North African immigrants, this language too seemed to be dying out rapidly. North Africans, unlike the East European Jews, did not seem to be making a collective effort to keep their language alive. Whereas Yiddish had overcome the common nineteenth-century prejudice against it as a 'jargon', the dialect of the North African Jews survived primarily as a spoken rather than a literary language and was regarded by most of its speakers as a patois.

The logical consequence of the decline of Jewish languages was that the Yiddish press declined almost into oblivion. In 1993 the communist paper *Di Naie Presse* closed after nearly sixty years of existence. Formerly a daily, in its last years it had appeared only once every three weeks and its circulation had dwindled to barely 1,000. The Zionist *Unzer Vort*, founded in 1946, clung precariously to life under its octogenarian editor, Jacques Cypel, but it was published only four days a week – and that irregularly: when Cypel fell ill or went away on holiday the paper would fail to appear for a while.

The French-language Jewish press catered for a very different audience and in a very different style. The weekly *Actualité Juive* claimed a circulation of 16,500 and came closest to serving as a national communal newspaper. Its closest rival was *Tribune Juive*. The glossy monthly magazine *L'Arche* aimed at an audience of bourgeois *consommateurs*. *Les Nouveaux Cahiers*, founded in 1965, catered to middlebrow intellectuals. None of these publications could compare with the hot-lead excitement of the old Yiddish daily press in its heyday. Nor did they approach the quality of the oldest and best Jewish newspaper in Europe, the *Jewish Chronicle* of London.

As a journalistic and communal phenomenon, the *Jewish Chronicle* was a remarkable success story. Even the North American Jewish communities, twenty times the size of Anglo-Jewry, could boast nothing comparable in the post-war period. The paper's success was built on a close affinity with the evolving collective mentality of its readership and on a long period of financial and editorial independence. With a circulation of about 50,000, the paper reached into most Jewish homes in Britain and many overseas. Indeed, as other forms of Jewish identification diminished, many readers who were otherwise unaffiliated seemed to cling to the paper as a last link with the community.

In its editorial stance the *Chronicle* was vigorously independent. In 1973 it took an early position against Israeli settlement in the occupied territories. The next year it published an interview with the London representative of the PLO, Said Hamami, a Palestinian moderate later murdered by extremists. Also in 1974 it proposed (twenty years too early to find general acceptance) talks between the PLO and Israel with a view to a two-state solution to the Arab–Israeli problem. In 1976 it argued: 'It is today beyond doubt that the Palestinians have developed a real sense of identity . . . They cannot be ignored or wished into silence.' In 1982 the Israeli attack on Beirut created, for the paper, 'a terrible unease, an anguish of soul', and in the aftermath of the massacres at Sabra and Shatila a leading article called for the resignations of the Israeli Prime Minister, Menahem Begin, and the Defence Minister, Ariel Sharon. In all this the paper's editors defied the conventional wisdoms of the majority of their readers. Letters of protest poured in; but the complainers carried on reading the paper.

No other Jewish newspaper in the Diaspora commanded comparable influence. None in Europe attained a comparable circulation. Elsewhere in the Continent the Jewish press could never recover its pre-war circulation or importance, although well-produced communal newspapers reappeared in the Netherlands, Belgium, Germany, Switzerland and Hungary.

In Istanbul, the lively *Shalom* was the last paper in the Diaspora to publish in Ladino, but only two or four pages in each issue appeared in the language. Even these were not printed in Hebrew characters. As a by-product of the romanization of the Turkish alphabet under Ataturk, printing in Hebrew characters became virtually impossible in the country. As a result Ladino was henceforth printed there in the Latin alphabet.★

Even as the Spanish language slowly disappeared among Jews at one end of the Mediterranean, however, it enjoyed a rebirth at the other. Although Jews remained formally banned from residence in Spain under the terms of the expulsion edict of 1492, a small number had entered the country during the war as refugees from Nazism and were permitted to remain. The Franco dictatorship's gradual opening to liberalization led in 1965 to legal recognition for the Jewish community in Madrid. Three years later, the country's first synagogue for nearly five centuries opened in the Spanish capital. Over the next few years, and particularly after the transition to democracy in the late 1970s, the Jewish population slowly increased, mainly as a result of immigration from North Africa. In 1990 a concordat signed by the Minister of Justice at last gave the country's Jews, by now numbering more than 10,000, a status as a religious community on a par with that of Roman Catholics. The quincentenary in 1992 of the expulsion of the Jews from Spain by Ferdinand and Isabella was commemorated with ceremonies both in Spain and in Turkey, the latter recalling the open door accorded to the Jewish refugees from Spain by the Ottoman government five centuries earlier.

In all the affluent Jewries of Western Europe a (perhaps *the*)

★ But not according to historic Spanish orthography: the letter 'q', for example, was not used in modern Turkish (allegedly Ataturk, while mulling over the details of the new alphabet, did not like the look of his own name with a 'q' and decided to ban the letter). In consequence, it was not used for romanized Ladino either. The result was that the Ladino pages of *Shalom*, and of the small number of Ladino books produced in recent years in Turkey, while easily comprehensible to any Spanish-speaker, bear a rebarbative aspect – a paradoxical outcome, given the pure preservation of the classical Castilian basis of the language.

characteristic feature of communal life in this period was fund-raising, especially for Israeli causes. The centrality of fund-raising in Jewish life was a function of growing affluence. In 1953 the Jewish National Fund (a Zionist collection agency) distributed 28,340 blue collection boxes to the estimated 82,000 Jewish house-holds in London. The 'blue box' was generally recognized as the most elementary means of contributing to Zionist funds; yet at that time no more than 30 per cent of London Jewry appeared to contribute. The 1967 crisis produced a significant increase not only in the total amounts raised but also in the numbers of contributors. The largest pro-Israeli fund-raising organization in Britain, the Joint Palestine (later Joint Israel) Appeal, was generally recognized as the most efficient mechanism for communal mobilization. In the mid-1980s it was estimated that about £48 million per annum was being collected in Britain each year for Jewish causes. About half of this was earmarked for Israel and the rest for domestic charities. Contributions to Jewish charities amounted to 3.5 per cent of all charitable giving in the country – £144 per head on average, as against £28 for the general population. Moreover, there was evidence that Jews, in addition to giving generously to specifically Jewish charities, also gave heavily to other ones. It was estimated that 15 per cent of the biggest 200 grant-making charities in Britain were established and operated by Jews. Even allowing for the general affluence of the Jewish community in the 1980s, these were impressive figures.[33]

In France too fund-raising assumed a growing importance in communal life. As prosperity returned, the number of contributors to the FSJU increased – from 8,000 in 1956 to 38,702 in 1977. In the early 1990s the Appel Juif Unifié was collecting about 120 million francs a year, of which about 40 per cent was spent in France and the remainder allocated to Israel.

By this time, however, a reaction had set in against the diversion of such a large part of communal resources to Israel. In part this reflected a change of outlook in some quarters in Israel, where the dependency relationship with the Diaspora was increasingly seen as unhealthy. In part it also reflected the diminishing size of most communities and the growing demands for welfare provision at home, particularly for the growing proportion of old people, many of them poor.

The reaction was not primarily political. Jewish money continued to flow to Israel in the 1980s in spite of the growing tendency to find fault with Israel's policies. Criticism, restricted to a small fringe in the 1970s, nevertheless grew after the Israeli adventure in Lebanon in 1982 and even more following the outbreak of the Palestinian *intifada* in December 1987. The weakness and isolation of Israel in the mid-1970s had constrained most critics from speaking their mind in public. In the 1980s, however, influential figures such as Nahum Goldmann and Pierre Mendès France condemned the policies of the Begin and Shamir governments and called for more dovish Israeli policies towards the Arabs. Acrimonious exchanges developed over the right of Diaspora Jews to express opinions on Israeli policy. Supporters of the Israeli government condemned such criticism as untoward interference. Opponents defended it as a necessary affirmation of Jewish values as they understood them. Rabbinical figures too entered the debate. Chief Rabbi Jakobovits of Britain was one of the few orthodox figures to criticize the Israeli occupation of the West Bank. In France Chief Rabbi Sirat went further: he criticized worship of the Land of Israel as idolatry. By contrast, Sirat's successor, Joseph Sitruk, offered unqualified support to the Shamir government and defended the extremist leader of Jewish settlers in Hebron, Rabbi Moshe Levinger.

Jewish criticism of the Israeli government was seen by some as evidence of a so-called 'Diaspora mentality' – an outlook supposedly conditioned primarily by the values of surrounding gentile society. In so far as the critics drew on basic liberal principles, there was no doubt something in this. But the readiness to criticize, like the growing reluctance to continue to funnel huge sums of money towards Israel at the expense of communal needs at home, also betokened a change in the nature of the 'Diaspora mentality' in the revolutionized conditions of post-1989 Europe. In the 1990s, concern for Israel's survival, until recently the governing idea in Jewish communities, was replaced by concern for the survival of the Diaspora itself.

CHAPTER ELEVEN

Jews in the New European Disorder

The renewed 'springtime of nations' in Eastern Europe in 1989 had an autumnal flavour for Jews. Except in the USSR and Hungary, few were left to participate in the rebirth of civil society. Conditions of economic and political insecurity in the following years brought about the largest wave of Jewish emigration from the region since before the First World War. The Jewish population of the continent as a result fell below 2 million for the first time since the eighteenth century. Of those who remained, the distribution shifted decisively: for the first time since the late Middle Ages there were, by the early 1990s, more Jews in Western than in Eastern Europe.

Within Jewish communities a miniature version of the larger political revolutions was enacted. Most of the old communal leaders, who had served as party-line enforcers and sometimes also as secret police informants, were ousted. In November 1988 a Hungarian Jewish Cultural Association, independent of the communist-controlled communal bodies, was founded with a membership of 600, mostly young intellectuals with a secular rather than a religious interest in Jewish matters. In Prague after the 'Velvet Revolution' of November 1989, František Kraus, who had outspokenly backed police action against student dissidents and denounced Zionist 'imperialism', was removed from the leadership of the community and returned to his old job as cook in the communal kitchen.

In the USSR an umbrella organization for all Jewish bodies, the Va'ad (Hebrew = 'committee'), was formed – the first secular

Jewish representative body since the dissolution of the Jewish Anti-Fascist Committee in 1948 and the first genuinely independent and legal Jewish organization since the 1920s. During the botched communist coup of August 1991, the Va'ad took the courageous course of proclaiming its support for the forces of democracy.

With the end of censorship, Jewish newspapers and periodicals revived. By 1991 at least fifty-five Jewish publications were appearing in the USSR, most of them in Russian. A few brave efforts were made to publish Yiddish papers, such as *Yerusholoyim d'Lita* in Vilna. They had little success: most Jews could no longer read the language. In Minsk a regular Jewish radio programme was broadcast by the local Jewish Cultural Society. These independent Jewish media breathed a radically different spirit from the communist-controlled press of the previous forty-five years. But unlike *Sovyetish Heymland*, which ceased publication in 1992, the new publications, such as the independent-minded *Di Yidishe Gas*, could no longer look to the state for subsidy and depended on income from subscriptions. Given their small potential readership, they could not hope to resurrect the politically and intellectually influential Yiddish and Hebrew press of earlier times. Many of the new publications fell by the wayside after a few issues.

Liberation from communism led to a revival of religious and cultural activity. Some Jewish men whose parents had not dared to have them circumcised at birth underwent the operation as a sign of Jewish commitment. Classes for Hebrew study were established. Hebrew summer camps for children were organized. By mid-1994 there were four yeshivas, four Jewish teachers' seminaries and four religious day schools in Moscow. St Petersburg too had four Jewish day schools. The 'Joint', free at last to operate in the USSR, made library provision a priority in its activities there and furnished a quarter of a million books, leading to the creation of eighty Jewish libraries. By 1993 the 'Joint' was spending $6 million per annum directly in the former Soviet Union, plus another $4 million through other organizations.

Other western Jewish and Israeli bodies became active in helping to revive Jewish life. In 1993 the Jewish Agency spent $10 million in the Commonwealth of Independent States. There and in East–Central Europe rabbis from the United States, Israel and even Australia were imported to fill the spiritual vacuum. The hasidic Lubavitch movement, based in New York, sent representatives to proselytize among Jews. In Moscow they took over a synagogue and founded an ultra-orthodox school. They also engaged in a bitter dispute with the Lenin Library, demanding the return of books once owned by the former Lubavitcher Rebbe which had been 'nationalized' by the Soviet authorities. The library claimed that it could not identify the books in question and refused to hand over any of its holdings, fearing that if it agreed to do so in one such case, it would be presented with an avalanche of similar demands. Also active in a kind of proselytizing among Russian Jews were representatives of American Reform Judaism, who enjoyed some limited success in a country where the movement had few indigenous roots.

The new freedoms did not lead to a religious revival. Five years after the fall of communism there were only five functioning synagogues in Moscow. No more than 1,500 of the Russian capital's quarter of a million Jews were reckoned to be religiously observant. On most Sabbaths the main synagogue was virtually empty. There was little demand for kosher meat. In spite of the intense educational effort, most Jewish children did not attend the newly established Jewish schools or Sunday classes. A father declared: 'I would never dream of putting my son in a Hebrew day school. Why should I? It would only mark my son for life and make him even more of a target.'[1] Meanwhile, the departure of many of the remaining orthodox Jews and Zionists drained the community of much of its life-blood.

The switch to complete freedom of emigration was the most consequential change in the Jewish position in Russia and its former dependencies. In 1989, 85,089 Soviet Jews were allowed to emigrate, as against only 22,403 the previous year. In 1990 the number of departures reached an all-time record, 229,510, of whom 185,227 went to Israel. This was a panic exodus by a mass of people who feared that, in the unsettled condition of the collapsing Soviet empire, prospects, particularly for Jews, were darkening. Unlike the majority of Jews who had left since 1977, most of this wave of emigrants went to the only country that had a completely open-door policy to them: Israel. The choice of destination was not entirely voluntary. From mid-1988 Soviet Jewish emigrants with Israeli entry visas were required to fly direct to Israel, with brief stopovers in Bucharest, thus virtually eliminating the possibility of 'dropping out'. From October 1991 regular direct flights of immigrants from the Soviet Union to Israel were permitted for the first time. These eventually left from many provincial cities and republican capitals – even from Biro-bidzhan, a final puncturing of the region's inflated pretensions to compete with Israel as a Jewish homeland.

Whereas the emigration of the 1970s had been composed dispro-portionately of young people, that of the early 1990s included large numbers of the aged and infirm, imposing heavy burdens on the Israeli welfare system. Soon it seemed as if the entire Jewish population of the country might be gone within a few years. In December 1990 alone, 34,000 immigrants arrived in Israel – the highest figure for a single month in the history of the state. In 1991 the number of Jewish emigrants from the USSR/CIS declined slightly to 194,715, of whom 148,000 went to Israel. By 1994 half a million had arrived in Israel since 1989, though the outward flow had slowed to about 100,000 a year, of whom about 60,000 settled in Israel (see Table 3, p. 200).

Of those who went elsewhere, the largest number, more than 200,000 between 1989 and 1994, moved to the USA. Even more would probably have gone there had it not been for the United States's abolition in 1989 of automatic recognition of Soviet emi-grants as 'refugees'. Informal understandings among the Israeli and American administrations and Jewish welfare organizations placed a ceiling of between 40,000 and 50,000 per annum on the number of Soviet Jewish arrivals in the USA.

After Israel and the USA, the next-largest recipient of Soviet Jews was Germany. In the aftermath of German reunification in 1990, an estimated 20,000 Soviet Jews emigrated there. The Jewish population of Berlin grew to nearly 10, 000, the highest level since the war. In communal elections in the city in March 1993, candidates published pamphlets in both German and Russian. A further 25,000 Soviet Jews were meanwhile reported to have applied for German visas. The readiness of the German government to admit such large numbers of Russian Jewish refugees produced angry reactions in Israel. In mid-1993 members of the immigration committee of the Knesset called on the German government to 'make it difficult' for Jews from the CIS to emigrate to Germany. That representatives of the Jewish state should call on Germany, of all countries, to bar entry to Jewish refugees seemed bizarre. The German ambassador told the committee candidly that the Jewish people would not countenance a German refusal to admit ex-Soviet Jews.[2] The flow of migrants continued; in June 1994 the lay head of the main Moscow synagogue settled in Germany.

Estimates of the size of potential further Jewish emigration from the former USSR varied widely. A study of potential emigrants published in early 1993 concluded that more than half of the remaining Jewish population might leave. Economic reasons were given by 59 per cent of those questioned, whereas 'ethnic-political' ones were mentioned by only 33 per cent. Only 16 per cent expressed a definite wish to go to Israel, whereas 23 per cent said they were planning to go elsewhere – mainly to the United States.[3] The fluid and uncertain situation in Russia, however, frightened even many Jews who did not intend to leave. A woman translator, for example, asked in 1992 whether she felt in danger as a Jew, replied: 'First of all, I feel threatened as a democratically oriented person of the intelligentsia. But I know for sure that if something does happen the first group threatened will be Jews.'[4]

The sudden, massive influx of Soviet Jews led inevitably to difficulties of absorption in Israel, where many immigrants were reduced to menial occupations: former concert violinists became street musicians and teachers became domestic servants. The Israeli public reaction soon changed from ecstatic rejoicing to resentment and even a questioning of Israel's policy of open Jewish immigration – long regarded as the very *raison d'être* of the state. Pressure on housing led to grumbling by veteran Israelis that the newcomers were being given unfair priority. In 1994 a government minister, Ora Namir, a member of the Labour Party, which owed its return to power in 1992 in large part to heavy support from Soviet Jewish immigrants, complained that Israel was being lumbered with problem cases, one-parent families, the aged and disabled persons. Although the statistical basis for the remark was disputed, it mirrored a certain public mood.

Absorption difficulties in Israel and partial stabilization in Russia ended the panic outflow in 1991. Thereafter more orderly emigration continued at a historically high rate. The numbers seeking entry to countries other than Israel once again increased. In 1992 only 64,441 immigrants from the ex-USSR arrived in Israel, while about 50,000 went to other countries. Several thousand found life in Israel so difficult that they returned to the USSR/CIS. Queues of Russian Jews formed outside the American consulate in Tel Aviv seeking US immigration visas. Some travelled to other countries and sought recognition as refugees, occasionally producing ugly incidents. In December 1991 Dutch police conducted a dawn raid on an immigrant hostel at Eindhoven, where they arrested forty-three ex-Soviet Jews, all recent arrivals from Israel. Some resisted arrest and refused to dress. They were deported back to Israel still barefoot and in their pyjamas. The Dutch government defended its action on the ground that 'these people didn't satisfy the conditions required to be granted refugee status on humanitarian grounds'.[5]

As during the earlier wave of Soviet Jewish emigration in the 1970s, the push out of the USSR seemed in many cases greater than the pull of Israel. The major cause of the exodus was by most accounts economic rather than political. Another was the reluctance of many young men to obey conscription calls. True, many of the emigrants complained bitterly of antisemitism and there were frequent rumours that pogroms were imminent. The actions of Pamyat and of other nationalist organizations frightened many Jews, but beyond minor incidents, such as the smashing of windows at the Moscow Central Synagogue, there were few serious antisemitic outbursts in Russia in the early post-communist years.

Surveys in Russia in 1990 and 1992 suggested that only a minority of fewer than 10 per cent of the population expressed strongly antisemitic attitudes.

In 1993, however, as the Russian economic crisis deepened, a worsening trend became apparent. There was an arson attack on a synagogue in Moscow. The anti-Jewish blood libel was revived with the support of some sections of the Russian Orthodox Church. Most disturbing was the success in parliamentary elections in December 1993 of the ultra-nationalist party led by Vladimir Zhirinovsky, which succeeded in garnering 24 per cent of the popular vote. The phenomenon was puzzling most especially because Zhirinovsky himself was reported to be of Jewish origin.* In spite of such developments, however, many assimilated Jews, particularly those married to non-Jews, felt no particular desire to leave. A sixty-nine-year-old woman painter from a family of Jewish intellectuals told a Western reporter that in spite of years of persecution, some of it petty, some of it vicious, she mused about leaving but did not seriously intend to do so:

> Deep in my soul I have the feeling I am not Russian, though we grew up on Russian culture. Being Jewish was a fact, but not much discussed . . . For me Moscow is the capital, the center, and it's important to me that I live here. If I emigrate, I couldn't live in a second-rate city in one-storey America or in some grassy English province. Here I feel I'm someone; there, I'm nobody.[6]

Events in Ukraine, Belarus and other former Soviet republics in the aftermath of the breakup of the USSR mirrored those in Russia. In Moldova, formerly Soviet Moldavia, the bulk of the Jewish population was evacuated to Israel after civil war broke out between Russian and Romanian ethnic groups. In Ukraine militant

---

* During a visit to the USA in November 1994, Zhirinovsky specifically denied that his father had been Jewish. There is no doubt, however, that Zhirinovsky had participated actively in the Moscow Jewish communal organization in the 1980s. Perhaps he had regarded this activity as some form of penetration of the enemy camp. More likely he had, in fact, considered himself as Jewish but later renounced and turned against that part of his identity, seeing an opportunity for wider acclaim as a Russian nationalist.

nationalists, drawing on a historic inventory of antisemitic doctrine, held public meetings in cities that still had large Jewish populations, such as Kiev and Lvov, and denounced the 'Jewish mafia' who, they alleged, were ruining the country. But in the general election in the spring of 1994 only three members of the extreme-rightist Ukrainian National Assembly were elected to the Rada (parliament) and other right-wing groups also performed poorly. At the same time four Jews were elected. Successive independent Ukrainian governments after 1991 took demonstrative actions to reassure Jews: among these were the establishment of friendly diplomatic relations with Israel.

In Poland a tiny community of orthodox Jews, led in the mid-1980s by two young men, Staszek Krajewski and Konstanty Gebert (a journalist on the Solidarity newspaper, *Gazeta Wyborcza*, who wrote under the pen-name David Warshawski), emerged from the shadows and re-established a fragment of Jewish religious life in Warsaw. A small independent paper, *Dos Yiddishe Vort*, began to appear with both Yiddish and Polish sections. Under an agreement signed with the Polish government in 1993, the 'Joint' undertook to spend nearly $1 million per annum on welfare and educational purposes in the country, while the government granted the organization tax-free status.

In the campaign for the first round of the Polish presidential election in 1990 Lech Wałęsa accused advisers to his rival, Prime Minister Tadeusz Mazowiecki, of 'hiding their Jewish origins'. For his part Wałęsa declared: 'I am a full-blooded Pole with documents going back to my ancestors to prove it.' The remark provoked widespread criticism. In the campaign for the second round he apologized: 'I stumbled on this. I crashed into anti-semitism.'[7] After his success in the election Wałęsa evinced remorse. He established a special council on Polish–Jewish relations, visited Israel and made a number of conciliatory statements. In 1994, however, the Jewish issue came to the fore again, this time in connection with the commemoration of the anti-German Warsaw rising of the Polish underground fifty years earlier. An article in *Gazeta Wyborcza* by Michal Cichy, noting that Jews had been murdered by Polish nationalists in the course of the rising, evoked a stream of protests against what some saw as a defamation of Polish patriots.

The Jewish question thus continued to occupy a place in Polish public discourse altogether out of proportion with the minuscule size of the remaining Jewish community. Konstanty Gebert commented wryly in 1991: 'If we only look at the numbers involved, the Buddhist question in Poland ought to be more prominent than the Jewish one, since there are more Buddhists than Jews in the country.'[8]

In 1991, with the Auschwitz convent affair still unresolved, the Roman Catholic hierarchy in Poland issued an unprecedented pastoral letter condemning antisemitism. It was read out from the pulpit in every parish in Poland. The document, the most far-reaching of its kind issued thus far, was nevertheless couched in defensive terms – as if by way of apology to those who still denounced the 'Zydo-Komuna':

> With the Jewish nation we Poles are linked by special ties ... We are aware that many of our compatriots still nurse in their memory the harm and injustice inflicted by post-war communist rule, in which people of Jewish origin participated as well. But we must admit that the source of inspiration for their actions cannot be seen in their Jewish origin or in their religion but came from the communist ideology from which Jews too suffered much injustice. We also express our sincere regret at all cases of antisemitism that have occurred on Polish soil.

How deep was the transformation represented by such statements? Whereas in 1975, according to an opinion poll, 41 per cent of Poles had harboured negative views of Jews, only 20 per cent did so by 1990. That a change of consciousness was taking place within Polish Catholicism was undeniable; no less so was the existence of a significant rearguard of old-style Catholic anti-semitism, whose most important exponent was the Polish Primate, Cardinal Glemp.

The few remaining Jews were by no means fully reassured that antisemitism was a thing of the past. Szymon Rudnicki, Professor of Polish History at Warsaw University, noted in 1990:

Antisemitism is conspicuous on the streets of Polish towns. Walls are covered with epithets such as 'Jude raus'. The word 'Jew' or the Star-of-David sign are painted on election posters . . . There have been more violent incidents too. During a performance given by a Jewish ensemble from the Soviet Union, a gas bomb exploded in the theatre hall, and the bus used by the actors was set on fire. This took place in Kielce, the site of the 1946 pogrom. A similar incident could have taken place in any other country, but what was particularly disturbing in this case was the silence of the bulk of the press and the absence of any condemnation.[9]

How can one explain the persistence of antisemitism in a country that was virtually without Jews? A residue of Christian anti-Jewish teaching was one cause. Another was simple ignorance: a survey in 1992 found that 10 per cent of Poles thought there were between 4 and 7 million Jews in the country; another 25 per cent put the number at between 750,000 and 3.5 million (the true number was around 6,000).[10] Adam Michnik, the Jewish editor-in-chief of *Gazeta Wyborcza*, argued that 'when anti-Semitic opinions are expressed in Poland, Jews are not the issue, whatever the authors of the opinions themselves may think. The question is whether there will or will not be a Polish democracy.'[11]

Elsewhere in Eastern Europe, antisemitic themes remained part of the armoury of extreme nationalism, particularly in Romania, where the right-wing press enjoyed a considerable circulation. Romanian Jews expressed alarm, mindful of the strong official and social antisemitism that had marked the country's entire independent non-communist history. Chief Rabbi Rosen declared in February 1990: 'Our killers are returning.'[12] In April 1991 the parliament stood for a minute of silence in honour of the wartime pro-Nazi dictator, Marshal Ion Antonescu. There was much talk of a 'red-brown' coalition between former communists and ultra-nationalists; the glue for such an alliance, it was said, would be antisemitism. In the event, elections in 1992 led to the return of the ruling Democratic National Salvation Front, but it was dependent in parliament on the support of ultra-nationalist factions such as the antisemitic Greater Romania Party. That the primary victims of Romanian nationalists remained Hungarians and

Gypsies gave Jews only limited reassurance. A renewed wave of emigration reduced the country's Jewish population to 10,000 by 1994.

In the first free elections in post-communist Hungary in 1990 Jews gave strong support to the Free Democrats, a liberal, centrist party with a heavily urban, intellectual constituency. Several of its candidates were Jews, one of them a rabbi, Tamás Raj. Antisemitic slogans and symbols were scrawled on Free Democrats' election posters. The victors were the right-wing Democratic Forum. The new government pursued a cautious, conservative policy and eschewed any form of antisemitism. A faction of the ruling party, however, led by the playwright and novelist István Csurka, engaged in outspoken anti-Jewish agitation. In a radio speech, Csurka called on Hungarians to 'wake up' to the threat from a 'dwarf minority' – by which he was generally understood to mean Jews.[13] But the traditional peasant base for antisemitism in Hungary had been weakened. A survey in May 1991 found that 67 per cent of the population viewed Jews favourably, while only 12 per cent had negative attitudes towards them.[14]

Nevertheless, the Jewish issue continued to rumble ominously in the background of Hungarian politics. Controversy was fanned by an interview given by the Chief Rabbi of Budapest, György Landeszmann, in which he observed indiscreetly that had it not been for the role of Jews in Hungarian culture, the Hungarians would have been 'left with only their wide peasants' pants'.[15] In 1993 Csurka founded a movement known as 'Hungarian Way', which accused the country's president, Árpád Goncz, of being an 'agent of Tel Aviv'.[16] In the 1994 general election, however, the Jewish issue did not re-emerge. The extreme right, represented by Csurka and Isabella Király (known as 'mother of the skinheads'), was annihilated at the polls. Most Jews continued to support the Free Democrats, but they were not perturbed by the return to power of the ex-communist Socialist Party, which embraced the free market and pursued a consensual style of government.

In Slovakia a sign of the revival of ultra-right nationalism in July 1990 was the unveiling of a plaque in memory of the wartime fascist leader, Father Josef Tiso, in the town of Banovce nad

Bebravou, where he had been parish priest. Among those attending the ceremony was Cardinal Korec. The plaque was removed a few days later after protests. But in October 1991 another was erected in Tiso's birthplace, Velka Bytca. The breakup of the Czechoslovak Federation in January 1993 heightened the anxiety of Slovak Jews. Fedor Gal, the Jewish leader of Public Against Violence, the democratic anti-Communist movement in Slovakia, felt obliged to leave Bratislava for Prague, complaining of antisemitic incitement against himself and his family.

In the Czech lands, faddish interest in all things Jewish developed in the wake of the fall of communism. Manifestations of this ranged from a pop group called 'Shalom' to the more lofty cultural aspirations of the Franz Kafka Society of Prague. Czech political culture had little room for antisemitism; latent xenophobia found an outlet in hostility to Gypsies. Anti-Jewish ideas, however, were given a forum in the newspaper *Politika*, founded in January 1991, which accused President Václav Havel of being an agent of the 'international Zionist conspiracy' and published a list of 100 prominent Czechs, purportedly all Jews, who controlled the country. The paper was eventually closed down by order of the public prosecutor.[17]

Of greater significance was an untoward dispute that broke out over the issue of restoration of Jewish property rights in the country. Opponents of restitution feared that the return of property formerly owned by Jews might open the door to claims by the former German population of Czechoslovakia. A parliamentary vote in early 1994 rejected a bill to return synagogues, communal buildings, cemeteries and other property, including the treasures of the Prague Jewish museum, to the Jewish communities from whom they had been confiscated, first by the Nazis and subsequently by the communists. President Havel denounced the decision as 'undignified' and 'insulting'.[18] After further controversy, a bill was passed in April 1994 facilitating the restitution to Jews of property confiscated by the Nazis. This did not, however, cover collectively owned property such as communal institutions or synagogues. The apparent reason was fear of setting another precedent that might lead to the return of the extensive lands once owned by the Roman Catholic Church. Following bitter Jewish protests and further negotiations, the government finally consented in May 1994 to restore most of the property. But by February 1995 only one-third of the agreed list of 202 properties had been returned, including only one (the Jewish museum) of the eighteen listed buildings in Prague.

The revolutions of 1989–91 cast light on some hitherto hidden corners of Jewish life in Eastern Europe. One such was the tiny Jewish community of Albania. In 'the first atheist state in the world', as the country's communist ruler Enver Hoxha proclaimed it in 1967, Jewish ritual, like all religious worship, was banned. There were no rabbis after the Second World War and by the 1980s the only remnants of Jewish practice were circumcision of males (in hospitals rather than religious ceremonies), observance of the Yom Kippur fast and clandestine festival celebrations at which participants ate traditional sweetmeats.[19] Following the overthrow of communism, the country's Jews suddenly found themselves free to leave. Given the desperate economic situation in this, the poorest country in Europe, most took the opportunity to move to Israel or the United States.

In neighbouring Bulgaria, the 5,000 Jews who remained following the large exodus upon the establishment of Israel had been able to maintain some of their synagogues and communal institutions, but the absence of a kosher butcher had compelled the few orthodox families to eat no meat save chicken for many years. After 1989, 3,000 or so Jews left the country, mostly for Israel. In spite of the diminutive size of the remaining community, Jews nevertheless played a role in the country's political evolution: six Jews were elected to parliament in the elections of 1990, three for the ex-communist Socialist Party and three for the opposition.

The outbreak of the Yugoslav civil war in 1991 brought a deterioration of the hitherto relatively satisfactory condition of that country's Jews. Under Tito the Jewish community of 12,000 (all that remained of the 71,000 Jews in pre-war Yugoslavia) had enjoyed religious freedom and had never suffered from antisemitic political campaigns like those that afflicted much of the rest of Eastern Europe at one stage or another under communist rule.

Tito was friendly with the president of the World Jewish Congress, Nahum Goldmann, and for a while seemed disposed to mildly amicable relations with Israel, though he joined the Soviet Union and its allies in breaking ties with the Jewish state after the 1967 war.

The collapse of the Yugoslav federation and the return of the greater part of its population to collective loyalties based on ethnicity and religion reopened the Jewish question in several painful ways. Serbia and Croatia each sought to impugn the other by drawing attention to collaborationist and antisemitic episodes during the Second World War. In the case of the Croats, some of the mud stuck. President Franjo Tudjman was widely condemned for the strangely ambivalent book he had written some years earlier that appeared to question the historicity of the mass murder of European Jewry. Leading members of the Jewish communities in Zagreb and Belgrade found themselves drawn into unedifying disputes over the extent to which Serbs and Croats had collaborated in Nazi genocide. The angry exchanges acquired a special contemporary significance because of the frequent comparisons in the Western media between Nazi atrocities and the 'ethnic cleansing' committed by all sides in the civil war. In Bosnia the 1,300 Jews of Sarajevo, a small but old-established community dating back to the expulsions from the Iberian peninsula at the end of the fifteenth century, found themselves no longer in a multi-ethnic society but in a predominantly Muslim state that looked for succour and inspiration to countries such as Pakistan and Saudi Arabia. Although not subject to any discrimination, Sarajevan Jews felt insecure and fearful. Most were evacuated in a special operation organized by Jewish welfare bodies. Some went to England; others to Israel. By 1994 only a handful of Jews remained in the city.

Overall, fears of a major revival of antisemitism in post-communist Europe turned out to have been exaggerated. In spite of the severe economic difficulties of the transition to a market economy, and notwithstanding the attempts by populist elements to revive anti-Jewish feeling, public opinion seemed to be relatively unmoved. A survey conducted in Poland, Czechoslovakia and Hungary in 1991 found that Poles were the most prone to hostility to Jews: 40 per cent said they would not want Jews living in their neighbourhood, as against 23 per cent of Czechoslovaks (more Slovaks than Czechs) and 17 per cent of Hungarians. But in all three cases hostility to other groups, such as Gypsies, Arabs and blacks, was much higher.[20] Although the post-1989 freedoms produced some disturbing public outbursts, antisemitism seemed to be in a long secular decline. The traditional role of the Jew as a hate figure in Eastern Europe seemed at last to be waning – too late for most Jews, who had either been killed or fled to happier climes.

The overthrow of the communist regimes led to profound changes in attitudes towards the past. Suddenly the entire modern history of the former Soviet empire was written afresh and the role played by each country's government and people during the years of Nazi occupation was reconsidered. In Hungary the liberal Christian political scientist István Bibó had written an essay in 1948, speaking of the moral bankruptcy of Hungarian society and urging Hungarians to acknowledge a share of responsibility for the fate of Hungarian Jews. At that time his was a lone voice. During the communist years the issue had been largely swept under the carpet. In April 1994, however, the Hungarian president, Árpád Goncz, registered the change of national mood in a moving statement at a ceremony commemorating the deportation fifty years earlier of Hungarian Jews to the death camps: 'On this side of Europe we are still waiting for an honest reckoning. And until we look into our own eyes, we wait in vain for inner peace and essential purification.'[21]

The Jews of Western Europe in the post-Cold War era continued on their path of slow demographic decline and assimilation. The tolerance of the open society rather than ethnic or religious hostility seemed to pose the main threat to collective Jewish survival. At the same time, however, a revival of the far right and accompanying manifestations of antisemitism threatened Jews more directly. The radical–right revival took several forms, ranging from the rise of new political parties to juvenile hooliganism and the chanting, particularly in Italy, England and the Netherlands, of antisemitic slogans at football matches.

Neo-Nazism in Germany, hitherto a marginal and politically insignificant phenomenon, assumed more substantial form after the country's reunification in October 1990. Gangs of unemployed teenage louts roamed through cities in both East and West Germany, attacking foreigners, burning immigrant hostels and reviving Nazi slogans and symbols. Although the primary targets of the violence were foreign immigrants, particularly Turks and Kurds, Jews were also threatened: in 1993 there were 656 anti-Jewish incidents in Germany, mainly desecrations of cemeteries and memorials.

Public opinion polls in Germany in the 1980s and early 1990s indicated a continuing decline in antisemitism, although a residue remained. A poll in 1992 showed that only 4 per cent of Germans held 'the Jews in general' to blame for the death of Jesus. At the same time 15 per cent (26 per cent of Catholics) held 'the Jews of the time' responsible. More than a third of those questioned declared that Jews 'have too much influence in the world'. Altogether, 13 per cent of Germans manifested strong antisemitic tendencies. The tendency was stronger in the West (16 per cent) than in the East (4 per cent) and among Christian Democrats and CSU supporters (17 per cent) than among Social Democrats (11 per cent) or Greens (5 per cent).

Sixty-two per cent now called for a 'Schlussstrich' (drawing a line) over the Nazi past. Here too a breakdown was revealing: two-thirds of West Germans answered 'yes', compared with fewer than half of East Germans. More than two-thirds of people aged over seventy said 'yes', as against a little over half of adults under thirty. The less-educated tended to answer affirmatively much more than those with higher education.[22] The expression in 1993 of support for a 'Schlussstrich' by a politician, Steffen Heitmann, cost him the Christian Democrats' nomination for the German presidency.[23] On this point a dangerous gulf was thus revealed between the polite conventions of political discourse in Germany and the real state of public feeling.

In spite of the violence in the streets, the overwhelming majority of Germans registered their support for democratic parties at the ballot-box. In the general election of 1994 the neo-Nazi Republican Party, led by a former SS officer, which had earlier won limited support in state elections, was trounced, receiving only a derisory level of support. Anti-Jewish themes did not emerge as issues in the election, in spite of the fact that the two most prominent candidates of Jewish origin, Gregor Gysi and the writer Stefan Heym, ran on the list of the PDS, successor to the former communist party. Both were elected.

By contrast with the failure of the German neo-Nazis at the polls, Jörg Haider's Freedom Party of Austria emerged as a serious contender for power: in 1990 it won 16.6 per cent of the vote and thirty-three parliamentary seats, and in the following general election in 1994 it performed even better, raising its share of the vote to 22 per cent. These results were disturbing, although some observers suggested that the strong radical-right performance was largely a protest vote against the grand coalition of the two main Austrian parties. Coming as it did, however, when Austria was seeking to repair its image as a democratic state in the wake of the Waldheim affair, the success of Haider's party was a disconcerting setback.

Italy was the only West European country where the extreme right succeeded in entering government in this period. The collapse of the centrist political parties as a result of the *tangentopoli* corruption scandal led in May 1994 to the formation of a coalition government that, for the first time since the war, included neo-fascists. Their presence in the Berlusconi coalition disquieted many non-Jews as well as Jews. The President of the European Union Commission, Jacques Delors, spoke of the 'rage in his heart' at comments by Gianfranco Fini, the neo-fascist leader.[24] Arrigo Levi, the former editor of *La Stampa* and one of Italy's most distinguished journalists, took particular issue with Fini's characterization of Mussolini's anti-Jewish laws as 'an error that led to a horror'. Levi argued that Fini's party 'has steadfastly refused to examine the tragic consequences of its acknowledged Fascist ideological roots'.[25]

Other elements in the new political constellation in Italy also gave rise to concern. The President of the Chamber of Deputies, Irene Pivetti, who was a prominent member of the Northern League, another partner in the government, attracted criticism for comments after an antisemitic incident in Milan. She declared the episode a 'witchhunt hysteria' and 'a pretext to give vent to ridiculous laments about resurgent antisemitism and to justify the susceptibilities of bands of young Jews with itchy fists'.[26] Some of her fellow politicians furnished their own 'pretexts', as when the Minister of Labour, a member of the small Christian Democrat Centre Party, complained that 'Jewish high finance' in New York was responsible for the fall in value of the lira – a remark that necessitated an apology to the Italian Chief Rabbi.[27]

Such lapses notwithstanding, there was little evidence that anti-semitism struck much of a chord in Italian society. The country's Jewish community of 31,000 felt secure and its chief concerns were not external hostility but internal decline and the dimming prospects for collective survival.

In France too the extreme right made significant gains in the late 1980s and early 1990s. For a time Jean-Marie Le Pen's Front National surpassed the traditional 10 per cent limit of support for the extreme right and overtook the Communist Party at the polls. Le Pen, like extreme rightists elsewhere in Europe, sought to exploit anti-immigrant feeling. His attitude towards Jews was one of coded hostility. While denying that he was an antisemite, he suggested that the gas chambers at Auschwitz were merely 'a detail' of the Second World War.

Although anti-Jewish terrorism in France died down by the early 1990s, lesser forms of violence and abuse continued. According to the French Ministry of the Interior, 372 anti-Jewish incidents of various kinds were reported in 1990. One in particular horrified the country: the desecration of the old Jewish cemetery in Carpentras, near Avignon, in May 1990. This outrage, in which a recently interred corpse was removed from the grave and abused, prompted a demonstration by 200,000 people, headed by President Mitterrand and including representatives of all political parties save the Front National.

No less disturbing than the incident itself was the readiness of some intellectuals to rationalize and excuse it. In the 1970s and 1980s the Palestinian cause had led some on the left to justify or extenuate the use of terror; now the violence of neo-Nazis too found sympathetic interpreters. After Carpentras, for example, the French sociologist Paul Yonnet complained of the exaggerated attention being paid to antisemitism. 'It is the Jews,' he said, 'who ghettoize themselves in a way that is racist towards non-Jews; they do not accept exogamous marriages; they keep their schools for their own children.'[28]

In spite of such episodes, the overall standing of Jews in French society had measurably improved since the end of the war. In 1947 the leading French public opinion poll, IFOP, had asked a representative sample, '*Les juifs sont-ils des Français comme les autres?*' Thirty-seven per cent said yes. The question was repeated over the years and on each occasion the proportion answering affirmatively increased, reaching 65 per cent by 1977 and 94 per cent in 1987.[29] A public opinion poll in early 1994 reported that 81 per cent of those questioned said they would have no problem in voting for a Jewish candidate for the presidency (40 per cent of Front National supporters, however, declared themselves hostile to any Jewish candidate).

In the United Kingdom, as in France and Italy, the position of Jews in society seemed more secure than ever. A survey in 1993 found that Jews were the least disliked ethnic minority in Britain. Only 8 per cent of those interviewed said that Jews had 'too much influence' and the same percentage said Jews did not behave in an agreeable manner. Twelve per cent said they would prefer not to have a Jewish neighbour, but that compared with 65 per cent who said they did not want Gypsies next door.[30]

British Jews, like those elsewhere in Western Europe, were more preoccupied by internal signs of weakness than by external threats – and with reason, since almost everywhere the knots binding Jews to Judaism and to Jewish communities seemed to be weakening. Statistics that seemed to point in a different direction were comforting, but misleading. In the case of Anglo-Jewry, for example, it was sometimes argued that high figures for synagogue membership indicated a strong continuing commitment to

Judaism. Eighty-eight per cent of Jews in the country were indeed estimated to belong to a synagogue. But this was probably an over-estimate, since the statisticians' net failed to catch some marginal Jews who did not belong to synagogues and who were, as a result, not counted as Jews at all. Many British Jews would echo the words of the French Jewish journalist Jean Daniel: 'There is no Jewish institution at the moment with which I feel I can identify.'[31] Moreover, for many Jews synagogue membership was little more than nominal, an insurance policy for Jewish burial. Beyond all that, the global membership figure concealed important shifts of balance within the community. The 'central orthodox' main-stream, in particular, was declining (in London, for example, from 72 to 58 per cent of synagogue members between 1970 and 1990) as affiliation polarized to the benefit of the strict orthodox on the right and the Liberal and Reform congregations on the left.

More telling than membership as a gauge of commitment were other measures such as attendance at services. Some synagogues in Britain were unable to muster a *minyan* for weekday services except by the expedient of building old-people's homes close by. More and more of those who attended orthodox synagogues on the Sabbath broke the religious law by driving there. Jewish butcher-shops grew steadily fewer as observance of the laws of *kashrut* declined.

By 1992 the largest grouping of Jewish congregations in the country, the United Synagogue, was in serious financial difficulties. A report by Stanley Kalms, a wealthy businessman, concluded that the body was £9 million in debt and faced insolvency. He warned that the United Synagogue's 'market share' of the commu-nity was in decline. His report called for various reforms and economies, including reductions in the pensions that had been promised to retired ministers. Venturing on to treacherous ground, Kalms made some tentative proposals that smacked of doctrinal reform – in particular, regarding the role of women in the commu-nity. The recently appointed Chief Rabbi, Jonathan Sacks, wel-comed the report, though he said it was 'a lay document couched in terms of finance, management and marketing' and lacked 'a spiritual dimension'.[32]

The aspect that proved to be most troublesome was the issue of women's participation, which, once raised, acquired a life of its own. On the one hand, the United Synagogue's chief competitors for 'market share', the Reform and Liberal movements, had already, like their counterparts in the United States, begun to ordain women rabbis – one of whom, Julia Neuberger, had become a well-known national figure. On the other hand, Sacks, like his predecessor, was determined to keep Anglo-Jewry within the confines of orthodoxy as it was understood in the greater part of the Jewish world. That precluded an equal role for women in communal prayer. Women members of the United Synagogue, however, were beginning to demand a greater role in religious life and pressure mounted, particularly for their increased participation in the synagogue service. Sacks commissioned a review of the issue which took two years to complete. When finally published in 1994, it noted widespread dissatisfaction among women while making modest proposals for change. Four-fifths of the women surveyed, for example, opposed use of the *mehitzah* (partition to divide men from women in synagogue) – regarded as *de rigueur* by orthodoxy. Sacks found himself in an awkward dilemma, since he did not dare to offend the ultra-orthodox right. Eventually he reaffirmed the traditional orthodox rejection of any significant role for women in public prayer. As a result, some feminists began holding all-women services in the synagogue of a sympathetic moderate orthodox rabbi in north London.

The main lay body of Anglo-Jewry, the Board of Deputies of British Jews, also underwent severe internal frictions and, like the United Synagogue, seemed to be suffering from institutional senility and inability to adapt to a changed social order. Under lacklustre leadership during the 1980s, the Board steadily lost influence. Its democratic basis, often gerrymandered by communal politicians, became increasingly unattractive to the new plutocracy who dominated the community. Efforts to 'reform' the Board (i.e. reduce its democratic character and parliamentary forms) collapsed in 1994. As it prepared to vacate its premises at Woburn House in central London, the Board's prestige seemed at a lower ebb than at any point since its formation in the eighteenth century.

A commentator noted that the 'funding fathers' now in any case bypassed the board as the 'Quangoization of Anglo-Jewry' proceeded apace.[33]

The new communal élite owed their positions neither to family connections nor to election but, American-style, to money. Wealthy businessmen such as Lord (David) Young, Stanley Kalms and the millionaire bookmaker Cyril Stein had become the new communal power brokers. Among the fifty or so Jews whose names figured on a list drawn up in 1994 of the 'richest 500' people in Britain, few belonged to the old patriciate. Apart from the Rothschilds, most were descendants of Russian-Jewish immigrants of the post-1881 period. Several were first-generation immigrants, among them the Hungarian-born financier George Soros, Leon Tamman, a Sudan-born industrialist, and the brothers Sami and David Shamoon, natives of Iraq.[34]

In France too the old communal élite had yielded to the pressure of social change although there the participation and commitment of North African Jews helped maintain more democratic control over communal affairs. Internal religious conflict continued between advocates of old-style laxity and a resurgent neo-orthodoxy. The latter was represented by the Tunisian-born Chief Rabbi, Joseph Sitruk, elected in 1987, who was supported by Benny Cohen, president of the Paris Consistoire from 1990. Their efforts provoked a backlash from more moderate elements. Such disputes also took on a socio-ethnic aspect: the orthodox militants were mainly of North African origin, while the more moderate elements were mainly Ashkenazi. The Sephardim had the weight of numbers on their side: although only about half the community overall was Sephardi, they were estimated by the 1990s to constitute as many as 80 per cent of religiously identifying Jews.

By the 1990s France had moved away from the centralizing tradition of Jacobin uniformity and embraced a new doctrine of multiculturalism. The origins of this change can be traced back to President Giscard d'Estaing's speech in Brittany in early 1977, affirming 'that there is no contradiction between the desire to be a fully-fledged French citizen and the aspiration to perpetuate traditions, customs and even a particular local or regional culture. French unity need not necessarily throttle and erase the naturally variegated character of our nation.'[35]

At some levels Jews found that the new doctrine opened opportunities for collective expression. One example was the new phenomenon of Jewish radio programmes or even radio stations. In 1993 three such stations were broadcasting in Paris and there were more in Marseilles, Lyons, Strasbourg and other French cities. In Britain, perhaps because of the continued importance of the *Jewish Chronicle*, there seemed to be less demand for Jewish radio, apart from the long-running 'You Don't Have to be Jewish . . .' programme, broadcast weekly in London.

More important was the expansion of Jewish education. Here, uniquely, a quantifiable increase in Jewish identification had taken place since the war in much of Western Europe.

Until the 1960s nearly all Jewish children in Western Europe were educated in secular, state schools. There were only two significant exceptions: the first was Antwerp, with its large hasidic community, where about 80 per cent of Jewish children attended state-aided Jewish schools. The second was Strasbourg. In Alsace and Lorraine, unlike the rest of France, confessional schools still received state financial support. As a result, more than 80 per cent of Jewish children in Strasbourg attended Jewish schools. In Britain the modern orthodox Jewish public (i.e. private) school, Carmel College, was founded in 1948 by Rabbi Kopul Rosen. A few public schools, for example Clifton, had separate Jewish houses, although these had mostly disappeared by the 1990s. Otherwise, such Jewish schools as existed in Britain in the early post-war period were sponsored mainly by strictly orthodox sections of the community and by the Zionist Federation. These attracted only a small segment of the community. In 1954 Jewish day schools in Britain were attended by a total of 4,400 pupils.

By 1991 the number had reached 16,000, representing about a third of the Jewish school-age population. The Jewish school system in France also grew significantly. In the early 1950s there had been fewer than 500 children in Jewish day schools there. By 1993 there were 21,000 — about a quarter of the age group. In

Britain about two-thirds of the day-school pupils were at the pre-
secondary level; in France, nearly half attended secondary schools.

Yet in spite of this expansion, all-Jewish schools were still
attended by only a minority of Jewish children in the 1990s. For
the majority, Jewish education was generally limited to a few
hours of Sunday school each week and ended with the bar or
bat mitzvah. Large numbers received no religious instruction at all.
Orthodox leaders laid great stress on the growth of Jewish education, seeing in it a basis for optimism that the decline in Jewish
observance might be arrested. The hope was probably misplaced:
a high percentage of Catholic children in Britain were educated in
Church schools but there seemed to be little relationship between
attendance at such schools and subsequent levels of religious observance, which, as in the case of all faiths in Britain, declined
precipitously between the 1960s and 1990s.

In any case, the greater openness to cultural differences still had
its limits both in France and in Britain. Jewish civil servants in
France were obliged to work on Saturdays and even on Yom
Kippur; Christmas, Easter and Ascension Day, on the other hand,
were official holidays in this secular republic. Another example of
the rigidity of the French state in the face of minority interests
arose in March 1994, when local elections were called on a date
that coincided with the first day of Passover. Chief Rabbi Sitruk
called on Jews 'not to vote on this particularly important day of
the Jewish calendar', on the ground that writing is forbidden to
orthodox Jews on Sabbaths and holy days. In the Italian general
election, which took place on the same date, special arrangements
were made to extend voting hours to enable observant Jews to
vote. But the French Minister of the Interior refused to make such
a concession in the French case, observing that 'there is no state
religion in France; freedom of worship is absolute'. The statement
was logical – though in Britain, which has an established Church,
elections are always timed in such a way as to enable observant
Jews to vote.

The issue divided Jews themselves. Jean Kahn, head of CRIF,
opposed the Chief Rabbi: 'Jews have rights. Jews have duties. The
foremost duty of the Jew is to vote.' But this ignored the plight of

the orthodox believer whose conscience forbade him to desecrate a holy day. Guy Konopnicki, a Jewish communist, seized the opportunity to hit back at the Chief Rabbi: 'In a country where Catholics and Protestants have agreed to cast their ballot on the Lord's Day, this display of religious particularism is extremely unfortunate . . . It may be hard for an observant Jew to sign his name on Passover, but what do these small concessions mean in view of the Jews' freedom in the French republic?'[36] The affair created such bitter feelings within the Jewish community that Sitruk's re-election as Chief Rabbi was threatened, although, in the event, he won reappointment to a second seven-year term in June 1994 by a wide margin. Kahn, however, consolidated his lay leadership of the community in 1995 by winning election to the presidency of the Consistoire Central.

As the political scientist Pierre Birnbaum pointed out, the episode, trivial in itself, raised large issues. It highlighted the unreceptivity of the French secular state to minority religious interests. Another example, so familiar as to encounter little Jewish protest, was the insistence of the French state school system that Jewish pupils, like others, must attend school on Saturday; the effect was to compel Jewish children either to breach the strict code of Sabbath observance or to attend private Jewish schools.[37]

A further minor but revealing illustration of the state's lack of flexibility was the case of Olivier Raimbaud, a Jewish publisher, whose parents had changed their name from Rubinstein when he was a child shortly after the war. Not wishing to hide his Jewish identity behind a Gallic-sounding appellation, he applied in 1991 for permission to change his surname back to Rubinstein. The Minister of Justice rejected the application on the ground that French law provided for name changes in exceptional cases where the 'foreign character' of the original name 'is of such a kind as to create difficulties in integration into the French community'. When Raimbaud/Rubinstein appealed to the Conseil d'Etat, he again encountered rejection on the ground that 'stability' in names was necessary.[38]

In Britain too there were occasional collisions involving differing interpretations of individual rights, minority interests and the role of the state. In 1992, for instance, a strange controversy erupted over a proposal for the erection of an *eruv* in north-west London. An *eruv* is an enclosure within which orthodox Jews may perform certain otherwise prohibited acts on the Sabbath – for example, wheeling invalid carriages or children's prams, carrying books or umbrellas and so on. The enclosure may take any form: the walls of a city (so long as they surround it completely), a fence or even a wire. In several cities in Israel and North America, orthodox Jews had erected a semi-symbolic *eruv*, generally a continuous wire, in order to make life easier for invalids, women and old people. The area of London proposed for enclosure encompassed 6.5 square miles of heavily Jewish suburban territory: Golders Green, Hendon, and parts of Hampstead Garden Suburb and Cricklewood. When the idea was broached, however, it encountered a barrage of opposition from a variety of quarters. Some ultra-orthodox circles condemned it as opening the way to breaches of the Sabbath. Non-orthodox Jewish ex-refugees who lived in the area complained that such a wire, even if invisible, would make them feel they were living once again in a concentration camp. Other opponents complained on aesthetic grounds – though the *eruv* would be almost invisible and strung high up beyond reach, like a telegraph wire. To these voices were added others from the extreme left and right of the general population, objecting on grounds ranging from antisemitism to environmentalism. As it happened, the minister responsible, Michael Howard, was himself a Jew, who was thus placed in a peculiarly awkward position. Eventually, in 1994, it fell to his successor as Minister for the Environment, John Gummer, a deeply engaged Christian, to approve construction of the *eruv*.

It might be argued that this faintly absurd controversy represented in symbolic form the basic dilemma of Jewish life in liberal societies in the late twentieth century. Could Jews, *should* Jews, maintain some form of separation, even an invisible one, between themselves and surrounding society – religiously, culturally or socially? If so, where would or should the lines be drawn, and by whom? If, on the other hand, no such separation was feasible or desirable under modern conditions, could the Jews survive outside

Israel? Or would disappearance by murder and emigration in Eastern Europe be matched in the West by dissolution into a society that killed by kindness?

Afterthoughts

Perhaps the most significant effect of the Nazi genocide on post-war Jewish life everywhere has been the obsession (this is not too strong a term) that it has created among Jewish leaders and thinkers, both religious and lay, with *survival*. Whatever the differences among religious and secular, orthodox and Reform, Zionists and non-Zionists, left and right, nearly all agree that collective Jewish survival should be the primary goal of Jewish communal life.★

This fundamental concern has shaped most organized Jewish activity, whether in Israel or the Diaspora, since 1945, giving it direction and a sense of purpose. Israel has provided the most distinctive and cohesive framework for such activity – a society unique in having a Jewish majority and in being created and maintained for the specific purpose of ensuring Jewish survival and creativity. Barring some cataclysm, Israel's survival is no longer in doubt.

The Jews in the Diaspora face, as a group, a much more clouded future. For the great majority of European Jews, particularly those living in the open societies of the west, where liberal values inevitably tend to draw them into an assimilative vortex, the prospects for collective survival are dim.

★ A rare dissenting voice is the former British Chief Rabbi, Lord Jakobovits, who warns against the 'survival complex now governing Jewish concerns for the first time in our history'. But his dissent is a limited one: what he questions is not survival in itself but rather the value of a contentless, spiritually empty survival for its own sake.[1]

The very beneficence of the surrounding environment tends to diminish the Jews' attachment to specific Jewish practices, languages, traditions and values – except, sometimes, in the case of the latter, values reinterpreted in such a watered-down sense as to be emptied of all but a faint remnant of specific Jewishness. In the 1990s, unlike the 1940s, it is very unusual for a Jew to convert to Christianity for reasons other than genuine spiritual conviction. Similarly the changing of names in order to try to pass for a non-Jew, not uncommon a generation or two ago, is now rare. These are two small signs of the change for the better in the relationship of the Jew in Europe to his external environment. In 1946 it was still possible for Sartre to write with some truth that 'even the most liberal democrat harbours a nuance of antisemitism: he is hostile to the Jew to the extent that the Jew continues to conceive of himself as a Jew . . . The antisemite reproaches the Jew for *being* Jewish; the democrat prefers to reproach him for *considering* himself Jewish.'[2] By the 1990s this is much less true. In multicultural, pluralist Western Europe, the Jew is no longer obliged to efface his Jewishness. This very fact has a *disintegrative* effect on Jews no longer bound by religious, cultural or political ties to their Jewishness.

In a provocative book, *Fin du peuple juif?*, published in 1964, the French Jewish sociologist Georges Friedmann argued that the solidarities that had bound Jews together in previous generations and had helped to create the State of Israel were dissolving. The process was retarded by antisemitism but that seemed to be diminishing in Western Europe. The Jews in the Diaspora were rapidly integrating into gentile society, those of Israel were becoming 'Hebrew-speaking gentiles'. Shortly after its appearance, some elements of this analysis seemed to be contradicted by events. The reaction of Diaspora Jewry to the Middle East crisis of 1967 did not suggest any loosening of the bonds of Jewish solidarity; rather the reverse. Antisemitism in the 1970s made a partial return in the form of terrorism and a revival of extremist political movements.

Yet from the longer perspective of the 1990s, the basic soundness of Friedmann's prediction seems undeniable. Demographic, social, religious and cultural trends over the past half-century point inexorably towards the dissolution of the Diaspora, at any rate in Europe.

The demographic outlook for Jews in all the major Diaspora centres is bleak. The Jewish family, that stereotypical pillar of Jewish continuity, is itself disappearing. In France, for example, only a minority of Jews between the ages of twenty and forty-four live in a conventional Jewish family. Jewish marriages are becoming fewer and tend to occur at a later age. In most of Europe a third to a half of Jews who marry have non-Jewish spouses. Most of the children of such marriages cannot be expected to identify themselves as Jews. Moreover, even within all-Jewish marriages, fertility rates are significantly below replacement level almost everywhere.

The reasons for the extraordinarily low Jewish birth-rate are unclear. Just a century ago Jews were among the most fertile peoples on earth and in areas of Jewish concentration such as the Russian 'Pale of Settlement' and Austrian Galicia families of eight or more children were common. In Palestine too in the inter-war period the Jewish birth-rate was very high, though this was partly a result of the low average age of the population. Yet since the war Jewish fertility has declined everywhere, including Israel. One possible explanation may be the general prosperity of Jews in the post-war period. Like Germans, whose rate of natural increase has similarly shrunk, the Jews may prefer consumption to child-rearing – perhaps as a matter of changing 'lifestyle' fashions. Another reason may be female emancipation, in which Jewish women played a particularly prominent role. The late Maurice Freedman tentatively suggested a further explanation 'without implying that I have any supporting evidence': 'the possibility that the low replacement rate may be connected . . . with a state of uncertainty and insecurity'.[3] Although Freedman was writing about Britain, his hypothesis may have a more general application. Existential angst, feminist ideology or selfish materialism? What-ever the reason, the fact remains that the professional and business élites to which European Jews increasingly belong are failing to reproduce themselves.

The Jews, unlike these social groups in general, cannot increase or even maintain their numerical strength by means of recruitment from other classes. The very success of Jewish social mobility in both Eastern and Western Europe over the past three generations has virtually eliminated the Jewish working class in the continent. Nor can Jews, like European societies in general, look to immigration to replenish the demographic deficit. There are no Jewish 'Gastarbeiter' available.

The only remaining significant reservoir of potential Jewish emigration lies in the lands of the former Soviet Union. The great majority of ex-Soviet Jews go either to Israel or to the United States. The smaller numbers who arrive in Western Europe, principally in Germany, in any case play little part in Jewish life.

A realistic demographic projection for European Jewry over the next few decades must therefore envisage continued steep decline.

The dissolution of European Jewry is not situated at some point in a hypothetical future. The process is taking place before our eyes and is already far advanced on at least three fronts.

1. We witness now the last scene of the last act of more than a millennium of Jewish life in Eastern Europe.

Within living memory the Eastern European heartland was the centre of the Jewish world. Today it has been reduced to a backwater. Nazism was the main reason, but not the only one. The decline had begun in the 1880s, with the start of mass emigration to the United States and, to a lesser extent, to Central and Western Europe. After 1917 the Russian Revolution, while formally emancipating Jews, cut them off from contact with the rest of world Jewry and increasingly placed obstacles in the way of their expression of a collective religious, cultural or ethnic identity. Then came Hitler. After 1945 most of the shattered remains of the Jewish communities of East–Central Europe emigrated, mainly to Israel. In 1971 the large-scale departure of Soviet Jews began; it was reduced to a trickle in the early 1980s but after 1988 assumed the proportions of a wholesale exodus. If emigration from the former Soviet Union continues at anything like its present level, only a tiny Jewish residue will remain anywhere in Eastern Europe by the turn of the century. The number of Jews in Europe by the year 2000 would then be not much more than 1 million – the lowest figure since the late Middle Ages.

2. We witness now the withering away of Judaism as a spiritual presence in the daily lives of most Jews in Europe.

All over the continent, Jews are steadily abandoning most elements of religious practice, apart from the entry and exit rituals of male circumcision and Jewish burial. Synagogue attendance and observance of *kashrut*, of the Sabbath and of rites such as barmitzvah are all declining. This should be seen within the context of the general secularizing trend in the continent. The tendency is most advanced in north-western Europe – precisely where the majority of Jews in the continent now live. In France, for example, the proportions of the Catholic population observing baptism, celebrating Christian weddings or attending Mass regularly have declined greatly since the 1950s. In Britain the decline in religious practice has been even more precipitous.

3. We witness now the end of an authentic Jewish culture in Europe.

Jewish languages, the living root without which no such culture can exist, have already practically died out in Europe. Fluent knowledge of Hebrew is limited to a handful of ex-Israelis and the small number of people who have spent some time in Israel. The majority of European Jews, when they pray (*if* they pray), still do so in Hebrew; but for the most part they recite the prayers by rote, without understanding what they mean. They are like medieval peasants awed by the sanctity of the Latin Mass. Yiddish, the lingua franca of an estimated 10 million people in the late 1930s, is now spoken on a daily basis by only a handful of old people and by pockets of ultra-orthodox Jews in cities such as Antwerp. Ladino, the Judaeo-Spanish language that was spoken by most Jews in Turkey and many in the Balkans before the war, has also dwindled virtually out of existence. Unlike Yiddish, Ladino has no last bastion of orthodox speakers: it will vanish completely within the present generation.

Jewish culture in the sense of traditional religious learning has already been virtually eliminated from Europe. A few fragments remain, such as the yeshiva in the north-eastern English town of Gateshead. But the major centres of such learning are now located in the United States and Israel.

Jewish culture in the sense of modern critical scholarship is also now almost gone from Europe. Germany's pre-war role as its home was ended by Hitler. A few European universities have developed departments of Jewish studies since the war (Strasbourg, Paris, Oxford, London and the Free University of Berlin are the most important), but they too look to Israel and the United States as the centres of their scholarly world.

Jewish secular culture in the form of the plastic arts, literature and music undeniably thrives at a certain level in parts of Europe. Jews have played a large, probably disproportionate, role in the cultures of European societies in the post-war period. But they did not thereby create a Jewish culture. Playwrights such as Harold Pinter, Arnold Wesker and Peter Shaffer, novelists such as Elias Canetti or Stefan Heym wrote for general, not Jewish, audiences. Some of their works echoed Jewish themes and reflected Jewish preoccupations, but these were not their central concerns. Even those who, like the French writers Albert Cohen and Marek Halter, did focus primarily on Jewish themes, had to transmute these for non-Jewish audiences if they wished to attain a broad readership. All this is a universe away from the internally coherent cultural world that existed in Eastern Europe until the early twentieth century. At most it is a Jewish ingredient in general European cultures. Often it is mere artificial flavouring, not food.

What remains is a thin patina of a commercialized popular culture: *Fiddler on the Roof*, *lokshen* soup, Jewish jokes. This, in fact, is what many European Jews today mean when they say that they remain attached to things Jewish. The attachment has little contemporary vitality; it is nostalgia for an obscurely perceived, dead past, not a basis for a living collective identity.

We are, then, witnessing the disappearance of the European Diaspora as a population group, as a cultural entity and as a significant force in European society and in the Jewish world.

Historically speaking, population panics based on extrapolations of present trends into the future, whether of huge increases or of sudden declines, are often exaggerated and sometimes disproved by events. Is there any countervailing evidence to suggest such an outcome in the case of the European Jews?

One segment of Jewish society does seem to be demographically healthy and to be able to preserve a distinct identity: the ultra-orthodox. They marry young, appear not to practise birth control and often have families of eight or ten children. Living as a minority in gentile societies, they spin for themselves a virtual cocoon of institutions, social behaviour and ideology that may ensure their survival as a group. But these are a very small percentage of the Jewish people and are mainly concentrated in Israel and the United States. Their family patterns have little bearing on the Jewish future in Europe.

Can one approach the question, as it were, from the other end of the religious spectrum and argue that the high intermarriage rate between Jews and non-Jews, deplorable in the eyes of the orthodox, represents an opportunity for Jewish population growth rather than a threat of contraction? A positive attitude towards intermarriage is expressed by the French Jewish writer Alain Finkielkraut: 'Marrying a non-Jew doesn't mean one is abandoning one's tradition. On the contrary, it demonstrates a desire to disseminate the message throughout the world. Those who wish to remain Jews in a world they don't care about are reducing Judaism to something no better than a lobby.'[4] But such affirmative attitudes are rare. Even Reform and Liberal Jews tend to have a permissive rather than a celebratory attitude towards intermarriage. The social reality is that the very act of intermarriage generally reflects weak interest in a continuing Jewish identity. While conversion of the non-Jewish spouse (in any case reprehended by the orthodox) may solve individual problems, it is most unlikely to occur in numbers sufficient to have any significant demographic impact.

Can education in all-Jewish schools, the favoured panacea of many communal leaders in Western Europe, recall the next generation to its roots? The example of Catholic schools in Britain and the United States should serve as a warning of the limitations of such an approach. Other diasporas too have travelled this route:

for example, the Russian emigration after the Bolshevik Revolution. With the aid of their Church, their schools and their language, the 'White' Russians succeeded in preserving a distinctive culture in exile – for a couple of generations. After that, it faltered, maintaining a tenuous hold on life thanks only to a new flow of emigrants. For the Jewish Diaspora in Europe, no such blood transfusion is in prospect.

What of Israel? Can this new Jewish world, having been called into existence, redress the balance of the old? The Israeli demographer Sergio DellaPergola has argued that 'just as the Jews of the Diaspora at the moment support their brethren in Israel, we can foresee a time when the Israelis will come to the support of their brethren [in the Diaspora] in order to prevent their cultural extinction'.[5] The intricate mechanism that might achieve the desired equilibium remains, however, to be designed.

Some Israeli and Diaspora figures were beginning to utter heretical thoughts on this issue in the early 1990s. The Israeli Deputy Foreign Minister, Yossi Beilin, shocked Jewish charitable audiences in Britain and France when he pointed out that Israel, a country that now stood in eighteenth place in the world league table of per-capita incomes, no longer had need of charitable handouts. The outraged reactions of his listeners merely served to confirm his point: fund-raising for Israel had developed into an activity that was less important for Israel than for the self-consciousness (unkind critics might have said the self-importance) of the donors. His argument, although it touched a raw nerve, reflected a growing current of thought throughout the Diaspora. The British Chief Rabbi, Jonathan Sacks, pointed out in 1994 that the dispatch of the greater part of Jewish charitable funds to Israel represented in a curious fashion the internalization by the Diaspora of the classical Zionist doctrine of *shelilat ha-golah* (negation of the Diaspora). He urged a diversion of resources in order to shift the relationship between Israel and the Diaspora 'from dependence to reciprocity'.[6]

The issue is much more than one of resources. It is existential; it goes to the very heart of the question of what sort of people, as individuals and as a collectivity, Jews want to be.

In some Israeli eyes the dissolution of the Diaspora may appear as a fulfilment of the Zionist dream of the 'ingathering of the exiles' – particularly since one element in the process has consisted of emigration to Israel. Against this there is the view of Simon Rawidowicz, one of the most far-sighted Jewish thinkers of the post-war period. He argued that it was a vulgar error to conceive of the elimination of the *galut* (exile) as a Zionist objective. An Israel without its Jewish hinterland in the Diaspora would be a miserably stunted entity.

At a superficial level Israel and the Diaspora today coexist in greater harmony than ever before. In 1945 most Jews in Europe would not have called themselves Zionists. Many opposed Zionism, either from a liberal assimilationist or from a communist viewpoint – or simply because they did not believe in the practicability of its claim to provide a solution to the Jewish problem. Over the past two generations, outright hostility to Zionism has almost disappeared from the scene among Jews in Europe. This does not mean that Jews will invariably support Israeli policy. The Diaspora has been a source of fierce criticism both of Israeli settlement policy after 1967 and of Israeli withdrawal from occupied territories more recently. But since 1967, unlike before, it has been increasingly rare to find Jews who question the legitimacy of Israel's existence.

Most Jews today are prepared to acknowledge a link of some sort with the Jewish state. Many fall into the category of vicarious or armchair Zionists. Some have made of Israel a secular god. An intervention by this *deus ex machina*, however, is unlikely to work miracles. Israel can, no doubt, continue to send 'emissaries' overseas, encourage the teaching of Hebrew, welcome Jewish youth to kibbutzim and Israeli universities, and engage in an energetic cultural diplomacy. But all this leads ultimately to a Catch-22: the more successful Israel is in such endeavours, the more likely it is to draw to Israel – and away from the Diaspora – the very elements that it seeks to revitalize.

Can the Diaspora, then, somehow summon up from within itself the capacity for renewal?

One of the most thoughtful of French Jewish intellectuals,

Richard Marienstras, in his book *Être un peuple en diaspora*, argues that the Diaspora can and should have a purpose, a meaning and a future. Though sometimes called a 'neo-Bundist',★ Marienstras does not propose a resuscitation of the Bund's autonomist ideology, which, of course, has no practicability, indeed no meaning, outside the traditional East European context. He insists that 'it is time to have done with the mistaken idea that one cannot "be a Jew" otherwise than by religion or by Zionist nationalism'.[7] What, then, remains? Marienstras's answer is to call for a revival of interest by secular Jews in Hebrew and Yiddish culture, Jewish history and 'a cultural politics of the Diaspora'.

The project might not be quite as quixotic as it sounds. Such a stress on the virtues of cultural pluralism concords with the general cultural shift in West European societies since the 1970s, arising in particular from the influx of millions of non-European and often non-Christian immigrants. Hitherto unitary, centralist societies such as France and England now display greater openness to cultural diversity. The problem is that there is little evidence that in the conditions of the contemporary European Diaspora, Jews have, any longer, the minimal internal resources to respond effectively to the challenge and the potentialities of a genuine cultural pluralism. The fact is that Marienstras's proposals (and similar efforts from other quarters), admirable though they may be, have not taken root in any significant form outside small circles of intellectuals.

In the last resort peoples decide their own fate. As Nahum Goldmann put it: 'Peoples disappear in history by suicide, not by murder.' If the Jews of Europe do, in the end, disappear, it will be because, as a collectivity, they lost the will to live.

There is a precedent for this. Some time before 1127 a small number of Jews arrived in China after travelling along the Silk Road. They settled at Kai-feng, where they built a temple and maintained their separate identity for several centuries. The Jesuit missionary Matteo Ricci interviewed one of them in 1605 and documented their practices. They appear to have encountered

★ See above, p. 102.

little or no hostility from their Chinese neighbours. Gradually they absorbed the values and practices of Confucian civilization. Eventually they lost touch with their own culture. In the nineteenth century they sold their remaining holy scrolls, which they were unable any longer to read. In the early twentieth century a few of them made contact with Baghdadi and European Jewish merchants established in Shanghai and appealed for help in maintaining their communal identity. But it was too late. After surviving for an astonishing eight centuries as a distinctive entity, they merged into the surrounding society.

In the 1990s there are still some clans in Kai-feng who are vaguely conscious of Jewish ancestry. Some even claim (when meeting foreign Jewish tourists) to recall that their grandparents abstained from eating pork or lit candles on Friday. The descendants of the Kai-feng Jews have appealed to the Chinese government for recognition as a national minority. But the Beijing authorities have rejected such requests – and rightly so. These people are Chinese in every significant sense.

The Jews of Europe now face a similar destiny. Slowly but surely, they are fading away. Soon nothing will be left save a disembodied memory.

Notes

Preface

1. Jean-Paul Sartre, *Réflexions sur la question juive* (Paris, 1966 edn), 14.
2. 'Dutch Jewry: A Demographic Analysis, Part Two', *JJS*, IV, 1 (June 1962), 47–71.
3. Sergio DellaPergola, 'Jews in the European Community: Sociodemographic Trends and Challenges', *AJYB*, vol. 93 (New York, 1993), 29.
4. W. Rabinowitch, 'État du Judaïsme français', *Esprit*, 114 (September 1945), 481.
5. M. Freedman, ed., *A Minority in Britain: Social Studies of the Anglo-Jewish Community* (London, 1955), 228.

Chapter 1. Displaced Persons

1. Martin Gilbert, *Auschwitz and the Allies* (London, 1981), 338.
2. Quoted in Abram L. Sachar, *The Redemption of the Unwanted: From the Liberation of the Death Camps to the Founding of Israel* (New York, 1983), 12.
3. 'Buchenwald: A Preliminary Report' by Egon Fleck and 1st Lieut. Edward A. Tenenbaum, Headquarters, 12th Army Group, Publicity and Psychological Warfare, 24 April 1945, PRO FO 371/46796/C1922/63/18.
4. R. H. S. Crossman, *Palestine Mission* (London, 1946), 21.
5. PRO FO 371/46796/C2391/63/18, extract from SHAEF G Division Displaced Persons Branch, 30 April 1945.
6. Ronald W. Zweig, 'The Liberation of the Camps' (unpublished paper), 1.
7. Quoted in Dina Porat, 'Attitudes of the Young State of Israel towards the Holocaust and Its Survivors: A Debate over Identity

and Values', in Laurence J. Silberstein, ed., *New Perspectives on Israeli History: The Early Years of the State* (New York, 1991), 162.

8. Cmd 6626, London, April 1945.

9. *Daily Express*, 10 April 1945.

10. Maurice Szafran, *Les Juifs dans la politique française: De 1945 à nos jours* (Paris, 1990), 35.

11. Ibid.

12. Dienke Hondius, 'A Cold Reception: Holocaust Survivors in the Netherlands and Their Return', *Patterns of Prejudice*, 28, 1 (1994), 56.

13. Issue dated 2 July 1945, quoted ibid., 59.

14. See Lucjan Dobroszycki, 'Restoring Jewish Life in Post-war Poland', *SJA*, III, 2 (1973), 66–7.

15. Quoted in Roger Daniels, 'American Refugee Policy in Historical Perspective', in Jarrell C. Jackman and Carla M. Borden, eds., *The Muses Flee Hitler: Cultural Transfer and Adaptation 1930–1945* (Washington, DC, 1983), 71.

16. L. N. Collins for Ministry of Economic Warfare to Displaced Persons Division, SHAEF, [early May] 1945, PRO FO 371/51117/WR1390/4/48.

17. Minute by Vyvyan, 2 July 1945, PRO FO 371/51119/WR1951/4/48.

18. See Dobroszycki, 'Post-war Poland', 64.

19. *The Times*, 21 July 1945.

20. Minute by Paul Mason, 25 July 1945, PRO FO 371/51120/WR 2226/4/48.

21 Attlee to Truman, 16 September 1945, quoted in Amikam Nachmani, *Great Power Discord in Palestine: The Anglo-American Committee of Inquiry into the Problems of European Jewry and Palestine, 1945–1946* (London, 1987), 12.

22. House of Commons Hansard, 15 May 1945.

23. Text of Harrison's report in Appendix B to Leonard Dinnerstein, *America and the Survivors of the Holocaust* (New York, 1982), 291–305.

24. Malcolm J. Proudfoot, *European Refugees: 1939–1952* (London, 1957), 325.

25. Quoted in Constantin Goschler, 'The Attitude towards Jews in Bavaria after the Second World War', *Leo Baeck Institute Year Book*, XXXVI (London, 1991), 447.

26. Reproduction of pamphlet in Dinnerstein, *America and the Survivors*, Appendix C, 307–13.

27. Peter Meyer et al., *The Jews in the Soviet Satellites* (Syracuse, NY, 1953), 256.

28. Dispatch from Warsaw to London dated 20 February 1946, quoted in Nachmani, *Great Power Discord*, 11.

29. See, for example, *Bamidbar: Wochncajtung fun di bafrajte Jidn* (Föhrenwald, 1946); *Jidisze Cajtung: Algemejn-Nacjonaler Organ* (Landsberg, 1946-7); and *Cum Ojfboj* (Deggendorf, 1946-7).

30. Quoted in Porat, 'Attitudes', 164.

31. Yehuda Bauer, *Out of the Ashes: The Impact of American Jews on Post-Holocaust European Jewry* (Oxford, 1989), 200.

32. ibid., 84.

33. Sachar, *Redemption*, 202.

34. Transcript of UNRRA report in Yuri Boshyk, ed., *Ukraine during World War II. History and Its Aftermath: A Symposium* (Edmonton, Alberta, 1986), 209-22.

35. Crossman, *Palestine Mission*.

36. Nachmani, *Great Power Discord*, 145.

37. Crossman, *Palestine Mission*, 100.

38. John Stetsinger, *Truman, the Jewish Vote, and the Creation of Israel* (Stanford, CA, 1974), 29.

39. Quoted in Michael Checinski, 'The Kielce Pogrom: Some Unanswered Questions', *SJA*, V, 1 (1975) 65.

40. Transcript of Cardinal Hlond's remarks to American newspapermen, Warsaw, 11 July 1946, USNA State Department decimal file 840.48 Refugees/7-1146.

41. Memorandum of conversation between Górka and Gerald Keith, Warsaw, 9 July 1946, USNA State Department decimal file 840.48 Refugees/7-2446.

42. Quoted in Checinski, 'Kielce Pogrom', 61.

43. US Embassy, Warsaw, to State Department [airgram], 25 July 1946, USNA State Department decimal file 840.48 Refugees/7-2546.

44. Steinhardt to State Department, 7 October 1946, USNA State Department decimal file 840.48 Refugees S/10-746.

45. Transcript of 'Report of the Executive Staff of the UNRRA, US Zone HQ, to the Director-General of UNRRA', September 1946, in Boshyk, ed., *Ukraine during World War II*, 225-32.

46. Proudfoot, *European Refugees*, 344.

47. Foreign Office memorandum, 2 September 1946, quoted in Nachmani, *Great Power Discord*, 13.

48. Israel Cohen, 'Jewish Interests in the Peace Treaties', *Jewish Social Studies*, XI, 2 (April 1949), 99–118.
49. Minutes dated 8 (signature indecipherable) and 11 (by A. W. H. Wilkinson) February 1947, PRO FO 371/64060 C2896/2722/3.
50. Bauer, *Out of the Ashes*, 130.
51. Quoted in David Cesarani, *Justice Delayed* (London, 1992), 79.
52. Ronald Webster, 'American Relief and Jews in Germany 1945–1960: Diverging Perspectives', *Leo Baeck Institute Year Book*, XXXVIII (London, 1993), 307.
53. Ibid., 314.
54. Ibid., 299.
55. Ibid., 300.
56. A 1954 'Joint' report quoted ibid., 320.
57. Report on Germany by AJDC Country Director Theodor Feder, AJDC 11th Country Directors' Conference, Paris, October 15–17 1956 (cyclostyled).

Chapter 2. Stalin's Last Victims, 1945–53

1. Bernard Weinryb, 'Poland', in Meyer et al., *Jews in Soviet Satellites*, 244.
2. Memorandum by R. B. B. Tollinton, Sofia, 16 May 1945, PRO FO 371/51117/WR 11683/4/48.
3. Minute by B. Horsfield, 28 May 1945, PRO FO 371/51117/WR 1437/4/48.
4. Lambert (Sofia) to Foreign Office, 10 May 1945, ibid.
5. Paul Mason to H. A. Goodman, 10 August 1945, PRO FO 371/51120/WR2156/4/48.
6. Peter Meyer, 'Czechoslovakia', in Meyer et al., *Jews in Soviet Satellites*, 81–2.
7. Kurt Wehle, 'The Jews in Bohemia and Moravia, 1945–1948', in Avigdor Dagan, ed., *The Jews of Czechoslovakia: Historical Studies and Surveys*, vol. III (Philadelphia, 1984), 511–12.
8. Eugene Duschinsky, 'Hungary', in Meyer et al., *Jews in Soviet Satellites*, 392.
9. Irena Hurwic-Nowakowska, *A Social Analysis of Post-war Polish Jewry* (Jerusalem, 1986), 54, 57.
10. Ibid., 101.
11. Sartre, *Réflexions*, 34.
12. Weinryb, 'Poland', in Meyer et al., *Jews in Soviet Satellites*, 244.
13. Duschinsky, 'Hungary', in ibid., 404.

14. Meyer, 'Czechoslovakia', in ibid., 85.
15. Duschinsky, 'Hungary', in ibid., 469.
16. *JC*, 14 January 1955.
17. Duschinsky, 'Hungary', in Meyer et al., *Jews in Soviet Satellites*, 479.
18. Nicolas Sylvain, 'Rumania', in ibid., 534.
19. Baruch Hazzan, 'The Jewish Community of Bulgaria', in Daniel J. Elazar et al., *The Balkan Jewish Communities: Yugoslavia, Bulgaria, Greece and Turkey* (Lanham, MD, 1984), 77.
20. See Yosef Goldkorn, *The Rise and Fall of a Jewish Newspaper: Dos Nyeh Lebn, Poland, 1945–50* (Tel Aviv, 1993).
21. Translated text in Benjamin Pinkus, *The Soviet Government and the Jews 1948–1967: A Documented Study* (Cambridge, 1984), 34.
22. Sylvain, 'Rumania', in Meyer et al., *Jews in Soviet Satellites*, 534.
23. *Folksshtime*, 12 November 1948; the translation of this passage that appears in Weinryb, 'Poland', in Meyer et al., 295, gives a somewhat misleading impression.
24. Issue dated 23 January 1953, quoted in Meyer, 'Czechoslovakia', in ibid., 162.
25. Ibid., 183.
26. Czech newspaper account quoted in Patrick Brogan, *The Captive Nations: Eastern Europe 1945–1990* (New York, 1990), 90.
27. Pinkus, *Soviet Government*, 196–7.
28. Not twenty-four as was earlier thought: see Zev Ben-Shlomo, 'Darkness at the Heart of a Legend', *JC*, 7 August 1992; also Avraham Greenbaum, 'A Note on the Tradition of the Twenty-four Soviet Martyrs', *SJA*, XVII, 1 (1987), 49–52.
29. Elie Wiesel, *The Jews of Silence* (New York, 1966).
30. Text of announcement in Pinkus, *Soviet Government*, 219–20.
31. Ibid., 222.
32. Chimen Abramsky, 'Soviet Jewry: A Bird's-eye View of their Problems, Past and Present', lecture in conference hall of Westminster Cathedral, 27 April 1977.

Chapter 3. Revival in Western Europe, 1945–73

1. Quoted in Joel Fishman, 'The Jewish Community in Post-War Netherlands, 1944–1975', *Midstream* (January 1976), 42–54.
2. Report by Country Director for Greece, AJDC 11th Country Directors' Conference, Paris, 15–17 October 1956 (cyclo).
3. Chaim to Vera Weizmann, 6 January 1921, in Bernard Wasserstein,

ed., *The Letters and Papers of Chaim Weizmann*, vol. X (New Brunswick, NJ, 1977), 124.

4. *JC*, 15 October 1976.

5. Leni Yahil, *The Rescue of Danish Jewry: Test of a Democracy* (Philadelphia, 1969), 378.

6. Quoted in Maxime Rodinson, *Peuple juif ou problème juif?* (Paris, 1981), 47.

7. See ibid., 46.

8. Pierre Birnbaum, *Anti-Semitism in France: A Political History from Léon Blum to the Present* (Oxford, 1992), 143.

9. Ibid., 77, 211–12.

10. Ibid., 43.

11. For example, Szafran in his *Juifs dans la politique*.

12. *Sondages*, XX, 2 (1967), 69 ff.

13. Doris Bensimon, 'Sondage Socio-Démographique auprès des Juifs en France: Résultats Préliminaires (Région Parisienne)', in *Papers in Jewish Demography 1977*, U. O. Schmelz, P. Glikson and S. DellaPergola, eds. (Jerusalem, 1980), 179–90.

14. Georges Benguigui, 'First-year Jewish Students at the University of Paris', in Benguigui et al., *Aspects of French Jewry* (London, 1969), 24–96.

15. Norman Bentwich, 'The Social Transformation of Anglo-Jewry, 1883–1960', *JJS* II, 1 (June 1960), 16–24.

16. See Chaim Bermant, *The Cousinhood: The Anglo-Jewish Gentry* (London, 1971).

17. Ernest Krausz, 'The Economic and Social Structure of Anglo-Jewry', in Julius Gould and Shaul Esh, eds., *Jewish Life in Modern Britain* (London, 1964), 32–3.

18. S. J. Prais and Marlena Schmool, 'The Social-Class Structure of Anglo-Jewry, 1961', *JJS*, XVII, 1 (June 1975), 5–15.

19. Quoted in Howard Brotz, 'The Outlines of Jewish Society in London', in Freedman, ed., *Minority in Britain*, 185.

20. Freedman, ibid., 112, 230.

21. Gerald Cromer, 'The Transmission of Religious Observance in the Contemporary Jewish Family: The Methodology and Findings of a Survey of a London Suburb', in Schmelz et al., *Papers in Jewish Demography 1977*, 225–33.

22. The results of the Edgware survey were published in three articles in the *JJS* by Ernest Krausz: 'The Edgware Survey: Demographic Results', *JJS*, X, 1 (June 1968), 83–100; 'The Edgware Survey:

Occupation and Social Class', *JJS*, XI, 1 (June 1969), 75–95; and 'The Edgware Survey: Factors in Jewish Identification', *JJS*, XI, 2 (December 1969), 151–63.

23. Norman Cohen, 'Trends in Anglo-Jewish Religious Life', in Gould and Esh, eds., *Jewish Life in Modern Britain*, 49.

24. Ursula R. Q. Henriques, ed., *The Jews of South Wales: Historical Studies* (Cardiff, 1993), 212–13.

25. Maurice Freedman, 'The Jewish Population of Great Britain', *JJS*, IV, 1 (June 1962), 92–106.

26. Kurt B. Mayer, 'The Evolution of the Jewish Population of Switzerland in the Light of the 1970 Census', in Schmelz et al., *Papers in Jewish Demography 1973*, 309–22.

27. Ibid.

28. Sergio DellaPergola, 'A Note on Marriage Trends among Jews in Italy', *JJS*, XIV, 2 (December 1972), 199–200.

29. Ph. van Praag, *Demography of the Jews in the Netherlands* (Jerusalem, 1976), 47.

30. See review by Jacques Gutwirth of S. Wijnberg, *De Joden in Amsterdam* (Assen, 1967), *JJS*, X, 1 (June 1968), 160–62.

31. Georges Levitte, 'A Changing Community', in Benguigui et al., *Aspects of French Jewry*, 20.

32. *Sondages*, XX, 2 (1967), 69 ff.

33. Edgar Morin, *La Rumeur d'Orléans* (Paris, 1968).

34. Benguigui, 'First-year Jewish Students'; Bernard Wasserstein, 'Jewish Identification among Students at Oxford', *JJS*, XIII, 2 (December 1971), 135–51.

Chapter 4. The Impact of Israel

1. Ben Zion Dinur, *Israel and the Diaspora* (Philadelphia, 1969), 100.

2. Annie Besse in 1953, quoted in Rodinson, *Peuple juif*, 47.

3. The phrase is used by the former British Chief Rabbi, Lord Jakobovits, to describe the attitude of the hasidic sect of Satmar: Immanuel Jakobovits, 'Religious Responses to Jewish Statehood', *Tradition*, 20, 3 (Fall 1982), 192.

4. Ibid, 200.

5. See, for example, the pro-Sternist newspaper *Eretz Israel*, Paris, 1948–9.

6. Gideon Shimoni, 'Non-Zionists in Anglo-Jewry, 1937–1948' *JJS*, XXVIII, 2 (December 1986), 104.

7. Szafran, *Juifs dans la politique*, 85.

8. Ibid.

9. Ibid., 91.

10. Quoted in Marion Berghahn, *German-Jewish Refugees in England: The Ambiguities of Assimilation* (London, 1984), 141.

11. Georges Friedmann, *Fin du peuple juif?* (Paris, 1965), 13.

12. Yehoshua A. Gilboa, 'The 1948 Zionist Wave in Moscow', *SJA*, I, 2 (November 1971), 36.

13. Ibid., 37.

14. Weinryb, 'Poland', in Meyer et al., *Jews in Soviet Satellites*, 312–13.

15. Pinkus, *Soviet Government*, 239.

16. Geoffrey Alderman, *The Jewish Community in British Politics* (Oxford, 1983), 131–2.

17. Ibid., 133.

18. See Alistair Hetherington, *Guardian Years* (London, 1981), 21.

19. Doris Bensimon-Donath, *L'intégration des Juifs nord-africains en France* (Paris, 1971), 216.

20. Symposium on 'Juifs, en France, aujourd'hui', *Esprit*, no. 370 (April 1968), 581–2.

21. Ibid.

22. Maxime Rodinson, 'Israël, fait colonial?', *Les Temps Modernes*, 253 bis (1967), reprinted in Rodinson, *Peuple juif*, 153–239.

23. Raymond Aron, *De Gaulle, Israël et les Juifs* (Paris, 1967), 37.

24. Rodinson, *Peuple juif*, 9.

25. S. E. Finer, 'Looking Forward in Perplexity', *JJS*, X, 1 (June 1968), 139–44.

26. Official text of press conference, 27 November 1967, issued by French Embassy, London.

27. Aron, *De Gaulle*, 47.

28. Richard Marienstras, *Être un peuple en diaspora* (Paris, 1975), 54.

Chapter 5. Facing the Past

1. Telford Taylor, *The Anatomy of the Nuremberg Trials: A Personal Memoir* (London, 1993), 26n.

2. Porat, 'Attitudes', 168.

3. Ronald W. Zweig, 'Politics of Commemoration', *Jewish Social Studies*, XLIX, 2 (Spring 1987), 158.

4. See David Barnouw and Gerrold van der Stroom, eds., *The Diary of Anne Frank: The Critical Edition* (New York, 1989).

5. Benjamin Netanyahu to UN Secretary-General, 12 May 1986, UN

General Assembly Economic and Social Council document A/41/337 E/1986/87.

6. J. L. Brierly, 'War Crimes: What the Law Can Do', *Observer*, 8 April 1945.

7. Cesarani, *Justice Delayed*, 169.

8. All-Party Parliamentary War Crimes Group, *Report on the Entry of Nazi War Criminals and Collaborators into the UK, 1945–1950* (London, 1988), 13:1.

9. Quoted in Sachar, *Redemption*, 127.

10. *The Times*, 9 July 1981.

11. *Sunday Times*, 19 July 1981.

12. *The Economist*, 12 February 1983.

13. See CIA documents released under the Freedom of Information Act (copies in possession of the author) and *Time*, 29 August 1983.

14. *NYT*, 13 February 1983.

15. *Le Monde*, 14 September 1994.

16. Ibid., 26 September 1990.

17. *JC*, 29 April 1994.

18. *Le Monde*, 21–2 October 1990.

19. *NYT*, 13 June 1993.

20. Ibid., 10 May 1992.

21. *Le Monde*, 7 January 1992.

22. Pierre Péan, *Une jeunesse française: François Mitterrand, 1934–1947* (Paris, 1994).

23. *Le Monde*, 14 September 1994.

24. Cesarani, *Justice Delayed*, 218, 223.

25. Ibid., 221.

26. *JC*, 8 December 1989.

27. Cesarani, *Justice Delayed*, 238; *JC*, 29 June 1990.

28. *JC*, 1 July 1994.

29. *NYT*, 26 January and 23 February 1984.

30. Tom Bower, 'Conspiracy in Whitehall', *The Times*, 21 August 1987. See also Tom Bower, *Blind Eye to Murder: Britain, America and the Purging of Nazi Germany* (London, 1981).

31. Hannah Arendt, *Eichmann in Jerusalem: A Report on the Banality of Evil* (London, 1963).

32. Jacob Robinson, *And the Crooked Shall be Made Straight: The Eichmann Trial, the Jewish Catastrophe and Hannah Arendt's Narrative* (New York, 1965).

33. S. J. Roth, 'The History of the Luxemburg Agreement', IJARR (September 1977), 12.

34. Ibid.

35. Jacques Fredj, 'La Creation du CRIF: 1943 à 1966', Maîtrise thesis, Université de Paris IV, 1988, 87–8.

36. Nahum Goldmann, *The Autobiography of Nahum Goldmann: Sixty Years of Jewish Life* (New York, 1969), 257–61.

37. Text in Konrad Adenauer, *Erinnerungen 1953–1955* (Stuttgart, 1966), 138–9.

38. See Kai Bird, 'The Secret Policemen's Historian', *New Statesman*, 3 April 1981, 16–19.

39. 'German Supreme Court's Landmark Decision', IJARR, 797/7 (November 1979).

40. Address to Memorial Foundation for Jewish Culture, Geneva, 3 July 1979.

41. Immanuel Jakobovits, 'The Holocaust: Remembering the Future', in William Frankel, ed., *Survey of Jewish Affairs 1983* (Cranbury, NJ, 1985), 234.

Chapter 6. Jews and the Christian Problem

1. Quotations and analysis of contents of the journal in Sister Charlotte Klein, 'In the Mirror of *Civiltà Cattolica*: Vatican View of Jewry, 1939–1962', *Christian Attitudes on Jews and Judaism*, 43 (August 1975), 12–16.

2. Crossman, *Palestine Mission*, 101.

3. Weinryb, 'Poland', in Meyer et al., *Jews in Soviet Satellites*, 249.

4. Quoted in Michal Borwicz, 'Polish–Jewish Relations, 1944–1947', in Chimen Abramsky, Maciej Jachimczyk and Antony Polonsky, eds., *The Jews in Poland* (Oxford, 1986), 195.

5. Saul Friedländer, *When Memory Comes* (New York, 1979).

6. See Maurice Rajsfus, *N'oublie pas le petit Jésus! L'Église catholique et les enfants juifs* (Levallois-Perret, 1994). On the Finaly case see also 'Rabi', *L'Affaire Finaly: Des faits, des textes, des dates* (Marseilles, 1953); Jules Isaac, *L'Affaire Finaly: Significations, enseignements* (Marseilles, 1953); Moïse Keller, *L'Affaire Finaly telle que je l'ai vécue* (Paris, 1960); Roger Berg, '"Mon" affaire Finaly', *Tribune Juive*, 18 March 1993; and Szafran, *Juifs dans la politique*, 65–71.

7. Joel S. Fishman, 'Jewish War Orphans in the Netherlands – the Guardianship Issue 1945–1950', *Wiener Library Bulletin*, XXVII, new series 30/31 (1973–4), 31–6.

8. Ibid.

9. Joel S. Fishman, 'The Anneke Beekman Affair and the Dutch News Media', *Jewish Social Studies*, XL, 1 (Winter 1978), 3–24.

10. See memorandum by Lola Hahn-Warburg, 19 April 1950, CBF 169/47.

11. See 'John Presland' (= Gladys Bendit), *The Great Adventure* (London, 1944), 5.

12. Chief Rabbi Hertz to Lord Gorell, 16 November 1943, CBF 166/359.

13. *The Child-Estranging Movement* (London, January 1944).

14. See, for example, memorandum by Rev. R. Smith of Scottish Christian Council, September 1941, CBF 166/126.

15. Unsigned memorandum, 12 December 1949, CBF 169/8.

16. Memorandum by Carlebach, 16 September 1951, CBF 169/92.

17. Ibid.

18. Geoffrey Wigoder, *Jewish–Christian Relations since the Second World War* (Manchester, 1988), 37.

19. Duschinsky, 'Hungary', in Meyer et al., *Jews in Soviet Satellites*, 414.

20. Wigoder, *Jewish–Christian Relations*, 165.

21. See record of conversation between Archbishop Heenan and A. L. Easterman, September 1963, Institute of Jewish Affairs: World Jewish Congress 'Old Archives 1958–66: Box 34: Vatican II'.

22. John Cardinal Willebrands, 'Champion of Christian Unity and of a New Relationship to the Jews', *Christian–Jewish Relations*, 14, 4 (December 1981), 13.

23. John Cardinal Willebrands, 'Christians and Jews: A New Vision', in Alberic Stacpoole, ed., *Vatican II by Those Who Were There* (London, 1986), 220.

24. *Relatio* on the schema, November 1963, English translation in *Christian–Jewish Relations*, 14, 4 (December 1981).

25. Heenan–Easterman conversation, September 1963, Institute of Jewish Affairs: World Jewish Congress 'Old Archives 1958–66: Box 34: Vatican II'.

26. See record of conversation between Cardinal Bea and Gerhart M. Riegner of the World Jewish Congress, 16 May 1966, Institute of Jewish Affairs: World Jewish Congress 'Old Archives 1958–1966: Box 34: Vatican II'.

27. Christopher Hollis, 'The Vatican Council and the Jews', 11th Noah Barou Memorial Lecture, London, 29 November 1966 (mimeo).

28. *Observer*, 24 October 1965.
29. George Bull, *Vatican Politics at the Second Vatican Council 1962–5* (London, 1966), 86.
30. *Relatio* on the schema, English translation in *Christian–Jewish Relations*, 14, 4 (December 1981).
31. Bull, *Vatican Politics*, 86n.
32. Saul Friedländer, *Pius XII and the Third Reich: A Documentation* (London, 1966).
33. *Actes et Documents du Saint Siège Relatifs à la Seconde Guerre Mondiale* (Vatican City, 1965–).
34. John F. Morley, *Vatican Diplomacy and the Jews During the Holocaust 1939–1943* (New York, 1980).
35. Text in Wigoder, *Jewish–Christian Relations*, 143–4; an alternative translation from the Latin may be found in Austin Flannery, OP, ed., *Vatican Council II: The Conciliar and Post Conciliar Documents* (rev. edn, Northport, NY, 1992), 741.
36. Bull, *Vatican Politics*, 149.
37. Wigoder, *Jewish–Christian Relations*, 78.
38. Account of the Declaration, 20 November 1964, English translation in *Christian–Jewish Relations*, 14, 4 (December 1981), 51–3.
39. JTADNB, 22 April 1966.
40. Hans Küng, *The Church* (London, 1967), 138.
41. Wigoder, *Jewish–Christian Relations*, 94.
42. Text of announcement in *Osservatore Romano*, 23 October 1974, as reproduced in the official English translation in *Christian–Jewish Relations*, 39 (December 1974), 1.
43. Text in *Christian Attitudes on Jews and Judaism*, Special Issue (January 1975).
44. Sister Charlotte Klein, 'Catholics and Jews – Ten Years after Vatican II', *Journal of Ecumenical Studies*, 12, 4 (Fall 1975), 475.
45. Wigoder, *Jewish–Christian Relations*, 91–2.
46. See analysis by Wigoder, ibid., 91–8.
47. Krister Stendahl, 'Judaism and Christianity II – After a Colloquium and a War', *Harvard Divinity Bulletin*, new series, I, 1 (Autumn 1967), 2–8.
48. Text in Wigoder, *Jewish–Christian Relations*, 159–67.
49. 'Change at Oberammergau', *Christian Attitudes on Jews and Judaism*, 44 (October 1975), 16.
50. See John J. Kelly, SM, 'The Dilemma of Oberammergau', *Christian–Jewish Relations*, 23, 1 (1990), 28–32.

51. Text of the Pope's speech, 7 June 1979, in *Christian Attitudes to Jews and Judaism*, 67 (August 1979), 1–2.

52. 'Une forteresse de la prière', Tract de Aide à l'Église en détresse, Spring 1985, reprinted in supplement on 'Carmel d'Auschwitz' to *La Documentation Catholique*, no. 1991, Paris, 1 October 1989.

53. Speech delivered at the Mémorial du Martyr Juif Inconnu in Paris, 17 April 1986, text ibid.

54. Text (in French translation) ibid. The article appeared originally in *Tygodnik Powszechny*, 22 June 1986.

55. Text of the two Geneva agreements, ibid.

56. Polish Press Agency bulletin, 12 April 1989, text in *Christian–Jewish Relations*, 22, 1 (Spring 1989), 49.

57. Deborah Lipstadt, 'Anti-Semitism in Eastern Europe: Old Wine in New Bottles', report for Anti–Defamation League of B'nai B'rith, New York, December 1991, 6.

58. Geoffrey Wigoder, 'The Affair of the Carmelite Convent at Auschwitz', in William Frankel, ed., *Survey of Jewish Affairs 1990* (Oxford, 1990), 199.

59. Ibid., 202.

60. *Le Monde*, 16 April 1993.

61. Szafran, *Juifs dans la politique*, 21–2.

62. *JC*, 31 December 1993; full text of papal allocution in International Catholic–Jewish Liaison Committee, *Fifteen Years of Catholic–Jewish Dialogue 1970–1985: Selected Papers* (Vatican City, 1988), 321–5.

63. *NYT*, 7 December 1990.

Chapter 7. Three Germanies and the Jews

1. Karen Gershon, *Postscript: A Collective Account of the Lives of Jews in West Germany since the Second World War* (London, 1969), 24.

2. L. F. Katten to Police President of Berlin, 2 July 1945, with enclosure, Landesarchiv Berlin (Ost), STA Rep. 9/0060/20–21.

3. Memorandum dated 8 July, ibid., Rep. 9/0060/23.

4. Dörfel to Pastor Buchholz, Beirat für kirchliche Angelegenheiten des Magistrats der Stadt Berlin, 25 September 1945, ibid., Rep. 9/0060/26.

5. Josef Joffe, 'Fifty Years after the Third Reich: The Jewish Community in Post-war Germany', in Frankel, ed., *Survey of Jewish Affairs 1983*, 227.

6. Monika Richarz, 'Jews in Today's Germanies', *Leo Baeck Institute Year Book*, XXX (London, 1985), 265.

7. Landesarchiv Berlin (Ost), STA Rep 9/0060/137.

8. Gershon, *Postscript*, 29.

9. Report from Jewish Central Information Office, London, on Jews of Berlin, 25 August 1945, PRO FO 371/46959 C5258/4162/18.

10. Robin Ostow, *Jews in Contemporary East Germany: The Children of Moses in the Land of Marx* (London, 1989), 3.

11. Bauer, *Out of the Ashes*, 268.

12. Gershon, *Postscript*, 76.

13. Goschler, 'Jews in Bavaria', 448–9.

14. Ibid., 450.

15. Ibid., 454–8.

16. Webster, 'American Relief', 312–14.

17. Adenauer, *Erinnerungen*, 279.

18. Frederick Weil, 'The Extent and Structure of Anti-Semitism in Western Populations since the Holocaust', in Helen Fein, ed., *The Persisting Question: Sociological Perspectives and Social Contexts of Modern Antisemitism* (Berlin, 1987), 164–89.

19. Gershon, *Postscript*, 61.

20. Joffe, 'Fifty Years', 230.

21. Peter Sichrovsky, *Strangers in Their Own Land: Young Jews in Germany and Austria Today* (New York, 1986).

22. Ibid., 54.

23. See Micha Barkol, 'The Social Aspect of the Process of Establishing a Jewish Day School in West Berlin (1985–1987) in Light of the Crisis of Contemporary Jewish Life in the Diaspora', Ph. D. dissertation, Free University of Berlin, 1989, 204.

24. *International Herald Tribune*, 27 May 1988.

25. See, for example, *Frankfurter Allgemeine Zeitung* and *Die Welt*, 20 May 1988; *Süddeutsche Zeitung*, 9 July 1988; *Der Spiegel*, 31 October 1988.

26. Jeffrey Herf, 'East German Communists and the Jewish Question: The Case of Paul Merker', *Journal of Contemporary History*, XXIX (1994), 627–61. See also Herf, 'Dokumentation. Antisemitismus in der SED: Geheime Dokumente zum Fall Paul Merker aus SED- und MfS-Archiven', *Vierteljahrshefte für Zeitgeschichte*, 4 (1994), 635–67, and *Die Zeit*, 14 October 1994.

27. Quoted in Lukasz Hirszowicz, ed., 'Documents: Jewish Communal Life in the German Democratic Republic', *SJA*, XVII, 1 (1987), 62.

28. Paul O'Doherty, 'The GDR, Its Jews and the USA', *Politics and*

Society in Germany, Austria and Switzerland, 4.2 (Spring 1992), 25–33.

29. Crossman, *Palestine Mission*, 103; see also Robert Knight, 'Restitution and Legitimacy in Post-war Austria 1945–1953', *Leo Baeck Institute Year Book*, XXXVI (London 1991), 420. The accuracy of Crossman's version of Renner's remarks was later questioned. Knight, however, shows that it was in line with Renner's general thinking on the issue, as recorded in Austrian state documents of the period.

30. Ibid., 437.

31. Aviel Roshwald, 'The Politics of Statelessness: Jewish Refugees in Austria after the Second World War', *JJS*, XXXI, 1 (June 1989), 51.

32. Bauer, *Out of the Ashes*, 64.

33. *NYT*, 5 April 1986.

34. Ibid., 28 April 1987.

35. Ibid., 9 December 1987.

36. Ibid., 10 February 1988.

37. Ibid., 17 February 1988.

38. Ibid., 13 March 1988.

39. Leon Brandt, 'Ein anormales Miteinander, ein Zustand ohne Zukunft', in Henryk M. Broder and Michel R. Lang, eds., *Fremd im eigenen Land: Juden in der Bundesrepublik* (Frankfurt am Main, 1979), 70.

Chapter 8. The Soviet Jewish Revolt

1. See, for example, *Encyclopaedia Judaica Year Book 1986–1987*, 363.

2. See Mordechai Altshuler, *Soviet Jewry since the Second World War: Population and Social Structure* (Westport, Conn., 1987), especially chapters 1 and 2.

3. U. O. Schmelz, 'New Evidence on Basic Issues in the Demography of Soviet Jews', *JJS*, XVI, 2 (December 1974), 209–23.

4. Benjamin Fain and Mervin F. Verbit, *Jewishness in the Soviet Union: Report of an Empirical Survey* (Jerusalem, 1984), 88–9.

5. Theodore H. Friedgut, 'Soviet Jewry: The Silent Majority', *SJA*, X, 2 (1980), 16.

6. Abraham Brumberg, '*Sovyetish Heymland* and the Dilemmas of Jewish Life in the USSR', *SJA*, 3 (May 1972), 28.

7. Pinkus, *Soviet Government*, 58.

8. Ibid., 62.

9. Brumberg, '*Sovyetish Heymland*', 32.

10. Pinkus, *Soviet Government*, 224–5.
11. 'Protest and Militancy – A New Trend in Soviet Jewry?', IJARR USSR/6 (June 1969).
12. 'Soviet Press Campaign on the Demand for Emigration to Israel', IJARR USSR/10 (December 1969).
13. Vladimir Lazaris, 'The Saga of Jewish Samizdat', *SJA*, IX, 1 (1979), 5.
14. 'EXODUS: A Jewish Underground Publication in the USSR', IJARR USSR/20 (November 1970).
15. Account of the trial based on that in the Russian *samizdat* paper, *Chronicle of Current Events*, no. 17 (December, 1970), of which an English translation appeared in IJARR USSR/26 (24 May 1971).
16. Edict dated 3 August 1972, *International Legal Materials*, 12 (1973), 427.
17. *Jews in the USSR*, II, 20 (18 May 1973).
18. Ibid., III, 27 (5 July 1974).
19. Martin Gilbert, *Shcharansky: Hero of Our Time* (London, 1986), 255.
20. Fain and Verbit, *Jewishness in the Soviet Union*, 66 ff.
21. Ibid., 119.
22. 'Twenty-five Years of Destalinization and Soviet Jewry', IJARR USSR/78/2 (March 1978).
23. See IJARR USSR/46a (January 1975), 4.
24. See Zvi Gitelman, 'Soviet Jewish Emigrants: Why are They Choosing America?', *SJA*, VII, 1 (1977), 33–4.
25. 'Chronicle', *JJS*, XVII, 2 (December 1976), 183.
26. See Theodore H. Friedgut, 'Passing Eclipse: The Exodus Movement in the 1980s', in Robert O. Freedman, ed., *Soviet Jewry in the 1980s* (Durham, NC, 1989), 3–25.
27. 'Soviet Jewry', memorandum to regional offices of Anti-Defamation League of B'nai B'rith, New York, 4 May 1983.
28. See Mordechai Altshuler, 'Who are the "Refuseniks"? A Statistical and Demographic Analysis', *SJA*, XVIII, 1 (1988), 3–15.
29. William Korey, 'Soviet Jews' Anxiety', *NYT*, 14 January 1984.
30. Ibid., 20 November 1985.
31. *AJYB 1989*, 358.

Chapter 9. East European Shadows, 1953–89

1. Harriet Pass Friedenreich, 'The Jewish Community of Yugoslavia', in Elazar et al., *Balkan Jewish Communities*, 18–19.
2. Ivor Millman, 'The Jewish Population of Romania: Continuity and

Decline', in *Papers in Jewish Demography 1981*, U. O. Schmelz, P. Glikson and S. DellaPergola, eds. (Jerusalem, 1983), 163–72.

3. Szyja Bronsztejn, 'A Questionnaire Inquiry into the Jewish Population of Wrocław', *JJS*, VII, 2 (December 1965), 255.

4. *Guardian*, 28 October 1977.

5. Typescript memorandum by David J. Wasserstein, Budapest, June 1983.

6. George Schöpflin, ed., 'Documents: Jews and Hungarians', *SJA*, XVII, 3 (1987), 55–66; see also *JC*, 8 March 1990.

7. See Jaff Shatz, *The Generation: The Rise and Fall of the Jewish Communists of Poland* (Berkeley, 1991), 272, 379.

8. See Anonymous [= Michael Checinski], 'USSR and the Politics of Polish Antisemitism 1956–68', *SJA*, I, 1 (June 1971), 22. This article, which claimed to draw on secret sources, is the basis for much of the information in this and succeeding paragraphs.

9. Ibid., 27.

10. Cynthia Stopnicka Heller, '"Anti-Zionism" and the Political Struggle within the Elite of Poland', *JJS*, XI, 2 (December 1969), 133–50; see also Shatz, *Generation*, 304.

11. Heller, 'Anti-Zionism'.

12. 'The Student Unrest in Poland and the Anti-Jewish and Anti-Zionist Campaign', Institute of Jewish Affairs Background Paper, 9 (April 1968).

13. 'The Anti-Jewish and Anti-Zionist Campaign in Poland II', Institute of Jewish Affairs Background Paper, 12 (1 July 1968).

14. Translated extracts in ibid.

15. Lukasz Hirszowicz, 'Jewish Themes in the Polish Crisis', IJARR, 10/11 (August 1981), 15.

16. 'The Anti-Jewish and Anti-Zionist Campaign in Poland II'.

17. The results of the survey, originally published in *Znak*, 339–40, February–March 1983, were reprinted in French translation in the supplement on 'Carmel d'Auschwitz' to *La Documentation Catholique*, no. 1991, 1 October 1989.

18. 'Polish Anti-Semitism – 1981', Memorandum of Anti-Defamation League of B'nai B'rith, 13 March 1981.

19. *NYT*, 15 March 1981.

20. Ibid., 22 April 1981.

21. Hirszowicz, 'Jewish Themes in the Polish Crisis', 7.

22. Ibid., 14.

23. *SJA*, XII, 1 (1982), 59–65; see also *JC*, 23 July 1982.

24. Ibid.; see also Abraham Brumberg, 'The Ghost in Poland', *New York Review of Books*, 2 June 1983, 41.
25. *NYT*, 15 January 1982.
26. Ibid., 17 April 1983.
27. Ibid., 3 March 1988.
28. The article originally appeared in *Tygodnik Powszechny*, 11 January 1987. An English translation appeared in *Christian–Jewish Relations*, 22, 3/4 (1989), 5–17. The entire article, as well as several other contributions to the ensuing debate, have been conveniently collected and translated into English in Antony Polonsky, ed., *My Brother's Keeper? Recent Polish Debates on the Holocaust* (London, 1990).
29. Ibid.
30. *NYT*, 10 May 1968.
31. 'Anti-Zionist and Anti-Israel Comment in Czechoslovak Press', IJARR Czechoslovakia/9 (May 1970).
32. A. Zwergbaum, 'Czechoslovak Jewry in 1979', *SJA*, X, 3 (1980), 43.
33. Peter Brod, ed., 'Documents. Czechoslovakia: Jewish Legacy and Jewish Present', *SJA*, XX, 1 (Spring, 1990), 63.

Chapter 10. West European Dilemmas, 1973–89

1. Text in John Norton Moore, *The Arab–Israeli Conflict* (Princeton, 1974), vol. III: Documents, 1146–8.
2. Henri Simonet, 'Energy and the Future of Europe', *Foreign Affairs* (April 1975).
3. 'Israeli Expansion', leaflet published by British Anti-Zionist Organization, *c*. 1978.
4. 'People of a Jewish Background Oppose Racist Zionism', BAZO leaflet, *c*. 1978.
5. S. J. Roth, 'Antisemitism in the Western World Today', IJARR, 7 (June 1981), 9.
6. Richard Eder, 'The Jewish Question in France', *NYT* (magazine section), 30 November 1980.
7. 'Antisemitism Today: A Symposium', *Patterns of Prejudice*, 16, 4 (October 1962), 9.
8. Ibid., 13.
9. Michel Abitbol, *Bituyei Hizdahut Leumit Be-Tsarfat* (Jerusalem, 1982), 25.
10. *Le Monde*, 29 June 1982.
11. Quoted in Helen Fein, 'Contemporary Conflicts: How Do Jewish

Claims and Jewish Nationhood Affect Antisemitism?', in Fein, ed., *Persisting Question*, 368.

12. 'French Jewry and the General Elections', IJARR, 78/3 March 1978), 2.
13. *Consistoire Central Israélite de France et d'Algérie: Bulletin Intérieur*, 19 February 1973.
14. Column by Serge Weill Goudchoux, *Journal des Communautés*, 12 January 1973.
15. *Presse Nouvelle Hebdo*, 23 February 1973.
16. *JTA Bulletin Quotidien d'Informations*, 1 February 1973.
17. Ibid., 12 February 1973.
18. *La Terre Retrouvée*, 15 February 1973.
19. Ibid.
20. Ibid.
21. Ibid., 1 March 1973.
22. *L'Arche*, 192, 26 February 1973.
23. Ibid.
24. Barry Kosmin et al., *Steel City Jews* (London, 1976).
25. DellaPergola, 'Jews in the European Community', 74.
26. For a full analysis, see Doris Bensimon and Sergio DellaPergola, *La Population Juive de la France: Socio-Démographie et Identité* (Jerusalem, 1984).
27. Gerald Cromer, 'Intermarriage and Communal Survival in a London Suburb', *JJS*, XVI, 2 (December 1974), 155–69.
28. Henriques, *Jews of South Wales*, 214.
29. *Dublin Jewish News* (new series), I, 1 (March 1984).
30. Bensimon and DellaPergola, *Population Juive de la France*, 246–7.
31. Ibid., 342–3.
32. *Jerusalem Post*, 1 March 1988.
33. See Avraham A. Kessler, 'Fund-raising and Finance in the British Jewish Community, 1983', in *Papers in Jewish Demography 1985*, U. O. Schmelz and S. DellaPergola, eds. (Jerusalem, 1989), 395–404.

Chapter 11. Jews in the New European Disorder

1. *JC*, 25 March 1994.
2. *Jerusalem Post*, 3 June 1993.
3. Robert J. Brym, 'The Emigration Potential of Jews in the Former Soviet Union', *East European Jewish Affairs*, 23, 2 (Winter 1993), 9–24.

4. 'Peter Brodsky' [pseud.], 'Are Russian Jews in Danger?', *Commentary*, 95, 5 (May 1993), 40.
5. *JTADNB*, 18 and 19 December 1991.
6. *NYT*, 19 September 1993.
7. Lipstadt, 'Anti-Semitism in Eastern Europe', 5–6.
8. 'Being a Jew in Poland' (interview with Gebert and others), *East European Reporter*, 4, 4 (Summer 1991), 106–7.
9. Quoted in Abraham Brumberg, 'Poland, the Polish Intelligentsia and Antisemitism', *SJA*, XX (1990), 2–3, 6.
10. *JJS* (December 1993), 159.
11. Adam Michnik, 'Poland and the Jews', *New York Review of Books*, 30 May 1991, 11.
12. 'Antisemitism in Central and Eastern Europe: A Current Survey', IJARR (November 1991), 4–6.
13. *NYT*, 20 February 1990.
14. Lipstadt, 'Anti-Semitism in Eastern Europe', 10.
15. 'Antisemitism in Europe in the first Quarter of 1993', Wiener Library, Tel Aviv, 1993, 26.
16. Ibid.
17. Ibid., 28.
18. Krystyna Sieradzka, 'Restitution of Jewish Property in the Czech Republic: New Developments', IJARR (August 1994), 7.
19. *NYT*, 30 August 1986 and 11 April 1991; *JC*, 4 January, 12 and 19 April 1991.
20. 'Antisemitism in Central and Eastern Europe: A Current Survey', Institute of Jewish Affairs (November 1991).
21. *AJR Information*, 49, 9 (September 1994), 14.
22. *Der Spiegel*, special issue, 'Juden und Deutsche', August 1992, 61–73.
23. *JC*, 11 March 1994.
24. *Independent* (London), 7 June 1994.
25. Quoted by Lisa Palmieri-Billig in an analysis of the Italian elections in 'West European Elections', Anti-Defamation League of B'nai B'rith memorandum, New York, 27 April 1994.
26. Ibid.
27. *Le Monde*, 14–15 August 1994.
28. Nelly Hanson, 'France: The Carpentras Syndrome and Beyond', *Patterns of Prejudice*, 25, 1 (Summer 1991), 32–45.
29. Szafran, *Juifs dans la politique*, 16–17.
30. *JJS* (December 1993), 159–60.
31. *Tribune Juive*, 14 July 1994.

32. *AJYB 1994*, 257–8.
33. Matthew Kalman on BBC Radio 4, 12 June 1994.
34. *JC*, 15 April 1994.
35. Abitbol, *Bituyei Hizdahut*, 14–15.
36. *JC*, 18 March 1994.
37. See Pierre Birnbaum, 'Le député et le grand rabbin', *L'Arche*, May 1994.
38. *Le Monde*, 2–3 January 1994.

Afterthoughts
1. Jakobovits, 'Holocaust', 235.
2. Sartre, *Réflexions*, 68–9.
3. Freedman, 'Jewish Population', 96.
4. *Le Monde*, 23 February 1990.
5. *Tribune Juive*, 10 February 1994.
6. *JC*, 20 May 1994.
7. Marienstras, *Être un peuple en diaspora*, 188.

Bibliography

A complete bibliography of this subject would run to many thousands of items. The following list consists mainly of published materials that have been of particular help to the author and that are recommended for further reading. The two foremost journals dealing with post-war European Jewry are the *Jewish Journal of Sociology* (*JJS*) and *Soviet Jewish Affairs* (*SJA*), renamed after the fall of the USSR *East European Jewish Affairs*. For Christian–Jewish relations a great deal of contemporary documentation was surveyed in the journal *Christian Attitudes on Jews and Judaism*, now, unfortunately, defunct. The research reports produced over the years by the Institute of Jewish Affairs in London and the Anti-Defamation League of the B'nai B'rith in New York also contain a wealth of reliable information. The foremost authority for recent demographic information is the annual survey of world Jewish population by U. O. Schmelz and Sergio DellaPergola, published in the *American Jewish Year Book*.

Abitbol, Michel, *Bituyei Hizdahut Leumit Be-Tsarfat* (Jerusalem, 1982)

Abramsky, Chimen, Jachimczyk, Maciej and Polonsky, Antony, eds., *The Jews in Poland* (Oxford, 1986)

Adenauer, Konrad, *Erinnerungen 1953–1955* (Stuttgart, 1966)

Alderman, Geoffrey, *The Jewish Community in British Politics* (Oxford, 1983)

– *London Jewry and London Politics 1889–1986* (London, 1989)

– *Modern British Jewry* (Oxford, 1992)

Altshuler, Mordechai, *Soviet Jewry since the Second World War: Population and Social Structure* (Westport, Conn., 1987)

– 'Who are the "Refuseniks"? A Statistical and Demographic Analysis', *SJA*, XVIII, 1 (1988), 3–15

American Jewish Joint Distribution Committee, *Statistical Abstract 1953* (New York, 1954)

Anglo-American Committee of Inquiry into the Problems of European Jewry and Palestine: Report, Cmd 6806 (London, 1946)

Arendt, Hannah, *Eichmann in Jerusalem: A Report on the Banality of Evil* (London, 1963)

Aron, Raymond, *De Gaulle, Israël et les Juifs* (Paris, 1967)

Ascherson, Neal, 'The *Shoah* Controversy', *SJA*, XVI, 1 (1986), 53–61

– 'The Prosecution of Nazi War Criminals: Vengeance or Justice?', in William Frankel, ed., *Survey of Jewish Affairs 1988* (Cranbury, NJ, 1989), 191–9

Azeroual, Yves and Derai, Yves, *Mitterrand, Israël et les Juifs* (Paris, 1990)

Balinska, Maria, 'A Year of Truth in Eastern Europe: Liberalization and the Jewish Communities', in William Frankel, ed., *Survey of Jewish Affairs 1990* (Oxford, 1990), 167–86

Barkol, Micha, 'The Social Aspect of the Process of Establishing a Jewish Day School in West Berlin (1985–1987) in Light of the Crisis of Contemporary Jewish Life in the Diaspora' (Ph.D. dissertation, Free University of Berlin, 1989)

Bauer, Yehuda, *Bricha: Flight and Rescue* (New York, 1970)

– *Out of the Ashes: The Impact of American Jews on Post-Holocaust European Jewry* (Oxford, 1989)

Benguigui, Georges, et al., *Aspects of French Jewry* (London, 1969)

Bensimon, Doris, 'Sondage Socio-Démographique auprès des Juifs en France: Résultats Préliminaires (Région Parisienne)', in *Papers in Jewish Demography 1977*, U. O. Schmelz, P. Glikson and S. DellaPergola, eds. (Jerusalem, 1980), 179–90

– 'Écologie urbaine des Juifs de la région parisienne vers 1975', *Papers in Jewish Demography, 1981* (Jerusalem, 1983), 363–79

– 'French Jewry Today', *Encyclopaedia Judaica Year Book 1986–1987*, 146–53

Bensimon-Donath, Doris, *L'Intégration des Juifs nord-africains en France* (Paris, 1971)

Bensimon, Doris and DellaPergola, Sergio, *La Population Juive de la France: Socio-Démographie et Identité* (Jerusalem, 1984)

Bentwich, Norman, *The Jews in Our Time* (Harmondsworth, 1960)

– 'The Social Transformation of Anglo-Jewry, 1883–1960', *JJS*, II, 1 (June 1960), 16–24

– 'Nazi Spoliation and German Restitution: The Work of the United

Restitution Office', *Leo Baeck Institute Year Book*, X (London, 1965), 204–24

Berghahn, Marion, *German-Jewish Refugees in England: The Ambiguities of Assimilation* (London, 1984)

Bermant, Chaim, *Troubled Eden: An Anatomy of British Jewry* (London, 1969)

– *The Cousinhood: The Anglo-Jewish Gentry* (London, 1971)

Birnbaum, Pierre, *Anti-Semitism in France: A Political History from Léon Blum to the Present* (Oxford, 1992)

British Parliamentary Delegation to Buchenwald Camp, Cmd 6626 (London, 1945)

Broder, Henryk M. and Lang, Michel R., eds., *Fremd im eigenen Land: Juden in der Bundesrepublik* (Frankfurt, 1979)

Brodetsky, Selig, *Memoirs: From Ghetto to Israel* (London, 1960)

Brodsky, Peter [pseud.], 'Are Russian Jews in Danger?', *Commentary*, 95, 5 (May 1993), 37–40

Bronsztejn, Szyja, 'A Questionnaire Inquiry into the Jewish Population of Wrocław', *JJS*, VII, 2 (December 1965) 246–75

Brumberg, Abraham, '*Sovyetish Heymland* and the Dilemmas of Jewish Life in the USSR', *SJA*, 3 (May 1972), 27–41

– 'Poland, the Polish Intelligentsia and Antisemitism', *SJA*, XX (1990), 2–3, 5–25

Brym, Robert, 'The Emigration Potential of Jews in the Former Soviet Union', *East European Jewish Affairs*, 23, 2 (Winter 1993), 9–24

– *The Jews of Moscow, Kiev and Minsk: Identity, Antisemitism, Emigration* (London, 1994)

Bull, George, *Vatican Politics at the Second Vatican Council 1962–5* (London, 1966)

Cesarani, David, ed., *The Making of Modern Anglo-Jewry* (Oxford, 1990)

– *Justice Delayed* (London, 1992)

– *The Jewish Chronicle and Anglo-Jewry 1841–1991* (Cambridge, 1994)

Checinski, Michael, 'The Kielce Pogrom: Some Unanswered Questions', *SJA*, V, 1 (1975), 57–72

Anonymous [= M. Checinski], 'USSR and the Politics of Polish Antisemitism 1956–68', *SJA*, I, 1 (June 1971), 19–39

Christian–Jewish Relations, 14, 4 (December 1981): special issue devoted to the work of Cardinal Augustin Bea, SJ

Cohen, Israel, 'Jewish Interests in the Peace Treaties', *Jewish Social Studies*, XI, 2 (April 1949), 99–118

Cromer, Gerald, 'Intermarriage and Communal Survival in a London Suburb', *JJS*, XVI, 2 (December 1974), 155–69
- 'The Transmission of Religious Observance in the Contemporary Jewish Family', in Schmelz et al., *Papers in Jewish Demography 1977* (Jerusalem, 1980), 225–33
Crossman, R. H. S., *Palestine Mission: A Personal Record* (London, 1946)
Dagan, Avigdor, ed., *The Jews of Czechoslovakia: Historical Studies and Surveys*, vol. III (Philadelphia, 1984)
Daniels, Roger, 'American Refugee Policy in Historical Perspective', in Jarrell C. Jackman and Carla M. Borden, eds., *The Muses Flee Hitler: Cultural Transfer and Adaptation 1930–1945* (Washington, DC, 1983), 61–77
DellaPergola, Sergio, 'A Note on Marriage Trends among Jews in Italy', *JJS*, XIV, 2 (December 1972), 197–205
- 'Jews in the European Community: Sociodemographic Trends and Challenges', *AJYB*, vol. 93 (New York, 1993), 25–82
DellaPergola, Sergio and Cohen, Leah, eds., *World Jewish Population: Trends and Policies* (Jerusalem, 1992)
Deutscher, Isaac, *The Non-Jewish Jew* (London, 1968)
Dijour, Ilja M., 'Jewish Migration in the Post-war Period', *JJS*, IV, 1 (June 1962), 72–81
Dinnerstein, Leonard, *America and the Survivors of the Holocaust* (New York, 1982)
Dinur, Ben Zion, *Israel and the Diaspora* (Philadelphia, 1969)
Dobroszycki, Lucjan, 'Restoring Jewish Life in Post-war Poland', *SJA*, III, 2 (1973), 58–72
Documentation Catholique, special supplement, 'Carmel d'Auschwitz', no. 1991, Paris, 1 October 1989
Dressen, Willi, 'The Investigation of Nazi Criminals in Western Germany', *Encyclopaedia Judaica Yearbook 1986–7*, 132–8
Dunn, Stephen P., 'The Roman Jewish Community: A Study in Historical Causation', *JJS*, II, 2 (November 1960), 185–201
Eatwell, Roger, 'Why are Fascism and Racism Reviving in Western Europe?', *Political Quarterly*, 65, 3 (July–September 1994), 313–25
Elazar, Daniel, et al., *The Balkan Jewish Communities: Yugoslavia, Bulgaria, Greece and Turkey* (Lanham, MD, 1984)
Epstein, Leon D., *British Politics in the Suez Crisis* (London, 1964)
Esprit, 114 (September 1945), special issue, 'Les Juifs parlent aux nations'
- 370 (April 1968), special issue, 'Juifs, en France, aujourd'hui'

Fain, Benjamin and Verbit, Mervin F., *Jewishness in the Soviet Union: Report of an Empirical Survey* (Jerusalem, 1984)

Fein, Helen, ed., *The Persisting Question: Sociological Perspectives and Social Contexts of Modern Antisemitism* (Berlin, 1987)

Ferencz, Benjamin, *Less than Slaves* (Cambridge, Mass., 1979)

Finer, S. E., 'Look Forward in Perplexity', *JJS*, X, 1 (June 1968), 139–44

Fishman, Joel, 'Jewish War Orphans in the Netherlands – the Guardianship Issue 1945–1950', *Wiener Library Bulletin*, XXVII, new series 30/31 (1973–4), 31–6

– 'The Jewish Community in Post-war Netherlands, 1944–1975', *Midstream* (January 1976), 42–54

– 'The Anneke Beekman Affair and the Dutch News Media', *Jewish Social Studies*, XL, 1 (Winter 1978), 3–24

Florsheim, Yoel, 'Soviet Jewish Immigration to Israel in 1990 – A Demographic Profile', *SJA*, XXI, 2 (1991), 3–10

Fredj, Jacques, 'La Création du CRIF: 1943 à 1946' (Maîtrise thesis, Université de Paris IV, 1988)

Freedman, Maurice, ed., *A Minority in Britain: Social Studies of the Anglo-Jewish Community* (London, 1955)

– 'The Jewish Population of Great Britain', *JJS*, IV, 1 (June 1962), 92–106

Freedman, Robert O., ed., *Soviet Jewry in the 1980s: The Politics of Anti-Semitism and Emigration and the Dynamics of Resettlement* (Durham, NC, 1989)

Friedenreich, Harriet, *The Jews of Yugoslavia* (Philadelphia, 1979)

Friedgut, Theodore H., 'Soviet Jewry: The Silent Majority', *SJA*, X, 2 (1980), 3–19

Friedländer, Saul, *When Memory Comes* (New York, 1979)

Friedmann, Georges, *Fin du peuple juif?* (Paris, 1964)

Friedmann, Joan, 'The Last Jews of Czechoslovakia?', *SJA*, XIX, 1 (1989), 49–68

Garai, George, 'Hungary's Liberal Policy and the Jewish Question', *SJA*, I, 1 (June 1971), 101–7

Gebert, Konstanty, et al., 'Being a Jew in Poland' [Symposium], *East European Reporter*, 4, 4 (Summer 1991), 106–7

Gershon, Karen, *Postscript: A Collective Account of the Lives of Jews in West Germany since the Second World War* (London, 1969)

Gilbert, Martin, *Shcharansky: Hero of Our Time* (London, 1986)

Gilboa, Yehoshua A., 'The 1948 Zionist Wave in Moscow', *SJA*, I, 2 (November 1971), 35–9

Gilman, Sander L., and Remmler, Karen, eds., *Reemerging Jewish Culture in Germany: Life and Literature since 1989* (New York, 1994)

Gitelman, Zvi, 'Soviet Jewish Emigrants: Why are They Choosing America?', *SJA*, VII, 1 (1977), 31–46

Glikson, Paul, 'Jewish Population in the Polish People's Republic, 1944–1972', *Papers in Jewish Demography 1973* (Jerusalem, 1977), 235–53

Goldkorn, Yosef, *The Rise and Fall of a Jewish Newspaper:* Dos Nyeh Leben, *Poland, 1945–50* (Tel Aviv, 1993)

Goldmann, Nahum, *The Autobiography of Nahum Goldmann: Sixty Years of Jewish Life* (New York, 1969)

Goschler, Constantin, 'The Attitude towards Jews in Bavaria after the Second World War', *Leo Baeck Institute Year Book*, XXXVI (London, 1991), 443–58

Gould, Julius, and Esh, Shaul, eds., *Jewish Life in Modern Britain* (London, 1964)

Greenbaum, Avraham, 'A Note on the Tradition of the Twenty-Four Soviet Martyrs', *SJA*, XVII, 1 (1987), 49–52

Greilshammer, Ilan, 'The Democratization of a Community: French Jewry and the Fonds Social Juif Unifié', *JJS*, XXI, 2 (December 1979), 109–24

Grizzard, Nigel, and Raisman, Paula, 'Inner-city Jews in Leeds', *JJS*, XXII, 1 (June 1980), 21–33

Gutwirth, Jacques, 'Antwerp Jewry Today', *JJS*, X, 1 (June 1968), 121–37

– *Vie juive traditionelle: Ethnologie d'une communauté hassidique* (Paris, 1970)

Hanson, Nelly, 'France: The Carpentras Syndrome and Beyond', *Patterns of Prejudice*, 25, 1 (Summer 1991), 32–45

Harris, David, 'A Note on the Problem of the *Noshrim*', *SJA*, VI, 2 (1976), 104–13

Heitman, Sidney, 'The Third Soviet Emigration', *SJA*, XVIII, 2 (1988), 17–42

– 'Soviet Emigration in 1990: A New "Fourth Wave"?', *SJA*, XXI, 2 (1991), 11–21

Heller, Celia Stopnicka, '"Anti-Zionism" and the Political Struggle within the Elite of Poland', *JJS*, XI, 2 (December 1969), 133–50

Henriques, Ursula R. Q., *The Jews of South Wales: Historical Studies* (Cardiff, 1993)

Herf, Jeffrey, 'East German Communists and the Jewish Question: The

Case of Paul Merker', *Journal of Contemporary History*, XXIX (1994), 627–61

— 'Dokumentation. Antisemitismus in der SED: Geheime Dokumente zum Fall Paul Merker aus SED- und MfS-Archiven', *Vierteljahrshefte für Zeitgeschichte*, 4 (1994), 635–67

Hondius, Dienke, 'A Cold Reception: Holocaust Survivors in the Netherlands and Their Return', *Patterns of Prejudice*, 28, 1 (1994), 47–65

Hurwic-Nowakowska, Irena, *A Social Analysis of Post-war Polish Jewry* (Jerusalem, 1986)

Institute of Jewish Affairs, *Antisemitism in Central and Eastern Europe: A Current Survey* (London, 1991)

International Catholic–Jewish Liaison Committee, *Fifteen Years of Catholic–Jewish Dialogue 1970–1985: Selected Papers* (Vatican City, 1988)

Isaac, Jules, *L'Affaire Finaly: Significations, enseignements* (Marseilles, 1953)

Jacobs, Louis, *We Have Reason to Believe* (London, 1962)

Jakobovits, Immanuel, 'Religious Responses to Jewish Statehood', *Tradition*, 20, 3 (Fall 1982), 188–204

— 'The Holocaust: Remembering the Future', in William Frankel, ed., *Survey of Jewish Affairs 1983* (Cranbury, NJ, 1985), 233–7

Jelinek, Yeshayahu, 'The Jews in Slovakia, 1945–1949', *SJA*, 8, 2 (1978), 45–56

— 'Slovaks and the Holocaust: An End to Reconciliation', *East European Jewish Affairs*, 22, 1 (Summer 1992) 5–22

Joffe, Josef, 'Fifty Years after the Third Reich: The Jewish Community in Post-war Germany', in William Frankel, ed., *Survey of Jewish Affairs 1983* (Cranbury, NJ, 1985), 225–32

Kaplan, Jacob, *Judaïsme français et sionisme* (Paris, 1976)

Keller, Moïse, *L'Affaire Finaly telle que je l'ai vécue* (Paris, 1960)

Kelner, Viktor, 'The Jewish Press in the USSR Today', *SJA*, XXI, 2 (1991), 23–9

Kessler, Avraham A., 'Fund-raising and Finance in the British Jewish Community, 1983', in *Papers in Jewish Demography 1985*, U. O. Schmelz and S. DellaPergola, eds. (Jerusalem, 1989), 395–404

Klein, Charlotte, 'In the Mirror of *Civiltà Cattolica*: Vatican View of Jewry, 1939–1962', *Christian Attitudes on Jews and Judaism*, 43 (August 1975), 12–16

— 'Catholics and Jews – Ten Years after Vatican II', *Journal of Ecumenical Studies*, 12, 4 (Fall 1975), 471–82

Knight, Robert, 'Restitution and Legitimacy in Post-war Austria 1945–1953', *Leo Baeck Institute Year Book*, XXXVI (London, 1991), 413–41

Kochan, Lionel, ed., *The Jews in the Soviet Union since 1917* (London, 1970)

Kochavi, Arieh J., *Akurim u-Politikah Beinleumit: Britanyah ve-ha-Akurim ha-Yehudim le-Ahar Milhemet ha-Olam ha-Shniyah* (Tel Aviv, 1992)

Koestler, Arthur, *Promise and Fulfilment: Palestine 1917–1949* (London, 1949)

Kosmin, Barry and Levy, Caren, 'Jewish Circumcisions and the Demography of British Jewry, 1965–82', *JJS*, XXVII, 1 (June 1985), 5–11

Kosmin, Barry and Waterman, Stanley, 'Recent Trends in Anglo-Jewish Marriages', *JJS*, XXVIII, 1 (June 1986), 49–57

Kosmin, Barry, Levy, C. and Wigodsky, P., *Steel City Jews* (London, 1976)

Krausz, Ernest, 'Occupation and Social Advancement in Anglo-Jewry', *JJS*, IV, 1 (June 1962), 82–90

– *Leeds Jewry: Its History and Social Structure* (Cambridge, 1964)

– 'The Edgware Survey: Demographic Results', *JJS*, X, 1 (June 1968), 83–100

– 'The Edgware Survey: Occupation and Social Class', *JJS*, XI, 1 (June 1969), 75–95

– 'The Edgware Survey: Factors in Jewish Identification', *JJS*, XI, 2 (December 1969), 151–63

Kushner, Tony, *The Persistence of Prejudice* (Manchester, 1989)

Laub, Morris, *Last Barrier to Freedom: Internment of Jewish Holocaust Survivors on Cyprus, 1946–1949* (Berkeley, CA, 1985)

Lazar, David, *L'Opinion Française et la naissance de l'État d'Israël 1945–1949* (Paris, 1972)

Lazaris, Vladimir, 'The Saga of Jewish Samizdat', *SJA*, IX, 1 (1979), 4–19

Levinson, Nathan Peter, *Ein Rabbiner in Deutschland: Aufzeichnungen zu Religion und Politik* (Gerlingen, 1987)

Levitte, Georges, 'French Jewry Today', *JJS*, II, 2 (November 1960), 172–84

Lipman, Sonia L. and Lipman, V. D., *Jewish Life in Britain 1962–1977* (New York, 1981)

Lipman, V. D., *Social History of the Jews in England 1850–1950* (London, 1954)

– 'Trends in Anglo-Jewish Occupations', *JJS*, II, 2 (November 1960), 202–18

– *A History of the Jews in Britain since 1858* (Leicester, 1990)

Litvinoff, Barnett, *A Peculiar People: Inside the Jewish World Today* (London, 1969)

Lowenthal, Richard, 'East–West Détente and the Future of Soviet Jewry', *SJA*, III, 1 (1973), 20–25

Malino, Frances and Wasserstein, Bernard, eds., *The Jews in Modern France* (Hanover, NH, 1985)

Marienstras, Richard, *Être un peuple en diaspora* (Paris, 1975)

Mattenklott, Gert, *Über Juden in Deutschland* (Frankfurt, 1992)

Mayer, Kurt B., 'The Evolution of the Jewish Population of Switzerland in the Light of the 1970 Census', in Schmelz et al., *Papers in Jewish Demography 1973* (Jerusalem, 1977), 309–22

Memmi, Albert, *Portrait d'un Juif* (Paris, 1962)

Memmi, Albert, Ackermann, W., Zoberman, N. and Zoberman, S., 'Differences and Perception of Differences among Jews in France', *JJS*, XII, 1 (June 1970), 7–19

Meyer, Peter, Weinryb, Bernard D., Duschinsky, Eugene and Sylvain, Nicolas, *The Jews in the Soviet Satellites* (Syracuse, NY, 1953)

Millman, Ivor I., 'The Jewish Population of Romania: Continuity and Decline', in *Papers in Jewish Demography 1981*, U. O. Schmelz, P. Glikson and S. DellaPergola, eds. (Jerusalem, 1983), 163–72

Morin, Edgar, *La Rumeur d'Orléans* (Paris, 1968)

Mosse, Werner, ed., *Second Chance: Two Centuries of German-speaking Jews in the United Kingdom* (Tübingen, 1991)

Nachmani, Amikam, *Great Power Discord in Palestine: The Anglo-American Committee of Inquiry into the Problems of European Jewry and Palestine, 1945–1946* (London, 1987)

Nathan, Naphtali, 'Notes on the Jews of Turkey', *JJS*, VI, 2 (December 1964), 172–89

New German Critique, 19 (Winter 1980), special issue: 'Germans and Jews'

Nezer, Zvi (Z. Alexander), 'Jewish Emigration from the USSR in 1981–82', *SJA*, XII, 3 (1982), 3–17

O'Doherty, Paul, 'The GDR, Its Jews and the USA', *Politics and Society in Germany, Austria and Switzerland*, 4, 2 (Spring 1992), 25–33

Oschlies, Wolf, 'The Jews in Bulgaria since 1944', *SJA*, XIV, 2 (May 1984), 41–54

Ostow, Robin, *Jews in Contemporary East Germany: The Children of Moses in the Land of Marx* (London, 1989)

Pinkus, Benjamin, *The Soviet Government and the Jews 1948–1967: A Documented Study* (Cambridge, 1984)

– 'National Identity and Emigration Patterns Among Soviet Jewry', *SJA*, XV, 3 (November 1985), 3–28

– *The Jews of the Soviet Union: The History of a National Minority* (Cambridge, 1988)

Pollins, Harold, 'Sociological Aspects of Anglo-Jewish Literature', *JJS*, II, 1 (June 1960), 25–41

– *Economic History of the Jews in England* (East Brunswick, NJ, 1982)

Polonsky, Antony, "Loving and Hating the Dead": Present-day Polish Attitudes to the Jews', *Religion, State and Society*, 20, 1 (1992), 69–79

Polonsky, Antony, ed., *My Brother's Keeper? Recent Polish Debates on the Holocaust* (London, 1990)

Porat, Dina, 'Attitudes of the Young State of Israel towards the Holocaust and Its Survivors: A Debate over Identity and Values', in Laurence J. Silberstein, ed., *New Perspectives on Israeli History: The Early Years of the State* (New York, 1991), 157–74

Praag, Ph. van, *Demography of the Jews in the Netherlands* (Jerusalem, 1976)

Prais, S. J. and Schmool, Marlena, 'The Size and Structure of the Anglo-Jewish Population 1960–1965', *JJS*, X, 1 (June 1968), 5–27

– 'The Fertility of Jewish Families in Britain 1971', *JJS*, XV, 2 (December 1973), 189–203

– 'The Social-class Structure of Anglo-Jewry, 1961', *JJS*, XVII, 1 (June 1975), 5–15

Proudfoot, Malcolm, *European Refugees: 1939–1952* (London, 1957)

'Rabi' [= Wladimir Rabinovitch], *L'Affaire Finaly: Des faits, des textes, des dates* (Marseilles, 1953)

Rajsfus, Maurice, *N'oublie pas le petit Jésus! L'Église catholique et les enfants juifs* (Levallois-Perret, 1994)

Rapaport, Lynn, 'The Cultural and Material Reconstruction of the Jewish Communities in the Federal Republic of Germany', *Jewish Social Studies*, XLIX, 2 (1987), 137–54

Rémond, René, *Forces religieuses et attitudes politiques dans la France contemporaine* (Paris, 1965)

Richarz, Monika, 'Jews in Today's Germanies', *Leo Baeck Institute Year Book*, XXX (London, 1985), 265–74

Robinson, Jacob, *And the Crooked Shall be Made Straight: The Eichmann Trial, the Jewish Catastrophe and Hannah Arendt's Narrative* (New York, 1965)

Rodinson, Maxime, *Peuple juif ou problème juif?* (Paris, 1981)

Roland, Charlotte, *Du Ghetto à l'Occident: Deux générations yiddiches en France* (Paris, 1962)

Rose, Ann, ed., *Judaism Crisis Survival* (Paris, 1966)

Roth, Stephen, 'Jewish Renewal in Europe: Hungary', in William Frankel, ed., *Survey of Jewish Affairs 1990* (Oxford, 1990), 205–23

Rousso, Henry, *Le syndrome de Vichy de 1944 à nos jours* (Paris, 1987)

Rubinstein, W. D., *The Left, the Right and the Jews* (London, 1982)

Sachar, Abram L., *The Redemption of the Unwanted: From the Liberation of the Death Camps to the Founding of Israel* (New York, 1983)

Sartre, Jean-Paul, *Réflexions sur la question juive* (Paris, 1946)

Schapiro, Leonard B., 'Antisemitism in the Communist World', *SJA*, IX, 1 (1979), 42–52.

Schatz, Jaff, *The Generation: The Rise and Fall of the Jewish Communists of Poland* (Berkeley, 1991)

Schmelz, U. O., 'New Evidence on Basic Issues in the Demography of Soviet Jews', *JJS*, XVI, 2 (December 1974), 209–23.

Schmelz, U. O., et al., *Papers in Jewish Demography* (Jerusalem, 1960–)

Seliktar, Ofira, 'The Political Attitudes and Behaviour of British Jews', University of Strathclyde Survey Research Centre Occasional Paper No. 1 (Glasgow, 1974)

Shafir, Michael, 'Marshall Ion Antonescu: Politik der Rehabilitierung', *Europäische Rundschau*, 22, 2 (Spring 1994), 55–70

Shimoni, Gideon, 'The Non-Zionists in Anglo-Jewry, 1937–1948', *JJS*, XXVIII, 2 (December 1986), 89–115

Sichrovsky, Peter, *Strangers in Their Own Land: Young Jews in Germany and Austria Today* (New York, 1986)

Der Spiegel, special issue (August, 1992), 'Juden und Deutsche'

Steinberg, Bernard, 'Jewish Schooling in Britain', *JJS*, VI, 1 (July 1964), 52–68

Stendahl, Krister, 'Judaism and Christianity II – After a Colloquium and a War', *Harvard Divinity Bulletin*, new series, I, 1 (Autumn 1967), 2–8

Szafran, Maurice, *Les Juifs dans la politique française: De 1945 à nos jours* (Paris, 1990)

Szaynok, Bozena, 'The Pogrom of Jews in Kielce, July 4, 1946', *Yad Vashem Studies*, XXII (1992), 199–235

Tapia, Claude, 'North African Jews in Belleville', *JJS*, XVI, 1 (June 1974), 5–23

Taylor, Telford, *The Anatomy of the Nuremberg Trials: A Personal Memoir* (London, 1993)

Tress, Madeleine, 'Soviet Jews in the Federal Republic of Germany: The Rebuilding of a Community', *JJS*, XXXVII, 1 (June 1995), 39–54

Trigano, Shmuel, *La République et les juifs* (Paris, 1982)

Vidal-Naquet, Pierre, *Les Juifs, la mémoire et le présent* (Paris, 1981)

– *Assassins of Memory: Essays on the Denial of the Holocaust* (New York, 1992)

La Vie Juive dans l'Europe Contemporaine, Colloque de l'Institut de Sociologie, Université de Bruxelles, September 1962 (Brussels, 1962)

Vinen, Richard C., 'The End of an Ideology? Right-wing anti-semitism in France 1944–1970', *Historical Journal*, 31, 2 (June 1994), 365–88

Waterman, Stanley, 'A Note on the Migration of Jews from Dublin', *JJS*, XXVII, 1 (June 1985), 23–7

Webster, Ronald, 'American Relief and Jews in Germany 1945–1960: Diverging Perspectives', *Leo Baeck Institute Year Book*, XXXVIII (London, 1993), 293–321

Wiesel, Elie, *The Jews of Silence* (New York, 1966)

Wigoder, Geoffrey, *Jewish–Christian Relations since the Second World War* (Manchester, 1988)

– 'The Affair of the Carmelite Convent at Auschwitz', in William Frankel, ed., *Survey of Jewish Affairs 1990* (Oxford, 1990), 187–204

– *The Vatican–Israel Agreement: A Watershed in Christian–Jewish Relations* (Institute of the World Jewish Congress Policy Forum 2, Jerusalem, November 1994)

Willebrands, Johannes, Cardinal, 'Christians and Jews: A New Vision', in Alberic Stacpoole, ed., *Vatican II by Those Who Were There* (London, 1986), 220–36

Wistrich, Robert S., 'Once Again, Anti-Semitism Without Jews', *Commentary*, 94, 2 (August 1992), 45–9

– 'Do the Jews Have a Future?', *Commentary*, 98, 1 (July 1994), 23–6

Zajka, Vital, 'Jewish Life in Belarus during the Past Decade', *East European Jewish Affairs*, 23, 1 (1993), 21–31

Zipes, Jack, 'Jewish Consciousness in Germany Today', *Telos*, 93 (Fall 1992), 159–72

Zitomirsky, Joseph, 'A Brief Survey of Research and Publications on the Jews of Sweden', *JJS* XXXII (June 1990), 31–40

Zweig, Ronald W., 'Politics of Commemoration', *Jewish Social Studies*, XLIX, 2 (Spring 1987), 155–66

Zwergbaum, Aaron, 'Czechoslovak Jewry in 1979', *SJA*, X, 3 (1980), 29–46

Index

Aberystwyth 245
Abs, Josef 126
Abusch, Alexander 173
Abusch, Moritz 161
Academic Assistance
  Council 71
Action Directe 232
Actualité Juive 248
Aden 73
Adenauer, Konrad 123–6,
  166, 168, 170
Admont camp 88
Adorno, Theodor 165
Afghanistan 202
Agudas Yisroel xix, 22, 49,
  231
Albania 265
Albu, Austen 95n.
Aleppo 70, 143
Alfrink, Monsignor B. J. 136
Algeria 62, 65–8, 238, 244
Allen, Jim 230
Alliance Israélite Universelle
  68, 154
Alter, Wyktor 220
Altmann, Alexander 73, 165
Altneuschul 225, 226
American Council for
  Judaism 87, 89
American Jewish
  Committee 11, 147, 217
American Jewish Joint
  Distribution Committee
  ('Joint') xix, 11, 56, 58–9;
  activities in Austria 37;
  activities in Bulgaria 55;
  activities in Czechoslovakia
  55, 222; activities in
  Germany 36, 161, 164;
  activities in Hungary 36;
  activities in Poland 36–7,
  55, 215, 219, 260; activities
  in Romania 36–7, 55, 211;
  activities in USSR/CIS
  205, 254; activities in

Yugoslavia 55, 207; and
  DPs 16, 26, 34, 36
Amson, Daniel 234
Amsterdam 60, 70, 81, 104,
  106, 136
Anglo-American Committee
  of Inquiry 22–3, 133, 175
Angry Brigade 83
Anti-Nazi League 230–31
antisemitism ix, 140, 141, 142,
  145, 148, 234, 281;
  definition of xii; in
  Austria 168, 175, 177; in
  Britain 78, 90, 138, 268; in
  Czechoslovakia 267; in
  Eastern Europe 42, 45, 53–
  6; in France 45, 65, 67, 82–
  3, 151, 168, 239–40, 270; in
  Germany 162, 167–8, 172–
  3, 268; in Hungary 207–8,
  263, 266–7; in Italy 270; in
  Poland 44, 151, 211–21,
  261–2, 266; in Romania
  210, 262; in USA 168; in
  USSR/CIS 64, 183, 186,
  188, 205, 258–60
Antonescu, Ion 262
Antwerp xix, 87, 231–2, 275,
  284
Appel Juif Unifié 251
Arafat, Yasir 152
Aragon, Louis 185
Arche, L' 229, 248
Arendt, Hannah 122
Argentina 113, 120, 122
Aron, Raymond 63, 66, 89,
  98, 100
Asche, Kurt 112
Ashkenazim 62, 69–70, 274;
  defined xix
Asscher, Abraham 60
assimilation, definition of
  xiii
Attali, Jacques 238, 239, 243
Auerbach, Dr Philip 164

Auschwitz 4, 22, 106, 107,
  128, 270; convent
  controversy 153–7, 220,
  261; deportations to 61,
  117, 134; liberation of 1;
  museum 105; postwar lack
  of interest in 7; trials 112;
  visit by Pope John Paul II
  152–3
Australia 33, 73, 199, 215
Austria: draft peace treaty 31;
  extreme right in 269;
  Jewish DPs in 16–18, 23,
  26–7, 33, 88; Jewish
  emigration from 71, 92;
  Jewish population of viii;
  Jewish question in vii, 174–
  6; Jewish wartime losses 4;
  Jews in 175–7; relations
  with Israel 178; war crimes
  trials 110

Baader–Meinhof gang 83
Babi Yar 105, 188
Babi Yar (Kuznetsov) 108
Babi Yar (Yevtushenko) 105
Bad Gastein 23
Badinter, Robert 238, 240
Bad Ischl 175
Banovce nad Bebravou 263–4
Barbie, Klaus 113
Barre, Raymond 231
Bart, Lionel 230
Bartoszewski, Władysław 218
Bass, Alfie 230
Bassani, Giorgio 107
Bauer, Yehuda xii
Baumann, Zygmunt 215
Bavaria 17, 21, 151, 164
Bayonne 62
Bea, Cardinal Augustin 141,
  142–3, 145–6
Beekman, Anneke 136
Begin, Menahem 88, 228, 235,
  249, 252

Begun, Iosif 204
Beilin, Yossi 287
Beirut 220, 249
Belarus 259; see also
    Byelorussia
Belfast 229
Belgium vii, 4, 33, 58, 92,
    153–4, 249
Belgrade 206, 266
Bell, Susan Groag 137n.
Belleville 67, 246
Beloff, Lord (Max) 119, 233
Belzer hasidim 86
Benassayag, Maurice 238
Bender, Georges 23
Benedek, Ladislas 55
Ben Gurion, David 4, 20,
    122
Bergelson, David 55
Bergen-Belsen 1–2, 3, 6, 7, 60,
    106
Berlin: Free University
    of 165, 285; Jewish
    movement through
    prohibited 17; Jews
    in 159–61, 162, 163, 165,
    167, 169, 172, 173–4, 256–7;
    Shcharansky freed in 197;
    terror attack 231
Berlusconi, Silvio 269
Berman, Jakub 43
Bermant, Chaim 118
Bernstein, Eduard 57
Besse, Annie: see Kriegel,
    Annie
Bevin, Ernest 23, 31
Bevis Marks Synagogue 70
Bibó, István 267
Birkenau 153
Birkett, Lord 111
Birmingham 79
Birnbaum, Pierre 235, 277
Birobidzhan 41, 51, 184, 194,
    256
Birobidzhaner Shtern 185
Bitburg 170
Black Book, The 108
Blaszczyk, L. D. 215
Bloch, Ernst 172
Błoński, Jan 220–21
Bloom, Claire 230
Bloom, Leopold 245
Blum, Léon 64, 89
B'nai B'rith 147
Board of Deputies of British
    Jews 9, 37, 72, 73, 90, 95,
    230, 273
Böhm, Franz 126
Bolkow 8
Bolsheviks 40
Bordeaux 62, 68, 116
Borowski, Wiktor 215
Bosnia 266
Bousquet, René 114–15, 117
Brailovskaya, Irina 195

Brandt, Willy 170, 233
Bratislava 11
Brezhnev, Leonid 189, 193
Brierly, J. L. 109
Briscoe, Robert 245
Britain: admission of war
    criminals 120–21; attitudes
    to war crimes trials 111,
    118–20; attitudes towards
    Jews 13, 271; Cabinet
    Office 8; condition of Jews
    in 70–81, 240–45, 271–4;
    decline in religious
    observance 276, 284; and
    DP issue 1–35; Foreign
    Office 9, 29–31, 38, 162;
    Home Office 118; House of
    Commons x, 74–5, 118–19,
    241; House of Lords 118–
    19; Jewish attitudes to Israel
    in 95–9; Jewish child
    refugees in 137; Jewish
    demographic characteristics
    viii, 4, 73, 76, 241; Jewish
    education 275–6; Jewish
    emigration to Israel
    from 91, 92, 101; Jewish
    fund-raising 251; Jewish
    immigration to 70–73, 208;
    Jewish inter-marriage 74,
    80; Jewish legal position xi;
    Jewish occupational
    distribution 74, 76; Jewish
    political behaviour 74–5,
    240–41; Jewish religious
    behaviour 75–7; Jewish
    social attitudes xiii; Jewish
    social geography 74; Jewish
    social mobility 76–7; and
    Jews in Bulgaria 37–8; and
    Jews in Hungary 38;
    Ministry of Economic
    Warfare 9; and 1967
    crisis 97; Post Office 13;
    'readmission' of Jews 70;
    synagogue membership 76,
    271–2
British Anti-Zionist
    Organization 228
Brodetsky, Selig 9, 72
Brodie, Israel 73, 78–9
Bronfmann, Edgar 174
Brun, Antoinette 134, 135
Buber, Martin 122, 165
Bucharest 259
Buchenwald 2, 6, 11
Budapest 5, 36, 40, 48, 55,
    208n., 209
Bueno de Mesquita family
    70
Buenos Aires 86
Bukovina 201
Bulganin, Nikolai 94–5
Bulgaria viii, 4, 26, 37, 49, 50,
    101, 265; at Paris Peace

Conference 30; Jewish
    emigration from 92, 94, 265
Bund xix, 19, 40, 49, 50, 52–
    3, 62–3, 86, 125, 220, 289
Byelorussia 201, 204, 205; see
    also Belarus

Callaghan, Lord (James) 119
Campbell (of Alloway),
    Lord 119
Canacos, Henry 238
Canada 20, 33–4, 73, 114, 120,
    121, 199, 208
Canetti, Elias 285
Caraolos 26
Cardiff 79–80, 245
Carlebach, Julius 139
Carli, Bishop Luigi 142, 146
'Carlos' (Illitch Ramirez
    Sanchez) 229
Carmel College 275
Carpentras 270–71
Carrington, Lord 119
Carvalho, Robert 89
Carvalho family 70
Ceauşescu, Nicolae 210
Central Committee of Polish
    Jews 49–50, 55
Centre de Documentation
    Juive Contemporaine 104
Chagrin et la Pitié, Le 113
'Charter 77' 226
Children's Movement 137–8
Chile 120
China 289–90
Chirac, Jacques 239
Chomsky, Noam 129
Christian Democratic Centre
    Party (Italy) 270
Christian Democratic Party
    (Germany) 268
Churchill, Winston 12, 13, 65,
    111
Cichy, Michal 260
Cicognani, Cardinal 142
Čierna nad Tisou 223
circumcision 77, 80, 212, 247,
    254, 284
Civiltà Cattolica 131–2
Clifton College 275
Clore, Charles 74
Club Méditerranée 229, 242
Cohen, Albert 285
Cohen, Benny 274
Cohen, Israel 30
Cohen family (London) 70
Cohn-Bendit, Daniel 83, 213
Cologne 112, 159, 168
Colville, Sir John 177
Commentary 217
Commonwealth of
    Independent States
    (CIS) 255, 283; see also
    Union of Soviet Socialist
    Republics

communism, Jewish attitudes to 5, 42–3
Communist Party: in Britain 74–5; in Czechoslovakia 38, 53; in France 57, 62, 63–7, 84, 89, 125, 237–8, 240, 270; in Germany 126, 172–3; in Hungary 38, 43, 46, 53, 207–8; in Poland 42–3, 45–6, 49–50, 217, 220; in Romania 43, 49; in USSR 40, 51, 183
Conference on Jewish Material Claims against Germany 124–7
Conseil Représentatif des Israélites de France (CRIF) 62, 63, 89–90, 125, 235, 243, 276
Conservative Judaism 79–80
Conservative Party (Britain) 74–5, 84, 240–41
Consistoire: Central xi, 62, 63, 236, 243, 277; of Paris 242, 274
conversion: from Judaism x, 61, 62, 134–9, 165, 207, 281; to Judaism x, 80
Cotton, Jack 74
Council of Christians and Jews 140, 143
Cracow 17, 153, 154, 216, 221
Créteil 237
Crimea 41, 55–6
Croatia 266
Crossman, Richard 2, 22, 121
Crum, Bartley C. 22
Csurka, István 263
Cypel, Jacques 248
Cyprus 26, 32
Cyrankiewicz, Josef 215
Czechoslovakia: anti-Zionist campaigns 54, 224–5; condition of Jews in 38–40, 54–5, 222–6; DPs permitted to pass through 17, 26–7; Evangelical Brethren 140; Germans expelled from 16; Jewish emigration from 71, 92, 94, 222, 225; Jewish population of viii; Jewish wartime losses 4, 222; relief of Jews in 11; restitution of Jewish property 46; show trials in 53–5; Soviet occupation of 224; supplies arms to Israel 51; 'Velvet Revolution' 253; war crimes trials 110; see also Czech Republic, Slovakia
Czech Republic 264–5
Czerniakow, Adam 60
Czestochowa 156

Dachau 1, 2–3, 83
Dacre, Lord 119
Daghestan 201
Daisenberger, Father Alois 151
Daniel, Jean 242, 272
Daniel, Yuli 186
Dann, Dr Rudolf 112
Dassault, Marcel 96
Debré, Michel 63
Debré, Robert 63
Defferre, Gaston 237
de Gaulle, Charles 63, 99–100, 233, 236
DellaPergola, Sergio 287
Delors, Jacques 269
Demjanjuk, John 121
Denmark viii, 4, 61, 92n.
Derczansky, Alex 98
Dernier des Justes, Le 106
Dernier Métro, Le 107
Diary of Anne Frank, The 106, 108
Displaced Persons (DPs) 8–35, 40, 52, 85, 163, 175; defined 8–9; Harrison report on 14–15
Displaced Persons Act (US) 32
D'Israeli family 70
Döblin, Alfred 165
'Doctors' Plot' 56, 63, 183
Doepfner, Cardinal 152
Domenach, Jean-Marie 157
Donaldson, Lord 119
Dreyfus, Pierre 239
Dreyfus affair 45
Dubček, Alexander 223–5
Dublin 229, 245–6
Dublin Jewish News 246
Dubnow, Simon 190
Duclos, Jacques 65, 89
Ducourtray, Cardinal Albert 116
Düsseldorf 168
Dymshits, Mark 191–2
Dzierzoniów 44–5

East Germany 171–4; war crimes trials 110
Ecuador 120
Edelman, Marek 219, 220
Edgware 76–7, 244
Edinburgh 118
Egypt 66, 73, 99, 100–101, 143
Ehrenburg, Ilya 52, 108
Eichmann, Adolf 122
Eichmann in Jerusalem 122
Eilat 97
Eindhoven 59, 258
Eisenhower, Dwight D. 6, 15, 28
El Al airline 229
Elef Milim 197

Elkabbach, Jean-Pierre 117–18, 242
Elleinstein, Jean 240
Entebbe 229
Erlangen 165
Erlich, Henryk 220
Eshkol, Levi 101
Esprit 157
Être un peuple en diaspora 289
European Commission 227, 269
European Community (Union) 179, 227–8
Evsektsiya 41
Exodus 190
Exodus 1947 31
Eynikeyt 51, 92

Faurisson, Robert 128, 129
Feffer, Itzig 55
Feigin, Anatol 43
Feldafing 17
Feuchtwanger, Lion 165
Fiddler on the Roof 285
Filderman, Wilhelm 49
Finaly, Gérald 134–5
Finaly, Robert 134–5
Finaly affair 133–4, 155
Fin du peuple Juif? 281
Finer, Samuel 99
Fini, Gianfranco 269
Finkielkraut, Alain 286
Finland 92, 193
Föhrenwald 33–5
Folksshtime 50, 215
Fonds Social Juif Unifié (FSJU) 63, 82, 242, 243, 251
France: attitudes towards Jews 233–4, 271; condition of Jews in 58, 61–70; Conseil d'Etat 277; decline in religious practice 284; DP issue 19, 26, 31, 33; emancipation of Jews in 62; extreme right in 270–71; Jewish attitudes to Israel in 88–9; Jewish charitable activity 82, 251; Jewish demographic characteristics viii, 61, 68, 241–2, 282; Jewish education 68, 275–6; Jewish emigration to Israel 91, 92, 101; Jewish intermarriage 243–4, 282; Jewish legal position xi; Jewish occupational distribution 68–9, 242; Jewish political behaviour 235–40; Jewish radio stations 275; Jewish religious practice 246–7, 274; Jewish wartime losses 4, 61; Ministry of Interior 270, 276; Ministry

of Justice 277; North
African Jewish influx 67–9,
96, 238; relations with
Israel 96–100; religious
behaviour 69; synagogue
attendance 69; war crimes
trials 110, 113–17; Yiddish
speakers in 67
Franco, Francisco 250
Frank, Anne 106
Frank, Hans 109
Frank, Otto 106
Frankfurt-am-Main 17
Franklin family 70
Free Democratic Party:
(Germany) 126; (Hungary)
263
Freedman, Maurice xiii, 282
Freud, Clement x
Friedländer, Saul 133, 143
Friedmann, Georges 91, 281
Front National 142n., 270–71

Gábor, Péter 55
Gaitskell, Hugh 95
Gal, Fedor 264
Galinski, Heinz 170
Garden of the Finzi-Continis 107
Garnethill Synagogue 79
Gateshead 87, 284
Gazeta Wyborcza 260, 262
Gebert, Konstanty 260–61
Geismar, Alain 83
Geneva 155, 156, 204
Geremek, Bronisław 216, 218
Gerlier, Cardinal 134, 155
Germany: antisemitic
outbreaks 268;
Bundestag 124–5, 126, 129,
168, 171; condition of Jews
in xi, 159–74; Jewish
emigration from 70, 71, 86,
92; Jewish immigration to
256–7, 283; Jewish
population of viii, 4, 10;
Protestant churches in 140,
168; see also East Germany,
West Germany
Gerö, Ernö 38
Giffnock 81
Giscard d'Estaing, Valéry 231,
239, 274
Glasgow 78, 79, 81, 208n., 245
Glatzer, Nahum 165
Glemp, Cardinal Józef 154,
155, 156, 157, 261
Globke, Hans 166
Goering, Hermann 109–10
Goldenberg's restaurant
bombing 232
Golders Green xix, 81, 278
Goldmann, Nahum 124–6,
252, 266, 289
Goldstuecker, Eduard 55, 223,
225

Gollancz, Victor 122
Gomułka, Władysław 94,
212–14
Goncz, Árpád 263, 267
Gorbachev, Mikhail 204
Gorbals 81
Górka, Olgierd 25
Graetz, Heinrich 190
Graff, Michael 177–8
Great Britain: see Britain
Greece viii, 92, 132, 232
Greenville synagogue 246
Greilsamer, Laurent 115
Grimond, Lord (Jo) 119
Gromyko, Andrei 51, 92
Grossman, Vasily 108, 186
Groupement de recherche et
d'études pour la civilisation
européenne (GRECE) 230
Grunwald Patriotic
Union 216–17
Gummer, John 278
Gysi, Gregor 269

Haider, Jörg 269
Hailsham, Lord 119
Hajdenberg, Henri 243
Halter, Marek 285
Hamami, Said 249
Hananel, Chief Rabbi 49
Hanukah 50, 81
Harrison, Earl G. 14, 23
hasidim xix, 86–7, 275
Havel, Václav 264
Heartfield, John 172
Heath, Edward 240
Hebrew 41, 50, 102, 190–91,
254, 284, 288, 289
Hebrew Immigrant Aid
Society (HIAS) 202, 215
Hebron 252
Heenan, Cardinal 140, 142,
143, 145
Heitmann, Steffen 268
Helmer, Oskar 175
Henriques family 70
Herf, Jeffrey 172
Hertz, Chief Rabbi J. H. 73,
138
Herzl, Theodor 208
Herzog, Chaim 245
Herzog, Chief Rabbi Isaac 245
Hess, Moses 57
Hess, Rudolf 109–10
Hetherington, Sir Thomas 118
Heuss, Theodor 123
Heym, Stefan 269, 285
Historikerstreit 128
Hlond, Cardinal 24–5, 133
Hochhuth, Rolf 143
Holocaust vii, ix, 1–8, 102–30,
148, 150, 233
Holocaust 107
'Holocaust denial' 128–9
Honecker, Erich 174

Hopkinson, Austin 13
Horkheimer, Max 165
Howard, Michael 278
Hoxha, Enver 265
Hungarian Way 263
Hungary: Anglo-American
Committee barred from 23;
anti-Jewish riot in 43–4;
arrests of Jews 55; attitudes
towards Jews in 207–9,
267; condition of Jews in
36, 38, 40, 47–8, 50, 207–9,
263; Jewish Cultural
Association 253; Jewish
emigration from 71, 73, 92;
Jewish population of viii;
Jewish press 249; Jewish
voting in 238, 263; Jewish
wartime losses 4, 36;
nationalization of Jewish
property 47–8; at Paris
peace conference 30;
Reformed Church 140;
restitution of Jewish
property in 46; show trials
in 53; war crimes trials 110;
White Terror 207
Hutcheson, Joseph C. 22

Indemnification Law (West
Germany) 127
International Jewish
Committee on Inter-
religious Consultations 147
International Refugee
Organization (IRO) 8, 33
Iraq 28, 274
Ireland viii, 4, 90, 245–6
Irgun Zvai Leumi 88
Irish Jewish Museum 246
Irving, David 106, 128
Isaac, Jules 141
Iskhod 189
Israel: attacked by
Ehrenburg 52;
commemoration of
Holocaust 104; declaration
of independence 32;
Diaspora Jewish attitudes
towards 77, 84, 85–102,
251–2, 280, 287–8;
emigration from 34;
European attitudes to 227–8;
immigration to 32, 91, 92,
101, 187–205, 208, 216, 255–
9, 265; Labour Party 228,
258; reparations issue 122–7;
war of 1947–9 94; war of
1956 94, 96–7; war of
1967 84, 96–102, 187, 212,
281; war of 1973 199, 227,
240; war of 1982 249, 252
Israel Interfaith Committee
147
Israel Radio 191

Istanbul 141, 232, 250
Italy viii, 4, 92, 132, 269–70;
    condition of Jews in 58, 81;
    DPs in 16–17, 27, 33
Iton 189, 192
Izvestiia 189

Jackson, Revd Jesse 204
Jackson–Vanik
    Amendment 198–9, 202
Jacob, Simone: *see* Veil, Simone
Jacobs, Rabbi Louis 78–80,
    247–8
Jakobovits, Chief Rabbi
    Immanuel 99, 119, 130,
    234, 241, 245, 247, 252, 280
Janner, Barnett 95
Jaruzelski, Wojciech 219
Jenninger, Philipp 171
Jerusalem 49
Jewish Agency 193, 202, 255
Jewish Anti-Fascist
    Committee 42, 51, 55, 108,
    254
Jewish Brigade 17
Jewish Chronicle x, xiv, 74, 78,
    88, 118, 248, 275
Jewish Councils (World War
    II) 59–61, 65, 122, 213
Jewish Defense League 230
Jewish Echo 245
Jewish Fellowship 89
Jewish Journal of Sociology 70
Jewish National Fund 251
Jews' College 78
Jochman, Rosa 178
John XXIII, Pope 141
John Paul II, Pope 103–4,
    152–4, 156, 157–8, 177
'Joint': *see* American Jewish
    Joint Distribution
    Committee
Joint Palestine (Israel)
    Appeal 251
Jordan 99
Jordan, Charles 34, 222
Joseph, Sir Keith 241
Juedische Rundschau 161–2
Juquin, Pierre 237

Kádár, János 208
Kafka, Franz 39
Kaganovich, Lazar 183
Kahane, Rabbi Meir 230
Kahn, Jean 276–7
Kai-feng 289–90
Kalms, Stanley 272, 274
Kamenev, Lev 40
Kaminska, Ida 107, 215
Kaplan, Chief Rabbi
    Jacob 100, 136
Karlin, Miriam 230–31
kashrut 49, 77–8, 79, 82, 247,
    272, 284
Kasman, Leon 215

Katten, Dr Fritz 160–61
Katz, Chief Rabbi Isidor 225
Katz, Rudolf 165
Katz-Suchy, Julius 215
Kharkov 109
Khrushchev, Nikita 56, 106,
    183–7, 212
Kielce 24, 44, 88, 217, 218, 262
Kiev 182, 188, 260
Király, Isabella 263
Klarsfeld, Beate 114
Klarsfeld, Serge 114
Kling, Jean 236
Knesset xix, 257
Knoch, Ara (Leiba) 192
Koestler, Arthur 90–91, 113
Kohl, Helmut 129, 170
Kohn, E. 54
Kołakowski, Leszek 215
Kolar, F. J. 224–5
Kolbe, Maximilian 153
Konopnicki, Guy 277
Kopecký, Václav 40
Korec, Cardinal 264
Kossecki, Jozef 218
Krajewski, Staszek 260
Krasnik 8
Krasnodar 109
Krasucki, Henri 240
Kraus, František 253
Krausz, Ernest 76
Kreisky, Bruno 176, 177, 178
Kriegel (Besse), Annie 62,
    63–4, 231
Kriegel, Frantisek 223–4
Kristallnacht 109, 171
Krivine, Alain 83
Kundamaras 43
Küng, Hans 146
Kurz, Hans Rudolf 177
Küster, Dr Otto 126
Kuznetsov, Anatoly 108,
    191–2
Kuznetsov, Eduard 191–2
Kychko, T. K. 186

Labour Party (Britain) 12,
    74–5, 84, 95, 240–41
Lacombe Lucien 107
Ladino xix, 59, 250, 284
Landeszmann, György 263
Landsberg 17, 21
Lang, Fritz 165
Lang, Jack 239
Lanzmann, Claude 107–8
Lassalle, Ferdinand 57
Lauderdale, Earl of 120
Laval, Pierre 61
Lebanon 232, 252
Leeds 75, 81, 215, 245
Lefebvre, Archbishop
    Marcel 115, 142
Leningrad 182, 205, 254;
    hijacking case 191–2; *see
    also* St Petersburg

Le Pen, Jean-Marie 270
Lerner, Aleksander 204
Lestchinsky, Jacob xv
Lever, Harold 95n.
Levetzowstrasse
    Synagogue 162
Levi, Arrigo 269
Levi, Primo 107
Levin, Bernard 118
Levinger, Rabbi Moshe 252
Levinson, Rabbi Peter 172
Lévy, Benny 83
Lévy, Bernard-Henri 114,
    235, 242
Lévy, Tony 83
Leylands (Leeds) 81
Liberal Judaism x, 72, 79–80,
    272, 273, 286
Linnas, Karl 121
Lithuania 56, 188–90
Liverpool 90, 245
Livingstone, Ken 240
Lodz 24, 36, 44, 46, 206, 215
Loewenthal, Richard 165
Loi Crémieux 66
Loi Gayssot 129
London 72, 99; East End 75,
    81, 90, 244–5; *eruv*
    controversy 278; hasidim
    in xix, 87; Holocaust
    memorial 105; Jewish
    movement to suburbs
    244–5; Jewish radio
    programme 275; Jewish
    working class 242; kosher
    butchers 75; Sephardim
    in 70; UN conference on
    refugees 23; University 285
Longford, Lord 119
Loshn un Lebn 71
Lubavitch hasidim 86, 255
Lubitsch, Ernst 165
Lublin 49
Ludwigsburg 111
Lukács, Georg 57
Lustig, Dr 160
Lustiger, Jean-Marie
    (Cardinal) 7, 155
Lutheran Church 132, 146,
    148–50
Luxemburg, Rosa 57
Luxemburg reparations
    agreement 122–6, 166
Lvov 186, 260
Lyons 62, 68, 113, 114, 116,
    128, 186, 236, 237, 275

Macharski, Cardinal 154–6
Madrid 250
Maisky, Ivan 42
Majdanek 1, 112
Malenkov, G. M. 183
Malle, Louis 107
Manchester 70, 73, 240, 245
Manchester Guardian 95–6

Mankowitz, Wolf 230
Mannheim 129
Mapam party 54, 125
Marais (Paris) 232
Marchais, Georges 237
Marcus, Claude-Gérard 237
Marienstras, Richard 97, 102, 289
Maritain, Jacques 132
Markish, Peretz 55
Marks family 74
Marseilles 68, 237, 275
Marx, Karl 57
Masaryk, Jan 17, 46–7
Masorti movement 247–8
Mauriac, François 134
Mauthausen 3
Mayhew, Lord (Christopher) 119
Mazowiecki, Tadeusz 260
McDonald, James G. 22
McNarney, General Joseph 27
Medveténc 209
Meir, Golda 52, 93, 101, 152
Memorial Foundation for Jewish Culture 167
Mendelsohn, Erich 160–61
Mendès France, Pierre 62, 64, 252
Menuhin, Yehudi 161
Merker, Paul 172–3
Merthyr Tydfil 245
Mexico 172, 173
Meyer, Julius 172
Meyer, Peter 39
Michnik, Adam 216, 262
Mickiewicz, Adam 216
Miesiecznik Literacki 214
Mikhoels, Shlomo 51, 56
Milan 81, 270
Miłosz, Czesław 221
Minc, Hilary 43
Minsk 51, 190, 204, 205, 254
Mitterrand, François 115, 117–18, 232, 237, 239, 270
Mizrachi party xx, 49, 161
Moczar, Mieczysław 213, 217
Moldavia: Romanian 211; Soviet 201, 259
Mollet, Guy 66
Monde, Le 115, 116
Montagu, Ewen 77–8, 89
Montagu family 70
Montefiore, Leonard 89
Montefiore family 70
Moortown 81
Morgan, General Sir Frederick 17–18
Morin, Edgar 83
Morley, Father John 144
Morocco 62, 67, 247
Mortara case 137
Moscow 56, 205, 259; Central Synagogue 93, 197, 257; Hebrew Teachers'

Association in 205; Jews in 52, 182, 186, 189, 191, 204, 254, 255; yeshivas 185, 254
Mossad le-Aliyah Bet 17
Moulin, Jean 113
Munich 152, 163–4
Muslims: in Algeria 66; in France 231, 239
Mussolini, Benito 269

Nachman, Werner 170
Nagy, Imre 207
Naie Presse, Di 65, 248
Namir, Ora 258
Nasser, Gamal Abdul 97, 143
National Democratic Party (NPD) 168, 230
National Front (Britain) 230
Natolin faction 211, 213
Nazi–Soviet Pact 64
Nekrasov, Viktor 105
Nelhans, Erich 160–61
Neolog Jews 50, 87
neo-Nazism 168, 230, 267–9
Netherlands: condition of Jews in 58–9; deportees return to 7; embassy in Moscow 193; Jewish collaboration in 59–61; Jewish demography of viii, 81; Jewish emigration to Israel from 92; Jewish press in 249; Jewish refugees in 33, 58, 258; Jewish religious behaviour in xi, 81–2; Jewish war orphans controversy 136–7; Jewish wartime losses 4; State Institute for War Documentation 61, 106
Neuberger, Joseph 165
Neuberger, Julia 273
New London Synagogue 78–9
New West End Synagogue 78
New York 23, 86, 194, 230, 247, 255
Night 107
Nixon, Richard M. 195
Noel-Baker, Philip 111
Nolte, Ernst 128
Northern League 270
Norway 92, 232
Nostra Aetate 144–7, 152, 157
Nouveaux Cahiers, Les 248
Nouvel Observateur, Le 242
Novotny, Antonin 224
Nudel, Ida 204
Nuit et brouillard 106
numerus clausus 48, 198, 214, 221
Nuremberg laws 109, 166
Nuremberg trials 103, 109–11, 119, 131
Nyeh Lebn, Dos 49–50

Oberammergau 151–2
Ochab, Edward 214–15
Oesterreicher, Monsignor John 141–2
Ohrdruf 6
Ohrenstein, Rabbi Aaron 164
Olszowski, Stefan 216
Ophuls, Marcel 113
Oran 242
Oranienburgerstrasse Synagogue 174
Oren, Mordechai 54
Organization for Rehabilitation and Training (ORT) 215
Orléans 83
orthodox Jews 19, 138, 146, 244, 247, 255, 272, 278, 284, 286
Oświęcim: see Auschwitz
Ottaviani, Cardinal Alfredo 140n., 142
Oxford 73, 84, 285

Pakenham, Lord 33
Palestine 12, 14, 17, 18–23, 26, 31–2, 41, 42, 72, 282; civil war in 88; partition of 51
Palestine Liberation Organization 220, 249
Palestinian Arabs 101, 227, 229, 231, 232, 252, 271
Pamiat' 205
Panov, Galina 195
Panov, Valery 195
Papen, Franz von 109
Papon, Maurice 114, 116–17
Paris: Bundists in 86; deportees return to 7; exhibition of Nazi crimes 104; 'grande rafle' 117; hasidim in xix, 87; intermarriage in 244, 286; Jewish occupational distribution 69; Jewish population in 237, 246; Jewish radio stations 275; Jewish students in 83–4; Jewish studies in 285; kosher butchers in 69; Mémorial du Martyr Juif Inconnu 105; Mossad headquarters near 17; 1919 peace conference 29; 1946 peace conference 30; North African Jewish influx 67–9; 'Pletzl' 81; pro-Israel demonstration in 243; terrorist attacks 229, 231, 232; Yiddish press in 63, 248
Parliamentary War Crimes Group 118
Passover 50, 69, 204, 276
Patriot, De 7
Patton, General 6, 15

Pauker, Ana 55
Paul VI, Pope 146, 152
Pax (Poland) 213, 218
Peerce, Jan 185
Perfidy 230
Pétain, Philippe 61, 117
Piasecki, Bolesław 213
pieds noirs 66–7
Pinter, Harold 285
Piratin, Phil 75
Pirkei Avot 226
Pius XI, Pope 132
Pius XII, Pope 132–3, 143
Pivetti, Irene 270
pogroms 17, 24–5, 43–4
Poland: Anglo-American
    Committee visits 23; anti-
    Zionist campaigns 53, 212–
    16, 223; attitudes to Jews
    in 5, 43–5, 211–21;
    condition of Jews in 44–6,
    49–50, 211–21, 260–62;
    Home Army 217; Jewish
    emigration from 16–18, 26,
    32, 44, 63, 92, 94, 215–16;
    Jewish population of viii, 4,
    36, 44; Jewish question
    in vii, 261; Ministry of
    Interior 216; Ministry of
    Public Security 43; PEN
    Club 218; postwar hostility
    to Jews 8, 17, 22, 24–5;
    reaction to *Shoah* 108; relief
    of Jews in 11; repatriation
    of Jews to 18, 44, 93, 187;
    Roman Catholic Church
    in 24–5, 217–18, 261;
    Sejm 49; State Jewish
    Theatre 50; war crimes
    trials 110
Polaniec 8
Politika 264
Polityka 214, 217
Pompidou, Georges 115
Pontifical Biblical
    Institute 141
Pontypridd 245
Porat, Dina 104
Portugal 70
Potsdam Conference 12
Poujade, Pierre 64–5
Prague 5, 11, 54, 222, 225,
    253, 264–5
'Prague Spring' 55, 222–4
Pravda (Bratislava) 54
Pravda (Moscow) 52
Presov 44
Presse Nouvelle Hebdo 236
Preysing, Cardinal 166n.
Prittie, Terence 166n.
Purim 50

Radkiewicz, Stanisław 43
Raimbaud, Olivier 277
Raj, Rabbi Tamás 263

Rajk, László 53
Rákosi, Mátyás 38, 207
Rakowski, Mieczysław
    214–15
Rapaport, Nathan 105
Raphael, Frederic 230
Rauff, Walter 120
Rawidowicz, Simon 288
Reagan, Ronald 170–71
Reform Judaism 79–80, 139,
    248, 255, 272, 273, 286;
    attitude towards
    conversion x, 80; attitude
    to Zionism 87
Reichsvereinigung der Juden
    in Deutschland 160
Rémond, René 116
Renner, Karl 175
Renouveau juif 243
reparations 82, 122–8, 166–7,
    174, 213
Republican Party
    (Germany) 269
Resnais, Alain 106
restitution 46
Revisionist Zionists xx, 22
Ribbentrop, Joachim von 109
Ricci, Matteo 289
Riegner, Gerhart 155
Riesenburger, Martin 173
Riga 185, 189, 191
Ringelblum, Emanuel xv
Ripps, Ilya 188
Robinson, Jacob 122
Rodinson, Maxime 98, 233
Rogosnitzky, Rabbi Ber 80
Roman Catholic Church:
    antisemitism of 42, 131;
    attitude to Jews and
    Judaism 131–6, 140–58; in
    France 116, 134; in
    Netherlands 136–7; in
    Poland 24–5; schools 286;
    Universal Catechism
    (1992) 158
Romania: Anglo-American
    Committee barred from 23;
    attitude to Israel 94, 211;
    condition of Jews in 50, 55,
    209–11, 262–3; Germans
    expelled from 16; hostility
    to Zionism 52; Hungarian
    Jews deported to 47; Jewish
    Democratic Committee
    48–9; Jewish educational
    attainments in 206; Jewish
    emigration from 32, 92,
    210–11; Jewish population
    of viii; Jewish wartime
    losses 4; at Paris peace
    conference 30
Romanian Orthodox
    Church 42, 132, 209–10
Rome 61, 81, 120, 157, 177,
    202, 232

Roosevelt, Franklin D. 12
Rosen, Chief Rabbi
    Moshe 154, 210–11, 262
Rosen, Rabbi Kopul 275
Rosenberg, Alfred 109
Roth, Cecil 190
Rothschild, Alain de 236, 243
Rothschild, Élie de 243
Rothschild, Guy de 105, 243
Rothschild family 62, 70, 274
Rousso, Henry 235
Rude Pravo 224
Rudnicki, Szymon 261–2
Ruppin, Arthur xv
Russell, Earl (Bertrand) 186
Russia 181, 203, 255–9; Jewish
    emigration from 63, 201,
    283; *see also* Union of Soviet
    Socialist Republics
Russian Orthodox Church 42,
    132, 259, 287
Rzeszów 17

Sabra and Shatila camps 232,
    249
Sachs, Nelly 107, 165
Sacks, Chief Rabbi
    Jonathan 272, 273, 287
Safran, Chief Rabbi
    Alexander 49, 211
St Albans, Bishop of 119
St John's Wood 244, 248
St John's Wood
    Synagogue 79
St Petersburg 254
Salonica (Thessaloniki) 59
samizdat literature 189–91, 194
Samuel, Lord (Herbert) 71
Samuel family 70
Sarajevo 206, 266
Sarcelles 237, 238
Sartre, Jean-Paul x, 45, 83,
    108, 190, 281
Sassoon family 70
Sator, Dezső 48
Schacht, Hjalmar 109
Schaefer, Emanuel 112
Schaff, Adam 215
Scheiber, Rabbi
    Alexander 209
Schnabel, Arthur 165
Schneerson, Rabbi M. M. 86
Schoeps, Hans-Joachim 165
Scholem, Gershom 165
Schonfeld, Rabbi
    Solomon 138
Schwammberger, Joseph 113
Schwarz-Bart, André 106
Scotland 118, 245
Sephardim xx, 62, 70, 80, 243,
    274
Serbia 266
Shaffer, Peter 285
Shalom 250
Shamir, Yitzhak 220, 252

Shamoon, David 274
Shamoon, Sami 274
Shanghai 165, 290
Sharett, Moshe 126
Sharon, Ariel 249
Shawcross, Lord 119
Shazar, Zalman 190
Shcharansky, Anatoly (Natan Sharansky) 196–7
She'ereit ha-Pletah 20
Sheffield 242
Shelest, P. E. 223–4
shelilat ha-golah 91, 287
Sherman, Sir Alfred 241
Shinwell, Emanuel 75, 95
shiva 77
Shoah 107
Shop on Main Street 107
Shostakovich, Dmitry 106
Shultz, George 204
Sieff, J. Edward 229
Sieff family 74
Siła-Nowicki, Władisław 221
Silesia 16, 44
Simon Wiesenthal Center 118
Singer, Isaac Bashevis 226
Singer's Hill Synagogue 79
Sinyavsky, Andrei 186
Sirat, Chief Rabbi René-Samuel 155, 247, 252
Siri, Cardinal 142
Sitruk, Chief Rabbi Joseph 252, 274, 276–7
Slánský, Rudolf 53–4, 63, 222, 223, 224
Slepak, Vladimir 204
Slovakia 8, 38, 43–4, 225, 226, 263–4
Smolar, Hersch 215
Smrkovsky, Josef 223
Sobibor 1, 136
Social Democrat Party (Germany) 164, 268
Socialisme et Judaïsme 238
Socialist Party: Bulgaria 265; France 237–9; Hungary 263
Socialist Zionist Movement of France 237
Socialist Zionists 40
Solidarity movement 216–19, 260
Sommerstein, Emil 49
Soper, Lord 119
Soros, George 274
SOS Racisme 231
South Africa 73
Sovyetish Heymland 185, 188, 254
Spain 70, 92, 250
Speer, Albert 109–10
Spinoza, Baruch 60
Stalin, Joseph 12, 45, 55–6
Stamford Hill xix, 244
Stampa, La 269
Steg, Ady 154, 155

Stein, Cyril 274
Stein, Edith 153
Steiner, Jean-François 107
Stellvertreter, Der 143
Stencl, A. 71
Stendahl, Bishop Krister 148–9
Stepney 75, 244
Stern Group (Lehi) 88
Stoeckler, Louis 55
Strasbourg 63, 69, 154, 243, 275, 285
Strauss, George 75
Stuttgart 28, 113
Stuttgart Declaration of Guilt 140
Subcarpathian Ruthenia 39
Suez crisis 66, 73, 94–6, 240
Suslov, Mikhail 184
Suzman, Janet 230
Swaythling, Lord 89
Sweden 4, 9, 33, 58, 61, 92, 165, 191
Switzerland 4, 58, 81, 92, 249
Synagogue Council of America 147
Syria 99, 100, 120, 238
Szabad Nép 46
Szirmai, Stephen 55

Tamman, Leon 274
Tartu 121
Tauber, Richard 165
Taylor, John (Bishop) 119
Taylor, Telford 103
Tel Aviv 258
Temps Modernes, Les 98, 108
terrorism: against Jews 228–33, 281; by Jews 12
Thatcher, Margaret 118, 240–41
Theresienstadt 3, 7, 39
Thrace 37
Tiran, Straits of 97
Tiso, Josef 263–4
Tito, Josip Broz 55
Tixier-Vignancour, J. L. 67
Topolcany 44
Toulouse 237
Touvier, Paul 114–16
Trades Advisory Council 90
Transnistria 210
Treblinka 1, 121
Treblinka 107
Tredegar 245
Tribune Juive 248
Trigano, Gilbert 242
Trigano, Shmuel 233
Troisier, Solange 238
Trotsky, Leon 57
Truffaut, François 107
Truman, Harry 10, 13, 14, 15, 32
Trybuna Ludu 214–15
Tuchmann, Dr Emil 175
Tudjman, Franjo 266

Tunisia 62, 67, 247
Turkey 62, 92, 250
Turner-Samuels, Moss 95n.
Turowicz, Jerzy 154–5
Tuwim, Julian 218
Tygodnik Powszechny 154–5, 220

Uj Élet 47–8
Ukraine 4, 8, 41, 56, 121, 184, 201, 205, 259–60
Ukrainians 33, 39, 120–21
Ungerová, Dr M. 39
Union Générale des Israélites Français (UGIF) 61
Union of Orthodox Hebrew Congregations 138
Union of Soviet Socialist Republics: annexations of territory 39, 41; army 1, 8; attitude to Israel 51, 100–101, 187–8; attitude to Jewish question 40–43, 50–52, 183–205; attitude to Jewish relief organizations 11, 37; commemoration of Holocaust 108; condition of Jews in xi, 40–42, 50–52, 55–6, 180–205, 253–60; DP issue 18, 19; emigration of Armenians from 202; emigration of Germans from 187n., 192–3, 199, 202; emigration tax 193–4; Hungarian Jews deported to 47; Jewish attitudes to Israel in 91–3; Jewish communists and 63–4; Jewish demographic characteristics viii, 180–82, 203; Jewish education in 56, 183, 197, 204–5; Jewish educational attainments 182–3; Jewish emigration from vii, 18, 92, 93, 187–205, 237, 255–9, 283; Jewish losses in World War II 42; Jewish occupational distribution 182–3; Jewish political participation 183; Jewish religious practice 197, 204; KGB 192, 195–6; pact with Hitler 41; revival of Jewish press 254; Suez crisis 94–5; Supreme Soviet 183; war crimes trials 109, 110; Yiddish in 181, 183–5, 194, 204, 254; Zionism 42, 52, 187–205
United Nations 189; Economic and Social Council 23; Emergency Force (UNEF) 97; General Assembly 31, 51, 93, 227; Relief and Rehabilitation

Organization (UNRRA)
16–17, 19, 21, 26–7, 31;
Secretariat 108n.;
Secretary-General 97, 189;
War Crimes Commission
108–9, 176
United Restitution
Organization 127
United States of America:
Army Counter-Intelligence
Corps 113; Central
Intelligence Agency 222;
Congress 198–9; DP issue
1–35; help given to war
criminals by 113–14, 120;
Jewish Anti-Fascist
Committee visits 42; Jewish
immigration to 13, 199,
200, 201–2, 208, 256–7, 265;
Jews in 10; Justice
Department 121, 176–7;
1967 crisis 97; Suez crisis 94;
support for Birobidzhan
from 41; War Department
15
United Synagogue 72–3,
77–80, 272–3
Unzer Vort 65, 248
Uris, Leon 190
Ustaša 120
U Thant 97, 189

Va'ad (USSR) 253, 254
Vatican 132; archives 143–4;
attitude to Israel 147, 148,
152, 158; Commission for
Religious Relations with
Judaism 147; Curia 143,
145; help given to war
criminals 120; Holy
Office 140; honours Kurt
Waldheim 177; Radio 153;
Second Vatican Council
131, 141–6, 151, 152, 221;
Secretariat for Christian
Unity 141, 143; shelters
Chief Rabbi Zolli 61
Veil, Simone 7, 62, 89, 239
Venice declaration 228
Vergelis, Aron 185
Vergès, Jacques 114
Vidal-Naquet, Pierre 66
Vienna 5, 26, 175–6, 193, 202,
231; Bishop of 133;
demonstration in 178; Jews
in 165, 176, 177
Villeurbanne 237
Vilna 56, 185, 189–90, 254
Voronel, Nina 196

Waldheim, Kurt 176–8, 269
Wales 245

Wałęsa, Lech 156, 260
Waley-Cohen, Sir Robert 77,
89
war crimes 127; allied
declaration on 42;
trials 108–22
War Crimes Act 119–20
Warsaw: anti-Jewish agitation
in 217, 218; British
Embassy in 18; ghetto
commemoration 105, 170,
219–20; Jewish Council in
60; Jewish Historical
Institute 104, 215; Jews
in 206, 216, 260–61;
radio 214; State Yiddish
Theatre 215; synagogue
219; University 215, 261
Wassenaar 126
Weichmann, Herbert 164
Weidenfeld, Lord (George)
177
Weill, Kurt 165
Weinreb, Friedrich 60–61
Weinstein, Yerahmiel 93
Weiss, Rabbi Avraham 156
Weissman, Baruch Mordechai
93
Weitzman, David 95n.
Weizmann, Chaim 30, 60
Weizsäcker, Richard von 171
Weltsch, Robert 161–2
Werblan, Andrzej 214
Wesker, Arnold 230, 285
West, Rebecca 111
West Germany: Central Office
for the Investigation of
National-Socialist Crimes
111; DPs in 1–35, 40;
Jewish immigration
to 164–5, 167, 169, 199;
Jewish press 249; Jews
in 166–71; relations with
Israel 170; reparations
payments 122–8; Supreme
Court 129; war crimes
trials 109–13
Whitechapel 71, 244
Wiener Library 104
Wiesel, Elie 56, 170–71
Wiesenthal, Simon 177, 178
Wigoder, Geoffrey 146, 148
Wilder, Billy 165
Winterton, Major-General 33
Wolfson, Sir Isaac 74, 77–8
Woolwich, Bishop of 78
World at War 107
World Council of
Churches 140, 150
World Jewish Congress 11,
12, 29, 55, 124, 147, 155,
174, 217, 266

World Zionist
Organization 124
Wrocław 44, 206
Wyszyński, Cardinal 218

Xylotymbou 26

Yad Vashem 104
Yeltsin, Boris 205
Yerusholoyim d'Lita 254
yeshivot xx, 5
Yevtushenko, Yevgeni 105–6
Yiddish xx, 6, 41, 45, 51, 56,
63, 211, 246, 248, 284, 289
Yiddish press xiv, 20, 41, 49–
50, 63, 71, 194, 215
Yidishe Gas, Di 254
Yidishe Vort, Dos 260
Yom Hashoah 104
Yom Kippur xx, 45, 69, 77,
246, 265, 276
Yonnet, Paul 271
Young, Lord (David) 274
Yugoslavia viii, 4, 16, 92, 94,
206, 265–6

Zagreb 206, 266
Zalmanson, Sil'va 191–2
Zambrowski, Roman 43,
212
Zevi, Tullia 155
Zhdanov, Andrei 51, 56
Zhirinovsky, Vladimir 259
Zinoviev, G. 40
Zionism 12, 19, 34, 60, 85–
102, 102, 287–8; in Britain
72, 85, 229; in France 62,
85, 96, 237, 238; in
Germany 86, 172–4; in
Hungary 208; in
USSR 205; orthodox
Jewish attitudes to 86–7;
Reform Jewish attitudes
to 87
Zionist Federation (Britain)
275
Zionist movement: in DP
camps 19–22; in Hungary
52; in Poland 46, 49–50, 52,
86; in Romania 52; in
USA 86; in USSR 41, 51,
86, 93
Zionists: attitudes towards
camp survivors 4; and
illegal immigration to
Palestine 26–7; reaction to
Anglo-American
Committee's report 23
Zolli, Israel 61
Zuckerman, Leo 173
Zurich 61, 154
Zweig, Arnold 172